Oliver Goldsmith, William Collins, Thomas Warton, George Gilfillan

The Poetical Works of Goldsmith, Collins, and Warton

Oliver Goldsmith, William Collins, Thomas Warton, George Gilfillan

The Poetical Works of Goldsmith, Collins, and Warton

ISBN/EAN: 9783743312579

Manufactured in Europe, USA, Canada, Australia, Japa

Cover: Foto ©Thomas Meinert / pixelio.de

Manufactured and distributed by brebook publishing software
(www.brebook.com)

Oliver Goldsmith, William Collins, Thomas Warton, George Gilfillan

The Poetical Works of Goldsmith, Collins, and Warton

THE WORKS

OF

OLIVER GOLDSMITH

A NEW EDITION, CONTAINING PIECES HITHERTO

UNCOLLECTED, AND A LIFE OF THE AUTHOR.

WITH NOTES FROM VARIOUS SOURCES BY

J. W. M. GIBBS.

IN FIVE VOLUMES.

VOL. II.

POEMS: PLAYS: "THE BEE:" COCK-LANE GHOST.

LONDON: GEORGE BELL AND SONS, YORK STREET,

COVENT GARDEN.

1885.

CONTENTS.

POEMS.

THE

TRAVELLER,

OR A

PROSPECT OF SOCIETY.

['The Traveller' was the first of Goldsmith's publications which bore his name. It was published and sold at 1*s.* 6*d.* by Mr. J. Newbery, of St. Paul's Churchyard, in Dec., 1764, the title-page being dated 1765. Goldsmith received twenty guineas for the work, which went through nine editions during his lifetime.]

THE TRAVELLER;

OR

A PROSPECT OF SOCIETY.

[DEDICATION.]

TO THE REV. HENRY GOLDSMITH.

DEAR SIR,—I am sensible that the friendship between us can acquire no new force from the ceremonies of a Dedication; and perhaps it demands an excuse thus to prefix your name to my attempts, which you decline giving with your own. But as a part of this poem was formerly written to you from Switzerland, the whole can now, with propriety, be only inscribed to you. It will also throw a light upon many parts of it, when the reader understands, that it is addressed to a man who, despising fame and fortune, has retired early to happiness and obscurity, with an income of forty pounds a-year.

I now perceive, my dear brother, the wisdom of your humble choice. You have entered upon a sacred office, where the harvest is great, and the labourers are but few; while you have left the field of ambition, where the labourers are many, and the harvest not worth carrying away. But of all kinds of ambition—what from the refinement of the times, from different systems of criticism, and from the divisions of party—that which pursues poetical fame is the wildest.[1]

---

[1] This passage the author altered twice. In the first edition it appears thus :—"But of all kinds of ambition as things are now circumstanced perhaps that which pursues poetical fame is the wildest. What from

Poetry makes a principal amusement among unpolished nations; but in a country verging to the extremes of refinement, painting and music come in for a share. As these offer the feeble mind a less laborious entertainment, they at first rival poetry, and at length supplant her; they engross all that favour once shown to her, and though but younger sisters, seize upon the elder's birthright.

Yet, however this art may be neglected by the powerful, it is still in greater danger from the mistaken efforts of the learned to improve it. What criticisms have we not heard of late in favour of blank verse and Pindaric odes, choruses, anapests and iambics, alliterative care and happy negligence! Every absurdity has now a champion to defend it; and as he is generally much in the wrong, so he has always much to say; for error is ever talkative.

But there is an enemy to this art still more dangerous, —I mean party. Party entirely distorts the judgment, and destroys the taste. When the mind is once infected with this disease, it can only find pleasure in what contributes to increase the distemper. Like the tiger, that seldom desists from pursuing man after having once preyed upon human flesh, the reader, who has once gratified his appetite with calumny, makes ever after the most agreeable feast upon murdered reputation. Such readers generally admire some half-witted thing, who wants to be thought a bold man, having lost the character of a wise one. Him they dignify with the name of poet: his tawdry[1] lampoons are called satires; his turbulence is said to be force, and his frenzy fire.

What reception a poem may find, which has neither abuse, party, nor blank verse to support it, I cannot tell,

the increased refinement of the times, from the diversity of judgments produced by opposing criticism, and from the more prevalent opinion influenced by party, the strongest and happiest efforts can expect to please but in a very narrow circle. [Though the poet were as sure of his aim as the imperial archer of antiquity, who boasted that he never missed the heart, yet would many of his shafts now fly at random, for the heart too often is in the wrong place."] In the second edition the bracketed paragraph was cut off; and in the sixth the final curtailment was effected.—ED.

[1] The word "tawdry" was first given in the sixth edition. Goldsmith is thought to have had Churchill in his mind in this sketch.—ED.

nor am I solicitous to know. My aims are right. Without espousing the cause of any party, I have attempted to moderate the rage of all. I have endeavoured to show, that there may be equal happiness in states that are differently governed from our own; that every state has a particular principle of happiness, and that this principle in each [state, and in our own in particular [1]] may be carried to a mischievous excess. There are few can judge better than yourself how far these positions are illustrated in this Poem.

I am, dear Sir,

Your most affectionate brother,

OLIVER GOLDSMITH.

[1] In the first five editions.—ED.

THE TRAVELLER.[1]

REMOTE, unfriended, melancholy, slow,
Or by the lazy Scheld, or wandering Po;
Or onward, where the rude Carinthian boor
Against the houseless stranger shuts the door;
Or where Campania's plain forsaken lies,   5
A weary waste expanding to the skies:
Where'er I roam, whatever realms to see,
My heart untravell'd fondly turns to thee;
Still to my brother turns, with ceaseless pain,
And drags at each remove a lengthening chain.   10

   Eternal blessings crown my earliest friend,
And round his dwelling guardian saints attend:
Blest be that spot, where cheerful guests retire
To pause from toil, and trim their ev'ning fire:
Blest that abode, where want and pain repair,   15
And every stranger finds a ready chair;
Blest be those feasts with simple plenty crown'd,[2]
Where all the ruddy family around
Laugh at the jests or pranks that never fail,
Or sigh with pity at some mournful tale,   20
Or press the bashful stranger to his food,
And learn the luxury of doing good!

---

[1] This poem is printed from the ninth edition, which was the last that appeared in the lifetime of the author. It underwent several alterations, and received some additional lines in the course of its successive visits to the press; and as it is interesting to trace the minutest efforts by which genius seeks to attain excellence, we have subjoined some of the more important various readings from the earlier editions.—B.

[2] *Variation.*—In the first five editions.—

    Blest be those feasts where mirth and peace abound,
    Where, &c.

But me, not destin'd such delights to share,
My prime of life in wandering spent and care,
Impell'd, with steps unceasing, to pursue   25
Some fleeting good, that mocks me with the view;
That, like the circle bounding earth and skies,
Allures from far, yet, as I follow, flies;
My fortune leads to traverse realms alone,
And find no spot of all the world my own.   30

E'en now, where Alpine solitudes ascend,
I sit me down a pensive hour to spend;
And, plac'd on high above the storm's career,
Look downward where a hundred realms appear;
Lakes, forests, cities, plains extending wide,   35
The pomp of kings, the shepherd's humbler pride.

When thus Creation's charms around combine,
Amidst the store, should thankless pride repine?[1]
Say, should the philosophic mind disdain
That good which makes each humbler bosom vain?   40
Let school-taught pride dissemble all it can,
These little things are great to little man;
And wiser he, whose sympathetic mind
Exults in all the good of all mankind.
Ye glitt'ring towns, with wealth and splendour crown'd; 45
Ye fields, where summer spreads profusion round,
Ye lakes, whose vessels catch the busy gale,
Ye bending swains, that dress the flow'ry vale,
For me your tributary stores combine;
Creation's heir, the world, the world is mine!   50

As some lone miser, visiting his store,
Bends at his treasure, counts, recounts it o'er;
Hoards after hoards his rising raptures fill,
Yet still he sighs, for hoards are wanting still:
Thus to my breast alternate passions rise,   55
Pleas'd with each good that heaven to man supplies:

[1] *Var.*—In the first edition.—
    Amidst the store 'twere thankless to repine:
    'Twere affectation all, and school-taught pride,
    To spurn the splendid things by heaven supplied,
    Let, &c.

Yet oft a sigh prevails, and sorrows fall,
To see the hoard [1] of human bliss so small;
And oft I wish, amidst the scene to find
Some spot to real happiness consign'd,   60
Where my worn soul, each wand'ring hope at rest,
May gather bliss to see my fellows blest.

But where to find that happiest spot below
Who can direct, when all pretend to know?
The shudd'ring tenant of the frigid zone   65
Boldly proclaims that happiest spot his own, [2]
Extols the treasures of his stormy seas,
And his long nights of revelry and ease:
The naked negro, panting at the Line,
Boasts of his golden sands and palmy wine,   70
Basks in the glare, or stems the tepid wave,
And thanks his gods for all the good they gave.
Such is the patriot's boast where'er we roam,
His first, best country, ever is at home.
And yet, perhaps, if countries we compare, [3]   75
And estimate the blessings which they share,
Though patriots flatter, still shall wisdom find
An equal portion dealt to all mankind;
As different good, by art or nature given,
To different nations makes their blessing even.   80

Nature, a mother kind alike to all,
Still grants her bliss at Labour's earnest call;
With food as well the peasant is supplied [4]
On Idra's cliffs as Arno's shelvy side;

---

[1] *Var.*—First five editions.—To see the sum, &c.
[2] *Var.*—Boldly asserts that country for his own, &c.—First edition.
[3] The first edition has—

> And yet, perhaps, if states with states we scan,
> Or estimate their bliss on Reason's plan,
> Though patriots flatter, and though fools contend,
> We still shall find uncertainty suspend,
> Find that each good, by art or nature given,
> To these or those but makes the balance even.
> Find that the bliss of all is much the same,
> And patriotic boasting Reason's shame.

[4] This and the following line are wanting in the first edition.

And though the rocky crested summits frown,[1] 85
These rocks by custom turn to beds of down.
From art more various are the blessings sent,—
Wealth, commerce, honour, liberty, content.
Yet these each other's power so strong contest,
That either seems destructive of the rest. 90
Where wealth and freedom reign, contentment fails,[2]
And honour sinks where commerce long prevails.
Hence every state, to one loved blessing prone,
Conforms and models life to that alone.
Each to the favourite happiness attends, 95
And spurns the plan that aims at other ends;
'Till carried to excess in each domain,
This favourite good begets peculiar pain.

But let us try these truths with closer eyes,
And trace them through the prospect as it lies; 100
Here, for a while, my proper cares resign'd,
Here let me sit in sorrow for mankind;
Like yon neglected shrub at random cast,
That shades the steep, and sighs at every blast.

Far to the right, where Apennine ascends, 105
Bright as the summer, Italy extends;
Its uplands sloping deck the mountain's side,
Woods over woods in gay theatric pride;
While oft some temple's mould'ring tops between
With venerable grandeur mark the scene. 110

Could Nature's bounty satisfy the breast,
The sons of Italy were surely blest:
Whatever fruits in different climes are found,
That proudly rise, or humbly court the ground;
Whatever blooms in torrid tracts appear, 115
Whose bright succession decks the varied year;
Whatever sweets salute the northern sky
With vernal lives, that blossom but to die;

---

[1] *Var.*—And though rough rocks or gloomy summits frown,
    These rocks, &c.—First edition.

[2] This and the following line are wanting in the first five editions.

These here disporting own the kindred soil,
Nor ask luxuriance from the planter's toil;   120
While sea-born gales their gelid wings expand,
To winnow fragrance round the smiling land.

But small the bliss that sense alone bestows,
And sensual bliss is all the nation knows.
In florid beauty groves and fields appear,   125
Man seems the only growth that dwindles here.
Contrasted faults through all his manners reign :
Though poor, luxurious ; though submissive, vain ;
Though grave, yet trifling; zealous, yet untrue,
And e'en in penance planning sins anew.   130
All evils here contaminate the mind,
That opulence departed leaves behind :
For wealth was theirs ; not far remov'd the date,
When commerce proudly flourish'd through the state :
At her command the palace learn'd to rise,   135
Again the long-fall'n column sought the skies,
The canvass glow'd beyond e'en nature warm,
The pregnant quarry teem'd with human form :
Till, more unsteady than the southern gale,
Commerce on other shores display'd her sail ; [1]   140
While nought remain'd, of all that riches gave, [2]
But towns unmann'd, and lords without a slave :
And late the nation found, with fruitless skill, [3]
Its former strength was but plethoric ill.

Yet, still the loss of wealth is here supplied [4]   145
By arts, the splendid wrecks of former pride :
From these the feeble heart and long-fall'n mind
An easy compensation seem to find.

----

[1] *Var.*—Soon Commerce turn'd on other shores her sail.—First five
editions.
[2] This and the following line are wanting in the first edition.
[3] *Var.*—This and the following line appeared in the first edition, were
omitted in the second, third, fourth, and fifth, and re-appeared in the
sixth. One of many instances of Goldsmith's pains-taking revision of
his poetical work.—Ed.
[4] *Var.*—Yet though to fortune lost, here still abide
         Some splendid arts, the wrecks of former pride :
         From which, &c.—First edition.

Here may be seen, in bloodless pomp array'd,
The pasteboard triumph and the cavalcade ;   150
Processions form'd for piety and love,
A mistress or a saint in every grove.
By sports like these are all their cares beguil'd ;
The sports of children satisfy the child.[1]
Each nobler aim, repress'd by long control,   155
Now sinks at last, or feebly mans the soul ;
While low delights succeeding fast behind,
In happier meanness occupy the mind :
As in those domes where Cæsars once bore sway,
Defac'd by time, and tottering in decay,   160
There in the ruin, heedless of the dead,
The shelter-seeking peasant builds his shed ;
And, wond'ring man could want the larger pile,
Exults, and owns his cottage with a smile.

My soul, turn from them ! turn we to survey   165
Where rougher climes a nobler race display,
Where the bleak Swiss their stormy mansions tread,
And force a churlish soil for scanty bread :
No product here the barren hills afford,
But man and steel, the soldier and his sword ;   170
No vernal blooms their torpid rocks array,
But winter ling'ring chills the lap of May ;
No zephyr fondly sues the mountain's breast,
But meteors glare, and stormy glooms invest.

Yet still, e'en here, content can spread a charm,   175
Redress the clime, and all its rage disarm.
Though poor the peasant's hut, his feasts though small,
He sees his little lot the lot of all ;
Sees no contiguous palace rear its head
To shame the meanness of his humble shed ;   180

[1] After this line followed, in the first edition,—
     At sports like these, while foreign arms advance,
     In passive ease they leave the world to chance ;
     When struggling Virtue sinks by long control,
     She leaves at last, or feebly mans the soul.
In the second to the fifth editions the last two lines were—
     When noble aims have suffer'd long control,
     They sink at last, or feebly man the soul.

No costly lord the sumptuous banquet deal,
To make him loathe his vegetable meal ;
But calm, and bred in ignorance and toil,
Each wish contracting, fits him to the soil.
Cheerful, at morn, he wakes from short repose,   185
Breasts [1] the keen air, and carols as he goes ;
With patient angle trolls the finny deep,
Or drives his vent'rous ploughshare to the steep ;
Or seeks the den where snow-tracks mark the way
And drags the struggling savage into day.   190
At night returning, every labour sped,
He sits him down the monarch of a shed ;
Smiles by his cheerful fire, and round surveys
His children's looks that brighten at the blaze ;
While his lov'd partner, boastful of her hoard,   195
Displays her cleanly platter on the board ;
And haply, too, some pilgrim, thither led,
With many a tale repays the nightly bed.

Thus every good his native wilds impart,
Imprints the patriot passion on his heart ;   200
And e'en those ills that round his mansion rise,[2]
Enhance the bliss his scanty fund supplies.
Dear is that shed to which his soul conforms,
And dear that hill which lifts him to the storms ;
And as a child, when scaring sounds molest,   205
Clings close and closer to the mother's breast,
So the loud torrent, and the whirlwind's roar,
But bind him to his native mountains more.

Such are the charms to barren states assign'd :
Their wants but few, their wishes all confin'd :   210
Yet let them only share the praises due,—
If few their wants, their pleasures are but few ;
For every want that stimulates the breast,
Becomes a source of pleasure when redrest.
Hence [3] from such lands each pleasing science flies,   215

[1] Some editions have "Breathes the keen air," but all the originals
have " Breasts," and Dr. Johnson added the passage to his ' Dictionary,'
in illustration of the word " breasts."—ED.
[2] This and the following line are wanting in the first edition.
[3] The ninth, and also the sixth edition reads, " Whence from," &c. ;

That first excites desire, and then supplies;
Unknown to them, when sensual pleasures cloy,
To fill the languid pause with finer joy;
Unknown those powers that raise the soul to flame,
Catch every nerve, and vibrate through the frame.　220
Their level life is but a smould'ring fire,
Unquench'd by want, unfann'd[1] by strong desire;
Unfit for raptures, or, if raptures cheer
On some high festival of once a-year,
In wild excess the vulgar breast takes fire,　225
Till, buried in debauch, the bliss expire.

　But not their joys alone thus coarsely flow,—
Their morals, like their pleasures, are but low;
For, as refinement stops, from sire to son
Unalter'd, unimproved the[2] manners run;　·　230
And love's and friendship's finely pointed dart
Fall blunted from each indurated heart.
Some sterner virtues o'er the mountain's breast
May sit, like falcons cow'ring on the nest;
But all the gentler morals,—such as play　235
Through life's more cultur'd walks, and charm the way,—
These, far dispers'd, on timorous pinions fly,
To sport and flutter in a kinder sky.

　To kinder skies, where gentler manners reign,
I turn; and France displays her bright domain.　240
Gay, sprightly land of mirth and social ease,
Pleas'd with thyself, whom all the world can please,
How often have I led thy sportive choir,
With tuneless pipe beside the murmuring Loire![3]
Where shading elms along the margin grew,　245
And, freshen'd from the wave, the zephyr flew;
And haply, though my harsh touch falt'ring still,
But mock'd all tune, and marr'd the dancer's skill;
Yet would the village praise my wondrous power,
And dance, forgetful of the noon-tide hour.　250

but "Hence," as in the earlier editions, seems to be the better word.
—Ed.
　[1] First, second, and sixth editions have "Nor quench'd," and "nor
fann'd."—Ed.　　　　[2] First edition has "their."—Ed.
　[3] Vide 'Vicar of Wakefield,' ch. xx.—Ed.

Alike all ages: dames of ancient days
Have led their children through the mirthful maze;
And the gay grandsire, skill'd in gestic lore,
Has frisk'd beneath the burthen of threescore.

So blest a life these thoughtless realms display;   255
Thus idly busy rolls their world away:
Theirs are those arts that mind to mind endear,
For honour forms the social temper here:
Honour, that praise which real merit gains,
Or ev'n imaginary worth obtains,   260
Here passes current; paid from hand to hand,
It shifts in splendid traffic round the land;
From courts to camps, to cottages it strays,
And all are taught an avarice of praise:
They please, are pleas'd; they give to get esteem;   265
Till, seeming blest, they grow to what they seem.

But while this softer art their bliss supplies,
It gives their follies also room to rise;
For praise too dearly lov'd, or warmly sought,
Enfeebles all internal strength of thought: 270
And the weak soul, within itself unblest,
Leans for all pleasure on another's breast.
Hence ostentation here, with tawdry art,
Pants for the vulgar praise which fools impart;
Here vanity assumes her pert grimace,   275
And trims her robes of frieze with copper lace;
Here beggar pride defrauds her daily cheer,
To boast one splendid banquet once a-year:
The mind still turns where shifting fashion draws,
Nor weighs the solid worth of self-applause.   280

To men of other minds my fancy flies,
Embosom'd in the deep where Holland lies.
Methinks her patient sons before me stand,
Where the broad ocean leans against the land,
And, sedulous to stop the coming tide,   285
Lift the tall rampire's [2] artificial pride.
Onward, methinks, and diligently slow, [1]

---

[1] This and the following couplet are transposed in the first edition.
[2] Rampire, the wall of a dyke or canal.—ED.

The firm connected bulwark seems to grow,
Spreads its long arms amidst the watery roar,
Scoops out an empire, and usurps the shore ;   290
While the pent ocean, rising o'er the pile,
Sees an amphibious world beneath him smile ;
The slow canal, the yellow-blossom'd vale,
The willow-tufted bank, the gliding sail,
The crowded mart, the cultivated plain,   295
A new creation rescued from his reign.

Thus, while around the wave-subjected soil
Impels the native to repeated toil,
Industrious habits in each bosom reign,[1]
And industry begets a love of gain.   300
Hence all the good from opulence that springs,
With all those ills superfluous treasure brings,
Are here display'd.   Their much loved wealth imparts
Convenience, plenty, elegance, and arts ;
But view them closer, craft and fraud appear ;   305
Even liberty itself is barter'd here:
At gold's superior charms all freedom flies,
The needy sell it, and the rich man buys.
A land of tyrants, and a den of slaves,
Here wretches seek dishonourable graves,   310
And, calmly bent, to servitude conform,
Dull as their lakes that slumber in the storm.

Heavens ! how unlike their Belgic sires of old !
Rough, poor, content, ungovernably bold,
War in each breast, and freedom on each brow ;   315
How much unlike the sons of Britain now !

Fired at the sound, my genius spreads her wing,
And flies where Britain courts the western spring ;
Where lawns extend that scorn Arcadian pride,
And brighter streams than famed Hydaspes glide.   320
There all around the gentlest breezes stray,
There gentle music melts on every spray ;
Creation's mildest charms are there combined,
Extremes are only in the master's mind !

[1] *Var.*—Industrious habits in each breast obtain.—First edition.

Stern o'er each bosom Reason holds her state,   325
With daring aims irregularly great,
Pride in their port, defiance in their eye,
I see the lords of human kind pass by;
Intent on high designs, a thoughtful band,
By forms unfashion'd, fresh from Nature's hand;   330
Fierce in their native hardiness of soul,
True to imagin'd right, above control,—
While e'en the peasant boasts these rights to scan,
And learns to venerate himself as man.[1]

Thine, Freedom, thine the blessings pictured here,   335
Thine are those charms that dazzle and endear!
Too blest indeed were such without alloy;
But, foster'd e'en by Freedom, ills annoy:
That independence Britons prize too high,
Keeps man from man, and breaks the social tie;   340
The self-dependent lordlings stand alone,[2]
All claims that bind and sweeten life unknown;
Here, by the bonds of nature feebly held,
Minds combat minds, repelling and repell'd;
Ferments arise, imprison'd factions roar,   345
Represt ambition struggles round her shore;
Till, overwrought, the general system feels
Its motion stop, or frenzy fire the wheels.

Nor this the worst.   As Nature's ties decay,
As duty, love, and honour fail to sway,   350
Fictitious bonds, the bonds of wealth and law,
Still gather strength, and force unwilling awe.
Hence all obedience bows to these alone,
And talent sinks, and merit weeps unknown:
Till time may come, when, stript of all her charms,   355
The land of scholars, and the nurse of arms,

---

[1] These last ten lines were greatly admired by Dr. Johnson, *vide* Boswell's 'Life,' v. v. p. 85.—ED.

[2] *Var.*—This and the following line are wanting in the first edition; where follows:—

      See, though by circling deeps together held,
      Minds, &c.

The second edition has :—

      All kindred claims that soften life, &c.

Where noble stems transmit the patriot flame,
Where kings have toil'd, and poets wrote for fame,[1]
One sink of level avarice shall lie,
And scholars, soldiers, kings, unhonour'd die.   360

Yet think not, thus when Freedom's ills I state,
I mean to flatter kings, or court the great :[2]
Ye powers of truth, that bid my soul aspire,
Far from my bosom drive the low desire !
And thou, fair Freedom, taught alike to feel   365
The rabble's rage, and tyrant's angry steel ;
Thou transitory flower, alike undone
By proud contempt, or favour's fostering sun—
Still may thy blooms the changeful clime endure,
I only would repress them to secure !   370
For just experience tells, in every soil,
That those who think must govern those that toil ;
And all that Freedom's highest aims can reach,
Is but to lay proportion'd loads on each.[3]
Hence, should one order disproportion'd grow,   375
Its double weight must ruin all below.

O, then, how blind to all that truth requires,
Who think it freedom when a part aspires !
Calm is my soul, nor apt to rise in arms,
Except when fast approaching danger warms :   380
But when contending chiefs blockade the throne,
Contracting regal power to stretch their own ;
When I behold a factious band agree
To call it freedom when themselves are free ;

[1] *Var.*—And monarchs toil, and poets pant for fame, &c.—First to fifth editions—except second, which has " paint for," &c.
[2] *Var.*—After this the following couplet is inserted in the first edition :—

> Perish the wish, for, inly satisfied,
> Above their pomp I hold my ragged pride.

And the next eighteen lines, to " But when contending chiefs," &c., are wanting.
[3] *Var.*—After this, in editions two to five,—

> Much on the low, the rest as rank supplies,
> Should in columnar diminution rise, &c.

This doctrine was probably esteemed rather too aristocratic.—B.

Each wanton judge new penal statutes draw,   385
Laws grind the poor, and rich men rule the law ;
The wealth of climes, where savage nations roam,
Pillag'd from slaves to purchase slaves at home,—
Fear, pity, justice, indignation, start,
Tear off reserve, and bare my swelling heart ;   390
'Till, half a patriot, half a coward grown,
I fly from petty tyrants to the throne.

Yes, brother, curse with me that baleful hour,
When first ambition struck at regal power ;
And thus, polluting honour in its source,   395
Gave wealth to sway the mind with double force.
Have we not seen, round Britain's peopled shore,
Her useful sons exchaug'd for useless ore ?
Seen all her triumphs but destruction haste,
Like flaring tapers brightening as they waste ?   400
Seen Opulence, her grandeur to maintain,
Lead stern Depopulation in her train,
And over fields where scatter'd hamlets rose,
In barren, solitary pomp repose ?
Have we not seen, at pleasure's lordly call,   405
The smiling, long frequented village fall ? [1]
Beheld the duteous son, the sire decay'd,
The modest matron, and the blushing maid,
Forced from their homes, a melancholy train,
To traverse climes beyond the western main,   410
Where wild Oswego spreads her swamps around,
And Niágara [2] stuns with thund'ring sound ?

E'en now, perhaps, as there some pilgrim strays
Through tangled forests, and through dangerous ways,
Where beasts with man divided empire claim,   415
And the brown Indian marks with murderous aim ;
There, while above the giddy tempest flies,
And all around distressful yells arise,

---

[1] This passage is viewed by several editors as disclosing the same
theme as that which inspired the ' Deserted Village,' published five
years later. Sir James Prior points to " Have not we " (the author addressing his brother) as evidence that Auburn was an Irish village.—Ed.
[2] Niágara, it will be observed. This, Prior says, was the old pronun-
ciation of the name of the American river.—Ed.

The pensive exile, bending with his woe,
* To stop too fearful, and too faint to go,   420
Casts a long look where England's glories shine,
And bids his bosom sympathize with mine.

Vain, very vain, my weary search to find
That bliss which only centres in the mind :
Why have I stray'd from pleasure and repose,   425
To seek a good each government bestows?
In every government, though terrors reign,
Though tyrant kings, or tyrant laws restrain,
* How small, of all that human hearts endure,
* That part which laws or kings can cause or cure ! 430
* Still to ourselves in every place consign'd,
* Our own felicity we make or find :
* With secret course, which no loud storms annoy,
* Glides the smooth current of domestic joy.
The lifted axe, the agonizing wheel,   435
Luke's [1] iron crown, and Damien's [2] bed of steel,
* To men remote from power but rarely known,
* Leave reason, faith, and conscience, all our own. [3]

[1] In 1514, two brothers, Luke and George Zeck, headed a desperate
rebellion in Hungary. When it was quelled, George, not Luke, was
punished by having his head encircled with a red-hot crown, in mockery
of his supposed ambitious views.—B. The real name of the brothers
seems to have been Dosa. Forster says they were of the race of the
Szeklers, or Zecklers, of Transylvania. Bolton Corney has on this account
substituted " Zeck's " for " Luke's " in the poem.—ED.
[2] Robert Francis Damien, a mad fanatic, who, in 1757, made an
attempt to assassinate Louis XV. of France. He was put to the most
exquisite tortures, and at last torn to pieces by horses.—B.
[3] The nine lines to which an asterisk is prefixed were written by Dr.
Johnson, when the poem was submitted to his friendly revision, previous
to publication.—B. [This is on the authority of Boswell, who states
(Boswell's ' Life of Johnson,' Bohn's ed., v. ii., p. 308) that Johnson
marked the above ten lines, and " added, ' These are all of which I can be
sure.' " In the original editions there are no asterisks, and no intimation of Johnson having contributed these lines ; and Boswell's work of
course was published after both Goldsmith and Johnson were dead.
See also note at p. 45.—ED.]

EDWIN AND ANGELINA;

A BALLAD.

[SOMETIMES ENTITLED "THE HERMIT."]

[The first publicly printed version of this ballad appeared in the 'Vicar of Wakefield' (1766). But a few copies of another version had been printed privately in 1764, or 1765, for the Countess of Northumberland, who having seen the MS. through Dr. Percy (then just bringing out his collection of similar ballads, the 'Reliques'), wished to see the poem in print. This version was titled 'Edwin and Angelina'; and as it differs somewhat from that in the 'Vicar of Wakefield' we give its text here, referring the reader to our edition of the 'Vicar' (chap. viii.) for the author's later adopted text. Mr. Forster has said that the care bestowed by Goldsmith in amending and again amending this ballad affords an example "that young writers should study and make profit of." We think also that a comparison of the first with the later versions of the poem, as shown in the following text, its variation notes, and the text of the 'Vicar of Wakefield,' cannot fail of being generally interesting. The privately printed edition of 'Edwin and Angelina' is now extremely rare. Prior ascertained that in his day not even the Duke of Northumberland's library possessed a copy; while in the present day the British Museum library is also without a copy. The title of this edition runs: 'Edwin and Angelina; a Ballad: By Mr. Goldsmith: Printed for the Amusement of the Countess of Northumberland.' We here give the poem its original title, though 'The Hermit' has somewhat unaccountably become its most usual title. Goldsmith seems never to have titled it 'The Hermit'—though he is said to have spoken of it thus :—"As to my 'Hermit,' that poem, Cradock, cannot be amended." On the contrary his first, or Countess of Northumberland edition, is titled, as we have seen, 'Edwin and Angelina,' and he used the same title when he included the work in his 'Poems for Young Ladies,' 1767 (and again in 1770); while in the publication in the 'Vicar of Wakefield' the heading is simply 'A Ballad.' Then, in the edition of the 'Essays and Poems' of the year after Goldsmith's death, which seems to be the first collection of the author's chief poems into one volume, the ballad still figures as 'Edwin and Angelina.' Other reasons for reverting to the original title are, it seems to us, indicated by the facts; (1) that Parnell, whose poems have been published with those of Goldsmith, (and whose ' Life ' Goldsmith wrote,) has a poem entitled, 'The Hermit'; and, (2) that Bishop Percy, whose work in the ' Reliques ' is otherwise mixed up with this poem (as is shown by Goldsmith's own letter now usually prefixed to it), is the author of ' The Hermit of Warkworth.' Some controversy as to the poem's originality (besides that dealt with in Goldsmith's letter here following) is noticed in a note at p. 30.—ED.]

THE FOLLOWING LETTER, ADDRESSED TO THE PRINTER OF THE ST. JAMES'S CHRONICLE, APPEARED IN THAT PAPER IN JULY, 1767.

SIR,—As there is nothing I dislike so much as newspaper controversy, particularly upon trifles, permit me to be as concise as possible in informing a correspondent of yours, that I recommended Blainville's Travels because I thought the book was a good one ; and I think so still. I said I was told by the bookseller that it was then first published ; but in that, it seems, I was misinformed, and my reading was not extensive enough to set me right.

Another correspondent of yours accuses me of having taken a ballad I published some time ago from one[1] by the ingenious Mr. Percy. I do not think there is any great resemblance between the two pieces in question. If there be any, his ballad is taken from mine. I read it to Mr. Percy some years ago; and he (as we both considered these things as trifles at best) told me, with his usual good humour, the next time I saw him, that he had taken my plan to form the fragments of Shakespeare into a ballad of his own. He then read me his little Cento,[2] if I may so

---

[1] Percy attached a note here pointing out that the ballad referred to is ' The Friar of Orders Gray,' ' Reliques of Ancient Poetry,' v. i. book 2, No. 18 [Bohn's edition, 1876, v. i. p. 176].—ED.

[2] Dr. Percy, in the Life of Goldsmith which is prefixed to the octavo edition of his Miscellaneous Works published in 1801, denies the statement in this letter, so far as regards his having adopted the plan of his ballad from that of our author. The truth is, the idea which is common to both pieces was suggested by an old ballad published in Percy's ' Reliques,' and there headed ' Gentle Herdsman, Tell to me : A Dialogue between a Pilgrim and Herdsman ;' Percy, however, appears to have

call it, and I highly approved it. Such petty anecdotes as
these are scarcely worth printing ; and, were it not for the
busy disposition of some of your correspondents, the public
should never have known that he owes me the hint of his
ballad, or that I am obliged to his friendship and learning
for communications of a much more important nature.—I
am, Sir, yours, &c.   OLIVER GOLDSMITH.

been indebted to Goldsmith for the idea of making the lady confess to
the lover himself.

Goldsmith's imitation of the old ballad is in some parts so close, that
the reader may not be displeased to have an opportunity of comparing
the two in this place. The following is a short abstract of the story :—

A young pilgrim inquires of a *gentle* herdsman the way to Walsingham,
where was, in popish times, a famous image of the Virgin Mary. The
herdsman, by way of discouraging him, urges the difficulty and uncertainty of the path ; but the young pilgrim replies that these are a very
inadequate penance for his offence. This leads to a confession of the
penitent's sex, who turns out to be a young female in male attire ; and
her crime is no less than having treated a beautiful and amiable youth,
her lover, with so much caprice and scorn, as to drive him to a secret
retreat, where he died. She soon repents of her cruelty, and is resolved,
first, to do penance for her fault, and then to die for her lover's sake.
Compare the following stanzas with the thirty-third and three following
stanzas of 'Edwin and Angelina' beginning, " Yet still," &c.

> And grew so coy and nice to please,
>   As women's lookes are often soe ;
> He might not kisse, nor hand forsooth,
>   Unlesse I willed him soo to doe.

> Thus, being wearyed with delayes,
>   To see I pityed not his greeffe,
> He gott him to a secrett place,
>   And there hee dyed without releeffe.

> And for his sake these weedes I weare,
>   And sacriffice my tender age ;
> And every day I'le begge my bread,
>   To undergoe this pilgrimage.

> Thus every day I fast and praye,
>   And ever will doe till I dye ;
> And gett me to some secrett place,
>   For soe did hee, and soe will I.

'Gentle Herdsman.' 'Reliques,' vol. ii. p. 72, 1765 [Bohn's
edition, 1876, v. i. p. 302].—B.

EDWIN AND ANGELINA.

I.

" DEIGN saint-like tenant of the dale,
To guide my nightly way,
To yonder fire, that cheers the vale
With hospitable ray.

II.

" For here forlorn and lost [1] I tread,
With fainting steps and slow,
Where wilds, immeasurably spread,
Seem length'ning as I go."

III.

" Forbear, my son," the hermit cries,[2]
" To tempt the dangerous [3] gloom ;
For yonder faithless phantom flies
To lure thee to thy doom.

IV.

" Here to the houseless child of want
My door is open still ;
And though my portion is but scant,
I give it with good will.

---

[1] *Var.*—For here deserted, &c.   N.B. The variations here given are
in Goldsmith's ' Poems for Young Ladies' (the 1770 edition).   The
principal and final variations of the poem will be found, as we have
already said, in the version given in our edition of the ' Vicar of Wakefield '' (chap. viii.).—ED.

[2] *Var.*—the sage replies.   [3] *Var.*—lonely gloom.

V.

" Then turn to-night, and freely share
　　Whate'er my cell bestows ;
My rushy couch and frugal fare,
　　My blessing and repose.

VI.

" No flocks that range the valley free
　　To slaughter I condemn ;
Taught by that Power that pities me,
　　I learn to pity them :

VII.

" But from the mountain's grassy side
　　A guiltless feast I bring ;
A scrip with herbs and fruits supplied,
　　And water from the spring.

VIII.

" Then, pilgrim,[1] turn ; thy cares forego ;
　　All earth-born[2] cares are wrong :
' Man wants but little here below,
　　Nor wants that little long.' " [3]

IX.

Soft as the dew from heaven descends,
　　His gentle accents fell :
The modest stranger lowly bends,
　　And follows to the cell.

[1] *Var.*—Then, trav'ller, &c.
[2] *Var.*—For earth-born cares, &c.
[3] Goldsmith has been accused of plagiarizing Young in this couplet ;
but in the earliest editions he points the two lines with quotation marks
(which we restore) ; though really Goldsmith's lines are a better rendering rather than a quotation of Young's—

　　Man wants but little ; nor that little long.

　　　　　　　　　　('Night Thoughts,' iv. l. 118.)—ED.

X.

Far shelter'd in a glade obscure
    The modest[1] mansion lay,
A refuge to the neighb'ring poor,[2]
    And strangers led astray.

XI.

No stores beneath its humble thatch
    Required a master's care ;
The door just op'ning[3] with a latch,
    Received the harmless pair.

XII.

And now, when worldly crowds retire
    To revel or to rest,
The hermit trimm'd his little fire,[4]
    And cheer'd his pensive guest :

XIII.

And spread his vegetable store,
    And gaily press'd, and smiled ;
And, skill'd in legendary lore,
    The ling'ring hours beguil'd.

XIV.

Around,[5] in sympathetic mirth,
    Its tricks the kitten tries,
The cricket chirrups in the hearth,
    The crackling fagot flies.

XV.

But nothing mirthful could assuage
    The pensive stranger's woe ;
For grief had seized his early age,
    And tears would often flow.

---

[1] *Var.*—The later version has " lonely " for " modest."
[2] *Var.*—th' unshelt'red poor.   [3] *Var.*—But the door op'ning, &c.
[4] *Var.*—pleasant fire.   [5] *Var.*—While round, &c.

XVI.

His rising cares the hermit spied,
  With answ'ring care oppress'd:
" And whence, unhappy youth," he cried,
  " The sorrows of thy breast?

XVII.

" From better habitations spurn'd,
  Reluctant dost thou rove?
Or grieve for friendship unreturn'd,
  Or unregarded love?

XVIII.

" Alas! the joys that fortune brings,
  Are trifling, and decay;
And those who prize the paltry things,
  More trifling still than they.

XIX.

" And what is friendship but a name,[1]
  A charm that lulls to sleep;
A shade that follows wealth or fame,
  But leaves the wretch to weep?

XX.

" And love is still an emptier sound,[2]
  The modern fair one's jest;
On earth unseen, or only found
  To warm the turtle's nest.

XXI.

" For shame, fond youth, thy sorrows hush,
  And spurn the sex," he said;
But while he spoke, a rising blush
  The bashful[3] guest betray'd.

---

[1] *Var.*—Say, what is friendship? But a name.
[2] *Var.*—And what is love? An empty sound.
[3] *Var.*—The love-lorn, &c.

XXII.

He sees unnumber'd beauties [1] rise,
 Expanding to the view;
Like clouds that deck the morning skies,
 As bright, as transient too.

XXIII.

Her looks, her lips, her panting breast,
 Alternate spread alarms:
The lovely stranger stands confess't
 A maid in all her charms.

XXIV.

And, " Ah ! forgive a stranger rude—
 A wretch forlorn," [2] she cried;
" Whose feet unhallow'd thus intrude
 Where heaven and you reside.

XXV.

" Forgive, and let thy pious care
 A heart's distress allay:
That seeks repose, but finds despair
 Companion of the way.

XXVI.

" My father liv'd of high degree,
 Remote beside the Tyne;
And as he had but only me,
 Whate'er he had [3] was mine.

XXVII.

" To win me from his tender arms,
 Unnumber'd suitors came,
Their chief pretence my flatter'd charms,
 My wealth perhaps their aim.

---

[1] *Var.*—new beauty rise.   [2] *Var.*—A thing forlorn, &c.
    [3] *Var.*—His opulence was mine.

XXVIII.

" Each hour a mercenary [1] crowd
    With richest proffers [2] strove ;
Among the rest young Edwin bow'd,
    But offer'd only love.

XXIX.

" In humble, simplest habit clad,
    No wealth nor power had he ;
A constant heart was all he had,
    But that was all to me.

XXX.

" And when, beside me in the dale,
    He carol'd lays of love,
His breath lent fragrance to the gale,
    And music to the grove. [3]

XXXI.

" Whene'er he spoke amidst the train,
    How would my heart attend !
And still [4] delighted e'en to pain,
    How sigh for such a friend !

XXXII.

" And when a little rest I sought,
    In sleep's refreshing arms,
How have I mended what he taught,
    And lent him fancied charms !

---

[1] *Var.*—the mercenary, &c.

[2] *Var.*—With glitt'ring proffers, &c.

[3] This stanza was added by Bishop Percy, and first printed in his edition of the Works, 1801. Percy states that he had the MS. from Mr. Richard Archdal, an Irish M.P., to whom it had been given by Goldsmith.—ED.

[4] Most of the editions misprint this " And till," &c. Here we have from Goldsmith's own ' Poems for Young Ladies ' (1770), " And still." —ED.

XXXIII.

" Yet still (and woe betide [1] the hour!)
    I spurn'd him from my side,
And still with ill-dissembled power,
    Repaid his love with pride.

XXXIV.

" Till, quite dejected with my scorn,
    He left me to deplore;
And sought a solitude forlorn,
    And ne'er was heard of more.

XXXV.

" Then since he perish'd by my fault,
    This pilgrimage I pay;
I'll seek the solitude he sought,
    And stretch me where he lay.

XXXVI.

" And there in shelt'ring thicket hid,
    I'll linger till I die;
'Twas thus for me my lover did,
    And so for him will I."

XXXVII.

" Thou shalt not thus!" the hermit cried,
    And clasp'd her to his breast:
Th' astonish'd fair one turn'd to chide—
    'Twas Edwin's self that prest!

XXXVIII.

For now no longer could he hide,
    What first to hide he strove;
His looks resume their youthful pride,
    And flush with honest love.

[1] *Var.*—and hapless be the hour. }

XXXIX.

" Turn, Angelina, ever dear,
   My charmer, turn to see
Thy own, thy long lost Edwin here,
   Restored to love and thee.

XL.

" Thus let me hold thee to my heart,
   And ev'ry care resign :
And shall we never, never part,
   My life [1]—my all that's mine?

XLI.

" No, never, from this hour to part,
   Our love shall still be new ;
And the last sigh that rends thy heart
   Shall break thy Edwin's too.

XLII.

" Here amidst sylvan bow'rs [2] we'll rove,
   From lawn to woodland stray ;
Blest as the songsters of the grove,
   And innocent as they.

XLIII.

" To all that want, and all that wail,
   Our pity shall be given,
And when this life of love shall fail,
   We'll love again [3] in heav'n." [4]

[1] *Var.*—My thou—my all that's mine ? [Some mistake here probably. —ED.]

[2] *Var.*—Here amidst streams and bow'rs, &c.

[3] *Var.*—We'll love it o'er in heav'n.

[4] In 1798 the ' Monthly Review' gave place to the charge that Goldsmith had taken his ballad from a French poem called ' Raimond et Angeline'; and the very same charge was repeated in 1812 through the 'European Magazine'. Upon both occasions, however, our poet's fame was very effectually vindicated by its being shown that ' Raimond et Angeline' bore date 1792—eighteen years later than the poet's death —and was really *a translation from Goldsmith's own work* done by a M. Leonard.—ED.

THE DESERTED VILLAGE.

A POEM.

[First published in May, 1770. Percy is wrong in dating It 1769. Seven editions were printed in the author's lifetime, the sixth appearing within a year of the first publication. The principal author's emendations occur in the third and fourth editions.—ED.]

[DEDICATION.]

TO SIR JOSHUA REYNOLDS.

DEAR SIR,—I can have no expectations, in an address of this kind, either to add to your reputation, or to establish my own. You can gain nothing from my admiration, as I am ignorant of that art in which you are said to excel; and I may lose much by the severity of your judgment, as few have a juster taste in poetry than you. Setting interest, therefore, aside, to which I never paid much attention, I must be indulged at present in following my affections. The only dedication I ever made was to my brother, because I loved him better than most other men. He is since dead. Permit me to inscribe this Poem to you.

How far you may be pleased with the versification and mere mechanical parts of this attempt, I don't pretend to enquire; but I know you will object, (and indeed several of our best and wisest friends concur in the opinion,) that the depopulation it deplores is no where to be seen, and the disorders it laments are only to be found in the poet's own imagination. To this I can scarce make any other answer, than that I sincerely believe what I have written ; that I have taken all possible pains, in my country excursions, for these four or five years past, to be certain of what I allege ; and that all my views and enquiries have led me to believe those miseries real, which I here attempt to display. But this is not the place to enter into an enquiry whether the country be depopulating or not : the discussion would take up much room, and I should prove myself, at best, an indifferent politician, to tire the reader with a long preface, when I want his unfatigued attention to a long poem.

In regretting the depopulation of the country, I inveigh against the encrease of our luxuries ; and here also I expect the shout of modern politicians against me. For twenty or thirty years past, it has been the fashion to consider luxury as one of the greatest national advantages ; and all the wisdom of antiquity in that particular as erroneous. Still, however, I must remain a professed ancient on that head, and continue to think those luxuries prejudicial to states by which so many vices are introduced, and so many kingdoms have been undone. Indeed, so much has been poured out of late on the other side of the question, that, merely for the sake of novelty and variety, one would sometimes wish to be in the right.

I am, dear sir, your sincere friend, and ardent admirer,

OLIVER GOLDSMITH.

THE DESERTED VILLAGE.[1]

Sweet Auburn! loveliest village of the plain,
Where health and plenty cheer'd the labouring swain,
Where smiling spring its earliest visit paid,
And parting summer's lingering blooms delay'd :
Dear lovely bowers of innocence and ease,   5
Seats of my youth, when every sport could please,
How often have I loiter'd o'er thy green,
Where humble happiness endear'd each scene !
How often have I paused on every charm,
The shelter'd cot, the cultivated farm,   10
The never-failing brook, the busy mill,
The decent church that topt the neighbouring hill,
The hawthorn bush, with seats beneath the shade,
For talking age and whisp'ring lovers made.
How often have I blest the coming day,   15
When toil remitting lent its turn to play,
And all the village train, from labour free,
Led up their sports beneath the spreading tree ;
While many a pastime circled in the shade,
The young contending as the old survey'd ;   20
And many a gambol frolick'd o'er the ground,
And sleights of art and feats of strength went round ;

---

[1] The locality of this poem is supposed to be Lissoy, near Ballymahon, where the poet's brother Henry had his living. As usual in such cases, the place afterwards became the fashionable resort of poetical pilgrims, and paid the customary penalty of furnishing relics for the curious. The *hawthorn bush* has been converted into snuff-boxes, and now adorns the cabinets of poetical virtuosi.—B. [See also p. 18, and Appendix to our 'Life of Goldsmith,' v. i. Notwithstanding the abundance of evidence in favour of Lissoy, many think the original of Auburn is in England ; among these are Mr. Bolton Corney, Mr. Forster, and Professor Masson.—Ed.]

And still as each repeated pleasure tired,
Succeeding sports the mirthful band inspired;
The dancing pair that simply sought renown,   25
By holding out to tire each other down;
The swain, mistrustless of his smutted face,
While secret laughter titter'd round the place;
The bashful virgin's sidelong looks of love,
The matron's glance that would those looks reprove: 30
These were thy charms, sweet village! sports like these,
With sweet succession, taught e'en toil to please;
These round thy bowers their cheerful influence shed,
These were thy charms—but all these charms are fled.

Sweet, smiling village, loveliest of the lawn,   35
Thy sports are fled, and all thy charms withdrawn!
Amidst thy bowers the tyrant's hand is seen,
And desolation saddens all thy green:
One only master grasps the whole domain,
And half a tillage stints thy smiling plain.   40
No more thy glassy brook reflects the day,
But, choked with sedges, works its weedy way;
Along thy glades, a solitary guest,
The hollow-sounding bittern guards its nest;
Amidst thy desert walks the lapwing flies,   45
And tires their echoes with unvaried cries:
Sunk are thy bowers in shapeless ruin all,
And the long grass o'ertops the mouldering wall;
And, trembling, shrinking from the spoiler's hand,
Far, far away, thy children leave the land.   50

Ill fares the land, to hastening ills a prey,
Where wealth accumulates, and men decay:
Princes and lords may flourish, or may fade;
A breath can make them, as a breath has made;
But a bold peasantry, their country's pride,   55
When once destroy'd, can never be supplied.

A time there was, ere England's griefs began,
When every rood of ground maintain'd its man:
For him light labour spread her wholesome store,
Just gave what life required, but gave no more: 60

His best companions, innocence and health,
And his best riches, ignorance of wealth.

But times are alter'd: trade's unfeeling train
Usurp the land, and dispossess the swain;
Along the lawn, where scatter'd hamlets rose,   65
Unwieldy wealth and cumbrous pomp repose,
And every want to opulence [1] allied,
And every pang that folly pays to pride.
These gentle hours that plenty bade to bloom,
Those calm desires that ask'd but little room,   70
Those healthful sports that graced the peaceful scene,
Lived in each look, and brighten'd all the green,—
These, far departing, seek a kinder shore,
And rural mirth and manners are no more.

Sweet Auburn! parent of the blissful hour,   75
Thy glades forlorn confess the tyrant's power.
Here, as I take my solitary rounds,
Amidst thy tangling walks and ruin'd grounds,
And, many a year elapsed, return to view [2]
Where once the cottage stood, the hawthorn grew. [3]   80
Remembrance wakes with all her busy train,
Swells at my breast, and turns the past to pain.

In all my wand'rings round this world of care,
In all my griefs—and God has given my share—
I still had hopes, my latest hours to crown,   85
Amidst these humble bowers to lay me down;
To husband out life's taper at the close, [4]

[1] Editions one and two have "luxury."—ED.
[2] At Lissoy it was believed that Goldsmith visited Ireland shortly after his return from his wanderings on the Continent, as he said he would in his letter to his brother-in-law Hodson (Dec. 27, 1757), and that part of this poem was actually written in the village. See Newell's account of his visit to Lissoy, 1811, p. 74.—ED.
[3] *Var.*—After this was the following couplet, in the first three editions:—

    Here as with doubtful, pensive steps I range,
    Trace every scene, and wonder at the change.

[4] *Var.*— My anxious day to husband near the close,
    And keep life's flame, &c.—Editions one to three.

And keep the flame from wasting, by repose :
I still had hopes—for pride attends us still—
Amidst the swains to show my book-learn'd skill,   90
Around my fire an evening group to draw,
And tell of all I felt, and all I saw;
And, as a hare, whom hounds and horns pursue,
Pants to the place from whence at first she flew,
I still had hopes, my long vexations past,   95
Here to return—and die at home at last.

O, blest retirement, friend to life's decline,
Retreats from care that never must be mine !
How happy[1] he who crowns, in shades like these,
A youth of labour with an age of ease ;   100
Who quits a world where strong temptations try,
And, since 'tis hard to combat, learns to fly !
For him no wretches, born to work and weep,
Explore the mine, or tempt the dang'rous deep;
No surly porter stands in guilty state,   105
To spurn imploring famine from the gate :
But on he moves to meet his latter end,
Angels around befriending virtue's friend ;
Bends to the grave with unperceived decay,
While resignation gently slopes the way ;   110
And, all his prospects brightening to the last,
His heaven commences ere the world be past ![2]

Sweet was the sound, when oft, at evening's close,
Up yonder hill the village murmur rose :
There, as I past with careless steps and slow,   115
The mingling notes came soften'd from below ;
The swain responsive as the milk-maid sung,
The sober herd that low'd to meet their young ;
The noisy geese that gabbled o'er the pool,

---

[1] " How blest is," in first and second editions.—ED.
[2] Sir Joshua Reynolds drew the idea of his ' Resignation' from these lines. When the picture was engraved by T. Watson, the painter inscribed it to Goldsmith, saying :—" This attempt to describe a character in ' The Deserted Village' is dedicated to Dr. Goldsmith by his sincere friend and admirer Joshua Reynolds." The painting was in Lord Inchiquin's collection.—ED.

The playful children just let loose from school;   120
The watch-dog's voice that bay'd the whispering wind,
And the loud laugh that spoke the vacant mind,—
These all in sweet confusion sought the shade,
And fill'd each pause the nightingale had made.
But now the sounds of population fail,   125
No cheerful murmurs fluctuate in the gale,
No busy steps the grass-grown footway tread,
But all the bloomy flush of life is fled!
All but yon widow'd, solitary thing,
That feebly bends beside the plashy spring ;   130
She, wretched matron, forced in age, for bread,
To strip the brook with mantling cresses spread,
To pick her wintry fagot from the thorn,
To seek her nightly shed, and weep till morn ;
She only left, of all the harmless train,   135
The sad historian of the pensive plain.

Near yonder copse, where once the garden smiled,
And still where many a garden flower grows wild,
There, where a few torn shrubs the place disclose,
The village preacher's modest mansion rose.   140
A man he was to all the country dear,
And passing rich with forty pounds a-year :
Remote from towns he ran his godly race,
Nor e'er had changed, nor wish'd to change, his place ;
Unpractis'd he to fawn, or seek for power,   145
By doctrines fashion'd to the varying hour ;
Far other aims his heart had learn'd to prize,
More skill'd to raise the wretched than to rise.[1]
His house was known to all the vagrant train,
He chid their wand'rings, but relieved their pain :   150
The long remember'd beggar was his guest,
Whose beard descending swept his aged breast ;
The ruin'd spendthrift, now no longer proud,
Claim'd kindred there, and had his claims allow'd ;
The broken soldier, kindly bade to stay,   155
Sat by his fire, and talk'd the night away,
Wept o'er his wounds, or, tales of sorrow done,

---

[1] *Var.*—More bent to raise, &c.—The editions prior to the fourth.

Shoulder'd his crutch, and show'd how fields were won.
Pleased with his guests, the good man learn'd to glow,
And quite forgot their vices in their woe :   160
Careless their merits or their faults to scan,
His pity gave ere charity began.

Thus to relieve the wretched was his pride,
And e'en his failings lean'd to virtue's side ;
But in his duty prompt at every call,   165
He watch'd and wept, he pray'd and felt, for all ;
And, as a bird each fond endearment tries
To tempt its new-fledged offspring to the skies,
He tried each art, reproved each dull delay,
Allured to brighter worlds, and led the way.   170

Beside the bed where parting life was laid,
And sorrow, guilt, and pain, by turns dismay'd,
The reverend champion stood. At his control,
Despair and anguish fled the struggling soul ;
Comfort came down the trembling wretch to raise,   175
And his last faltering accents whisper'd praise.

At church, with meek and unaffected grace,
His looks adorn'd the venerable place ;
Truth from his lips prevail'd with double sway,
And fools who came to scoff, remain'd to pray.   180
The service past, around the pious man,
With steady [1] zeal, each honest rustic ran ;
E'en children followed, with endearing wile,
And pluck'd his gown, to share the good man's smile.
His ready smile a parent's warmth exprest,   185
Their welfare pleased him, and their cares distrest ;
To them his heart, his love, his griefs were given,
But all his serious thoughts had rest in heaven.
As some tall cliff that lifts its awful form,
Swells from the vale, and midway leaves the storm,   190
Though round its breast the rolling clouds are spread,
Eternal sunshine settles on its head.

Beside yon straggling fence that skirts the way,

---

[1] So in third, fourth, and other editions. Some editions, however,
have " ready."—ED.

With blossom'd furze unprofitably gay,
There, in his noisy mansion, skill'd to rule, 195
The village master taught his little school.
A man severe he was, and stern to view;
I knew him well, and every truant knew:
Well had the boding tremblers learn'd to trace
The day's disasters in his morning face; 200
Full well they laugh'd, with counterfeited glee, \
At all his jokes, for many a joke had he;
Full well the busy whisper, circling round,
Convey'd the dismal tidings when he frown'd:
Yet he was kind; or, if severe in aught, 205
The love he bore to learning was in fault.
The village all declared how much he knew;
'Twas certain he could write, and cypher too;
Lands he could measure, terms and tides presage,
And e'en the story ran—that he could gauge: 210
In arguing, too, the parson own'd his skill,
For ev'n though vanquish'd he could argue still;
While words of learned length, and thund'ring sound,
Amazed the gazing rustics ranged around;
And still they gazed, and still the wonder grew, 215
That one small head could carry all he knew.
But past is all his fame. The very spot
Where many a time he triumph'd, is forgot.

Near yonder thorn, that lifts its head on high,
Where once the sign-post caught the passing eye, 220
Low lies that house where nut-brown draughts inspired,
Where greybeard mirth, and smiling toil retired,
Where village statesmen talk'd with looks profound,
And news much older than their ale went round.
Imagination fondly stoops to trace 225
The parlour splendours of that festive place:
The white-wash'd wall, the nicely sanded floor,
The varnish'd clock that click'd behind the door;
The chest contrived a double debt to pay,
A bed by night, a chest of drawers by day; 230
The pictures placed for ornament and use,
The Twelve Good Rules,[1] the Royal Game of Goose;

[1] King Charles's ‘Twelve Good Rules,’ a wall decoration of the time,

The hearth, except when winter chill'd the day,
With aspin boughs, and flowers, and fennel gay;
While broken teacups, wisely kept for show,   235
Ranged o'er the chimney, glisten'd in a row.

Vain, transitory splendours! Could not all
Reprieve the tottering mansion from its fall?
Obscure it sinks, nor shall it more impart
An hour's importance to the poor man's heart: 240
Thither no more the peasant shall repair,
To sweet oblivion of his daily care;
No more the farmer's news, the barber's tale,
No more the woodman's ballad shall prevail;
No more the smith his dusky brow shall clear,   245
Relax his pond'rous strength, and lean to hear;
The host himself no longer shall be found
Careful to see the mantling bliss go round;
Nor the coy maid, half willing to be prest,
Shall kiss the cup to pass it to the rest.[1]   250

Yes! let the rich deride, the proud disdain,
These simple blessings of the lowly train;
To me more dear, congenial to my heart,
One native charm, than all the gloss of art.
Spontaneous joys, where nature has its play,   255
The soul adopts, and owns their firstborn sway;
Lightly they frolic o'er the vacant mind,
Unenvied, unmolested, unconfined:
But the long pomp, the midnight masquerade,
With all the freaks of wanton wealth array'd,—   260
In these, ere triflers half their wish obtain,
The toiling pleasure sickens into pain;
And, e'en while fashion's brightest arts decoy,
The heart, distrusting, asks—if this be joy?

Ye friends to truth, ye statesmen, who survey   265

as also mentioned by Goldsmith in his ' Description of an Author's Bed-
chamber' (p. 82). Crabbe likewise mentions them in his 'Parish Register.'—ED.
    [1] The Lissoy ale-house, then or afterwards called the Three Pigeons,
is sketched here, no doubt. It figures again as the " Three Jolly
Pigeons" in 'She Stoops to Conquer,' Act I., sc. 2.—ED.

The rich man's joys increase, the poor's decay,
'Tis yours to judge, how wide the limits stand
Between a splendid and a happy land.
Proud swells the tide with loads of freighted ore,
And shouting Folly hails them from her shore;   270
Hoards, e'en beyond the miser's wish, abound,
And rich men flock from all the world around.
Yet, count our gains.   This wealth is but a name
That leaves our useful products still the same.
Not so the loss.   The man of wealth and pride   275
Takes up a space that many poor supplied;
Space for his lake, his park's extended bounds;
Space for his horses, equipage, and hounds:
The robe that wraps his limbs in silken sloth,
Has robb'd the neighbouring fields of half their growth;
His seat, where solitary sports are seen,   281
Indignant spurns the cottage from the green;
Around the world each needful product flies,
For all the luxuries the world supplies:—
While thus the land adorn'd for pleasure, all   285
In barren splendour feebly waits the fall.

As some fair female, unadorn'd and plain,
Secure to please while youth confirms her reign,
Slights every borrow'd charm that dress supplies,
Nor shares with art the triumph of her eyes;   290
But when those charms are past—for charms are frail—
When time advances, and when lovers fail,
She then shines forth, solicitous to bless,
In all the glaring impotence of dress:
Thus fares the land, by luxury betray'd;   295
In Nature's simplest charms at first array'd:
But verging to decline, its splendours rise,
Its vistas strike, its palaces surprise;
While, scourged by famine from the smiling land,
The mournful peasant leads his humble band;   300
And while he sinks, without one arm to save,
The country blooms—a garden, and a grave.

Where, then, ah! where, shall Poverty reside,
To 'scape the pressure of contiguous pride?

If to some common's fenceless limits stray'd,   305
He drives his flock to pick the scanty blade,
Those fenceless fields the sons of wealth divide,
And ev'n the bare-worn common is denied.

If to the city sped—what waits him there?
To see profusion that he must not share;   310
To see ten thousand baneful arts combined
To pamper luxury and thin mankind;
To see those joys the sons of pleasure know
Extorted from his fellow-creatures' woe.
Here, while the courtier glitters in brocade,   315
There the pale artist plies his sickly trade;
Here, while the proud their long drawn pomps display,
There the black gibbet glooms beside the way.
The dome where Pleasure holds her midnight reign,
Here, richly deck'd, admits the gorgeous train;   320
Tumultuous grandeur crowds the blazing square,
The rattling chariots clash, the torches glare.
Sure scenes like these no troubles e'er annoy,
Sure these denote one universal joy!
Are these thy serious thoughts?—Ah, turn thine eyes
Where the poor houseless shivering female lies: 326
She once, perhaps, in village plenty blest,
Has wept at tales of innocence distrest;
Her modest looks the cottage might adorn,
Sweet as the primrose peeps beneath the thorn: 330
Now lost to all—her friends, her virtue fled,
Near her betrayer's door she lays her head,
And, pinch'd with cold and shrinking from the shower,
With heavy heart deplores that luckless hour,
When idly first, ambitious of the town,   335
She left her wheel and robes of country brown.

Do thine, sweet Auburn, thine, the loveliest train,
Do thy fair tribes participate her pain?
E'en now, perhaps, by cold and hunger led,
At proud men's doors they ask a little bread!   340

Ah, no. To distant climes, a dreary scene,
Where half the convex world intrudes between,

Through torrid tracts with fainting steps they go,
Where wild Altama [1] murmurs to their woe.
Far different there from all that charm'd before,   345
The various terrors of that horrid shore :
Those blazing suns that dart a downward ray,
And fiercely shed intolerable day ;
Those matted woods, where birds forget to sing,
But silent bats in drowsy clusters cling ;   350
Those poisonous fields, with rank luxuriance crown'd,
Where the dark scorpion gathers death around ;
Where at each step the stranger fears to wake
The rattling terrors of the vengeful snake ;
Where crouching tigers [2] wait their hapless prey,   355
And savage men, more murd'rous still than they ;
While oft in whirls the mad tornado flies,
Mingling the ravaged landscape with the skies.
Far different these from every former scene,
The cooling brook, the grassy-vested green,   360
The breezy covert of the warbling grove,
That only shelter'd thefts of harmless love.

Good Heaven ! what sorrows gloom'd that parting day
That call'd them from their native walks away ;
When the poor exiles, every pleasure past,   365
Hung round their bowers, and fondly look'd their last,
And took a long farewell, and wish'd in vain
For seats like these beyond the western main ;
And, shuddering still to face the distant deep,
Return'd and wept, and still return'd to weep !   370
The good old sire, the first prepared to go
To new-found worlds, and wept for others' woe ;
But for himself, in conscious virtue brave,
He only wish'd for worlds beyond the grave :
His lovely daughter, lovelier in her tears,   375
The fond companion of his helpless years,
Silent went next, neglectful of her charms,
And left a lover's for a father's arms :
·With louder plaints the mother spoke her woes,

---

[1] The Altama (or Altamaha) is a river in the province of Georgia, United States.—B.
[2] The jaguar is the American tiger.—NOAH WEBSTER.

And blest the cot where every pleasure rose ;   380
And kiss'd her thoughtless babes with many a tear,
And clasp'd them close, in sorrow doubly dear ;
Whilst her fond husband strove to lend relief
In all the silent manliness of grief.[1]

·O, luxury ! thou curst by Heaven's decree,   385
How ill exchanged are things like these for thee !
How do thy potions, with insidious joy,
Diffuse their pleasures only to destroy !
Kingdoms by thee, to sickly greatness grown,
Boast of a florid vigour not their own :   390
At every draught more large and large they grow,
A bloated mass of rank unwieldy woe ;
Till, sapp'd their strength, and every part unsound,
Down, down they sink, and spread a ruin round.

E'en now the devastation is begun,   395
And half the business of destruction done ;
E'en now, methinks, as pond'ring here I stand,
I see the rural virtues leave the land.
Down where yon anchoring vessel spreads the sail,
That idly waiting flaps with every gale,   400
Downward they move, a melancholy band,
Pass from the shore, and darken all the strand :
Contented toil, and hospitable care,
And kind connubial tenderness are there ;
And piety, with wishes placed above,   405
And steady loyalty, and faithful love.
And thou, sweet Poetry, thou loveliest maid,
Still first to fly where sensual joys invade ;
Unfit, in these degenerate times of shame,
To catch the heart, or strike for honest fame ;   410
Dear, charming nymph, neglected and decried,
My shame in crowds, my solitary pride ;
Thou source of all my bliss, and all my woe,
That found'st me poor at first, and keep'st me so ;
Thou guide by which the nobler arts excel,   415
Thou nurse of every virtue, fare thee well !

[1] *Var.*—In all the decent manliness, &c.—Editions one, two, and three.

Farewell; and O ! where'er thy voice be tried,
On Torno's cliffs, or Pambamarca's side,[1]
Whether where equinoctial fervours glow,
Or winter wraps the polar world in snow,　　　420
Still let thy voice, prevailing over time,
Redress the rigours of th' inclement clime ;
Aid slighted truth with thy persuasive strain ;
Teach erring man to spurn the rage of gain ;
Teach him, that states of native strength possess'd, 425
Though very poor, may still be very blessed ;
* That trade's proud empire hastes to swift decay,
* As ocean sweeps the labour'd mole away ;
* While self-dependent power can time defy,
* As rocks resist the billows and the sky.[2]　　　430

[1] Tornea, Gulf of Bothnia, Sweden. Pambamarca is said to be a mountain near Quito, South America.—ED.

[2] The four lines marked with an asterisk were written by Dr. Johnson, according to Boswell; vide ' Life of Johnson,' Bohn's edition, vol. ii., p. 309 :—" At the same time Dr. Johnson favoured me by marking the lines which he furnished to Goldsmith's ' Deserted Village,' which are only the last four." But, as we have said at p. 19, there was no evidence of this fact till Boswell wrote ; and, what is perhaps stranger still, even after Boswell had written, Percy, the friend and literary executor of Goldsmith, in his edition of the ' Works ' (1801) makes no mention of Johnson's contribution of these lines. Evans's first collected edition of the Poems and Plays (1780-86) is likewise without any indication of these contributions. See also Appendix to the Poems, p. 141.—ED.

THE HAUNCH OF VENISON;

A POETICAL EPISTLE TO LORD CLARE.

[Written about 1771, but not published until 1776, two years after
the poet's death. A second edition also appeared in 1776, having "additions and corrections taken from the author's last transcript." Our
text is mainly that of the second edition; but as some of the "corrected"
lines of that edition have been thought to be inferior to the correspond-
ing lines in the first edition, we add the latter as variations.—ED.]

THANKS, my lord, for your venison, for finer or fatter
Never rang'd in a forest, or smok'd in a platter.
The haunch was a picture for painters to study,
The fat was so white, and the lean was so ruddy;[1]
Though my stomach was sharp, I could scarce help re-
      gretting   5
To spoil such a delicate picture by eating:[2]
I had thoughts, in my chambers to place it in view,
To be shown to my friends as a piece of *virtù*;
As in some Irish houses, where things are so so,
One gammon of bacon hangs up for a show;   10
But for eating a rasher of what they take pride in,
They'd as soon think of eating the pan it is fried in.
But hold—let me pause—don't I hear you pronounce,
This tale of the bacon a damnable bounce?
Well, suppose it a bounce—sure a poet may try,   15
By a bounce now and then, to get courage to fly.

  But, my lord, it's no bounce: I protest, in my turn,
It's a truth—and your lordship may ask Mr. Burn.[3]

[1] *Var.*—The white was so white, and the red was so ruddy.—First
edition.

[2] This couplet is one of the additions to the second edition.—ED.

[3] Mr. Byrne, Lord Clare's nephew.—ED.

To go on with my tale: as I gazed on the haunch,
I thought of a friend that was trusty and staunch;   20
So I cut it, and sent it to Reynolds undrest,
To paint it, or eat it, just as he lik'd best.
Of the neck and the breast I had next to dispose—
'Twas a neck and a breast that might rival M—r—e's:[1]
But in parting with these I was puzzled again,   25
With the how, and the who, and the where, and the when.
There's H—d, and C—y, and H—rth, and H—ff—[2]
I think they love venison—I know they love beef;
There's my countryman, H—gg—ns [3]—oh, let him alone,
For making a blunder, or picking a bone: 30
But, hang it! to poets, who seldom can eat,
Your very good mutton's a very good treat;
Such dainties to them their health it might hurt,
It's like sending them ruffles, when wanting a shirt. [4]
While thus I debated, in reverie center'd,   35
An acquaintance—a friend, as he call'd himself—enter'd;
An under-bred, fine spoken fellow was he,
And he smiled as he look'd at the venison and me,—[5]

---

[1] The full word "Monroe's" is in the first, and in editions after the second. Dorothy Monroe was a beauty celebrated in Lord Townshend's verse.—ED.

[2] The full names, "Coley, and Williams, and Howard, and Hiff," are in the first edition. "Hiff—" stands for Paul Hiffernan, M.D., a turbulent Irishman of the Grub Street class of authors. He was associated with Burke in that celebrity's youthful squabbles with the theatrical managers of Dublin; and, later, was a hack writer, and half friend, half pensioner of Goldsmith in London. The others alluded to are now unknown, though probably they were characters of the same genus as "Hiff—." Mr. Bolton Corney queries whether Howard is the author of the "Choice Spirits' Museum" (1765), and whether "H——rth" is Hogarth, the surgeon of Golden Square.—ED.

[3] This couplet first appeared in the second edition. The full name "Higgins" appeared later. It is in the 1777 edition, and Percy also gives it, though without telling us who Higgins was. Mr. B. Corney thinks he may have been Captain Higgins, the officious military "friend" who helped Goldsmith to, rather than in, his quarrel with Evans the bookseller; see our 'Life' of the poet, p. 33, vol. i.—ED.

[4] *Var.*—Such dainties to them! It would look like a flirt,
                Like sending 'em ruffles, when wanting a shirt.
                                                        First edition.

[5] *Var.*—A fine spoken Custom-house officer he,
                Who smil'd as he gaz'd on the ven'son and me.
                                                        First edition.

" What have we got here ?—Why, this is good eating !
Your own, I suppose—or is it in waiting ? "   40
" Why, whose should it be ? " cried I, with a flounce,
" I get these things often ; "—but that was a bounce.
" Some lords, my acquaintance, that settle the nation,
Are pleas'd to be kind—but I hate ostentation." [1]

   " If that be the case, then," cried he, very gay,   45
" I'm glad I have taken this house in my way :
To-morrow you take a poor dinner with me ;
No words—I insist on't—precisely at three :
We'll have Johnson, and Burke, all the wits will be there ;
My acquaintance is slight, or I'd ask my lord Clare.   50
And, now that I think on't, as I am a sinner !
We wanted this venison to make out the dinner.
What say you—a pasty ? it shall, and it must,
And my wife, little Kitty, is famous for crust.
Here, porter—this venison with me to Mile-end :   55
No stirring, I beg—my dear friend—my dear friend ! " [2]
Thus, snatching his hat, he brusht off like the wind,
And the porter and eatables followed behind.

   Left alone to reflect, having emptied my shelf,
And " nobody with me at sea but myself ; " [3]   60
Though I could not help thinking my gentleman hasty,
Yet Johnson, and Burke, and a good venison pasty,
Were things that I never disliked in my life,
Though clogg'd with a coxcomb, and Kitty his wife.
So next day, in due splendour, to make my approach,   65
I drove to his door in my own hackney coach.

   When come to the place where we all were to dine,
(A chair lumber'd closet, just twelve feet by nine,)
My friend bade me welcome, but struck me quite dumb
With tidings that Johnson and Burke would not come ;

---

[1] This couplet is an addition to the second edition.—ED.
[2] *Var.*—No words, my dear Goldsmith ! my very good friend !
                                      First edition.
[3] A quotation from some love-letters that passed between his Royal
Highness the Duke of Cumberland and Lady Grosvenor (12mo., 1769), of
which the newspapers were at the time making fun.—ED.

"For I knew it," he cried, "both eternally fail,   71
The one with his speeches, and t' other with Thrale : [1]
But no matter, I'll warrant we'll make up the party
With two full as clever, and ten times as hearty.
The one is a Scotchman, the other a Jew ;   75
They both of them merry, and authors like you : [2]
The one writes the *Snarler*, the other the *Scourge ;*
Some think he writes *Cinna*—he owns to *Panurge*."
While thus he describ'd them, by trade and by name,
They enter'd, and dinner was served as they came.   80

At the top, a fried liver and bacon were seen ;
At the bottom, was tripe in a swingeing tureen ;
At the sides, there was spinnage, and pudding made hot ;
In the middle, a place where the pasty—was not.
Now, my Lord, as for tripe, it's my utter aversion, ·   85
And your bacon I hate like a Turk or a Persian ;
So there I sat stuck like a horse in a pound,
While the bacon and liver went merrily round : [3]
But what vex'd me most was that d——'d Scottish rogue, [4]
With his long-winded speeches, his smiles and his brogue, 90
And, "Madam," quoth he, "may this bit be my poison,
A prettier dinner I never set eyes on :
Pray, a slice of your liver, though, may I be curst,
But I've eat of your tripe till I'm ready to burst."
"The tripe !" quoth the Jew, with his chocolate cheek, 95
"I could dine on this tripe seven days in the week :
I like these here dinners, so pretty and small ;
But your friend there, the Doctor, eats nothing at all."
"O-ho !" quoth my friend, "he'll come on in a trice,
He's keeping a corner for something that's nice :   100

---

[1] An eminent London brewer, M.P. for the borough of Southwark, at whose table Dr. Johnson was a frequent guest.—B.
[2] *Var.*—Who dabble and write in the papers—like you.
                                        First edition.
[3] This couplet is one of the additions to the second edition.—Ed.
[4] Prior ['Life,' v. ii., p. 277] and Forster [v. ii., p. 262], say this Scotchman is "Parson Scott," who was a paid writer in support of the North ministry. He wrote in the *Public Advertiser* with the signatures Panurge and Anti-Sejanus; and it was he who unsuccessfully offered pay to Goldsmith to induce him to write for the North faction.—Ed.

There's a pasty."—"A pasty!" repeated the Jew,
"I don't care if I keep a corner for't too."
"What the deil mon, a pasty!" re-echo'd the Scot,
"Though splitting, I'll still keep a corner for thot." [1]
"We'll all keep a corner," the lady cried out;   105
"We'll all keep a corner," was echo'd about.
While thus we resolved, and the pasty delay'd,
With looks that quite petrified, enter'd the maid:
A visage so sad, and so pale with affright,
Wak'd Priam, in drawing his curtains by night.   110
But we quickly found out—for who could mistake her?—
That she came with some terrible news from the baker:
And so it fell out; for that negligent sloven
Had shut out the pasty on shutting his oven.
Sad Philomel thus—but let similes drop—   115
And now that I think on't, the story may stop. [2]

   To be plain, my good Lord, it's but labour misplac'd,
To send such good verses to one of your taste:
You've got an odd something—a kind of discerning—
A relish—a taste—sicken'd over by learning;   120
At least it's your temper, 'tis [3] very well known,
That you think very slightly of all that's your own:
So, perhaps, in your habits of thinking amiss,
You may make a mistake—and think slightly of this. [4]

---

   [1] The second edition has "that;" but we think "thot," as in the
first edition, preferable. The four lines here ending are an amplifica-
tion of two in the first edition.—ED.
   [2] The description of the dinner party in this poem is imitated from
one of Boileau's satires. Boileau himself took the hint from Horace, Lib.
ii. Sat. 8, which has also been imitated by Regnier, Sat. 10.—B.
   [3] From the first edition. The second has " as."—ED.
   [4] Robert Nugent, created Viscount Clare in 1766, was a man of parts
and also a merry companion. He published poems anonymously, through
Dodsley. He and Goldsmith seem to have been fast friends : see ' Life,'
p. 24, &c., v. i.—ED.

RETALIATION:

A POEM.

INCLUDING EPITAPHS ON THE MOST DISTINGUISHED WITS
OF THIS METROPOLIS.

[First published April 18, 1774, just a fortnight after the author's death. Several editions were published in the same year, the second being " corrected, with explanatory notes and observations." To the fourth (or, ? fifth) the " Postscript " was added. In 1777, Kearsley, the publisher who had issued all the preceding editions, issued an eighth edition. Evans gives the following account of the origin of the poem :— " Dr. Goldsmith and some of his friends occasionally dined at the St. James's Coffee-house. One day, it was proposed to write epitaphs on him. His country, dialect, and person furnished subjects of witticism. He was called on for ' Retaliation,' and at their next meeting produced the following poem."—Introduction to the poem, ' Poems and Plays,' 1786. Other and somewhat contradictory accounts are given by Cumberland and others. The late Mr. Peter Cunningham added to these by being the first to print (in his edition of Goldsmith's Works, 4 vols. 8vo., 1854) Garrick's account, from a MS. found amongst that famous actor's papers and lent to Mr. Cunningham by the late Mr. George Daniel of Canonbury House, Islington. We are indebted to Mr. Cunningham's edition for the following extract from the Garrick MS., which is signed " D. Garrick."—" At a meeting of a company of gentlemen, who were well known to each other, diverting themselves, among many other things, with the peculiar oddities of Dr. Goldsmith, who never would allow a superior in any art, from writing poetry down to dancing a hornpipe, the Doctor, with great eagerness, insisted upon trying his epigrammatic powers with Mr. Garrick, and each of them was to write the other's epitaph. Mr. Garrick immediately said that his epitaph was finished, and he spoke the following distich extempore :—

    ' Here lies Nolly Goldsmith, for shortness call'd Noll,
    Who wrote like an angel, but talk'd like poor Poll.'

Goldsmith, upon the company's laughing very heartily, grew very thoughtful, and either would not, or could not, write anything at that time : however, he went to work, and some weeks after he produced the following printed poem called ' Retaliation,' which has been much admired, and gone through several editions." [1]—ED.]

OF old, when Scarron his companions invited,
Each guest brought his dish, and the feast was united ;
If our landlord [2] supplies us with beef and with fish,
Let each guest bring himself—and he brings the best dish :
Our Dean [3] shall be venison, just fresh from the plains ; 5
Our Burke [4] shall be tongue, with a garnish of brains ;
Our Will [5] shall be wild-fowl, of excellent flavour,
And Dick [6] with his pepper shall heighten the savour.
Our Cumberland's [7] sweetbread its place shall obtain ;
And Douglas [8] is pudding, substantial and plain ;   10
Our Garrick's [9] a salad, for in him we see

[1] Garrick's epitaph, no doubt the chief, though not the sole, provocation of ' Retaliation ' had been hitherto given (by Dr. M'Donnell):—

> " Here lies Poet Goldsmith, for shortness call'd Noll,
> Who wrote like an angel, but talk'd like poor Poll."

and by another—

> " Here lies poor Goldsmith, &c.
> Who wrote like Apollo, &c."—ED.

[2] The master of the St. James's Coffee-house, where the Doctor, and the friends he has characterized in this poem occasionally dined. [The foot-notes here given with ' Retaliation,' are mostly founded upon those given with the revised editions of the poem (two to eight, 1774 to 1777). Those notes were of course not by Goldsmith, who left even the text of his poem unfinished, and, no doubt, in more ways than one unlike what it would have been had he himself given it out for publication. Mitford asks, " Why is there no portrait of Johnson in ' Retaliation ?' was it affection or fear that withheld the poet's hand ? " Had Goldsmith ever completed his poem, no doubt Johnson and others would have had their places. " Affection " did not exclude Reynolds ; neither did " fear " deter from the inclusion of Burke.—ED.]

[3] Dr. Barnard, Dean of Derry [afterwards successively Bishop of Killaloe and Limerick].

[4] The Rt. Hon. Edmund Burke.

[5] Mr. William Burke, a kinsman of Edmund, formerly secretary to General Conway, and member for Bedwin.

[6] Mr. Richard Burke, younger brother of Edmund. He held a post in Spain at this time.

[7] Mr. Richard Cumberland, author of ' The West Indian,' ' The Jew,' and other dramatic works.

[8] Dr. John Douglas, Canon of Windsor, and afterwards Bishop of Salisbury, was himself a native of Scotland, and obtained considerable reputation by his detection of the forgeries of his countrymen, Lauder and Bower. *Vide post*, notes.—B.

[9] David Garrick, actor, and manager of Drury Lane Theatre.

Oil, vinegar, sugar, and saltness agree :
To make out the dinner, full certain I am,
That Ridge[1] is anchovy, and Reynolds[2] is lamb ;
That Hickey's[3] a capon ; and, by the same rule,   15
Magnanimous Goldsmith a gooseberry fool.
At a dinner so various—at such a repast,
Who'd not be a glutton, and stick to the last?
Here, waiter, more wine! let me sit while I'm able,
Till all my companions sink under the table ;   20
Then, with chaos and blunders encircling my head,
Let me ponder, and tell what I think of the dead.

Here lies the good Dean, reunited to earth,
Who mixt reason with pleasure, and wisdom with mirth :
If he had any faults, he has left us in doubt,   25
At least, in six weeks, I could not find 'em out ;
Yet some have declar'd, and it can't be denied 'em,
That sly-boots was cursedly cunning to hide 'em.

Here lies our good Edmund, whose genius was such,
We scarcely can praise it or blame it too much ;   30
Who, born for the universe, narrow'd his mind,
And to party gave up what was meant for mankind :
Though fraught with all learning, yet straining his throat,
To persuade Tommy Townshend[4] to lend him a vote ;
Who, too deep for his hearers, still went on refining,   35
And thought of convincing, while they thought of dining :[5]
Though equal to all things, for all things unfit ;
Too nice for a statesman, too proud for a wit ;
For a patriot, too cool ; for a drudge, disobedient ;
And too fond of the *right* to pursue the *expedient*.   40
In short, 'twas his fate, unemploy'd or in place, sir,
To eat mutton cold, and cut blocks with a razor.

[1] Counsellor John Ridge, a gentleman belonging to the Irish bar.
[2] Sir Joshua Reynolds.   [3] An eminent attorney.
[4] Mr. T. Townshend, member for Whitchurch, afterwards Lord Sydney.
[5] Mr. Burke's speeches in Parliament, though distinguished by all the characteristic force of reasoning and eloquence of their highly gifted author, were not always listened to with patience by his brother members, who not unfrequently took the opportunity of retiring to dinner when he rose to speak. To this circumstance, which procured for the orator the *sobriquet* of the *Dinner Bell*, the poet here alludes.—B.

Here lies honest William, whose heart was a mint,
While the owner ne'er knew half the good that was in't;
The pupil of impulse, it forced him along,   45
His conduct still right, with his argument wrong;
Still aiming at honour, yet fearing to roam,
The coachman was tipsy, the chariot drove home:
Would you ask for his merits? alas! he had none;   49
What was good was spontaneous, his faults were his own.

Here lies honest Richard, whose fate I must sigh at;
Alas, that such frolic should now be so quiet!
What spirits were his! what wit and what whim!
Now breaking a jest, and now breaking a limb![1]
Now wrangling and grumbling to keep up the ball,   55
Now teasing and vexing, yet laughing at all!
In short, so provoking a devil was Dick,
That we wish'd him full ten times a-day at Old Nick;
But missing his mirth and agreeable vein,
As often we wish'd to have Dick back again.   60

Here Cumberland lies, having acted his parts,
The Terence of England, the mender of hearts;
A flattering painter, who made it his care
To draw men as they ought to be, not as they are.
His gallants are all faultless, his women divine,   65
And Comedy wonders at being so fine;
Like a tragedy queen he has dizen'd her out,
Or rather like Tragedy giving a rout.
His fools have their follies so lost in a crowd
Of virtues and feelings, that folly grows proud;   70
And coxcombs, alike in their failings alone,
Adopting his portraits, are pleased with their own.
Say, where has our poet this malady caught,
Or wherefore his characters thus without fault?
Say, was it, that vainly directing his view   75
To find out men's virtues, and finding them few,
Quite sick of pursuing each troublesome elf,
He grew lazy at last, and drew from himself?[2]

---

[1] Mr. Richard Burke having slightly fractured an arm and a leg at different times, the Doctor has rallied him on these accidents, as a kind of retributive justice, for breaking his jests upon other people.
[2] Mrs. Piozzi says this portrait of Cumberland is ironical.—Ed.

Here Douglas retires from his toils, to relax,
The scourge of impostors, the terror of quacks :   80
Come all ye quack bards, and ye quacking divines,
Come and dance on the spot where your tyrant reclines :
When satire and censure encircl'd his throne,
I fear'd for your safety—I fear'd for my own ;
But now he is gone, and we want a detector,   85
Our Dodds [1] shall be pious, our Kenricks [2] shall lecture ;
Macpherson [3] write bombast, and call it a style ;
Our Townshend make speeches, and I shall compile :
New Lauders [4] and Bowers [5] the Tweed shall cross over,
No countryman living their tricks to discover ;   90

[1] The Rev. Dr. Dodd, who was executed for forgery.

[2] Dr. Kenrick, who read lectures at the Devil Tavern, under the title of ' The School of Shakespeare.' [Kenrick was a well-known writer upon town, of prodigious versatility, and some talent. Dr. Johnson once observed of him, " Sir, he is one of the many who have made themselves *public*, without making themselves *known*." He was a man of no principle, and frequently wrote the severest libels against those with whom he was living on terms of apparent friendship. Amongst those who experienced the bitterness of his abuse was our author himself, which led to the altercation with Evans the bookseller.—See ' Life of Goldsmith' prefixed to v. i., p. 33. He was the original editor of the *Morning Chronicle*, but was afterwards dismissed for negligence.—B.]

[3] James Macpherson, Esq., who lately, from the mere *force of his style*, wrote down the first poet of all antiquity. [Macpherson's claim to original genius rests chiefly upon what has not yet been ascertained with sufficient accuracy, viz., his own share in the publication which he gave to the world as a translation of Ossian's Poems. He was, however, unquestionably a man of considerable talents, and not deficient in classical learning. The popularity of his Ossian induced him to publish a version of Homer in the same style of measured prose ; but this work, which is the one alluded to in the first part of this note, certainly added nothing to his reputation.—B.]

[4] William Lauder, a Scottish schoolmaster, who, by interpolating certain passages from the ' Adamus Exul ' of Grotius, from Masenius, and others, with translations from ' Paradise Lost,' endeavoured to fix on Milton a charge of extensive plagiarism from the modern Latin poets. Dr. Douglas, in a pamphlet entitled, ' Milton no Plagiary,' detected and exposed this impudent imposture, and extorted from the author a confession and apology, dictated by Dr. Johnson, who had been so far imposed upon by the forgery as to furnish a preface and postscript to Lauder's pamphlet.—B.

[5] Archibald Bower, a Scottish Jesuit, and author of a ' History of the Popes from St. Peter to Lambertini.' He also published, about the year 1755, his ' Motives of Conversion from Popery to Protestantism.' Dr. Douglas published a critical examination of this pamphlet, in which he

Detection her taper shall quench to a spark,
And Scotchman meet Scotchman, and cheat in the dark.

   Here lies David Garrick, describe me who can,
An abridgment of all that was pleasant in man ;
As an actor, confess't without rival to shine,   95
As a wit, if not first, in the very first line :
Yet, with talents like these, and an excellent heart,
The man had his failings, a dupe to his art.
Like an ill-judging beauty, his colours he spread,
And beplaster'd with rouge his own natural red.   100
On the stage he was natural, simple, affecting ;
'Twas only that when he was off he was acting.
With no reason on earth to go out of his way,
He turn'd and he varied full ten times a-day :
Though secure of our hearts, yet confoundedly sick   105
If they were not his own by finessing and trick :
He cast off his friends, as a huntsman his pack,
For he knew when he pleased he could whistle them back.
Of praise a mere glutton, he swallow'd what came,
And the puff of a dunce, he mistook it for fame ;   110
Till his relish, grown callous almost to disease,
Who pepper'd the highest, was surest to please.
But let us be candid, and speak out our mind,
If dunces applauded, he paid them in kind.
Ye Kenricks, ye Kellys,[1] and Woodfalls[2] so grave,   115
What a commerce was yours, while you got and you gave !
How did Grub Street re-echo the shouts that you raised,
While he was be-Roscius'd, and you were be-praised !
But peace to his spirit wherever it flies,
To act as an angel and mix with the skies :   120
Those poets who owe their best fame to his skill,
Shall still be his flatterers, go where he will,

convicted Bower of gross imposture, and totally destroyed the credit of
his history.—B.
  [1] Mr. Hugh Kelly, originally a staymaker, afterwards a newspaper
editor and dramatist, and latterly a barrister, was a native of Ireland.
His comedies of ' False Delicacy' and the ' School for Wives,' had considerable success. He also wrote ' Clementina,' ' A Word to the Wise,'
&c.—B.
  [2] Mr. William Woodfall, editor of the *London Packet*, and afterwards
of the *Morning Chronicle*.

Old Shakespeare receive him with praise and with love,
And Beaumonts and Bens be his Kellys above.[1]

Here Hickey reclines, a most blunt pleasant creature,
And slander itself must allow him good nature; 126
He cherish'd his friend, and he relish'd a bumper ;
Yet one fault he had, and that one was a thumper.
Perhaps you may ask if the man was a miser ?
I answer, No, no, for he always was wiser. 130
Too courteous, perhaps, or obligingly flat ?
His very worst foe can't accuse him of that.

[1] The following poems by Garrick are quoted by some editors, who think they " may in some measure account for the severity exercised by Dr. Goldsmith in respect to that gentleman." But these editors have been set right by others, who show that both *jeux d'esprit* were produced *after* ' Retaliation.' The ' Fable ' appeared in the *Annual Register*, 1776, and in Davies's ' Garrick,' 1780, v. ii., p. 157.—ED.

JUPITER AND MERCURY ;

A FABLE.

HERE, Hermes, says Jove, who with nectar was mellow,
Go fetch me some clay—I will make an odd fellow !
Right and wrong shall be jumbled,—much gold and some dross :
Without cause be he pleas'd, without cause be he cross ;
Be sure, as I work, to throw in contradictions,
A great love of truth, yet a mind turn'd to fictions :
Now mix these ingredients, which, warm'd in the baking,
Turn to learning and gaming, religion and raking.
With the love of a wench, let his writings be chaste ;
Tip his tongue with strange matter, his pen with fine taste;
That the rake and the poet o'er all may prevail,
Set fire to the head, and set fire to the tail.
For the joy of each sex, on the world I'll bestow it,
This scholar, rake, Christian, dupe, gamester, and poet ;
Though a mixture so odd, he shall merit great fame,
And among brother mortals—be GOLDSMITH his name :
When on earth this strange meteor no more shall appear,
You, Hermes, shall fetch him to make us sport here.

ON DR. GOLDSMITH'S CHARACTERISTICAL COOKERY.

A JEU D'ESPRIT.

ARE these the choice dishes the Doctor has sent us ?
Is this the great poet whose works so content us ?
This Goldsmith's fine feast, who has written fine books ?—
Heaven sends us good meat, but the Devil sends cooks.[*]

---

[*] God sends meat, and the Devil sends cooks.—*Ray's Proverbs.*—ED.

Perhaps he confided in men as they go,
And so was too foolishly honest? Ah, no!
Then what was his failing? come tell it, and burn ye:
He was, could he help it?—a special attorney!　　136

　Here Reynolds is laid, and, to tell you my mind,
He has not left a wiser or better behind;
His pencil was striking, resistless, and grand,
His manners were gentle, complying, and bland:　　140
Still born to improve us in every part,
His pencil our faces, his manners our heart.
To coxcombs averse, yet most civilly steering,
When they judg'd without skill, he was still hard of
　　hearing:
When they talk'd of their Raphaels, Correggios, and stuff,
He shifted his trumpet,[1] and only took snuff.[2]　　146

*　　*　　*　　*　　*　　*

POSTSCRIPT.

After the fourth edition of this Poem was printed, the publisher received an epitaph on Mr. Whitefoord, from a friend of the late Dr. Goldsmith, inclosed in a letter of which the following is an abstract:—

"I have in my possession a sheet of paper containing nearly forty lines in the Doctor's own handwriting; there are many scattered, broken verses, on Sir Jos. Reynolds, Counsellor Ridge, Mr. Beauclerk, and Mr. Whitefoord. The Epitaph on the last-mentioned gentleman is the only one that is finished, and therefore I have copied it, that you may add it

---

[1] Sir Joshua Reynolds was so deaf as to be under the necessity of using an ear trumpet in company.

[2] Malone, in his 'Memoir of Sir Joshua Reynolds' (1797), quotes these lines upon Reynolds, and says:—"These were the last lines the author wrote. He had written half a line more of this character, when he was seized with the fever which carried him in a few days to the grave. He intended to have concluded with his own character." Mr. Forster, quoting the same lines, gives an additional half-line, making the fragment end—

　　Shifted his trumpet, and only took snuff.
　　By flattery unspoiled . . . .

But none of the early editions have this half-line; nor has Percy; nor do these make any mention of this additional half-line. The stars end the poem in the original editions.—Ed.

to the next edition. It is a striking proof of Doctor Goldsmith's good-nature. I saw this sheet of paper in the Doctor's room, five or six days before he died; and, as I had got all the other Epitaphs, I asked him if I might take it. '*In truth you may, my boy*' (replied he), '*for it will be no use to me where I am going*'"[1] [" Introduction to the Postscript," in Kearsley's eighth edition (1777)].

HERE Whitefoord reclines, and, deny it who can,
Though he merrily lived, he is now a grave man :[2]
'Rare compound of oddity, frolic, and fun !
Who relish'd a joke, and rejoiced in a pun ;[3]
Whose temper was generous, open, sincere ;   5
A stranger to flatt'ry, a stranger to fear ;
Who scatter'd around wit and humour at will ;
Whose daily *bon mots* half a column might fill :
A Scotchman, from pride and from prejudice free ;
'A scholar, yet surely no pedant was he.   10

What pity, alas ! that so liberal a mind
Should so long be to newspaper essays confined !
Who perhaps to the summit of science could soar,
Yet content " if the table be set on a roar : "
Whose talents to fill any station were fit,   15
Yet happy if Woodfall[4] confess'd him a wit.

[1] The genuineness of the epitaph on Whitefoord has been doubted on account of, among other things, (1) its length, taking into account Whitefoord's comparative unimportance, and (2) the fact that the publisher did not have the MS. in the poet's handwriting. Whitefoord himself has been suspected of having written this epitaph. Prior thinks the words attributed to Goldsmith in the letter as "beyond doubt an untruth." Forster thinks the POSTSCRIPT "doubtful." Nevertheless, Percy has accepted it without comment; and succeeding editors have mostly followed Percy.—ED.

[2] Mr. Caleb Whitefoord, author of many humorous essays. Mr. Whitefoord was not, as Colman erroneously observes in his ' Random Records,' a member of THE LITERARY CLUB, but he was of the party at the St. James's Coffee-house which provoked ' Retaliation.' In the ' Foundling Hospital for Wit ' are some apologetical verses by him for having read in that club a ludicrous epitaph on the supposed death of Goldsmith.—B.

[3] Mr. Whitefoord was so notorious a punster, that Dr. Goldsmith used to say it was impossible to keep him company, without being *infected* with the *itch* of *punning*.

[4] Mr. H. S. Woodfall, editor of the *Public Advertiser*, and so editor of the original Junius Letters.

Ye newspaper witlings! ye pert scribbling folks!
Who copied his squibs, and re-echo'd his jokes;
Ye tame imitators, ye servile herd, come,
Still follow your master, and visit his tomb: 20
To deck it, bring with you festoons of the vine,
And copious libations bestow on his shrine;
Then strew all around it (you can do no less)
Cross Readings, Ship News, and *Mistakes of the Press.*[1]

Merry Whitfoord, farewell! for *thy* sake I admit   25
That a Scot may have humour, I'd almost said wit.
This debt to thy mem'ry I cannot refuse,
" Thou best humour'd man with the worst humour'd
      Muse."

[1] Mr. Whitefoord had frequently indulged the town with humorous
pieces under those titles in the *Public Advertiser.*

THE CAPTIVITY: AN ORATORIO.[1]

[Though two autograph MSS. of this work exist, it was scarcely known in the author's lifetime. And even after his death it remained unprinted till 1820.' It was set to music by R. J. S. Stevens (vide George Steevens's letter to Percy, Sept. 3, 1797), whose score has been lately (1880) added to the British Museum; but it does not appear to have been performed. Two extracted songs, however, got into print soon after the poet's death, and these (given at p. 83) have duly appeared in successive editions of the 'Poems.' The 'Oratorio' was first printed in the four vol. edition of the 'Works' dated 1820. The MS. of the version there given is supposed to bear date 1761. Some years later a second MS. turned up, and got printed in Prior's edition of the 'Works,' 1837. This latter is evidently a revised version of the first; and an accompanying document, dated 1764 (see Letters, &c., in vol. i.), shows that it was sold by Goldsmith to Dodsley for £10. Our text is from this second and corrected MS. The variations are from the first MS., some being erasures in that MS. The story of the oratorio is a combination of that of the captivity of the Jews under Zedekiah, B.C. 587, with that of their release at the destruction of Babylon by Cyrus, B.C. 538.—ED.]

THE PERSONS.

First Jewish Prophet.   First Chaldean Priest.
Second Jewish Prophet.   Second Chaldean Priest.
Israelitish Woman.   Chaldean Woman.
          Chorus of Youths and Virgins.·

SCENE.—*The Banks of the River Euphrates, near Babylon.*

[1] Both MSS. are untitled, though, as the extracted songs, given to the world soon after, if not before, Goldsmith's death, purport to be "From the Oratorio of 'The Captivity,'" it is clear 'The Captivity' was meant to be the title. When the original MS. was first printed in 1820 the work was merely titled 'An Oratorio.'—ED.

ACT I.

SCENE.—*Israelites sitting on the banks of the Euphrates.*

FIRST PROPHET.

Recitative.

YE captive tribes, that hourly work and weep,
Where flows Euphrates murmuring to the deep,
Suspend awhile the task, the tear[1] suspend,
And turn to God, your father and your friend:
Insulted, chain'd, and all the world a foe,　　　　5
Our God alone is all we boast below.

Air.

Our God is all we boast below,
　To him we turn our eyes;
And every added weight of woe,
　Shall make our homage rise.　　　　10

SECOND PROPHET.

And though no temple richly drest,
　Nor sacrifice is here,
We'll make his temple in our breast,
　And offer up a tear.
　　　　[*The first stanza repeated by the* CHORUS.

SECOND PROPHET.

Recitative.

That strain once more! it bids remembrance rise,　　15
And calls my long lost country to mine eyes:
Ye fields of Sharon, dress'd in flowery pride,
Ye plains where Jordan[2] rolls its glassy tide,
Ye hills of Lebanon, with cedars crown'd,
Ye Gilead groves, that fling perfumes around:—　　20

---

[1] *Var.*—Suspend your woes awhile, the task, &c.—*First MS.*
[2] *Var.*—Kidron.—*First MS.*

These hills how sweet! those plains how wond'rous fair![1]
But sweeter still when Heaven was with us there![2]

Air.

O Memory! thou fond deceiver,
　Still importunate and vain;
To former joys recurring ever,　　　　　　　　25
　And turning all the past to pain:

Hence, deceiver most distressing!
　Seek[3] the happy and the free:
The wretch who wants each other blessing,
　Ever wants a friend in thee.[4]　　　　　　　30

FIRST PROPHET.

Recitative.

Yet, why repine? What though by bonds confin'd,
Should bonds repress the vigour of the mind?
Have we not cause for triumph, when we see
Ourselves alone from idol worship free?
Are not, this very morn, those feasts begun,　　35
Where prostrate error hails the rising sun?
Do not our tyrant lords this day ordain
For superstitious rites and mirth profane?
And should we mourn? Should coward virtue fly,
When impious[5] folly rears her front[6] on high?　　40
No! rather let us triumph still the more,
And as our fortune sinks, our wishes[7] soar.

Air.

The triumphs that on vice attend
Shall ever in confusion end;
The good man suffers but to gain,　　　　　　45
And every virtue springs from pain:

---

[1] *Var.*—How sweet those groves! that plain, &c.—*First MS.*
[2] *Var.*—How doubly sweet when, &c.—*First MS.*
[3] *Var.*—Fly to.—*Erasure, first MS.*
[4] This song is one of the two that were re-written and published separately. See Poems, p. 83.—ED.　　[5] *Var.*—vaunting.—*First MS.*
[6] *Var.*—head.—*First MS.*　　　　[7] *Var.*—spirits.—*First MS.*

As aromatic plants bestow
No spicy fragrance while they grow ;
But crush'd, or trodden to the ground,
Diffuse their balmy sweets around.   50

SECOND PROPHET.

But hush, my sons ! our tyrant lords are near,
The sounds of barbarous mirth offend [1] mine ear ;
Triumphant music floats along the vale,
Near, nearer still, it gathers on the gale ;
The growing sound their swift approach declares— 55
Desist, my sons, nor mix the strain with theirs.

Enter CHALDEAN PRIESTS *attended.*

FIRST PRIEST.

Air.

Come on, my companions, the triumph display,
  Let rapture the minutes employ ;
The sun calls us out on this festival day,
  And our monarch partakes in the joy.   60

SECOND PRIEST.

Like the sun, our great monarch all rapture supplies,
  Both similar blessings bestow :
The sun with his splendour illumines the skies,
  And our monarch enlivens below.

A CHALDEAN WOMAN.

Air.

Haste, ye sprightly sons of pleasure,   65
Love presents its [2] fairest treasure,
  Leave all other joys for me.

A CHALDEAN ATTENDANT.

Or rather, Love's delights despising,
Haste to raptures ever rising :
  Wine shall bless the brave and free.   70

---

[1] *Var.*—pleasure strike.—*First MS.*   [2] *Var.*—the.—*First MS.*

FIRST PRIEST.

Wine and beauty thus inviting,
Each to different joys exciting,
　　Whither shall my choice incline?

SECOND PRIEST.

I'll waste no longer thought in choosing,
But, neither this nor that refusing,   75
　　I'll make them both together mine.

Recitative.

But whence, when joy should brighten o'er the land
This sullen gloom in Judah's captive band?
Ye sons of Judah, why the lute unstrung?
Or why those harps on yonder willows hung?   80
Come, take the lyre, and pour the strain along,
The day demands it; sing us Sion's song,
Dismiss your griefs, and join our warbling choir,
For who like you can wake the sleeping lyre?

SECOND PROPHET.

Bow'd down with chains,[1] the scorn of all mankind,   85
To want, to toil, and every ill consign'd,
Is this a time to bid us raise the strain,
Or mix in rites that Heaven regards with pain?
No, never! May this hand forget each art
That speeds the power of music to the heart,[2]   90
Ere I forget the land that gave me birth,
Or join with sounds profane its sacred mirth!

FIRST PRIEST.

Insulting slaves! if gentler methods fail,
The whip and angry tortures shall prevail.[3]
　　　　　　　　　　　　[*Exeunt* CHALDEANS.

---

[1] *Var.*—Chain'd as we are, &c.—*First MS.*
[2] *Var.*—That wakes to finest joys the human heart.—*First MS.*
[3] *Var.*—Rebellious slaves! if soft persuasion fail,
　　　More formidable terrors, &c.—*First MS.*

FIRST PROPHET.

Why, let them come; one good remains to cheer,—   95
We fear the Lord, and know no [1] other fear.

CHORUS.

Can whips or tortures hurt [2] the mind
On God's supporting breast reclin'd?
Stand fast, and let our tyrants see
That fortitude is victory! [3]   100
[*Exeunt.*

ACT II.

SCENE *as before.*

Chorus of ISRAELITES.

O Peace of Mind, angelic guest!
Thou soft companion of the breast,
    Dispense thy balmy store!
Wing all our thoughts to reach the skies,
Till earth, receding from our eyes,   5
    Shall vanish as we soar!

FIRST PRIEST.

Recitative.

No more!   Too long has justice been delay'd,
The king's commands must fully be obey'd:
Compliance with his will your peace secures,
Praise but our gods, and every good is yours.   10
But if, rebellious to his high command,
You spurn the favours offer'd from his hand,
Think, timely think, what terrors are behind,
Reflect, nor tempt to rage the royal mind.

[1] *Var.*—scorn all.—*First MS.*
[2] *Var.*—Can chains or tortures bend, &c.—*First MS.*
[3] *Var.*— Can chains or tortures bind the mind
        That leans on heaven for all felicity?
        Stand fast and let our tyrants find
        Our sufferings are victory.—*Erasure.*

SECOND PRIEST.

Air.

Fierce is the whirlwind [1] howling   15
O'er Afric's sandy plain,
And fierce the tempest [2] rolling
Along the furrow'd main ;
    But storms that fly
    To rend the sky,   20
Every ill presaging,
    Less dreadful show
    To worlds below
Than angry monarch's raging.

ISRAELITISH WOMAN.

Recitative.

Ah me ! what angry terrors round us grow ;   25
How shrinks my soul to meet the threaten'd blow!
Ye prophets, skill'd in Heaven's eternal truth,
Forgive my sex's fears, forgive my youth !
If shrinking thus, when frowning power appears,
I wish for life, and yield me to my fears : [3]   30
Let us one hour, [4] one little hour obey ;
To-morrow's tears may wash our stains away.

Air.

To the last moment of his breath,
    On hope the wretch relies ;
And e'en the pang preceding death   35
    Bids expectation rise. [5]
Hope, like the gleaming taper's light,
    Adorns and cheers our way ; [6]

---

[1] *Var.*—tempest.—*First MS.*   [2] *Var.*—whirlwind.—*First MS.*
[3] These two lines are not in the first MS.—Ed.
[4] *Var.*—Ah ! let us one, one little hour obey.—*First MS.*
[5] *Var.*—Fatigued with life, yet loth to part,
    On hope the wretch relies ;
And every blow that sinks the heart
    Bids the deluder rise.—*First MS.*
[6] *Var.*—Hope like the taper's gleamy light,
    Adorns and cheers our way, &c.—*First MS.*
    Adorns the gloomy way.—*Erasure.*

And still, as darker grows the night,
Emits a brighter ray.[1]   40

SECOND PRIEST.

Why this delay?   At length for joy prepare :
I read your looks, and see compliance there.
Come on, and bid the warbling rapture rise,
Our monarch's fame the noblest theme supplies.
Begin, ye captive bands, and strike the lyre,   45
The time, the theme, the place, and all conspire.

CHALDEAN WOMAN.

Air.

See the ruddy morning smiling,
Hear the grove to bliss beguiling ;
Zephyrs through the woodland playing,
Streams along the valley straying.   50

FIRST PRIEST.

While these a constant revel keep,
Shall Reason only teach to weep ?
Hence, intruder ! we'll pursue
Nature, a better guide than you.

SECOND PRIEST.

Air.

Every moment as it flows   55
Some peculiar pleasure owes :
Come, then, providently wise,
Seize the debtor as it flies.

Think not to-morrow can repay
The pleasures that we lose [2] to-day :   60
To-morrow's most unbounded store [3]
Can but pay its proper score.

---

[1] This is the other of the two songs which were extracted, re-written, and published in 1776, or earlier; see Poems, p. 83.—ED.
[2] *Vars.*—The debt of pleasure lost.—*First MS.*
       The pleasures we have lost, &c.—*Erasure.*
       The debt that we have lost, &c.—*Erasure.*
[3] *Var.*—Alas ! to-morrow's richest store.—*First MS.*

FIRST PRIEST.

Recitative.

But, hush![1] see, foremost of the captive choir,
The master prophet grasps his full-toned lyre.
Mark where he sits, with executing art,   65
Feels for each tone, and speeds it to the heart ;
See, how prophetic rapture fills his form,
Awful as clouds that nurse the growing storm !
And now his voice, accordant to the string,
Prepares our monarch's victories to sing.   70

FIRST PROPHET.

Air.

From north, from south, from east, from west,
   Conspiring nations come :
Tremble, thou vice-polluted breast ;
   Blasphemers, all be dumb.

The tempest gathers all around,   75
   On Babylon it lies ;
Down with her ! down—down, to the ground,
   She sinks, she groans, she dies.

SECOND PROPHET.

Down with her, Lord, to lick the dust,
   Ere yonder[2] setting sun ;   80
Serve her as she has served the just !
   'Tis fix'd—it shall be done.

FIRST PRIEST.

Recitative.

No more ! when slaves thus insolent presume,
The king himself shall judge, and fix their doom.
Unthinking wretches ! have not you and all   85
Beheld our power in Zedekiah's fall ?

---

[1] *Var.*—hold !—*First MS.*
[2] *Var.*—Before yon setting sun.—*First MS.*

To yonder gloomy dungeon turn your eyes :
See where dethron'd your captive monarch lies,
Deprived of sight, and rankling in his chain ;
See where he mourns his friends and children slain.
Yet know, ye slaves, that still remain behind   91
More ponderous chains, and dungeons more confin'd.

CHORUS OF ALL.

Arise, all potent ruler, rise,
    And vindicate thy people's cause,
Till every tongue in every land   95
    Shall offer up unfeign'd applause.

                        [Exeunt.

ACT III.

Scene *as before.*

FIRST PRIEST.

Recitative.

Yes, my companions, Heaven's decrees are pass'd,
And our fix'd empire shall for ever last :
In vain the madd'ning prophet threatens woe,
In vain rebellion aims her secret blow ;
Still shall our fame [1] and growing power be spread,   5
And still our vengeance [2] crush the traitor's head.

Air.

Coeval with man
Our empire began,
And never shall fall
Till ruin shakes all.   10
When ruin shakes all,
Then shall Babylon fall.

FIRST PROPHET.

Recitative.

'Tis thus that pride [3] triumphant rears the head :
A little while, and all their power is fled.

---

[1] *Var.*—name.—*First MS.*   [2] *Var.*—justice.—*First MS.*
[3] *Var.*—the proud.—*First MS.*

But, ha! what means yon sadly plaintive train,   15
That this way [1] slowly bends along the plain?
And now, methinks,[2] to yonder bank they bear
A pallid corse, and rest the body there.
Alas! too well mine eyes indignant trace
The last remains of Judah's royal race: 20
Our monarch falls, and now[3] our fears are o'er,
Unhappy Zedekiah is no more!

Air.

Ye wretches who by fortune's hate,
    In want and sorrow groan,
Come, ponder his severer fate,   25
    And learn to bless your own.

You vain, whom youth and pleasure guide,[4]
    Awhile the bliss suspend;
Like yours, his life began in pride,
    Like his, your lives shall end.   30

SECOND PROPHET.

Behold his wretched corse, with sorrow worn,
His squalid limbs with ponderous fetters torn;
Those eyeless orbs that shock with ghastly glare,
These ill-becoming rags—that matted hair!
And shall not Heaven for this its terrors show,[5]   35
Grasp the red bolt, and lay the guilty low?[6]
How long, how long, Almighty God of all,
Shall wrath vindictive threaten ere it fall!

ISRAELITISH WOMAN.

Air.

As panting flies the hunted hind,
    Where brooks refreshing stray;   40

---

[1] *Var.*—onward.—*First MS.*   [2] *Var.*—behold.—*First MS.*
[3] *Var.*—Fall'n is our king, and all, &c.—*First MS.*
[4] *Var.*—Ye sons from Fortune's lap supplied, &c.
[5] *Var.*—avenge the foe.—*First MS.*
[6] *Var.*—And deal its angry vengeance on the foe?

And rivers through the valley wind,
That stop the hunter's way:

Thus we, O Lord, alike distrest,[1]
For streams of mercy long;
Those streams[2] which cheer the sore opprest,   45
And overwhelm the strong.

FIRST PROPHET.

Recitative.

But, whence that shout? Good heavens! amazement all!
See yonder tower just nodding to the fall:
See where[3] an army covers all the ground,
Saps the strong wall, and[4] pours destruction round!   50
The ruin smokes, destruction pours along—
How low the great, how feeble are the strong![5]
The foe prevails, the lofty walls[6] recline—
O, God of hosts, the victory is Thine!

CHORUS OF ISRAELITES.

Down with them, Lord, to lick the dust;   55
Thy vengeance be begun:
Serve them as they have serv'd the just,
And let[7] Thy Will be done.

FIRST PRIEST.

Recitative.

All, all is lost! The Syrian army fails,[8]
Cyrus, the conqueror of the world, prevails!   60
The ruin smokes, the torrent pours along—
How low the proud, how feeble are the strong!
Save us, O Lord! to Thee, though late, we pray,
And give repentance but an hour's delay.

[1] *Var.*—deprest.—*Erasure.*   [2] *Var.*—Streams.—*First MS.*
[3] *Var.*—Behold.—*First MS.*
[4] *Var.*—'Tis Cyrus here that pours, &c.—*First MS.*
[5] These two lines are not in the first MS.—ED.
[6] *Var.*—And now, behold, the battlements recline.—*First MS.*
[7] *Var.*—O Lord.—*Erasure.*
[8] *Var.*—Whither shall we fly.—*Erasure.*

FIRST AND SECOND PRIEST.

Thrice[1] happy, who in happy hour ·65
To heaven[2] their praise bestow,
And own his all-consuming power
Before they feel the blow !

FIRST PROPHET.

Recitative.

Now, now's our time ! ye wretches bold and blind,[3]
Brave but to God, and cowards to mankind ; 70
Too late you seek that power [4] unsought before,
Your wealth, your pride,[5] your kingdom, are no more !

Air.

O, Lucifer, thou son of morn,
Alike of Heaven and man the foe,—[6]
Heaven, men, and all, 75
Now press thy fall,
And sink thee lowest of the low.

FIRST PROPHET.

O, Babylon, how art thou fallen !
Thy fall more dreadful from delay !
Thy streets forlorn 80
To wilds shall turn,
Where toads shall pant,[7] and vultures prey.

SECOND PROPHET.

Recitative.

Such be her fate !   But listen ! [8] from afar
The clarion's note proclaims the finish'd war !

[1] *Var.*—O happy.—*First MS.*   [2] *Var.*—To God.—*First MS.*
[3] *Var.*—Ye haughty sons of earth.—*Erasure.*
[4] *Var.*—Ye seek in vain the Lord, &c.—*First MS.*
[5] *Var.*—Your wealth, your lives, &c.—*First MS.*
[6] *Var.*—Heaven's bold usurper, mankind's foe.—*Erasure.*
[7] *Var.*—Where foxes haunt, &c.—*Erasure.*
[8] *Var.*—But hark ! how from afar.—*First MS.*

Cyrus, our great restorer, is at hand,   85
And this way leads his formidable band.
Give, give your songs of Zion to the wind,
And hail the benefactor of mankind :
He comes, pursuant to divine decree,
To chain the strong, and set the captive free.   90

CHORUS OF YOUTHS.

Rise to transports past expressing,
    Sweeter by remember'd woes ;
Cyrus comes, our wrongs redressing,
    Comes to give the world repose.

CHORUS OF VIRGINS.

Cyrus comes, the world redressing,   95
    Love and pleasure in his train ;
Comes to heighten every blessing,
    Comes to soften every pain.

SEMI-CHORUS.

Hail to him with mercy reigning,
    Skill'd in every peaceful art ;   100
Who, from bonds our limbs unchaining,
    Only binds the willing heart.

LAST CHORUS.

But chief to Thee, our God, defender, friend,
    Let praise be given to all eternity ;
O Thou, without beginning, without end,   105
    Let us, and all, begin and end in Thee ! [1]

---

[1] Washington Irving ('Life of Goldsmith,' chap. **xv.**) says of this work—"Most of the Oratorio has passed into oblivion ; but the following song from it will never die." He then quotes " The wretch condemned," &c. (see pp. 83 and 67).—ED.

MISCELLANEOUS POEMS.

THE CLOWN'S REPLY.

[This piece is traced in print no farther back than 1777, though the date attached shows that it was written while Goldsmith was a medical student in Edinburgh.—ED.]

JOHN TROTT was desir'd by two witty peers
To tell them the reason why asses had ears ;
" An't please you," quoth John, " I'm not given to letters,
Nor dare I pretend to know more than my betters ;
Howe'er, from this time, I shall ne'er see your graces—
As I hope to be sav'd !—without thinking on asses."
Edinburgh, 1753.

A PROLOGUE,

WRITTEN AND SPOKEN BY THE POET LABERIUS,[1] A ROMAN KNIGHT, WHOM CÆSAR FORCED UPON THE STAGE.

PRESERVED BY MACROBIUS.

[First printed in the chapter on the stage in Goldsmith's ' Enquiry into the Present State of Polite Learning,' 1759. In the second edition of the ' Enquiry' (1774), which the author revised just before his death, this poem was amongst the matter omitted. Goldsmith has translated, or rather imitated, only about the fore-half of the Latin original.—ED.]

WHAT ! no way left to shun th' inglorious stage,
And save from infamy my sinking age !
Scarce half alive, oppress'd with many a year,
What in the name of dotage drives me here ?

[1] Decimus Laberius, a Roman knight and popular farce-writer. Julius Cæsar commanded his appearance in one of his own plays.— —ED.

A time there was, when glory was my guide,
Nor force nor fraud could turn my steps aside ;
Unaw'd by power, and unappal'd by fear,
With honest thrift I held my honour dear :
But this vile hour disperses all my store,
And all my hoard of honour is no more ;
For, ah ! too partial to my life's decline,
Cæsar persuades, submission must be mine ;
Him I obey, whom heaven itself obeys,
Hopeless of pleasing, yet inclin'd to please.
Here then at once I welcome every shame,
And cancel, at threescore, a life of fame :
No more my titles shall my children tell,
The old buffoon will fit my name as well :
This day beyond its term my fate extends,
For life is ended when our honour ends.

THE LOGICIANS REFUTED.[1]

[IN IMITATION OF DEAN SWIFT.]

[First appeared in the ' Busy Body,' No. 5, Oct. 18, 1759, where it
is heralded by the statement that it is " an original poem by the late
Dean Swift, communicated to the ' Busy Body' by a nobleman of distinguished learning and taste." It seems to have first appeared as the
work of Goldsmith in Evans's edition of the Poems, 1780, where it got
the sub-heading (which we put in brackets), " In imitation of Dean
Swift." Percy and his successors have since included the poem in the
' Works,' though the doubt of its being by Goldsmith, caused by
Faulkner's claiming it for Swift (as mentioned in the note below), has
never been set at rest.—ED.]

LOGICIANS have but ill defined
As rational, the human kind : [2]

[1] This singularly happy imitation was adopted by Mr. Faulkner, the
Dublin publisher of Swift, as a genuine poem by that author, and as
such it has been reprinted in almost every successive edition of the
Dean's works. Even Sir Walter Scott has fallen into the same mistake,
and has inserted this piece, without any remark, in his excellent edition
of Swift's ' Works' published in 1814.—B. [It also appears in Scott's
second edition, 1824.]—ED.

[2] So in ' Busy Body ' edition. Nearly all the editors have substituted
" mind" for " kind."—ED.

REASON, they say, belongs to man,
But let them prove it if they can.
Wise Aristotle and Smiglesius,[1]   5
By ratiocinations specious,
Have strove to prove with great precision,
With definition and division,
Homo est ratione præditum ;
But for my soul I cannot credit 'em ;   10
And must in spite of them maintain,
That man and all his ways are vain ;
And that this boasted lord of nature
Is both a weak and erring creature.
That instinct is a surer guide   15
Than reason, boasting mortals' pride ;[2]
And that brute beasts are far before 'em—
Deus est anima brutorum.
Who ever knew an honest brute
At law his neighbour prosecute,   20
Bring action for assault and battery ?
Or friend beguile with lies and flattery ?
O'er plains they ramble unconfined,
No politics disturb their mind ;
They eat their meals, and take their sport   25
Nor know who's in or out at court ;
They never to the levee go
To treat as dearest friend a foe ;
They never importune his Grace,
Nor ever cringe to men in place ;   30
Nor undertake a dirty job,
Nor draw the quill to write for B—b.[3]
Fraught with invective they ne'er go
To folks at Pater-Noster Row :
No judges, fiddlers, dancing-masters,   35
No pickpockets, or poetasters,
Are known to honest quadrupeeds ;

---

[1] Smiglecius, a Polish logician : died 1618.—ED.
[2] 'Busy Body' edition reads "reason-boasting mortal's pride."—ED.
[3] So in 'Busy Body.' The editors make the word Bob, and annotate
it as a reference to Sir Robert Walpole. This no doubt is right, whether
the piece was written by Goldsmith or Swift, though Walpole was the
contemporary of Swift, and not of Goldsmith.—ED.

No single brute his fellows leads.
Brutes never meet in bloody fray,
Nor cut each others' throats for pay.   40
Of beasts, it is confess'd, the ape
Comes nearest us in human shape:
Like man, he imitates each fashion,
And malice is his ruling passion:
But both in malice and grimaces,   45
A courtier any ape surpasses.
Behold him humbly cringing wait
Upon the minister of state:
View him soon after to inferiors
Aping the conduct of superiors: 50
He promises with equal air,
And to perform takes equal care.
He in his turn finds imitators;
At court, the porters, lacqueys, waiters,
Their master's manners still contract,   55
And footmen lords and dukes can act.
Thus at the court, both great and small
Behave alike,—for all ape all.

[STANZAS]

ON THE TAKING OF QUEBEC,

[AND DEATH OF GENERAL WOLFE.]

[First published in the 'Busy Body,' Oct. 22, 1759, on receipt of the
news of General Wolfe's victory and death (Sept. 13, 1759).—ED.]

AMIDST the clamour of exulting joys,
    Which triumph forces from the patriot heart,
Grief dares to mingle her soul-piercing voice,
    And quells the raptures which from pleasures start.

O Wolfe![1] to thee a streaming flood of woe,
    Sighing we pay, and think e'en conquest dear;
Quebec in vain shall teach our breast to glow,
    Whilst thy sad fate extorts the heart-wrung tear.

[1] Goldsmith claimed relationship with this gallant soldier, whose
character he greatly admired, and whose death he thus laments in his

Alive, the foe thy dreadful vigour fled,
  And saw thee fall with joy pronouncing eyes :
Yet they shall know thou conquerest, though dead !
  Since from thy tomb a thousand heroes rise.

ON A BEAUTIFUL YOUTH,

STRUCK BLIND BY LIGHTNING.

Imitated from the Spanish.

[This seems to have been first printed in ' The Bee,' No. 1, 1759.
—Ed.]

SURE 'twas by Providence design'd,
  Rather in pity than in hate,
That he should be, like Cupid, blind,
  To save him from Narcissus' fate.

A SONNET.

[First printed in ' The Bee,' No. 3, 1759. Mr. Bolton Corney says
it is an imitation from the French of Saint-Pavin.—Ed.]

WEEPING, murmuring, complaining,
  Lost to every gay delight,
Myra, too sincere for feigning,
  Fears th' approaching bridal night.

Yet, why this killing soft dejection,
  Why dim thy beauty with a tear ?[1]
Had Myra follow'd my direction,
  She long had wanted cause of fear.

' History of England' (first edition, 1771, v. iv., p. 400): " Perhaps
the loss of the English that day was greater, than the conquest of
Canada was advantageous.   But it is the lot of mankind only to know
true merit on that dreadful occasion when they are going to lose it."—B.
Prior says Wolfe's mother was Henrietta Goldsmith, of Limerick.—Ed.

[1] We restore ' The Bee' text here. Most editions have in lieu of this
couplet—

> " Yet why impair thy bright perfection,
>   Or dim, &c."

The change was made in the first collected edition of the Poems and
Plays, that by Evans, 1780, and thence has been adopted by most of the
succeeding editors, Percy included.—Ed.

THE GIFT.

TO IRIS, IN BOW-STREET, COVENT GARDEN.

[First printed in 'The Bee,' 1759. It is an imitation of a French piece titled, 'Etrene a Iris,' and given by La Monnoye in the 'Ménagiana,' 1715, v. iii. p. 397.—ED.]

SAY, cruel Iris, pretty rake,
    Dear mercenary beauty,
What annual offering shall I make
    Expressive of my duty?

My heart, a victim to thine eyes,   5
    Should I at once deliver,
Say, would the angry fair one prize
    The gift, who slights the giver?

A bill, a jewel, watch, or toy,
    My rivals give—and let 'em ;   10
If gems, or gold, impart a joy,
    I'll give them—when I get 'em.

I'll give—but not the full-blown rose,
    Or rosebud more in fashion ;
Such short-lived off'rings but disclose   15
    A transitory passion.

I'll give thee something yet unpaid,
    Not less sincere than civil,—
I'll give thee—ah ! too charming maid !—
    I'll give thee—to the Devil !   20

'AN ELEGY

ON THAT GLORY OF HER SEX,

MRS. MARY BLAIZE.

[First printed in 'The Bee,' 1759. See introductory note to 'Elegy on the Death of a Mad Dog,' p. 89.—ED.]

GOOD people all, with one accord,
    Lament for Madam Blaize,
Who never wanted a good word—
    From those who spoke her praise.

The needy seldom pass'd her door,   5
    And always found her kind ;
She freely lent to all the poor—
    Who left a pledge behind.

She strove the neighbourhood to please,
    With manners wond'rous winning,   10
And never follow'd wicked ways—
    Unless when she was sinning.

At church, in silks and satins new,
    With hoop of monstrous size,
She never slumber'd in her pew—   15
    But when she shut her eyes.

Her love was sought, I do aver,
    By twenty beaux and more ;
The king himself has follow'd her—
    When she has walk'd before.   20

But now, her wealth and finery fled,
    Her hangers-on cut short all ;
The doctors found, when she was dead—
    Her last disorder mortal.

Let us lament, in sorrow sore,   25
    For Kent Street well may say,
That had she lived a twelvemonth more—
    She had not died to-day.

DESCRIPTION

OF AN

AUTHOR'S BED-CHAMBER.

[1759-60. Goldsmith intended this for the commencement of a " heroi-comic poem." After the description below, the hero of the piece, Scroggen, indulges in a soliloquy, which is interrupted by the entrance of the landlord, to dun him for his reckoning :—

> " Not with that face, so servile and so gay,
> That welcomes every stranger that can pay ;
> With sulky eye he smok'd the patient man,
> Then pull'd his breeches tight, and thus began," &c.

Our author does not appear to have proceeded farther with his plan, which is to be regretted, as he would in all probability have made it a very humorous account of the shifts and adventures of a needy author.—B. The above, with the extra lines of the fragment, are gleaned from Goldsmith's letter to his brother Henry, 1759 ; see Letters, vol. i. The lines of our text following differ otherwise slightly from the version in the letter. As here given they are the same as Goldsmith gave them, a year later, in his ' Citizen of the World' (Letter XXX.), where, probably, they first appeared in print.—ED.]

WHERE the Red Lion, staring o'er the way,
Invites each passing stranger that can pay ;
Where Calvert's butt, and Parson's black champagne,
Regale the drabs and bloods of Drury-lane :
There, in a lonely room, from bailiffs snug,
The Muse found Scroggen stretch'd beneath a rug.
A window, patch'd with paper, lent a ray,
That dimly show'd the state in which he lay ;
The sanded floor that grits beneath the tread ;
The humid wall, with paltry pictures spread ;
The Royal Game of Goose was there in view,
And the Twelve Rules the Royal Martyr drew ; [1]
The Seasons, fram'd with listing, found a place,
And brave Prince William show'd his lamp-black face. [2]

---

[1] See ' Deserted Village,' p. 39, and the note there.—ED.
[2] *Var.*—The version in the letter gives, " And Prussia's monarch show'd ", &c. " Prince William " applied to Prince William Augustus, Duke of Cumberland, the hero of Culloden, who died in 1765.—ED.

The morn was cold ; he views with keen desire
The rusty grate unconscious of a fire :
With beer and milk arrears the frieze was scor'd,[1]
And five crack'd teacups dress'd the chimney-board ; [2]
A nightcap deck'd his brows instead of bay,
A cap by night—a stocking all the day !

FROM THE ORATORIO OF THE CAPTIVITY.

[The publication of this and the following song we have traced back
to 1776, when they appeared, as here given, added to the first edition of
'The Haunch of Venison' (4to, Kearsley and Ridley, 1776). The
oratorio from which they were extracted, though probably written
about 1761, was not printed till 1820. See p. 61 for the Oratorio, and
pp. 63 and 67, for the previous forms of these two songs.—ED.]

SONG.

THE wretch condemn'd with life to part,
    Still, still on hope relies ;
And ev'ry pang that rends the heart
    Bids expectation rise.

Hope, like the glim'ring taper's light,
    Adorns and cheers the way ;
And still, as darker grows the night,
    Emits a brighter ray.

SONG.

O MEMORY ! thou fond deceiver,
    Still importunate and vain,
To former joys recurring ever,
    And turning all the past to pain.

Thou, like the world, th' oppress'd oppressing,
    Thy smiles increase the wretch's woe :
And he who wants each other blessing,
    In thee must ever find a foe.

[1] *Var.*—An unpaid reck'ning on the frieze, &c.
[2] The author has given a similar, or rather, with a very slight altera-
tion, the same description of the alehouse, in the 'Deserted Village.'
—PRIOR.

THE DOUBLE TRANSFORMATION:

A TALE.

[This and the next poem have not been traced farther back in print than the 'Essays' volumes (1765-6), though, doubtless, as Goldsmith's motto for the 'Essays' was "Collecta revirescunt," these two poems, which were respectively Essays XXVI. and XXVII. in the first edition, and XXVIII. and XXIX. in the second edition, had appeared in print before. Our text is that of the author-revised second edition of the 'Essays,' 1766, the variations being from the first edition.—ED.]

SECLUDED from domestic strife,
Jack Book-worm led a college life;
A fellowship at twenty-five
Made him the happiest man alive;
He drank his glass, and crack'd his joke, 5
And freshmen wonder'd as he spoke.[1]

 Such pleasures, unalloy'd with care,
Could any accident impair?
Could Cupid's shaft at length transfix
Our swain, arrived at thirty-six? 10
O, had the archer ne'er come down
To ravage in a country town!
Or Flavia been content to stop
At triumphs in a Fleet Street shop!
O, had her eyes forgot to blaze! 15
Or Jack had wanted eyes to gaze!
O!—but let exclamation cease,
Her presence banish'd all his peace;[2]

[1] The following additional couplet is in the first edition:—
  Without politeness aim'd at breeding,
  And laugh'd at pedantry and reading.

[2] After this, the following lines were in the first edition:—
  Our alter'd parson now began
  To be a perfect ladies' man;
  Made sonnets, lisp'd his sermons o'er,
  And told the tales he told before,
  Of bailiffs pump'd, and proctors bit;
  At college how he show'd his wit;
  And, as the fair one still approv'd,
  He fell in love—or thought he lov'd.
  So, &c.

So, with decorum all things carried,
Miss frown'd, and blush'd, and then was—married.

Need we expose to vulgar sight   21
The raptures of the bridal night?
Need we intrude on hallow'd ground,
Or draw the curtains clos'd around?
Let it suffice that each had charms: 25
He clasp'd a goddess in his arms;
And though she felt his usage rough,[1]
Yet in a man 'twas well enough.

The honey-moon like lightning flew,
The second brought its transports too;   30
A third, a fourth, were not amiss,
The fifth was friendship mix'd with bliss:
But, when a twelvemonth pass'd away,
Jack found his goddess made of clay;
Found half the charms that deck'd her face   35
Arose from powder, shreds, or lace;
But still the worst remain'd behind,—
That very face had robb'd her mind.

Skill'd in no other arts was she,
But dressing, patching, repartee;   40
And, just as humour rose or fell,
By turns a slattern or a belle.
'Tis true she dress'd with modern grace,
Half naked at a ball or race;
But when at home, at board or bed,   45
Five greasy nightcaps wrapp'd her head.
Could so much beauty condescend
To be a dull, domestic friend?
Could any curtain lectures bring
To decency so fine a thing?   50
In short, by night, 'twas fits or fretting;
By day, 'twas gadding or coquetting.
Fond to be seen, she kept a bevy [2]

---

[1] *Var.*—And though she felt his visage rough.—*First edition.*
[2] *Var.*—Now tawdry Madam kept a bevy.—*First edition.*

Of powder'd coxcombs at her levy ;
The 'squire and captain took their stations,   55
And twenty other near relations :
Jack suck'd his pipe, and often broke
A sigh in suffocating smoke ;[1]
While all their hours were pass'd between
Insulting repartee and spleen.   60

Thus, as her faults each day were known,[2]
He thinks her features coarser grown ;
He fancies every vice she shows,
Or thins her lip, or points her nose :
Whenever rage or envy rise,   65
How wide her mouth, how wild her eyes !
He knows not how, but so it is,
Her face is grown a knowing phiz ;
And though her fops are wondrous civil,
He thinks her ugly as the devil.   70

Now,[3] to perplex the ravell'd noose,
As each a different way pursues,
While sullen or loquacious strife
Promised to hold them on for life,
That dire disease, whose ruthless power   75
Withers the beauty's transient flower,—
Lo ! the small-pox, whose horrid glare
Levell'd its terrors at the fair ;
And, rifling every youthful grace,
Left but the remnant of a face.   80

The glass, grown hateful to her sight,
Reflected now a perfect fright :
Each former art she vainly tries
To bring back lustre to her eyes ;

[1] After this line, followed in the first edition :—

> She, in her turn, became perplexing,
> And found substantial bliss in vexing.
> Thus every hour was pass'd, &c.

[2] *Var.*—Each day, the more her faults were known.—*First edition.*
[3] Thus to perplex, &c.—*First edition.*

In vain she tries her paste and creams,   85
To smooth her skin, or hide its seams ;
Her country beaux and city cousins,
Lovers no more, flew off by dozens ;
The 'squire himself was seen to yield,
And ev'n the captain quit the field.   90

Poor madam, now condemn'd to hack
The rest of life with anxious Jack,
Perceiving others fairly flown,
Attempted pleasing him alone.
Jack soon was dazzl'd to behold   95
Her present face surpass the old :
With modesty her cheeks are dy'd,
Humility displaces pride ;
For tawdry finery is seen
A person ever neatly clean ;   100
No more presuming on her sway,
She learns good nature every day :
Serenely gay, and strict in duty,
Jack finds his wife—a perfect beauty.

A NEW SIMILE

IN THE MANNER OF SWIFT.

[1765, or earlier.   See Introduction to 'The Double Transformation,'
p. 84.]

Long had I sought in vain to find [1]
A likeness for the scribbling kind—
The modern scribbling kind, who write
In wit, and sense, and nature's spite—
Till reading—I forget what day on—   5
A chapter out of Tooke's *Pantheon*,[2]
I think I met with something there
To suit my purpose to a hair.

---

[1] *Var.*—I long had rack'd my brains to find.—*First edition.*
[2] The Rev. Andrew Tooke's ' Pantheon,' a popular illustrated mytho-
logy of the time.—ED.

But let us not proceed too furious;—
First please to turn to god Mercurius: 10
You'll find him pictured at full length,
In book the second, page the tenth:
The stress of all my proofs on him I lie,
And now proceed we to our simile.

Imprimis; pray observe his hat,   15
Wings upon either side—mark that.
Well! what is it from thence we gather?
Why, these denote a brain of feather.
A brain of feather! very right,
With wit that's flighty, learning light;   20
Such as to modern bard's decreed:
A just comparison—proceed.

In the next place, his feet peruse,
Wings grow again from both his shoes;
Design'd, no doubt, their part to bear,   25
And waft his godship through the air:
And here my simile unites;
For in a modern poet's flights,
I'm sure it may be justly said,
His feet are useful as his head.   30

Lastly, vouchsafe t'observe his hand,
Fill'd with a snake-encircled wand,
By classic authors term'd caduceus,
And highly famed for several uses:
To wit,—most wond'rously endued,   35
No poppy water half so good;
For let folks only get a touch,
Its soporific virtue's such,
Though ne'er so much awake before,
That quickly they begin to snore;   40
And, too, what certain writers tell,
With this he drives men's souls to hell.

Now to apply, begin we then:—
His wand's a modern author's pen;
The serpents round about it twined   45
Denote him of the reptile kind;

Denote the rage with which he writes,
His frothy slaver, venom'd bites : ,
An equal semblance still to keep,
Alike, too, both conduce to sleep.   50
This diff'rence only, as the god
Drove souls to Tart'rus with his rod,
With his goose-quill the scribbling elf,
Instead of others, damns himself.

And here my simile almost tript,   55
Yet grant a word by way of postcript.
Moreover Merc'ry had a failing :
Well ! what of that ? out with it—stealing ;
In which all modern bards agree,[1]
Being each as great a thief as he.   60
But ev'n this deity's existence
Shall lend my simile assistance :
Our modern bards ! why, what a pox
Are they but senseless stones and blocks ?
                                        * J. B.[2]

AN ELEGY ON THE DEATH OF A MAD DOG.

[This burlesque elegy is supposed to have been first printed in the
'Vicar of Wakefield' (chap. xvii.), 1766; though probably it was
written about the time of the popular scare concerning mad dogs (1760),
which Goldsmith has otherwise immortalized in his 'Citizen of the
World,' letter lxix.   Mr. Croker has pointed out that this and the similarly constructed 'Elegy on Mrs. Mary Blaize' (p. 81), are close imi-
tations of the popular French song 'Le fameux La Galisse, homme
imaginaire.'—ED.]

GOOD people all, of every sort,
    Give ear unto my song,
And if you find it wond'rous short,—
    It cannot hold you long.

---

[1] *Var.*—In which our scribbling bards agree.—*First edition.*
[2] The poem in both editions of the 'Essays' has this siguature.
Evans dropped it out; and Percy, and the rest, have followed Evans;
but, as a possible clue to the original publication, we now restore it.
Perhaps "J. B." stands for "Jack Book-worm," the name of the hero
of 'The Double Transfurmation,' which appeared with this poem in the
'Essays.'—ED.

In Isling town there was a man,⠀⠀⠀⠀⠀5
⠀⠀Of whom the world might say,
That still a godly race he ran,—
⠀⠀Whene'er he went to pray.

A kind and gentle heart he had,
⠀⠀To comfort friends and foes :⠀⠀⠀⠀10
The naked every day he clad,—
⠀⠀When he put on his clothes.

And in that town a dog was found,
⠀⠀As many dogs there be,
Both mongrel, puppy, whelp, and hound,⠀⠀15
⠀⠀And curs of low degree.

This dog and man at first were friends ;
⠀⠀But when a pique began,
The dog, to gain some private ends,[1]
⠀⠀Went mad, and bit the man.⠀⠀⠀⠀20

Around from all the neighb'ring streets
⠀⠀The wond'ring neighbours ran,
And swore the dog had lost his wits,
⠀⠀To bite so good a man.

The wound it seem'd both sore and sad⠀⠀25
⠀⠀To every Christian eye ;
And while they swore the dog was mad,
⠀⠀They swore the man would die.

But soon a wonder came to light,
⠀⠀That show'd the rogues they lied :⠀⠀30
The man recover'd of the bite—
⠀⠀The dog it was that died.

[1] The first edition has—"his private ends."—ED.

STANZAS ON WOMAN.

[Olivia's song in the 'Vicar of Wakefield,' chap. xxiv., where it seems to have been first published (1766).—ED.]

WHEN lovely woman stoops to folly,
And finds, too late, that men betray,
What charm can soothe her melancholy,
What art can wash her guilt away?

The only art her guilt to cover,
To hide her shame from every eye,
To give repentance to her lover,
And wring his bosom, is—to die.

EPITAPH ON EDWARD PURDON.[1]

[We have not found this in print earlier than 1777, when it appeared with the eighth edition of 'Retaliation.' Poor Purdon, however, died "suddenly" ten years before that date.—ED.]

HERE lies poor Ned Purdon, from misery freed,
Who long was a bookseller's hack;
He led such a damnable life in this world,
I don't think he'll wish to come back.

EPITAPH ON DR. PARNELL.

[This epitaph on Thomas Parnell, the poet-Archdeacon of Clogher, whose life Goldsmith wrote, seems to have been first printed in 1776 with 'The Haunch of Venison,' though probably it was written at the time of the 'Life of Parnell,' 1770.—ED.]

THIS tomb, inscribed to gentle PARNELL's name,
May speak our gratitude, but not his fame.
What heart but feels his sweetly moral lay,
That leads to truth through pleasure's flowery way?

[1] This gentleman was educated at Trinity College, Dublin; but having wasted his patrimony, he enlisted as a foot soldier. Growing tired of that employment, he obtained his discharge, and became a scribbler in the newspapers. He translated Voltaire's 'Henriade.'—*Note in edit.* 1777. [Goldsmith revised the translation: see Voltaire in vol. iv.—ED.]

Celestial themes confess'd his tuneful aid;
And Heav'n, that lent him genius, was repaid.
Needless to him the tribute we bestow,
The transitory breath of fame below:
More lasting rapture from his works shall rise,
While converts thank their poet in the skies.

EPILOGUE TO THE COMEDY OF THE SISTER.[1]

[This Epilogue was spoken by Mrs. Bulkley, who played Miss Autumn
in the comedy, and was afterwards the original Miss Hardcastle in
'She Stoops to Conquer.' 'The Sister' was produced Feb. 18. 1769.
The editors of Goldsmith, including the much relied upon, but often
fallible, Percy, very persistently misprint the name 'The Sisters.' Our
text is that of the first and second editions of the comedy, 1769.—ED.]

WHAT? five long acts—and all to make us wiser!
Our auth'ress sure has wanted an adviser.
Had she consulted *me*, she should have made
Her moral play a speaking masquerade;
Warm'd up each bustling scene, and, in her rage,   5
Have emptied all the green-room on the stage.
My life on't, this had kept her play from sinking,
Have pleased our eyes, and saved the pain of thinking.
Well, since she thus has shown her want of skill,
What if I give a masquerade?—I will.   10
But how? ay, there's the rub! [*pausing*] I've got my cue:
The world's a masquerade! the masquers, you, you, you.
                              [*To Boxes, Pit, and Gallery.*
Lud! what a group the motley scene discloses!
False wits, false wives, false virgins, and false spouses!
Statesmen with bridles on; and, close beside 'em,   15
Patriots in party-colour'd suits that ride 'em.
There Hebes, turn'd of fifty. try once more
To raise a flame in Cupids of threescore:

[1] 'The Sister' was by Mrs. Charlotte Lennox, author of 'The Female
Quixote,' 'Shakespeare Illustrated,' &c. It was performed one night
only at Covent Garden, in 1769, but in print it achieved a second
edition. The author, who was praised by Dr. Johnson, as the cleverest
female writer of her age (vide Boswell's 'Life of Johnson,' Bohn's ed.,
v. viii., p. 272), died in distressed circumstances, Jan. 4, 1804.—ED.

These, in their turn, with appetites as keen,
Deserting fifty, fasten on fifteen :   20
Miss, not yet full fifteen, with fire uncommon,
Flings down her sampler, and takes up the woman ;
The little urchin smiles, and spreads her lure,
And trys to kill, ere she's got power to cure.
Thus 'tis with all : their chief and constant care   25
Is to seem every thing—but what they are.
Yon broad, bold, angry spark, I fix my eye on,
Who seems t' have robb'd his vizor from the lion ;
Who frowns, and talks, and swears, with round parade,
Looking, as who should say, *Damme ! whose afraid ?*   30
                                  [*Mimicking.*
Strip but this vizor off, and, sure I am,
You'll find his lionship a very lamb.
Yon politician, famous in debate,
Perhaps, to vulgar eyes, bestrides the state ;
Yet, when he deigns his real shape t' assume,   35
He turns old woman, and bestrides a broom.
Yon patriot, too, who presses on your sight,
And seems, to every gazer, all in white,
If with a bribe his candour you attack,
He bows, turns round, and, whip—the man's a black ! 40
You critic, too—but whither do I run ?
If I proceed, our bard will be undone !
Well, then, a truce, since she requests it too :
Do you spare her, and I'll for once spare you.

VERSES IN REPLY TO AN INVITATION
TO DINNER AT DR. BAKER'S.[1]

[Written about 1769. It was first published from his family papers by Major-Gen. Sir Henry Bunbury, Bart., through Prior's edition of Goldsmith's Works, 1837.—ED.]

" This *is* a poem ! This *is* a copy of verses ! "

      YOUR mandate I got,
      You may all go to pot ;

[1] Sir Joshua Reynolds' physician. He became Sir George Baker.— ED.

Had your senses been right,
You'd have sent before night;
As I hope to be saved,   5
I put off being shaved;
For I could not make bold,
While the matter was cold,
To meddle in suds,
Or to put on my duds;   10
So tell Horneck[1] and Nesbitt,
And Baker and his bit,
And Kauffman[2] beside,
And the Jessamy bride,[3]
With the rest of the crew,   15
The Reynoldses two,
Little Comedy's[4] face,
And the Captain in lace.[5]
(By the bye you may tell him,
I have something to sell him;   20
Of use I insist,
When he comes to enlist.
Your worships must know
That a few days ago,
An order went out,   25
For the foot guards so stout
To wear tails in high taste,
Twelve inches at least:
Now I've got him a scale
To measure each tail,   30
To lengthen a short tail,
And a long one to curtail.)—
Yet how can I when vext,
Thus stray from my text?

[1] Mrs. Horneck, the widow of Capt. Kane Horneck.—Ed.

[2] Angelica Kauffman, the at that time popular artist, whose romantic story Miss Thackeray has told in her ' Miss Angel.'—Ed.

[3] Miss Mary Horneck, afterwards Mrs. Gwyn. She lived to 1840, and gave some reminiscences of Goldsmith to Hazlitt, which he published in his ' Conversations of Northcote.' See also p. 108.—Ed.

[4] Miss Catharine Horneck, afterwards (1771) the wife of Henry Bunbury, the caricaturist, who sometimes drew, and wrote, under the name of Geoffrey Gambado. See also p. 108.—Ed.

[5] Ensign, afterwards General Horneck: see v. i., p. 33.—Ed.

Tell each other to rue 35
Your Devonshire crew,
For sending so late
To one of my state.
But 'tis Reynolds's way
From wisdom to stray, 40
And Angelica's whim
To be frolick like him,
But alas! your good worships, how could they be wiser,
When both have been spoiled in to-day's *Advertiser?* [1]

OLIVER GOLDSMITH.

PROLOGUE TO ZOBEIDE.

['Zobeide' was a tragedy founded upon Voltaire's 'Les Scythes,' and written by Joseph Cradock, a gentleman of fortune, and friend of Goldsmith. The play was produced at Covent Garden Theatre, Dec. 11, 1771, and the prologue was spoken by the comedian Quick in the character of a sailor. Our text is from the edition of 1772, which it will be seen varies considerably from the earlier editions.—ED.]

IN these bold times, when Learning's sons explore
The distant climate and the savage shore;
When wise astronomers to India steer,
And quit for Venus many a brighter here;
While botanists,[2] all cold to smiles and dimpling, 5
Forsake the fair, and patiently—go simpling;
When every bosom swells with wond'rous scenes,
Priests, cannibals, and *hoity-toity* queens,[3]
Our bard into the general spirit enters,
And fits his little frigate for adventures. 10
With Scythian stores, and trinkets deeply laden,
He this way steers his course, in hopes of trading—

[1] In allusion to some verse in the 'Public Advertiser' on Angelica Kauffman's portrait of Sir Joshua Reynolds.—ED.

[2] At this time Captain Cook had just returned from his first voyage round the world, a voyage projected by the Royal Society and Mr. (afterwards Sir Joseph) Banks for scientific purposes. Cook and Mr. Charles Green were the astronomers of the expedition, and were charged with the observation of the transit of Venus, &c., while Mr. Banks and Dr. Solander, of the British Museum, were the botanists.—ED.

[3] These two lines are not in the earliest editions.—ED.

Yet ere he lands he's order'd me before,
To make an observation on the shore.
Where are we driven? our reckoning sure is lost!   15
This seems a barren[1] and a dangerous coast.
Lord, what a sultry climate am I under!
Yon ill-forboding cloud seems big with thunder:
            [*Upper Gallery.*
There mangroves spread, and larger than I've seen 'em—
                [*Pit.*
Here trees of stately size—and turtles in 'em.[2]   20
             [*Balconies.*
Here ill-condition'd oranges abound—   [*Stage.*
And apples, [*takes up one and tastes it*] bitter apples strew
  the ground.
The place is uninhabited,[3] I fear:
I heard a hissing—there are serpents here!
Oh, there the natives are, a dreadful race!   25
The men have tails, the women paint the face.
No doubt the're all barbarians.—Yes, 'tis so;
I'll try to make palaver with them though:
           [*Making signs.*[4]
'Tis best, however, keeping at a distance.
Good savages, our Captain craves assistance:[5]   30
Our ship's well stored—in yonder creek we've laid her,
His Honour is no mercenary trader.[6]
This is his first adventure; lend him aid,
Or you may chance to spoil[7] a thriving trade.
His goods, he hopes, are prime, and brought from far, 35
Equally fit for gallantry and war.
What? no reply to promises so ample?
—I'd best step back—and order up a sample.[8]

[1] *Var.*—a rocky, &c.   [2] *Var.*—billing turtles in 'em.
[3] *Var.*—The inhabitants are cannibals, &c.
[4] These four lines are not in the early editions.—ED.
[5] *Var.*—Oh, there the people are—best keep my distance:
   Our Captain, gentle natives, craves assistance.
[6] Cradock gave the profits of the performance to Mrs. Yates, who
played the heroine.—ED.
[7] *Var.*—And we may chance to drive, &c.
[8] Goldsmith's note, sent to Cradock with this Prologue, will be found
with the Letters at the end of vol. i.—ED.

THRENODIA AUGUSTALIS:

SACRED TO THE MEMORY OF HER LATE ROYAL HIGHNESS THE

PRINCESS DOWAGER OF WALES.

[This piece was produced upon the occasion of the death of Augusta of Saxe Gotha, the relict of Frederick, Prince of Wales, and mother of George III., and was performed at Mrs. Conely's, or " the Great Room," Soho Square, Feb. 20, 1772. The only separate edition, which so appeared without Goldsmith's name, seems to have been the usual pamphlet one for selling " at the doors," on the evening of performance. This exists, but is very rare. The poet's name does not appear upon the work, probably because he deemed it, as he says below, " a compilation rather than a poem." Steevens and Reed suggested that it should be included in Goldsmith's works; and Chalmers first (1810) so included it, printing from a copy given by the author to Cradock, and then in the possession of Nichols. See also note 2 at p. 106, and the letter to Cradock dated " *Sunday Morning*," with the Letters in vol. i.—ED.]

ADVERTISEMENT.

The following may more properly be termed a compilation than a poem. It was prepared for the composer in little more than two days: and may therefore rather be considered as an industrious effort of gratitude than of genius.

In justice to the composer, it may likewise be right to inform the public, that the music was adapted in a period of time equally short.

SPEAKERS—*Mr. Lee and Mrs. Bellamy.*

SINGERS—*Mr. Champnes, Mr. Dine, and Miss Jameson; with Twelve Chorus Singers.*

THE MUSIC PREPARED AND ADAPTED BY SIGNOR VENTO.

II.   H

THRENODIA AUGUSTALIS.

OVERTURE.—A SOLEMN DIRGE.

AIR.—TRIO.

ARISE, ye sons of worth, arise,
　And waken every note of woe.
When truth and virtue reach the skies,
　'Tis ours to weep the want below!

CHORUS.

When truth and virtue, &c.   5

MAN SPEAKER.

The praise attending pomp and power,
　The incense given to kings,
Are but the trappings of an hour—
　Mere transitory things.
The base bestow them; but the good agree   10
To spurn the venal gifts as flattery.
　But when to pomp and power are join'd
　An equal dignity of mind—
When titles are the smallest claim—
　When wealth, and rank, and noble blood,   15
　But aid the power of doing good—
Then all their trophies last; and flattery turns to fame.

Blest spirit thou, whose fame, just born to bloom,
Shall spread and flourish from the tomb,
　How hast thou left mankind for heaven!   20
Even now reproach and faction mourn,
And, wondering how their rage was born,
　Request to be forgiven!
Alas! they never had thy hate;
　Unmoved, in conscious rectitude,   25
　Thy towering mind self-centred stood,
Nor wanted man's opinion to be great.
In vain, to charm thy ravish'd sight,
　A thousand gifts would fortune send;

In vain, to drive thee from the right,   30
  A thousand sorrows urged thy end:
Like some well-fashion'd arch thy patience stood,
And purchased strength from its increasing load.
Pain met thee like a friend to set thee free,
Affliction still is virtue's opportunity!   35

SONG.—BY A MAN,[1] AFFETTUOSO.

Virtue, on herself relying,
  Every passion hush'd to rest,
Loses every pain of dying
  In the hopes of being blest.
Every added pang she suffers   40
  Some increasing good bestows,
And ev'ry shock that malice offers
  Only rocks her to repose.

WOMAN SPEAKER.

Yet ah! what terrors frown'd upon her fate,
  Death, with its formidable band,   45
Fever, and pain, and pale consumptive care,
  Determined took their stand.

Nor did the cruel ravagers design
  To finish all their efforts at a blow;
  But, mischievously slow,   50
They robb'd the relic and defac'd the shrine.
    With unavailing grief,
    Despairing of relief,
  Her weeping children round
    Beheld each hour   55
    Death's growing pow'r,
And trembled as he frown'd.

As helpless friends who view from shore
The labouring ship, and hear the tempest roar,

---

[1] Chalmers's version runs this song on to the lines for the "Man Speaker," but has the same words then repeated under "Song by a man," &c.—ED.

While winds and waves their wishes cross,—   60
They stood, while hope and comfort fail,
Not to assist, but to bewail
   The inevitable loss.
Relentless tyrant, at thy call
How do the good, the virtuous fall!   65
Truth, beauty, worth, and all that most engage,
But wake thy vengeance and provoke thy rage.

SONG.   BY A MAN.—BASSO, STACCATO, SPIRITOSO.

  When vice my dart and scythe supply,
  How great a King of Terrors I!
  If folly, fraud, your hearts engage,   70
  Tremble, ye mortals, at my rage!

  Fall, round me fall, ye little things,
  Ye statesmen, warriors, poets, kings,
  If virtue fail her counsel sage,
  Tremble, ye mortals, at my rage!   75

MAN SPEAKER.

Yet let that wisdom, urged by her example,
Teach us to estimate what all must suffer;
Let us prize death as the best gift of nature—
As a safe inn, where weary travellers,
When they have journey'd through a world of cares,   80
May put off life, and be at rest for ever.
Groans, weeping friends, indeed, and gloomy sables,
May oft distract us with their sad solemnity:
The preparation is the executioner.
Death, when unmask'd, shows me a friendly face,   85
And is a terror only at a distance;
For as the line of life conducts me on
To Death's great court, the prospect seems more fair,
'Tis Nature's kind retreat, that's always open
To take us in when we have drain'd the cup   90
Of life, or worn our days to wretchedness.
   In that secure, serene retreat,
  Where all the humble, all the great,

    Promiscuously recline ;
  Where, wildly huddled to the eye,   95
  The beggar's pouch and prince's purple lie,
    May every bliss be thine !
And, ah ! blest spirit, wheresoe'er thy flight,
Through rolling worlds, or fields of liquid light,
May cherubs welcome their expected guest ;   100
May saints with songs receive thee to their rest ;
May peace, that claim'd, while here, thy warmest love,
May blissful, endless peace be thine above !

            SONG.   BY A WOMAN.—AMOROSO.

    Lovely, lasting Peace below,
    Comforter of every woe,   105
    Heavenly born, and bred on high,
    To crown the favourites of the sky—
    Lovely, lasting Peace, appear !
    This world itself, if thou art here,
    Is once again with Eden blest,   110
    And man contains it in his breast.

                  WOMAN SPEAKER.

Our vows are heard ! Long, long to mortal eyes,
Her soul was fitting to its kindred skies :
Celestial-like her bounty fell,
Where modest want and patient sorrow dwell,   115
    Want pass'd for merit at her door,
      Unseen the modest were supplied,
    Her constant pity fed the poor,—
      Then only poor, indeed, the day she died.
And, oh ! for this, while sculpture decks thy shrine, 120
    And art exhausts profusion round,
The tribute of a tear be mine,
    A simple song, a sigh profound.
There Faith shall come—a pilgrim grey,
To bless the tomb that wraps thy clay :   125
And calm Religion shall repair
To dwell a weeping hermit there.

Truth, Fortitude, and Friendship, shall agree
To blend their virtues while they think of thee !

AIR.—CHORUS.—POMPOSO.

Let us—let all the world agree,　　　　　　130
To profit by resembling thee.

PART II.

OVERTURE.—PASTORALE.

MAN SPEAKER.

FAST by that shore where Thames'[1] transluceut stream
　Reflects new glories on his breast,
Where, splendid as the youthful poet's dream,
　He forms a scene beyond Elysium blest—　　135
Where sculptur'd elegance and native grace
Unite to stamp the beauties of the place ;
While, sweetly blending, still are seeu
The wavy lawn, the sloping green—
　While novelty, with cautious cunning,　　·　140
　Through every maze of fancy running,
From China borrows aid to deck the scene—
There, sorrowing by the river's glassy bed,
　Forlorn, a rural band complain'd,
All whom AUGUSTA's bounty fed,　　　　　　145
　All whom her clemency sustain'd ;
The good old sire, unconscious of decay,
The modest matron, clad in home-spun grey,
The military boy, the orphan'd maid,
The shatter'd veteran, now first dismay'd,—　　150
These sadly join beside the murmuring deep,
　And, as they view the towers of Kew,
Call on their mistress—now no more—and weep.

---

[1] The scene is Kew Palace, where the Princess resided, and the gardens of which she greatly improved, employing the famous architect-gardener of the time, Chambers (afterwards Sir William), for the purpose.—ED.

CHORUS.—AFFETTUOSO, LARGO.

Ye shady walks, ye waving greens,
Ye nodding towers, ye fairy scenes— 155
Let all your echoes now deplore,
That she who form'd your beauties is no more.

MAN SPEAKER.

First of the train the patient rustic came,
  Whose callous hand had form'd the scene,
Bending at once with sorrow and with age, 160
  With many a tear, and many a sigh between :
" And where," he cried, " shall now my babes have bread,
  Or how shall age support its feeble fire ?
No lord will take me now, my vigour fled,
  Nor can my strength perform what they require : 165
Each grudging master keeps the labourer bare,
A sleek and idle race is all their care.
My noble mistress thought not so :
  Her bounty, like the morning dew,
Unseen, though constant, us'd to flow, 170
  And as my strength decay'd, her bounty grew."

WOMAN SPEAKER.

In decent dress, and coarsely clean,
The pious matron next was seen,—
Clasp'd in her hand a godly book was borne,
By use and daily meditation worn ; 175
That decent dress, that holy guide,
AUGUSTA's care had well supplied.
" And, ah ! " she cries, all woe-begone,
  " What now remains for me ?
Oh ! where shall weeping want repair, 180
  To ask for charity ?
Too late in life for me to ask,
  And shame prevents the deed,
And tardy, tardy are the times
  To succour, should I need. 185
But all my wants, before I spoke,

Were to my mistress known;
　She still reliev'd, nor sought my praise,
　Contented with her own.
But every day her name I'll bless—　　　　　190
　My morning prayer, my evening song;
I'll praise her while my life shall last,
　A life that cannot last me long."

SONG.—BY A WOMAN.

Each day, each hour, her name I'll bless—
　My morning and my evening song;　　　　195
And when in death my vows shall cease,
　My children shall the note prolong.

MAN SPEAKER.

The hardy veteran after struck the sight,
　Scarr'd, mangled, maim'd in every part,
Lopp'd of his limbs in many a gallant fight,　　200
　In nought entire—except his heart:
Mute for awhile, and sullenly distress'd,
At last the impetuous sorrow fir'd his breast.
　" Wild is the whirlwind rolling
　　O'er Afric's sandy plain,　　　　　　205
　And wild the tempest howling
　　Along the billow'd main:
　But every danger felt[1] before,
　The raging deep, the whirlwind's roar—
　Less dreadful struck me with dismay　　210
　Than what I feel this fatal day.
　Oh, let me fly a land that spurns the brave,
　Oswego's dreary shores shall be my grave;
　I'll seek that less inhospitable coast,
　And lay my body where my limbs were lost."　215

SONG.—BY A MAN.—BASSO, SPIRITOSO.

Old Edward's sons, unknown to yield,
Shall crowd from Crecy's laurell'd field,
　To do thy memory right:

---

[1] Reed's text (Prior) has "danger fell."—ED.

For thine and Britain's wrongs they feel,
Again they snatch the gleamy steel, 220
And wish th' avenging fight.[1]

WOMAN SPEAKER.

In innocence and youth complaining,
　Next appear'd a lovely maid—
Affliction, o'er each feature reigning,
　Kindly came in beauty's aid : 225
Every grace that grief dispenses,
　Every glance that warms the soul,
In sweet succession charm'd the senses,
　While pity harmoniz'd the whole.
" The garland of beauty,"—'tis thus she would say— 230
" No more shall my crook or my temples adorn ;
I'll not wear a garland—AUGUSTA's away—
I'll not wear a garland until she return.
But, alas ! that return I never shall see :
The echoes of Thames shall my sorrows proclaim, 235
There promised a lover to come—but, ah me !
'Twas death—'twas the death of my mistress that came.
But ever, for ever, her image shall last :
I'll strip all the Spring of its earliest bloom ;
On her grave shall the cowslip and primrose be cast, 240
And the new-blossom'd thorn shall whiten her tomb."

SONG.—BY A WOMAN.—PASTORALE.

With garlands of beauty the Queen of the May
　No more will her crook or her temples adorn ;
For who'd wear a garland when she is away,
　When she is remov'd, and shall never return ? 245

On the grave of AUGUSTA these garlands be plac'd,
　We'll rifle the Spring of its earliest bloom ;
And there shall the cowslip and primrose be cast,
　And the new blossom'd thorn shall whiten her tomb.

---

[1] These six lines are almost word for word the same as are lines 30-
36 of Collins' 'Ode to a Lady, on the death of Col. Ross.' See also
note 1 on next page.—ED.

CHORUS.—ALTRO MODO.

On the grave of AUGUSTA this garland be placed,   250
  We'll rifle the Spring of its earliest bloom;[1]
And there shall the cowslip and primrose be cast,
  And the tears of her country shall water her tomb.[2]

LETTER, IN PROSE AND VERSE, TO
MRS. BUNBURY.

[Written in 1772, according to Sir Henry Bunbury, when he first published the piece through Prior's edition of the poet's works, 1837; but when, in the following year, Sir Henry included it in his 'Correspondence,' &c., of his kinsman Sir T. Hanmer, he said that it was "probably written in 1773 or 1774." The letter was in reply to a rhyming invitation to visit the Bunburys (Mr. and Mrs. H. Bunbury) at Barton, their country seat in Suffolk.—ED.]

MADAM:

I READ your letter with all that allowance which critical candour could require, but after all find so much to object to, and so much to raise my indignation, that I cannot help giving it a serious answer. I am not so ignorant, Madam, as not to see there are many sarcasms contained in it, and solecisms also, (solecism is a word that comes from the town of Soleis, in Attica, among the Greeks, built by Solon, and applied as we use the word Kidderminster for curtains from a town also of that name; but this is learning you have no taste for!)—I say, Madam, there are

---

[1] Here there seems to be a recollection of Collins's Cymbeline Dirge:—

   "Each opening sweet, of earliest bloom,
   And rifle all the breathing Spring."

And similar echoes of Collins, and others, will be found elsewhere in this poem. The haste attendant upon its production, however, and the author's own admission in his "Advertisement" (p. 97) that it is "a compilation rather than a poem" will excuse these shortcomings.—ED.

[2] There are three texts of this work—(1) That of the printed pamphlet of 1772 (used by Mr. B. Corney, and adopted also by us in the main); (2) That of the Cradock MS. (used by Chalmers); and (3) That of the copy owned by Isaac Reed (which Prior mostly adhered to).—ED.

sarcasms in it, and solecisms also. But, not to seem an ill-natured critic, I'll take leave to quote your own words, and give you my remarks upon them as they occur. You begin as follows :—

> "I hope, my good Doctor, you soon will be here,
> And your spring-velvet coat very smart will appear,
> To open our ball the first day in the year."

Pray, Madam, where did you ever find the epithet "good" applied to the title of Doctor? Had you called me learned Doctor, or grave Doctor, or noble Doctor, it might be allowable, because they belong to the profession. But, not to cavil at trifles, you talk of my "spring-velvet coat," and advise me to wear it the first day in the year, that is in the middle of winter!—a spring-velvet in the middle of winter!!! That would be a solecism indeed! and yet, to increase the inconsistence, in another part of your letter you call me a beau. Now on one side or other, you must be wrong. If I am a beau I can never think of wearing a spring-velvet in winter; and if I am not a beau—why—then—that explains itself. But let me go on to your two next strange lines :—

> "And bring with you a wig that is modish and gay,
> To dance with the girls that are makers of hay."

The absurdity of making hay at Christmas you yourself seem sensible of; you say your sister will laugh, and so indeed she well may ! The Latins have an expression for a contemptuous sort of laughter, *Naso contemnere adunco;* that is to laugh with a crooked nose; she may laugh at you in the manner of the ancients, if she thinks fit.—But now I am come to the most extraordinary of all extraordinary propositions, which is, to take your and your sister's advice in playing at loo. The presumption of the offer raises my indignation beyond the bounds of prose; it inspires me at once with verse and resentment. I take advice ! And from whom ? You shall hear.—

First let me suppose, what may shortly be true,
The company set, and the word to be—Loo:
All smirking, and pleasant, and big with adventure,
And ogling the stake which is fix'd in the centre.

Round and round go the cards, while I inwardly damn,
At never once finding a visit from Pam.
I lay down my stake, apparently cool,
While the harpies about me all pocket the pool;
I fret in my gizzard, yet, cautious and sly,
I wish all my friends may be bolder than I:
Yet still they sit snug; not a creature will aim,
By losing their money, to venture at fame.
'Tis in vain that at niggardly caution I scold,
'Tis in vain that I flatter the brave and the bold;
All play their own way, and they think me an ass,—
" What does Mrs. Bunbury ? " " I, Sir ? I pass."
"Pray what does Miss Horneck?[1] take courage, come, do!"—
" Who, I? Let me see, Sir; why I must pass too."
Mr. Bunbury frets, and *I* fret like the devil,
To see them so cowardly, lucky, and civil;
Yet still I sit snug, and continue to sigh on,
'Till made by my losses as bold as a lion,
I venture at all; while my avarice regards
The whole pool as my own. " Come, give me five cards."
" Well done ! " cry the ladies; "ah ! Doctor, that's good !
The pool's very rich. Ah ! the Doctor is loo'd ! "
Thus foil'd in my courage, on all sides perplext,
I ask for advice from the lady that's next.
" Pray, Ma'am, be so good as to give your advice;
Don't you think the best way is to venture for 't twice ? "
" I advise," cries the lady, " to try it, I own.—
Ah ! the Doctor is loo'd. Come, Doctor, put down."
Thus playing and playing, I still grow more eager,
And so bold, and so bold, I'm at last a bold beggar.
Now ladies, I ask, if law matters you're skilled in,
Whether crimes such as yours should not come before
      Fielding ?[2]
For giving advice that is not worth a straw,
May well be called picking of pockets in law;

---

[1] Miss Mary Horneck, " the Jessamy Bride." See *ante*, p. 94; also
'Life,' v. i., pp. 32, 41; and, for some charming speculation as to the
Jessamy Bride and Goldsmith, see Washington Irving's 'Life' of the
poet.—ED.

[2] Sir John Fielding, the half-brother of Henry Fielding, the novelist.
He was a famous magistrate at Bow Street Police Court.—ED.

And picking of pockets, with which I now charge ye,
Is by *quinto Elizabeth*, death without clergy.
What justice, when both to the Old Bailey brought!
By the gods I'll enjoy it, though 'tis but in thought!
Both are plac'd at the bar, with all proper decorum,
With bunches of fennel and nosegays before 'em;
Both cover their faces with mobs and all that,
But the judge bids them angrily take off their hat.
When uncover'd, a buzz of enquiry goes round,—
" Pray what are their crimes?" " They've been pilfering
   found."
" But, pray whom have they pilfer'd?" " A Doctor, I
   hear;"
" What, yon solemn-faced, odd-looking man that stands
   near?"
" The same." " What a pity! How does it surprise
   one!
Two handsomer culprits I never set eyes on!"
Then their friends all come round me with cringing and
   leering,
To melt me to pity and soften my swearing.
First Sir Charles advances with phrases well strung :
" Consider, dear Doctor, the girls are but young."
" The younger the worse," I return him again,
" It shows that their habits are all dyed in grain."
" But then they're so handsome; one's bosom it grieves."
" What signifies *handsome* when people are thieves?"
" But where is your justice? Their cases are hard.
" What signifies *justice?* I want the *reward.*"—

" There's the parish of Edmonton offers forty pounds;
there's the parish of St. Leonard's, Shoreditch, offers
forty pounds; there's the parish of Tyburn, from the
Hog-in-the-Pound to St. Giles's watchhouse, offers forty
pounds,—I shall have all that if I convict them."—

" But consider their case,—it may yet be your own!
And see how they kneel! is your heart made of stone?"
This moves :—so at last I agree to relent,
For ten pounds in hand and ten pounds to be spent.

I challenge you all to answer this: I tell you, you cannot. It cuts deep;—but now for the rest of the letter; and next—but I want room. So I believe I shall battle the rest out at Barton some day next week.

I don't value you all !

O. G.

SONG.[1]

[Intended to have been sung in the comedy of 'She Stoops to Conquer' [1773]; but omitted, because Mrs. Bulkley, who acted the part of Miss Hardcastle, could not sing.—BOSWELL: *vide note below.*]

AH me ! when shall I marry me ?
  Lovers are plenty ; but fail to relieve me.
He, fond youth, that could carry me,
  Offers to love, but means to deceive me.

But I will rally, and combat the ruiner:
  Not a look, not[2] a smile shall my passion discover.
She that gives all to the false one pursuing her,
  Makes but a penitent—loses a lover.[3]

EPILOGUE

SPOKEN BY

MRS. BULKLEY AND MISS CATLEY.

[This Epilogue, headed as above, first appeared in Percy's edition of the 'Works,' 1801. It seems pretty certain, however, from the following letter by Goldsmith, that the heading should have been different, and that the epilogue was intended for 'She Stoops to Conquer,' but never delivered. Writing without date, but evidently just after the production of his comedy, Goldsmith says to his friend Cradock, "The play has met with a success much beyond your expectations or mine. I thank

---

[1] This song was communicated, after Goldsmith's death, to the editor of the 'London Magazine' (June, 1774), by Boswell, the biographer of Dr. Johnson. Goldsmith himself, says Boswell, used to sing it to a pretty Irish air called the 'Humours of Ballamagairy,' to which he confessed that he found it very difficult to adapt words.—ED.

[2] So in 'London Magazine.' The usual version is—"nor a smile."—ED.

[3] So in 'London Magazine.' The usual reading is—"and loses a lover."—ED.

you sincerely for your epilogue, which, however, could not be used, but with your permission shall be printed. The story in short is this; Murphy sent me rather the outline of an epilogue than an epilogue, which was to be sung by Mrs. Catley, and which she approved. Mrs. Bulkley hearing this, insisted on throwing up her part, unless, according to the custom of the theatre, she were permitted to speak the epilogue. In this embarrassment I thought of making a quarrelling epilogue between Catley and her, debating who should speak the epilogue, but then Mrs. Catley refused after I had taken the trouble of drawing it out. I was then at a loss indeed; an epilogue was to be made, and for none but Mrs. Bulkley. I made one, and Colman thought it too bad to be spoken; I was obliged therefore to try a fourth time, and I made a very mawkish thing as you'll shortly see.[1] Such is the history of my stage adventures, and which I have at last done with. I cannot help saying that I am very sick of the stage; and though I believe I shall get three tolerable benefits, yet I shall on the whole be a loser, even in a pecuniary light; my ease and comfort I certainly lost while it was in agitation" (Letters, v. i.). It seems clear, therefore, that this is the " quarrelling epilogue " *rejected* by Miss Catley, and that its heading should be " Epilogue intended to have been spoken by," &c.—ED.]

Enter Mrs. Bulkley, who curtsies very low, as beginning to speak; then enter Miss Catley, who stands full before her and curtsies to the audience.

Mrs. Bulkley. HOLD, Ma'am, your pardon. What's your business here?

Miss Catley. The Epilogue.

Mrs. B. The Epilogue?

Miss C. Yes, the Epilogue, my dear.

Mrs. B. Sure you mistake, Ma'am. The Epilogue? *I* bring it.

Miss C. Excuse me, Ma'am. The author bid *me* sing it.

Recitative.

Ye beaux and belles, that form this splendid ring,
Suspend your conversation while I sing.

Mrs. B. Why, sure the girl's beside herself! an Epilogue of singing?
A hopeful end, indeed, to such a blest beginning.
Besides, a singer in a comic set!—
Excuse me, Ma'am, I know the etiquette.

---

[1] The epilogue actually spoken, which will be found at the end of ' She Stoops to Conquer.'—ED.

Miss C. What if we leave it to the house?

Mrs. B. The house!—Agreed.

Miss C. Agreed.

Mrs. B. And she whose party's largest shall proceed.
And first, I hope you'll readily agree
I've all the critics and the wits for me.
They, I am sure, will answer my commands:
Ye candid judging few, hold up your hands.
What! no return? I find, too late, I fear,
That modern judges seldom enter here.

Miss C. I'm for a different set:—Old men, whose trade is
Still to gallant and dangle with the ladies.

Recitative.

Who mump their passion, and who, grimly smiling,
Still thus address the fair with voice beguiling:

AIR.—*Cotillon.*

Turn, my fairest, turn, if ever
　　Strephon caught thy ravish'd eye,
Pity take on your swain so clever,
　　Who without your aid must die.
　　　　Yes, I shall die, hu, hu, hu, hu!
　　　　Yes, I must die, ho, ho, ho, ho!
　　　　　　　　　　　　[*Da Capo.*

Mrs. B. Let all the old pay homage to your merit;
Give me the young, the gay, the men of spirit.
Ye travell'd tribe, ye macaroni train,
Of French friseurs and nosegays justly vain,
Who take a trip to Paris once a-year
To dress, and look like awkward Frenchmen here,—
Lend me your hands: O fatal news to tell,
Their hands are only lent to the Heinel.[1]

Miss C. Ay, take your travellers—travellers indeed!
Give me my bonny Scot, that travels from the Tweed.
Where are the chiels? Ah, ah! I well discern
The smiling looks of each bewitching bairn.

---

[1] Mlle. Heinel, a French dancer at the Opera House, in great vogue
in 1773.—ED.

AIR.—*A bonny young lad is my Jockey.*

I'll sing to amuse you by night and by day,
And be unco merry when you are but gay;
When you with your bagpipes are ready to play,
My voice shall be ready to carol away
   With Sandy, and Sawney, and Jockey,
   With Sawney, and Jarvie, and Jockey.

Mrs. B. Ye gamesters, who, so eager in pursuit,
Make but of all your fortune one *va toute :*
Ye jockey tribe, whose stock of words are few,
" I hold the odds.—Done, done, with you, with you ! "
Ye barristers, so fluent with grimace,
" My Lord, your Lordship misconceives the case ; "
Doctors, who cough, and answer every misfortuner—
" I wish I'd been call'd in a little sooner ; "
Assist my cause with hands and voices hearty,
Come, end the contest here, and aid my party !

AIR.—*Ballinamony.*

Miss C. Ye brave Irish lads, hark away to the crack,
Assist me, I pray, in this woful attack ;
For—sure I don't wrong you—you seldom are slack,
When the ladies are calling, to blush and hang back.
  For you're always polite and attentive,
  Still to amuse us inventive,
  And death is your only preventive :
  Your hands and your voices for me.

Mrs. B. Well, Madam, what if, after all this sparring,
We both agree, like friends, to end our jarring ?
Miss C. And that our friendship may remain unbroken,
What if we leave the Epilogue unspoken ?
Mrs. B. Agreed.
Miss C. Agreed.
Mrs. B. And now with late repentance, '
Un-epilogued the Poet waits his sentence.
Condemn the stubborn fool who can't submit
To thrive by flattery, though he starves by wit.
        [*Exeunt.*

AN EPILOGUE,

INTENDED FOR MRS. BULKLEY.

[This epilogue was first printed in Percy's edition, 1801. The editor added, in a note, that the MS. was given to him by Goldsmith, but that he, Percy, had forgotten to which comedy it belonged. Later editors, however, have viewed it as being one of the several unused epilogues written for ' She Stoops to Conquer,' of which Goldsmith has himself given the history in the letter quoted in the introduction to the preceding epilogue. Mr. Bolton Corney thought it was the one which Goldsmith says Colman judged as " too bad to be spoken."—ED.]

THERE is a place—so Ariosto sings—
A treasury for lost and missing things;
Lost human wits have places there assign'd them,
And they who lose their senses, there may find them.
But where's this place, this storehouse of the age?   5
The Moon, says he; but *I* affirm, the Stage:
At least, in many things, I think I see
His lunar and our mimic world agree:
Both shine at night, for, but at Foote's[1] alone,
We scarce exhibit till the sun goes down;   10
Both prone to change, no settled limits fix,
And sure the folks of both are lunatics.
But in this parallel my best pretence is,
That mortals visit both to find their senses:
To this strange spot, rakes, macaronies, cits,   15
Come thronging to collect their scatter'd wits.
The gay coquette, who ogles all the day,
Comes here at night, and goes a prude away.
Hither the affected city dame advancing,
Who sighs for operas, and doats on dancing,   20
Taught by our art, her ridicule to pause on,
Quits the *ballet*, and calls for *Nancy Dawson*.[2]
The gamester, too, whose wit's all high or low,
Oft risks his fortune on one desperate throw,

[1] " Foote's " was " the little theatre in the Haymarket," where morning performances were sometimes given.—ED.

[2] A popular air of the time; also the name of a famous hornpipe dancer.—ED.

Comes here to saunter, having made his bets, 25
Finds his lost senses out, and pays his debts.
The Mohawk,[1] too—with angry phrases stor'd—
As, " Damme, Sir ! " and, " Sir, I wear a sword ! "—
Here lesson'd for awhile, and hence retreating,
Goes out, affronts his man, and takes a beating. 30
Here come the sons of scandal and of news,
But find no sense—for they had none to lose.
Of all the tribe here wanting an adviser,
Our Author's the least likely to grow wiser ;
Has he not seen how you your favour place 35
On sentimental queens[2] and lords in lace ?
Without a star, a coronet, or garter,
How can the piece expect or hope for quarter ?
No high-life scenes, no sentiment : the creature
Still stoops among the low to copy Nature. 40
Yes, he's far gone :—and yet some pity fix,
The English laws forbid to punish lunatics.

EPILOGUE,

SPOKEN BY MR. LEE LEWES, IN THE CHARACTER OF
HARLEQUIN, AT HIS BENEFIT.

[The " benefit " took place at Covent Garden Theatre, May 7, 1773.
Charles Lee Lewes, though famous as harlequin, was not a comedian of
standing till, through the lucky refusal of the part by Smith, he became
the original Young Marlow in ' She Stoops to Conquer.'—ED.]

HOLD ! Prompter, hold ! a word before your nonsense :
I'd speak a word or two, to ease my conscience.
My pride forbids it ever should be said
My heels eclips'd the honours of my head ;

[1] Or Mohock, = London bully.—ED.
[2] In this allusion to *sentimental queens*, it is probable that Goldsmith
glanced in particular at Mr. Murphy's tragedy of ' Zenobia,' though his
splenetic attack is directed generally against the comedy which was
brought into fashion about this time by the great popularity of Kelly's
' False Delicacy,' and effectually exploded some years after by Foote's
clever satire of ' Piety in Pattens.'—B.

That I found humour in a pye-bald vest,   5
Or ever thought that jumping was a jest. [*Takes off his mask.*
Whence, and what art thou, visionary birth?
Nature disowns, and reason scorns thy mirth :
In thy black aspect every passion sleeps,
The joy that dimples, and the woe that weeps.   10
How hast thou fill'd the scene with all thy brood
Of fools pursuing, and of fools pursued!
Whose ins and outs no ray of sense discloses,
Whose only plot it is to break our noses ;
Whilst from below the trap-door demons rise,   15
And from above the dangling deities :
And shall I mix in this unhallow'd crew?
May rosin'd lightning[1] blast me if I do!
No—I will act—I'll vindicate the stage :
Shakespeare himself shall feel my tragic rage.   20
Off! off! vile trappings! a new passion reigns!
The madd'ning monarch revels in my veins.
Oh! for a Richard's voice to catch the theme,—
" Give me another horse! bind up my wounds!—soft—
          'twas but a dream."
Ay, 'twas but a dream, for now there's no retreating,   25
If I cease Harlequin, I cease from eating.
'Twas thus that Æsop's stag, a creature blameless,
Yet something vain, like one that shall be nameless,
Once on the margin of a fountain stood,
And cavill'd at his image in the flood :   30
" The deuce confound," he cries, " these drumstick shanks
They never have my gratitude nor thanks ;
They're perfectly disgraceful! strike me dead!
But for a head, yes, yes, I have a head :
How piercing is that eye! how sleek that brow!   35
My horns!—I 'm told horns are the fashion now."

Whilst thus he spoke, astonish'd, to his view,
Near, and more near, the hounds and huntsmen drew ;
" Hoicks! hark forward! " came thund'ring from behind :
He bounds aloft, outstrips the fleeting wind ;   40
He quits the woods, and tries the beaten ways ;

---

[1] Rosin'd lightning = stage lightning.—BOLTON CORNEY.

He starts, he pants, he takes the circling maze :
At length, his silly head, so prized before,
Is taught his former folly to deplore ;
Whilst his strong limbs conspire to set him free,   45
And at one bound he saves himself—like me.
> [*Taking a jump through the stage door.*

VIDA'S GAME OF CHESS,

AS IT HAS BEEN FOUND TRANSCRIBED IN THE HANDWRITING OF

OLIVER GOLDSMITH.

[The MS. of the following translation in the handwriting of Goldsmith was one of the literary treasures of Mr. Bolton Corney, and the
publishers have to thank him for permission to reprint it. Mr. Corney
did not become possessed of it until after he had published his own
edition of the Poems, and he first gave printed publicity to this before
quite unknown work through Mr. Cunningham's edition, 1854. Mr.
Forster, to whom Mr. B. Corney also lent the MS., concurs in believing
it to be the work of Goldsmith. He describes the MS. as follows (' Life
of Goldsmith,' 1854, v. ii., p. 265) :—" It is a small quarto manuscript
of thirty-four pages, containing 679 lines, to which a fly-leaf is appended,
in which Goldsmith notes the differences of nomenclature between Vida's
chessmen and our own. It has occasional interlineations and corrections, but rather such as would occur in transcription, than in a first or
original copy. Sometimes, indeed, choice appears to have been made
between two words equally suitable to the sense and verse, as ' to ' for
' toward ; ' but the insertions and erasures refer almost wholly to words
or lines accidentally omitted and replaced." From the evidences of
extra care which the MS. discloses, as well as from the apparent effort
at "taking up" (as Mr. Forster says) "the manner of the great master
of translation, Dryden," the work may be viewed as belonging to the
middle-period of Goldsmith's career, that is, to the time immediately
subsequent to the publication of the ' Traveller,' 1765.

Marco Vida (b. about 1480; d. 1567), the Italian poet whom Clement
VII. made Bishop of Alba, was but little known in England till Alexander Pope praised his work in his juvenile ' Essay on Criticism ' (1709),
thus :—

> " Immortal Vida ! on whose honoured brow
> The poet's bays and critic's ivy grow :
> Cremona now shall ever boast thy name,
> As next in place to Mantua, next in fame ! "
> *Essay on Criticism*, ll. 705-8.

Later, viz., in 1736, an English translation of the 'Scacchiæ Ludus'
(Game of Chess) was published by one George Jeffreys.   It was Vida's
' Scacchiæ Ludus' which procured for its author the patronage of Pope
Leo X., and subsequently advanced him in the Church and otherwise.
He afterwards published the 'Christiad' and other works.—ED.]

ARMIES of box that sportively engage
And mimic real battles in their rage,
Pleased I recount; how, smit with glory's charms,
Two mighty Monarchs met in adverse arms,
Sable and white : assist me to explore,   5
Ye Serian Nymphs, what ne'er was sung before.
No path appears : yet resolute I stray
Where youth undaunted bids me force my way.
O'er rocks and cliffs while I the task pursue,
Guide me, ye Nymphs, with your unerring clue.   10
For you the rise of this diversion know,
You first were pleased in Italy to show
This studious sport ; from Scacchis was its name,
The pleasing record of your Sister's fame.
    When Jove through Ethiopia's parch'd extent   15
To grace the nuptials of old Ocean went,
Each god was there ; and mirth and joy around
To shores remote diffused their happy sound.
Then when their hunger and their thirst no more
Claim'd their attention, and the feast was o'er;   20
Ocean, with pastime to divert the thought,
Commands a painted table to be brought.
Sixty-four spaces fill the chequer'd square ;
Eight in each rank eight equal limits share.
Alike their form, but diff'rent are their dyes,   25
They fade alternate, and alternate rise,
White after black; such various stains as those
The shelving backs of tortoises disclose.
Then to the Gods, that mute and wondering sate,
You see (says he) the field prepared for fate.   30
Here will the little armies please your sight,
With adverse colours hurrying to the fight :
On which so oft, with silent sweet surprise,
The Nymphs and Nereids used to feast their eyes,
And all the neighbours of the hoary deep,   35

When calm the sea, and winds were lull'd asleep.
But see, the mimic heroes tread the board;
He said, and straightway from an urn he pour'd
The sculptured box, that neatly seem'd to ape
The graceful figure of a human shape :—　　　　40
Equal the strength and number of each foe,
Sixteen appear'd like jet, sixteen like snow.
As their shape varies various is the name,
Different their posts, nor is their strength the same.
There might you see two Kings with equal pride　　45
Gird on their arms, their Consorts by their side;
Here the Foot-warriors glowing after fame,
There prancing Knights and dexterous Archers came,
And Elephants that on their backs sustain
Vast towers of war, and fill and shake the plain.　　50
　And now both hosts, preparing for the storm
Of adverse battle, their encampments form.
In the fourth space, and on the farthest line,
Directly opposite the Monarchs shine;
The swarthy on white ground, on sable stands　　55
The silver King; and thence they send commands.
Nearest to these the Queens exert their might;
One the left side, and t'other guards the right :
Where each, by her respective armour known,
Chooses the colour that is like her own.　　　　60
Then the young Archers,[1] two, that, snowy-white,
Bend the tough yew, and two, as black as night;
(Greece call'd them Mars's favourites heretofore,
From their delight in war, and thirst of gore).
These on each side the Monarch and his Queen　　65
Surround obedient; next to these are seen
The crested Knights in golden armour gay;
Their steeds by turns curvet, or snort, or neigh.
In either army on each distant wing
Two mighty Elephants their castles bring,　　　70
Bulwarks immense! and then at last combine

---

[1] Goldsmith notes in the MS. that he adheres to Vida's chess terms and other arrangements in the mimic war thus—"Archers are what we call Bishops; Horse are what we call Knights; Elephants are what we call Towers, Castles, or Rooks. Apollo has the White men, Mercury the Black."—ED.

Eight of the Foot to form the second line,
The vanguard to the King and Queen ; from far
Prepared to open all the fate of war.
So moved the boxen hosts, each double-lined,   75
Their different colours floating in the wind :
As if an army of the Gauls should go,
With their white standards, o'er the Alpine snow
To meet in rigid fight on scorching sands
The sun-burnt Moors and Memnon's swarthy bands.   80
    Then Father Ocean thus : You see them here,
Celestial Powers, what troops, what camps appear.
Learn now the sev'ral orders of the fray,
For ev'n these arms their stated laws obey.
To lead the fight, the Kings from all their bands   85
Choose whom they please to bear their great commands.
Should a black hero first to battle go,
Instant a white one guards against the blow ;
But only one at once can charge or shun the foe.
Their gen'ral purpose on one scheme is bent,   90
So to besiege the King within the tent,
That there remains no place by subtle flight
From danger free ; and that decides the fight.
Meanwhile, howe'er, the sooner to destroy
Th' imperial Prince, remorseless they employ   95
Their swords in blood ; and whosoever dare
Oppose their vengeance, in the ruin share.
Fate thins their camp ; the parti-coloured field
Widens apace, as they o'ercome or yield,
But the proud victor takes the captive's post ;   100
There fronts the fury of th' avenging host
One single shock ; and (should he ward the blow),
May then retire at pleasure from the foe.
The Foot alone (so their harsh laws ordain)
When they proceed can ne'er return again.   105
    But neither all rush on alike to prove
The terror of their arms : the Foot must move
Directly on, and but a single square ;
Yet may these heroes, when they first prepare
To mix in combat on the bloody mead,   110
Double their sally, and two steps proceed ;
But when they wound, their swords they subtly guide

With aim oblique, and slanting pierce his side.
But the great Indian beasts, whose backs sustain
Vast turrets arm'd, when on the redd'ning plain   115
They join in all the terror of the fight,   ·
Forward or backward, to the left or right,
Run furious, and impatient of confine
Scour through the field, and threat the farthest line. 119
Yet must they ne'er obliquely aim their blows;
That only manner is allowed to those
Whom Mars has favour'd most, who bend the stubborn
    bows.
These glancing sidewards in a straight career,
Yet each confined to their respective sphere,
Or white or black, can send th' unerring dart   125
Wing'd with swift death to pierce through ev'ry part.
The fiery steed, regardless of the reins,
Comes prancing on; but sullenly disdains   128
The path direct, and boldly wheeling round,
Leaps o'er a double space at ev'ry bound:
And shifts from white or black to diff'rent colour'd
    ground.
But the fierce Queen, whom dangers ne'er dismay,
The strength and terror of the bloody day,
In a straight line spreads her destruction wide,
To left or right, before, behind, aside.   135
Yet may she never with a circling course
Sweep to the battle like the fretful Horse;
But unconfined may at her pleasure stray,
If neither friend nor foe block up the way;
For to o'erleap a warrior, 'tis decreed   140
Those only dare who curb the snorting steed.
With greater caution and majestic state
The warlike Monarchs in the scene of fate
Direct their motions, since for these appear
Zealous each hope, and anxious ev'ry fear.   145
While the King's safe, with resolution stern
They clasp their arms; but should a sudden turn
Make him a captive, instantly they yield,
Resolved to share his fortune in the field.
He moves on slow; with reverence profound   150
His faithful troops encompass him around,

And oft, to break some instant fatal scheme,
Rush to their fates, their sov'reign to redeem ;
While he, unanxious where to wound the foe,
Need only shift and guard against a blow.   155
But none, however, can presume t' appear
Within his reach, but must his vengeance fear ;
For he on ev'ry side his terror throws ;
But when he changes from his first repose,
Moves but one step, most awfully sedate,   160
Or idly roving, or intent on fate.
These are the sev'ral and establish'd laws :
Now see how each maintains his bloody cause.
   Here paused the God, but (since whene'er they wage
War here on earth the Gods themselves engage   165
In mutual battle as they hate or love,
And the most stubborn war is oft above),
Almighty Jove commands the circling train
Of Gods from fav'ring either to abstain,
And let the fight be silently survey'd ;   170
And added solemn threats if disobey'd.
Then call'd he Phœbus from among the Powers
And subtle Hermes, whom in softer hours
Fair Maia bore : youth wanton'd in their face ;
Both in life's bloom, both shone with equal grace.   175
Hermes as yet had never wing'd his feet ;
As yet Apollo in his radiant seat
Had never driv'n his chariot through the air,
Known by his bow alone and golden hair.
These Jove commission'd to attempt the fray,   180
And rule the sportive military day ;
Bid them agree which party each maintains,
And promised a reward that's worth their pains.
The greater took their seats ; on either hand
Respectful the less Gods in order stand,   185
But careful not to interrupt their play,
By hinting when t' advance or run away.
   Then they examine, who shall first proceed
To try their courage, and their army lead.
Chance gave it for the White, that he should go   190
First with a brave defiance to the foe.
Awhile he ponder'd which of all his train

Should bear his first commission o'er the plain;
And then determined to begin the scene
With him that stood before to guard the Queen.   195
He took a double step : with instant care
Does the black Monarch in his turn prepare
The adverse champion, and with stern command
Bid him repel the charge with equal hand.
There front to front, the midst of all the field,   200
With furious threats their shining arms they wield;
Yet vain the conflict, neither can prevail
While in one path each other they assail.
On ev'ry side to their assistance fly
Their fellow soldiers, and with strong supply   205
Crowd to the battle, but no bloody stain
Tinctures their armour ; sportive in the plain
Mars plays awhile, and in excursion slight
Harmless they sally forth, or wait the fight.   .
    But now the swarthy Foot, that first appear'd   210
To front the foe, his pond'rous jav'lin rear'd
Leftward aslant, and a pale warrior slays,
Spurns him aside, and boldly takes his place.   ı
Unhappy youth, his danger not to spy !
Instant he fell, and triumph'd but to die.   215
At this the sable King with prudent care
Removed his station from the middle square,
And slow retiring to the farthest ground,
There safely lurk'd, with troops entrench'd around.
Then from each quarter to the war advance   220
The furious Knights, and poise the trembling lance :
By turns they rush, by turns the victors yield,
Heaps of dead Foot choke up the crimson'd field :
They fall unable to retreat; around
The clang of arms and iron hoofs resound.   225
    But while young Phœbus pleased himself to view
His furious Knight destroy the vulgar crew,
Sly Hermes long'd t' attempt with secret aim
Some noble act of more exalted fame.
For this, he inoffensive pass'd along   230
Through ranks of Foot, and midst the trembling throng
Sent his left Horse, that free without confine
Roved o'er the plain, upon some great design

Against the King himself. At length he stood,
And having fix'd his station as he would,   235
Threaten'd at once with instant fate the King
And th' Indian beast that guarded the right wing.
Apollo sigh'd, and hast'ning to relieve
The straiten'd Monarch, grieved that he must leave
His martial Elephant exposed to fate,   240
And viewed with pitying eyes his dang'rous state.
First in his thoughts however was his care
To save his King, whom to the neighbouring square
On the right hand, he snatch'd with trembling
          flight;
At this with fury springs the sable Knight,   245
Drew his keen sword, and rising to the blow,
Sent the great Indian brute to shades below.
O fatal loss! for none except the Queen
Spreads such a terror through the bloody scene.   249
Yet shall you ne'er unpunish'd boast your prize,
The Delian God with stern resentment cries;
And wedged him round with foot, and pour'd in fresh
          supplies.
Thus close besieged, trembling he cast his eye
Around the plain, but saw no shelter nigh;
No way for flight; for here the Queen opposed,   255
The Foot in phalanx there the passage closed:
At length he fell; yet not unpleased with fate,
Since victim to a Queen's vindictive hate.
With grief and fury burns the whiten'd host,
One of their Tow'rs thus immaturely lost.   260
As when a bull has in contention stern
Lost his right horn, with double vengeance burn
His thoughts for war, with blood he's cover'd o'er,
And the woods echo to his dismal roar,
So look'd the flaxen host, when angry fate   265
O'erturn'd the Indian bulwark of their state.
Fired at this great success, with double rage
Apollo hurries on his troops t' engage,
For blood and havoc wild; and, while he leads
His troops thus careless, loses both his steeds: 270
For if some adverse warriors were o'erthrown,
He little thought what dangers threat his own.

But slyer Hermes with observant eyes
March'd slowly cautious, and at distance spies
What moves must next succeed, what dangers next arise.
Often would he, the stately Queen to snare, 276
The slender Foot to front her arms prepare,
And to conceal his scheme he sighs and feigns
Such a wrong step would frustrate all his pains.
Just then an Archer, from the right-hand view, 280
At the pale Queen his arrow boldly drew,
Unseen by Phœbus, who, with studious thought,
From the left side a vulgar hero brought.
But tender Venus, with a pitying eye,
Viewing the sad destruction that was nigh, 285
Wink'd upon Phœbus (for the Goddess sat
By chance directly opposite); at that
Roused in an instant, young Apollo threw
His eyes around the field his troops to view ; 289
Perceived the danger, and with sudden fright
Withdrew the Foot that he had sent to fight,
And saved his trembling Queen by seasonable flight.
But Maia's son with shouts fill'd all the coast :
The Queen, he cried, the important Queen is lost.
Phœbus, howe'er, resolving to maintain 295
What he had done, bespoke the heavenly train.
    What mighty harm, in sportive mimic fight,
Is it to set a little blunder right,
When no preliminary rule debarr'd ?
If you henceforward, Mercury, would guard 300
Against such practice, let us make the law :
And whosoe'er shall first to battle draw,
Or white, or black, remorseless let him go
At all events, and dare the angry foe.
    He said, and this opinion pleased around : 305
Jove turn'd aside, and on his daughter frown'd,
Unmark'd by Hermes, who, with strange surprise,
Fretted and foam'd, and roll'd his ferret eyes,
And but with great reluctance could refrain
From dashing at a blow all off the plain. 310
Then he resolved to interweave deceits,—
To carry on the war by tricks and cheats.
Instant he call'd an Archer from the throng,

And bid him like the courser wheel along :
Bounding he springs, and threats the pallid Queen.   315
The fraud, however, was by Phœbus seen ;
He smiled, and, turning to the Gods, he said :
Though, Hermes, you are perfect in your trade,
And you can trick and cheat to great surprise,
These little sleights no more shall blind my eyes ;
Correct them if you please, the more you thus disguise.
The circle laugh'd aloud ; and Maia's son   322
(As if it had but by mistake been done)
Recall'd his Archer, and with motion due,
Bid him advance, the combat to renew.   325
But Phœbus watch'd him with a jealous eye,
Fearing some trick was ever lurking nigh,
For he would oft, with sudden sly design,
Send forth at once two combatants to join
His warring troops, against the law of arms,   330
Unless the wary foe was ever in alarms.
  Now the white Archer with his utmost force
Bent the tough bow against the sable Horse,
And drove him from the Queen, where he had stood
Hoping to glut his vengeance with her blood.   335
Then the right Elephant with martial pride
Roved here and there, and spread his terrors wide :
Glittering in arms from far a courser came,
Threaten'd at once the King and Royal Dame ;
Thought himself safe when he the post had seized,   340
And with the future spoils his fancy pleased.
Fired at the danger a young Archer came,
Rush'd on the foe, and levell'd sure his aim ;
(And though a Pawn his sword in vengeance draws,
Gladly he'd lose his life in glory's cause).   345
The whistling arrow to his bowels flew,
And the sharp steel his blood profusely drew ;
He drops the reins, he totters to the ground,
And his life issued murm'ring through the wound.   349
Pierced by the Foot, this Archer bit the plain ;
The Foot himself was by another slain ;
And with inflamed revenge, the battle burns again.
Towers, Archers, Knights, meet on the crimson ground,
And the field echoes to the martial sound.

Their thoughts are heated, and their courage fired,   355
Thick they rush on with double zeal inspired ;
Generals and Foot, with different colour'd mien,
Confusedly warring in the camps are seen,—
Valour and Fortune meet in one promiscuous scene.
Now these victorious, lord it o'er the field ;   360
Now the foe rallies, the triumphant yield:
Just as the tide of battle ebbs or flows.
As when the conflict more tempestuous grows
Between the winds, with strong and boisterous sweep
They plough th' Ionian or Atlantic deep !   365
By turns prevails the mutual blustering roar,
And the big waves alternate lash the shore.
    But in the midst of all the battle raged
The snowy Queen, with troops at once engaged,
She fell'd an Archer as she sought the plain,—   370
As she retired an Elephant was slain :
To right and left her fatal spears she sent,
Burst through the ranks, and triumph'd as she went ;
Through arms and blood she seeks a glorious fate,
Pierces the farthest lines, and nobly great   375
Leads on her army with a gallant show,
Breaks the battalions, and cuts through the foe.
At length the sable King his fears betray'd,
And begg'd his military consort's aid :
With cheerful speed she flew to his relief,   380
And met in equal arms the female chief.
    Who first, great Queen, and who at last did bleed ?
How many Whites lay gasping on the mead ?
Half dead, and floating in a bloody tide,
Foot, Knights, and Archer lie on every side.   385
Who can recount the slaughter of the day?
How many leaders threw their lives away ?
The chequer'd plain is fill'd with dying box,
Havoc ensues, and with tumultuous shocks
The different colour'd ranks in blood engage,   390
And Foot and Horse promiscuously rage.
With nobler courage and superior might
The dreadful Amazons sustain the fight,
Resolved alike to mix in glorious strife,
Till to imperious fate they yield their life.   395

Meanwhile each Monarch, in a neighbouring cell,
Confined the warriors that in battle fell,
There watch'd the captives with a jealous eye,
Lest, slipping out again, to arms they fly.
But Thracian Mars, in stedfast friendship join'd   400
To Hermes, as near Phœbus he reclined,
Observed each chance, how all their motions bend,
Resolved if possible to serve his friend.
He a Foot-soldier and a Knight purloin'd
Out from the prison that the dead confined;   405
And slyly push'd 'em forward on the plain;   ⎫
Th' enliven'd combatants their arms regain,   ⎬
Mix in the bloody scene, and boldly war again.   ⎭
   So the foul hag, in screaming wild alarms
O'er a dead carcase muttering her charms,   410
(And with her frequent and tremendous yell
Forcing great Hecate from out of hell)
Shoots in the corpse a new fictitious soul;   ⎫
With instant glare the supple eyeballs roll,   ⎬
Again it moves and speaks, and life informs the whole.   ⎭
   Vulcan alone discern'd the subtle cheat;   416
And wisely scorning such a base deceit,
Call'd out to Phœbus.   Grief and rage assail
Phœbus by turns; detected Mars turns pale.
Then awful Jove with sullen eye reproved   420
Mars, and the captives order'd to be moved
To their dark caves; bid each fictitious spear
Be straight recall'd and all be as they were.
   And now both Monarchs with redoubled rage
Led on their Queens, the mutual war to wage.   425
O'er all the field their thirsty spears they send,
Then front to front their Monarchs they defend.
But lo! the female White rush'd in unseen,
And slew with fatal haste the swarthy Queen;
Yet soon, alas! resign'd her royal spoils,   430
Snatch'd by a shaft from her successful toils.
Struck at the sight, both hosts in wild surprise
Pour'd forth their tears, and fill'd the air with cries;
They wept and sigh'd, as pass'd the fun'ral train,
As if both armies had at once been slain.   435
   And now each troop surrounds its mourning chief,

To guard his person, or assuage his grief.
One is their common fear; one stormy blast
Has equally made havoc as it pass'd.
Not all, however, of their youth are slain;   440
Some champions yet the vig'rous war maintain.
Three Foot, an Archer, and a stately Tower,
For Phœbus still exert their utmost power.
Just the same number Mercury can boast,
Except the Tower, who lately in his post   445
Unarm'd inglorious fell, in peace profound,
Pierced by an Archer with a distant wound;
But his right Horse retain'd its mettled pride,—
The rest were swept away by war's strong tide.
   But fretful Hermes, with despairing moan,   450
Grieved that so many champions were o'erthrown,
Yet reassumes the fight; and summons round
The little straggling army that he found,—
All that had 'scaped from fierce Apollo's rage,—
Resolved with greater caution to engage   455
In future strife, by subtle wiles (if fate
Should give him leave) to save his sinking state.
The sable troops advance with prudence slow,
Bent on all hazards to distress the foe.
More cheerful Phœbus, with unequal pace,   460
Rallies his arms to lessen his disgrace.
But what strange havoc everywhere has been!
A straggling champion here and there is seen;
And many are the tents, yet few are left within.
   Th' afflicted Kings bewail their consorts dead,   465
And loathe the thoughts of a deserted bed;
And though each monarch studies to improve
The tender mem'ry of his former love,
Their state requires a second nuptial tie.
Hence the pale ruler with a love-sick eye   470
Surveys th' attendants of his former wife,
And offers one of them a royal life.
These, when their martial mistress had been slain,
Weak and despairing tried their arms in vain;
Willing, howe'er, amidst the Black to go,   475
They thirst for speedy vengeance on the foe.
Then he resolves to see who merits best,

By strength and courage, the imperial vest ;
Points out the foe, bids each with bold design
Pierce through the ranks, and reach the deepest line: 480
For none must hope with monarchs to repose
But who can first, through thick surrounding foes,
Through arms and wiles, with hazardous essay,
Safe to the farthest quarters force their way.
Fired at the thought, with sudden, joyful pace   485
They hurry on ; but first of all the race
Runs the third right-hand warrior for the prize,—
The glitt'ring crown already charms her eyes.
Her dear associates cheerfully give o'er
The nuptial chase ; and swift she flies before,
And Glory lent her wings, and the reward in store.
Nor would the sable King her hopes prevent,   492
For he himself was on a Queen intent,
Alternate, therefore, through the field they go.
Hermes led on, but by a step too slow,   495
His fourth left Pawn : and now th' advent'rous White
Had march'd through all, and gain'd the wish'd for site.
Then the pleased King gives orders to prepare
The crown, the sceptre, and the royal chair,
And owns her for his Queen : around exult   500
The snowy troops, and o'er the Black insult.
  Hermes burst into tears,—with fretful roar
Fill'd the wide air, and his gay vesture tore.
The swarthy Foot had only to advance
One single step ; but oh ! malignant chance !   505
A tower'd Elephant, with fatal aim,
Stood ready to destroy her when she came :
He keeps a watchful eye upon the whole,
Threatens her entrance, and protects the goal.
Meanwhile the royal new-created bride,   510
Pleased with her pomp, spread death and terror wide ;
Like lightning through the sable troops she flies,
Clashes her arms, and seems to threat the skies.
The sable troops are sunk in wild affright,
And wish th' earth op'ning snatch'd 'em from her sight. 515
In burst the Queen, with vast impetuous swing :
The trembling foes come swarming round the King,
Where in the midst he stood, and form a valiant ring.

So the poor cows, straggling o'er pasture land,
When they perceive the prowling wolf at hand,   520
Crowd close together in a circle full,
And beg the succour of the lordly bull;
They clash their horns, they low with dreadful sound,
And the remotest groves re-echo round.
 But the bold Queen, victorious, from behind   525
Pierces the foe; yet chiefly she design'd
Against the King himself some fatal aim,
And full of war to his pavilion came.
Now here she rush'd, now there; and had she been
But duly prudent, she had slipp'd between,   530
With course oblique, into the fourth white square,
And the long toil of war had ended there,
The King had fall'n, and all his sable state;
And vanquish'd Hermes cursed his partial fate.
For thence with ease the championess might go,   535
Murder the King, and none could ward the blow.
 With silence, Hermes, and with panting heart,
Perceived the danger, but with subtle art,
(Lest he should see the place) spurs on the foe,
Confounds his thoughts, and blames his being slow.   540
For shame! move on; would you for ever stay?
What sloth is this, what strange perverse delay?—
How could you e'er my little pausing blame?—
What! you would wait till night shall end the game?
Phœbus, thus nettled, with imprudence slew   545
A vulgar Pawn, but lost his nobler view.
Young Hermes leap'd, with sudden joy elate;
And then, to save the monarch from his fate,
Led on his martial Knight, who stepp'd between,
Pleased that his charge was to oppose the Queen—   550
Then, pond'ring how the Indian beast to slay,
That stopp'd the Foot from making farther way,—
From being made a Queen; with slanting aim
An archer struck him; down the monster came,
And dying shook the earth: while Phœbus tries   555
Without success the monarch to surprise.
The Foot, then uncontroll'd with instant pride,
Seized the last spot, and moved a royal bride.
And now with equal strength both war again,

And bring their second wives upon the plain;   560
Then, though with equal views each hoped and fear'd,
Yet, as if every doubt had disappear'd,   .
As if he had the palm, young Hermes flies
Into excess of joy; with deep disguise,
Extols his own Black troops, with frequent spite   565
And with invective taunts disdains the White.
Whom Phœbus thus reproved with quick return—
As yet we cannot the decision learn
Of this dispute, and do you triumph now?
Then your big words and vauntings I'll allow,   570
When you the battle shall completely gain;
At present I shall make your boasting vain.
He said, and forward led the daring Queen;
Instant the fury of the bloody scene
Rises tumultuous, swift the warriors fly   575
From either side to conquer or to die.
They front the storm of war: around 'em Fear,
Terror, and Death, perpetually appear.
All meet in arms, and man to man oppose,
Each from their camp attempts to drive their foes;   580
Each tries by turns to force the hostile lines;
Chance and impatience blast their best designs.
The sable Queen spread terror as she went
Through the mid ranks: with more reserved intent
The adverse dame declined the open fray,   585
And to the King in private stole away:
Then took the royal guard, and bursting in,
With fatal menace close besieged the King.
Alarm'd at this, the swarthy Queen, in haste,
From all her havoc and destructive waste   590
Broke off, and her contempt of death to show,
Leap'd in between the monarch and the foe,
To save the King and state from this impending blow.
But Phœbus met a worse misfortune here:
For Hermes now led forward, void of fear,   595
His furious Horse into the open plain,
That onward chafed, and pranced, and pawed amain.
Nor ceased from his attempts until he stood
On the long-wished-for spot, from whence he could
Slay King or Queen. O'erwhelm'd with sudden fears, 600

Apollo saw, and could not keep from tears.
Now all seem'd ready to be overthrown;
His strength was wither'd, ev'ry hope was flown.
Hermes, exulting at this great surprise,
Shouted for joy, and fill'd the air with cries ;   605
Instant he sent the Queen to shades below,
And of her spoils made a triumphant show.
But in return, and in his mid career,
Fell his brave Knight, beneath the Monarch's spear.
  Phœbus, however, did not yet despair,   610
But still fought on with courage and with care.
He had but two poor common men to show,
And Mars's favourite with his iv'ry bow.
The thoughts of ruin made 'em dare their best
To save their King, so fatally distress'd.   615
But the sad hour required not such an aid ;
And Hermes breath'd revenge where'er he stray'd.
Fierce comes the sable Queen with fatal threat,
Surrounds the monarch in his royal seat ;
Rush'd here and there, nor rested till she slew   620
The last remainder of the whiten'd crew.
Sole stood the King, the midst of all the plain,
Weak and defenceless, his companions slain.
As when the ruddy morn ascending high
Has chased the twinkling stars from all the sky,   625
Your star, fair Venus, still retains its light,
And, loveliest, goes the latest out of sight.
No safety's left, no gleams of hope remain ;
Yet did he not as vanquish'd quit the plain,   629
But tried to shut himself between the foe,—
Unhurt through swords and spears he hoped to go,
Until no room was left to shun the fatal blow.
For if none threaten'd his immediate fate,
And his next move must ruin all his state,   634
All their past toil and labour is in vain,
Vain all the bloody carnage of the plain,—
Neither would triumph then, the laurel neither gain.
Therefore through each void space and desert tent,
By different moves his various course he bent:
The Black King watch'd him with observant eye,   640
Follow'd him close, but left him room to fly.

Then when he saw him take the farthest line,
He sent the Queen his motions to confine,
And guard the second rank, that he could go
No farther now than to that distant row.   645
The sable monarch then with cheerful mien
Approach'd, but always with one space between.
But as the King stood o'er against him there,
Helpless, forlorn, and sunk in his despair,   649
The martial Queen her lucky moment knew,
Seized on the farthest seat with fatal view,
Nor left th' unhappy King a place to flee unto.
At length in vengeance her keen sword she draws,
Slew him, and ended thus the bloody cause :
And all the Gods around approved it with applause.
    The victor could not from his insults keep,   656
But laugh'd and sneer'd to see Apollo weep.
Jove call'd him near, and gave him in his hand
The powerful, happy, and mysterious wand
By which the Shades are call'd to purer day,   660
When penal fire has purged their sins away ;
By which the guilty are condemn'd to dwell
In the dark mansions of the deepest hell ;
By which he gives us sleep, or sleep denies,
And closes at the last the dying eyes.   665
    Soon after this, the heavenly victor brought
The Game on earth, and first th' Italians taught.
For (as they say) fair Scacchis he espied
Feeding her cygnets in the silver tide,
(Scacchis, the loveliest Seriad of the place)   670
And as she stray'd, took her to his embrace.
Then, to reward her for her virtue lost,
Gave her the men and chequer'd board, emboss'd
With gold and silver curiously inlay'd,
And taught her how the game was to be play'd.   675
Ev'n now 'tis honour'd with her happy name ;
And Rome and all the world admire the game.
All which the Seriads told me heretofore,
When my boy-notes amused the Serian shore.

TRANSLATIONS.

[Under this head some editors of Goldsmith's Poems give a number of small pieces extracted from the prose works. Most of these, however, are really not translations by Goldsmith, as will be seen by reference to (for instance) those in the 'Belles Lettres' essays (v. i.), which are translations by Francis and others. Of the few that remain, we give the following from works by Goldsmith not included in the present edition.—ED.]

FROM THE 'HISTORY OF THE EARTH AND ANIMATED NATURE.'

[1774, vol. v., p. 312.]

Addison, in some beautiful Latin lines inserted in the 'Spectator,' is entirely of opinion that birds observe a strict chastity of manners, and never admit the caresses of a different tribe.[1]

CHASTE are their instincts, faithful is their fire,
No foreign beauty tempts to false desire :
The snow-white vesture, and the glittering crown,
The simple plumage, or the glossy down
Prompt not their love.—The patriot bird pursues
His well acquainted tints, and kindred hues.
Hence through their tribes no mix'd, polluted flame,
No monster breed to mark the groves with shame ;
But the chaste blackbird, to its partner true,
Thinks black alone is beauty's favourite hue ;
The nightingale, with mutual passion blest,
Sings to its mate, and nightly charms the nest :
While the dark owl to court its partner flies,
And owns its offspring in their yellow eyes.

[1] 'Spectator,' No. 412.—ED.

FROM THE SAME.

[V. iii., p. 6—Of the Salmon.]

OF all the fish that graze beneath the flood,
He only ruminates his former food.

OVID.

FROM 'THE COMIC ROMANCE' OF SCARRON.[1]

THUS when soft love subdues the heart
 With smiling hopes, and chilling fears,
The soul rejects the aid of art,
 And speaks in moments more than years.

SOME OTHER PIECES OF POETRY

by Goldsmith will be found in his prose works as follows:—

IN THE 'CITIZEN OF THE WORLD' [1760-2].

On Seeing Mrs. * * Perform, &c.

Letter LXXXV. See v. iii.

On the Death of the Right Hon. * * * *.

Letter CVI. See v. iii.

---

[1] 'The Comic Romance of Monsieur Scarron, translated by Oliver
Goldsmith:' London, W. Griffin, 2 vols. 12mo, 1776. This was put
forth two years after Goldsmith's death as being mainly by him; and it
is generally admitted that the poet had at least undertaken to furnish
such a translation. But most of the poetical pieces in these two volumes
have been traced to a previous translation, and the work generally is
now classed with those bearing Goldsmith's name which are denominated
"doubtful"—though the above four lines are viewed by Mr. Bolton
Corney and others as being certainly from Goldsmith's hand.—ED.

Epigram to the Gentlemen Reflected on in the 'Rosciad.'

Letter CXIII. See v. iii.

To G. C. and R. L.

Letter CXIII. See v. iii.

Translation of a South American Ode.

Letter CXVII. See v. iii.

IN 'THE GOOD-NATURED MAN' [1768].

Epilogue; spoken by Mrs. Bulkley.

IN 'SHE STOOPS TO CONQUER' [1773].

Song: Let Schoolmasters puzzle their Brain.

Act I. See v. ii.

Epilogue; spoken by Mrs. Bulkley in the character of Miss Hardcastle.

APPENDIX TO THE POEMS.

LOCALITY OF AUBURN:

(THE 'DESERTED VILLAGE.')

It has been disputed among the admirers of Goldsmith, whether the scene of the 'Deserted Village' is laid in England or in Ireland, and quotations from the poem itself have been adduced, in support of their opinion, by both parties. The truth seems to be, however, that while the poem generally refers to England—and, indeed, there are particular allusions which cannot possibly apply to Ireland—the author, at the same time, naturally referred for his village description to the locality most familiar to his memory, and most intimately connected with his fondest associations. That his reflections refer to England is evident, from his dedication to Sir Joshua Reynolds, where he says, " I know you will object, (and indeed several of our best and wisest friends concur in the opinion,) that the depopulation it deplores is no where to be seen, and the disorders it laments are only to be found in the poet's own imagination. To this I can scarce make any other answer, than that I sincerely believe what I have written ; that I have taken all possible pains, in my country excursions, for these four or five years past, to be certain of what I allege ; and that all my views and enquiries have led me to believe those miseries real, which I here attempt to display." [1]

That in his particular description of Auburn he drew from a scene endeared to him by many fond recollections, and that Auburn and Lissoy are the same, will, we think, be proved to the satisfaction of the most sceptical, by the following extracts :—

" The poem of the 'Deserted Village,'" says Dr. Strean,[2] in a letter printed in Mr. Mangin's ' Essay on Light Reading,'[3] " took its origin from the circumstance of General Robert Napier,[4] the grandfather of

---

[1] Supposing the preface to ' Goody Two-shoes' (1764-5) to have been written by Goldsmith, it constitutes an earlier and a similarly forcible appeal by the poet against the depopulation of villages, &c.—Ed.

[2] He succeeded Henry Goldsmith in the curacy of Kilkenny, West. —Ed.   [3] 12mo, 1808.—Ed.

[4] Or Napper. The Rev. Mr. Hancock said his family came from Germany.—Ed.

the gentleman who now lives in the house, within half a mile of Lissoy, built by the General, having purchased an extensive tract of the country surrounding Lissoy, or *Auburn;* in consequence of which, many families, here called *cottiers,* were removed to make room for the intended improvements of what was now to become the wide domain of a rich man, warm with the idea of changing the face of his new acquisition, and were forced, 'with fainting steps,' to go in search of ' torrid tracts,' and ' distant climes.'

" This fact alone might be sufficient to establish the seat of the poem ; but there cannot remain a doubt in any unprejudiced mind, when the following are added; viz., that in the character of the Village Preacher, Henry, the brother of the Poet, is copied from nature. He is described exactly as he lived ; and his ' modest mansion ' as it existed. Burn, the name of the village master, and the site of his school-house, and Catharine Giraghty, a lonely widow,—

" ' The wretched matron, forced in age, for bread,
To strip the brook with mantling cresses spread '

(and to this day the brook and ditches near the spot where her cabin stood abound with cresses), still remain in the memory of the inhabitants, and Catharine's children live in the neighbourhood. The pool, the busy mill, the house where ' nut-brown draughts inspired,' are still visited as the poetic scene ; and the ' hawthorn bush,' growing in an open space in front of the house, which I knew to have three trunks, is now reduced to one, the other two having been cut, from time to time, by persons carrying pieces of it away to be made into toys, &c., in honour of the bard, and of the celebrity of his poem. All these contribute to the same proof; and the ' decent church,' which I attended for upwards of eighteen years, and which ' tops the neighbouring hill,' is exactly described as seen from Lissoy, the residence of the Preacher."

The next extract is taken from a notice in a respectable periodical, and confirms the description given by Dr. Strean :—

" About three miles from Ballymahon, a very central town in the sister kingdom, is the mansion and village of Auburn, so called by their present possessor, Captain Hogan. Through the taste and improvement of this gentleman, it is now a beautiful spot, although fifteen years since it presented a very bare and unpoetical aspect. This, however, was owing to a cause which serves strongly to corroborate the assertion, that Goldsmith had this scene in view when he wrote his poem of the "Deserted Village.' The then possessor, General Napier, turned all his tenants out of their farms, that he might enclose them in his own private domain. Littleton, the mansion of the General, stands not far off, a complete emblem of the desolating spirit lamented by the poet, dilapidated and converted into a barrack.

" The chief object of attraction is Lissoy, once the parsonage-house of Henry Goldsmith, that brother to whom the poet dedicated his ' Traveller,' and who is represented as the Village Pastor,

" ' Passing rich with forty pounds a-year.'

" When I was in the country, the lower chambers were inhabited by pigs and sheep, and the drawing-rooms by oats. Captain Hogan, how ever, has, I believe, got it since into his possession, and has, of course, improved its condition.

"Though at first strongly inclined to dispute the identity of Auburn, Lissoy House overcame my scruples. As I clambered over the rotten gate, and crossed the grass-grown lawn, or court, the tide of association became too strong for casuistry: here the poet dwelt and wrote, and here his thoughts fondly recurred when composing his 'Traveller,' in a foreign land. Yonder was the decent church, that literally 'topped the neighbouring hill.' Before me lay the little hill of Knockrue, on which he declares, in one of his letters, he had rather sit with a book in hand, than mingle in the proudest assemblies. And above all, startlingly true, beneath my feet was

> "'Yonder copse, where once the garden smiled,
> And still where many a garden flower grows wild.'

"A painting from the life could not be more exact. 'The stubborn currant-bush' lifts its head above the rank grass, and the proud holyhock flaunts where its sisters of the flower-knot are no more.

"In the middle of the village stands the old 'hawthorn tree,' built up with masonry, to distinguish and preserve it: it is old and stunted, and suffers much from the depredations of post-chaise travellers, who generally stop to procure a twig. Opposite to it is the village alehouse, over the door of which swings 'The Three Jolly Pigeons.'[1] Within, every thing is arranged according to the letter:—

> "'The white-wash'd wall, the nicely sanded floor,
> The varnish'd clock, that click'd behind the door,
> The chest contrived a double debt to pay,
> A bed by night, a chest of drawers by day;
> The pictures placed for ornament and use,
> The Twelve Good Rules, the Royal Game of Goose.'

"Captain Hogan, I have heard, found great difficulty in obtaining 'The Twelve Good Rules,' but at length purchased them at some London book stall, to adorn the white-washed parlour of 'The Three Jolly Pigeons.' However laudable this may be, nothing shook my faith in the reality of Auburn so much as this exactness, which had the disagreeable air of being got up for the occasion. The last object of pilgrimage is the quondam habitation of the schoolmaster,

> "'There in his noisy mansion skill'd to rule.'

"It is surrounded with fragrant proofs of its identity in

> "'The blossom'd furze, unprofitably gay.'

* * * * * * * *

"The controversy concerning the identity of this Auburn, was formerly a standing theme of discussion among the learned of the neighbourhood, but since the *pros* and *cons* have been all ascertained, the argument has died away. Its abettors plead the singular agreement between the local

---

[1] See 'She Stoops to Conquer,' Act i., sc. ii.—ED.

history of the place and the Auburn of the poem, and the exactness with which the scenery of the one answers to the description of the other. To this is opposed the mention of the nightingale,

> " ' And fill'd each pause the nightingale had made,'

there being no such bird in the island. The objection is slighted, on the other hand, by considering the passage as a mere poetical licence. Besides, say they, ' the Robin is the Irish nightingale.' "—B.

The Rev. R. H. Newell, however, found an Auburn, so called, in Ireland on his visit, about 1810 : *vide* his ' Remarks on the Actual Scene of the Deserted Village,' with illustrations by Alken from drawings taken on the spot, 4to. 1811. But this, as he tells us, came by its name since, and in consequence of the fame of Goldsmith's ' Deserted Village.' This Auburn, too, Mr. Newell adds, is a house, not a village. It is near Athlone, and belonged to Goldsmith's nephew, Daniel Hodson, who, having made a fortune in India, built the house on his return, about 1790, and named it Auburn in honour of the poet.

Very few of those who contend for an English site for Auburn venture upon naming a locality. But Springfield, in Essex, has been so named. Here, it is said, while residing at a farm-house, " opposite the church," Goldsmith wrote the ' Deserted Village ; " and hence it is assumed that Springfield is pictured by the poet as Auburn.[1] See also for the Springfield theory, *Notes and Queries*, 5th Series, v. x., pp. 88 and 294, and Lewis's ' Topographical Dictionary,—England,' 1831, Gronin's ' Excursions in Essex,' 1818, and the ' Antiquarian Handbook of England and Wales,' 1849, there quoted.—ED.

THE JOHNSON LINES IN GOLDSMITH'S POEMS.

To test the view taken in our notes at pp. 19 and 45, the view, namely, that the attribution of these lines to Dr. Johnson rests solely upon Boswell's statements (' Life of Johnson,' Bohn's edition, v. ii., p. 309), the present writer lately (January, 1883) added to the substance of those notes the following in *Notes and Queries*:—" It need not be assumed that Boswell has stated anything more than what he believed to be true; still less need it be assumed that Johnson stated anything which was not true ; but I think, as the case stands, it may be at least admitted that Boswell may have made some mistake. The ascription of the good things of the time, in both verse and prose, to Dr. Johnson was, as is well known, quite a common occurrence. Miss Reynolds, for instance, states in reference to the ' Traveller ' (' Recollections,' published in the ' Johnsoniana ' at the end of Bohn's edition of Boswell's ' Life '), that ' Dr. Johnson told her that he had written ' the ten lines descriptive of the Englishman commencing ' Stern o'er each bosom.' Nobody, I suppose, believes this ; and yet no doubt the lady was, generally speaking, as worthy belief as Boswell. The explanation, of course, is that she

---

[1] Mr. Newell, however, in his work above mentioned, states that at Lissoy it was believed that the ' Deserted Village ' was written while the poet was on a visit there : see *ante*, p. 35.—ED.

was mistaken. Again, Johnson himself relates that Chamier went away with the belief that he (Johnson) had written the first line of the 'Traveller,' because he in conversation interpreted Goldsmith's meaning as to the word *slow* seemingly better than Goldsmith did himself (*vide* Boswell's 'Johnson,' vol. ii., p. 85). I should be glad if any further light could be thrown upon this matter; but so far it seems to me the above-stated facts point to at least a doubt as to whether the nine lines in the 'Traveller' and four lines in the 'Deserted Village,' usually marked as Johnson's, were really written by him." This elicited no contradiction; and we may therefore conclude that our plea that the question may be looked upon as an open one is virtually allowed.—ED.

PLAYS.

GOOD-NATURED MAN,

A COMEDY.

[This admirable comedy was represented, for the first time, at Covent Garden, January 29, 1768. It kept possession of the stage for nine nights, but was considered by the author's friends not to have met with all the success it deserved. Dr. Johnson spoke of it as the best comedy which had appeared since 'The Provoked Husband,' and Burke estimated its merits still higher.—B. The first edition, published in the usual 8vo. play-book form, bears date 1768, with the imprint—" Printed for W. Griffin, in Catharine-street, Strand." Five editions in this form appeared in the same year.—Ed.]

PREFACE.

WHEN I undertook to write a comedy, I confess I was strongly prepossessed in favour of the poets of the last age, and strove to imitate them. The term *genteel comedy* was then unknown amongst us, and little more was desired by an audience than nature and humour, in whatever walks of life they were most conspicuous. The author of the following scenes never imagined that more would be expected of him, and, therefore, to delineate character has been his principal aim. Those who know anything of composition, are sensible that, in pursuing humour, it will sometimes lead us into the recesses of the mean : I was even tempted to look for it in the master of a spunging-house ; but, in deference to the public taste—grown of late, perhaps, too delicate—the scene of the bailiffs was retrenched in the representation.[1] In deference also to the judgment of a few friends, who think in a particular way, the scene is here

---

[1] This scene (Act III.) was struck out after the first representation, at the desire of the manager, Mr. Colman.—B. Besides being restored in the printed copy, this scene—one of the most humorous in the play —was afterwards restored to the acting version.—Ed.

restored. The author submits it to the reader in his closet; and hopes that too much refinement will not banish humour and character from ours, as it has already done from the French theatre. Indeed, the French comedy is now become so very elevated and sentimental, that it has not only banished humour and Moliere from the stage, but it has banished all spectators too.

Upon the whole, the author returns his thanks to the public, for the favourable reception which the *Good-Natured Man* has met with; and to Mr. Colman in particular, for his kindness to it. It may not also be improper to assure any who shall hereafter write for the theatre, that merit, or supposed merit, will ever be a sufficient passport to his protection.

DRAMATIS PERSONÆ.

[THE CAST OF THE PLAY AS IT WAS FIRST ACTED AT COVENT GARDEN.]

MEN.

Mr. Honeywood, ...	MR. POWELL.
Croaker, ...	MR. SHUTER.
Lofty, ...	MR. WOODWARD.
Sir William Honeywood, . . .	MR. CLARKE.
Leontine, ...	MR. BENSLEY.
Jarvis, ...	MR. DUNSTALL.
Butler, ...	MR. CUSHING.
Bailiff, ...	MR. R. SMITH.
Dubardieu, ...	MR. HOLTOM.
Postboy, ...	MR. QUICK.

WOMEN.

Miss Richland, ...	MRS. BULKLEY.
Olivia, ...	MRS. MATTOCKS.
Mrs. Croaker, ...	MRS. PITT.
Garnet, ...	MRS. GREEN.
Landlady, ...	MRS. WHITE.

Scene.—LONDON.

THE

GOOD-NATURED MAN.

PROLOGUE.

WRITTEN BY DR. JOHNSON, SPOKEN BY MR. BENSLEY.

PRESS'D by the load of life, the weary mind
Surveys the general toil of human kind,
With cool submission joins the lab'ring train,
And social sorrow loses half its pain :[1]
Our anxious bard, without complaint, may share
This bustling season's epidemic care,
Like Cæsar's pilot, dignified by fate,
Toss'd in one common storm with all the great ;
Distress'd alike, the statesman and the wit,
When one a Borough courts, and one the Pit.
The busy candidates for power and fame
Have hopes, and fears, and wishes, just the same ;
Disabled both to combat or to fly,
Must hear all taunts, and hear without reply ;
Uncheck'd, on both loud rabbles vent their rage,

---

[1] In the Prologue as given in the *Public Advertiser* of Feb. 3, 1768, these lines are followed by—

> " Amidst the toils of this returning year,
> When senators and nobles learn to fear,
> Our little bard, without complaint," &c.

The alterations here and in other lines of the Prologue were made for the first edition as printed.—ED.

As mongrels bay the lion in a cage.[1]
Th' offended burgess hoards his angry tale,
For that blest year when all that vote may rail ;
Their schemes of spite the poet's foes dismiss,
Till that glad night, when all that hate may hiss.
" This day, the powder'd curls and golden coat,"
Says swelling Crispin, " begg'd a cobbler's vote."
" This night, our wit," the pert apprentice cries,
"Lies at my feet—I hiss him, and he dies."[2]
The great, 'tis true, can charm th' electing tribe :
The bard may supplicate, but cannot bribe.
Yet, judged by those whose voices ne'er were sold,
He feels no want of ill-persuading gold ;
But confident of praise, if praise be due,
Trusts, without fear, to merit,[3] and to you.

ACT I.

SCENE.—AN APARTMENT IN YOUNG HONEYWOOD'S HOUSE.

Enter Sir William Honeywood and Jarvis.

Sir William. GOOD Jarvis, make no apologies for this
honest bluntness.   Fidelity like yours, is the best excuse
for every freedom.

Jarvis. I can't help being blunt, and being very angry
too, when I hear you talk of disinheriting so good, so
worthy a young gentleman as your nephew, my master.
All the world loves him.

Sir William. Say rather, that he loves all the world ;
that is his fault.

Jarvis. I'm sure there is no part of it more dear to him
than you are, though he has not seen you since he was a
child.

[1]   " Uncheck'd, on both caprice may vent its rage,
         As children fret the lion in a cage."
                                        Public Advertiser.

[2] These four lines are not in the *Public Advertiser* version.—ED.
[3] The word is "candour" in the *Public Advertiser.*—ED.

Sir William. What signifies his affection to me? or how can I be proud of a place in a heart where every sharper and coxcomb find an easy entrance?

Jarvis. I grant you that he is rather too good-natured; that he's too much every man's man; that he laughs this minute with one, and cries the next with another; but whose instructions may he thank for all this?

Sir William. Not mine, sure. My letters to him during my employment in Italy, taught him only that philosophy which might prevent, not defend his errors.

Jarvis. Faith, begging your honour's pardon, I'm sorry they taught him any philosophy at all; it has only served to spoil him. This same philosophy is a good horse in the stable, but an arrant jade on a journey. For my own part, whenever I hear him mention the name on 't, I'm always sure he's going to play the fool.

Sir William. Don't let us ascribe his faults to his philosophy, I entreat you. No, Jarvis, his good-nature arises rather from his fears of offending the importunate, than his desire of making the deserving happy.

Jarvis. What it arises from, I don't know; but, to be sure, every body has it that asks it.

Sir William. Ay, or that does not ask it. I have been now for some time a concealed spectator of his follies, and find them as boundless as his dissipation.

Jarvis. And yet, faith, he has some fine name or other for them all. He calls his extravagance, generosity; and his trusting every body, universal benevolence. It was but last week he went security for a fellow whose face he scarce knew, and that he called an act of exalted mu—mu—munificence; ay, that was the name he gave it.

Sir William. And upon that I proceed, as my last effort, though with very little hopes, to reclaim him. That very fellow has just absconded, and I have taken up the security. Now, my intention is to involve him in fictitious distress, before he has plunged himself into real calamity: to arrest him for that very debt; to clap an officer upon him, and then let him see which of his friends will come to his relief.

Jarvis. Well, if I could but any way see him thoroughly vexed, every groan of his would be music to me; yet, faith, I believe it impossible. I have tried to fret him myself every morning these three years; but instead of being angry, he sits as calmly to hear me scold, as he does to his hair-dresser.

Sir William. We must try him once more, however, and I'll go this instant to put my scheme into execution: and I don't despair of succeeding, as, by your means, I can have frequent opportunities of being about him without being known. What a pity it is, Jarvis, that any man's good-will to others should produce so much neglect of himself, as to require correction! Yet we must touch his weaknesses with a delicate hand. There are some faults so nearly allied to excellence, that we can scarce weed out the vice without eradicating the virtue.   [*Exit.*

Jarvis. Well, go thy ways, Sir William Honeywood. It is not without reason, that the world allows thee to be the best of men. But here comes his hopeful nephew— the strange, good-natured, foolish, open-hearted—And yet, all his faults are such, that one loves him still the better for them.

Enter Honeywood.

Honeywood. Well, Jarvis, what messages from my friends this morning?

Jarvis. You have no friends.

Honeywood. Well, from my acquaintance then?

Jarvis. (*Pulling out bills.*) A few of our usual cards of compliment, that's all. This bill from your tailor; this from your mercer; and this from the little broker in Crooked-lane. He says he has been at a great deal of trouble to get back the money you borrowed.

Honeywood. That I don't know; but I am sure we were at a great deal of trouble in getting him to lend it.

Jarvis. He has lost all patience.

Honeywood. Then he has lost a very good thing.

Jarvis. There's that ten guineas you were sending to the poor gentleman and his children in the Fleet. I believe that would stop his mouth, for a while at least.

Honeywood. Ay, Jarvis, but what will fill their mouths in the mean time? Must I be cruel, because he happens to be importunate; and, to relieve his avarice, leave them to insupportable distress?

Jarvis. 'Sdeath! Sir, the question now is how to relieve yourself. Yourself—Haven't I reason to be out of my senses, when I see things going at sixes and sevens?

Honeywood. Whatever reason you may have for being out of your senses, I hope you'll allow that I'm not quite unreasonable for continuing in mine.

Jarvis. You are the only man alive in your present situation that could do so—Every thing upon the waste. There's Miss Richland and her fine fortune gone already, and upon the point of being given to your rival—

Honeywood. I'm no man's rival.

Jarvis. Your uncle in Italy preparing to disinherit you; your own fortune almost spent; and nothing but pressing creditors, false friends, and a pack of drunken servants that your kindness has made unfit for any other family.

Honeywood. Then they have the more occasion for being in mine.

Jarvis. Soh! What will you have done with him that I caught stealing your plate in the pantry? In the fact—I caught him in the fact.

Honeywood. In the fact? If so, I really think that we should pay him his wages, and turn him off.

Jarvis. He shall be turned off at Tyburn, the dog: we'll hang him, if it be only to frighten the rest of the family.

Honeywood. No, Jarvis: it's enough that we have lost what he has stolen; let us not add to it the loss of a fellow-creature!

Jarvis. Very fine! Well, here was the footman just now, to complain of the butler: he says he does most work, and ought to have most wages.

Honeywood. That's but just; though perhaps here comes the butler to complain of the footman.

Jarvis. Ay, it's the way with them all, from the scullion to the privy-counsellor. If they have a bad master, they keep quarrelling with him; if they have a good master, they keep quarrelling with one another.

Enter Butler, drunk.

Butler. Sir, I'll not stay in the family with Jonathan; you must part with him, or part with me, that's the ex—ex—exposition of the matter, Sir.

Honeywood. Full and explicit enough. But what's his fault, good Philip?

Butler. Sir, he's given to drinking, Sir, and I shall have my morals corrupted by keeping such company.

Honeywood. Ha! ha! he has such a diverting way—

Jarvis. Oh, quite amusing.

Butler. I find my wine's a-going, Sir; and liquors don't go without mouths, Sir—I hate a drunkard, Sir.

Honeywood. Well, well, Philip, I'll hear you upon that another time; so go to bed now.

Jarvis. To bed! let him go to the devil.

Butler. Begging your honour's pardon, and begging your pardon, master Jarvis, I'll not go to bed, nor to the devil neither. I have enough to do to mind my cellar. I forgot, your honour, Mr. Croaker is below. I came on purpose to tell you.

Honeywood. Why didn't you show him up, blockhead?

Butler. Show him up, Sir? With all my heart, Sir. Up or down, all's one to me.   [*Exit.*

Jarvis. Ay, we have one or other of that family in this house from morning till night. He comes on the old affair, I suppose. The match between his son that's just returned from Paris, and Miss Richland, the young lady he's guardian to.

Honeywood. Perhaps so. Mr. Croaker, knowing my friendship for the young lady, has got it into his head that I can persuade her to what I please.

Jarvis. Ah! if you loved yourself but half as well as she loves you, we should soon see a marriage that would set all things to rights again.

Honeywood. Love me! Sure, Jarvis, you dream. No, no; her intimacy with me never amounted to more than friendship—mere friendship. That she is the most lovely woman that ever warmed the human heart with desire, I own: but never let me harbour a thought of making her unhappy, by a connection with one so unworthy her merits as I am. No, Jarvis, it shall be my study to serve her, even in spite of my wishes; and to secure her happiness, though it destroys my own.

Jarvis. Was ever the like? I want patience.

Honeywood. Besides, Jarvis, though I could obtain Miss Richland's consent, do you think I could succeed with her guardian, or Mrs. Croaker, his wife; who, though both very fine in their way, are yet a little opposite in their dispositions, you know.

Jarvis. Opposite enough, Heaven knows! the very reverse of each other; she all laugh, and no joke; he always complaining, and never sorrowful—a fretful poor soul, that has a new distress for every hour in the four-and-twenty—

Honeywood. Hush, hush! he's coming up, he'll hear you.

Jarvis. One whose voice is a passing-bell—

Honeywood. Well, well; go, do.

Jarvis. A raven that bodes nothing but mischief—a coffin and cross bones—a bundle of rue—a sprig of deadly nightshade—a— (*Honeywood, stopping his mouth, at last pushes him off.*)   [*Exit Jarvis.*

Honeywood. I must own my old monitor is not entirely wrong. There is something in my friend Croaker's conversation that quite depresses me. His very mirth is an antidote to all gaiety, and his appearance has a stronger effect on my spirits than an undertaker's shop—Mr. Croaker, this is such a satisfaction—

Enter Croaker.

Croaker. A pleasant morning to Mr. Honeywood, and many of them. How is this! you look most shockingly to-day, my dear friend. I hope this weather does not affect your spirits. To be sure, if this weather continues—I say nothing; but God send we be all better this day three months!

Honeywood. I heartily concur in the wish, though, I own, not in your apprehensions.

Croaker. May be not. Indeed, what signifies what weather we have in a country going to ruin like ours?

taxes rising and trade falling; money flying out of the kingdom, and Jesuits swarming into it. I know, at this time, no less than a hundred and twenty-seven Jesuits between Charing Cross and Temple Bar.

Honeywood. The Jesuits will scarce pervert you or me, I should hope.

Croaker. May be not. Indeed, what signifies whom they pervert, in a country that has scarce any religion to lose? I'm only afraid for our wives and daughters.

Honeywood. I have no apprehensions for the ladies, I assure you.

Croaker. May be not. Indeed, what signifies whether they be perverted or no? The women in my time were good for something. I have seen a lady drest from top to toe in her own manufactures formerly: but now-a-days, the devil a thing of their own manufactures about them, except their faces.

Honeywood. But, however these faults may be practised abroad, you don't find them at home, either with Mrs. Croaker, Olivia, or Miss Richland?

Croaker. The best of them will never be canonized for a saint when she's dead.—By the by, my dear friend, I don't find this match between Miss Richland and my son much relished, either by one side or t'other.

Honeywood. I thought otherwise.

Croaker. Ah! Mr. Honeywood, a little of your fine serious advice to the young lady might go far: I know she has a very exalted opinion of your understanding.

Honeywood. But would not that be usurping an authority that more properly belongs to yourself?

Croaker. My dear friend, you know but little of my authority at home. People think, indeed, because they see me come out in a morning thus, with a pleasant face, and to make my friends merry, that all's well within. But I have cares that would break a heart of stone. My wife has so encroached upon every one of my privileges, that I'm now no more than a mere lodger in my own house.

Honeywood. But a little spirit exerted on your side might perhaps restore your authority.

Croaker. No, though I had the spirit of a lion! I do rouse sometimes; but what then? always haggling and

haggling.   A man is tired of getting the better before his
wife is tired of losing the victory.

Honeywood. It's a melancholy consideration, indeed, that
our chief comforts often produce our greatest anxieties, and
that an increase of our possessions is but an inlet to new
disquietudes.

Croaker. Ah! my dear friend, these were the very words
of poor Dick Doleful to me, not a week before he made
away with himself.   Indeed, Mr. Honeywood, I never see
you but you put me in mind of poor Dick. Ah! there was
merit neglected for you! and so true a friend! we loved
each other for thirty years, and yet he never asked me to
lend him a single farthing!

Honeywood. Pray what could induce him to commit so
rash an action at last?

Croaker. I don't know: some people were malicious
enough to say it was keeping company with me; because
we used to meet now and then, and open our hearts to each
other.   To be sure, I loved to hear him talk, and he loved
to hear me talk; poor dear Dick!   He used to say that
Croaker rhymed to joker; and so we used to laugh.—Poor
Dick !   (*Going to cry.*)

Honeywood. His fate affects me.

Croaker. Ay, he grew sick of this miserable life, where
we do nothing but eat and grow hungry, dress and undress,
get up and lie down; while reason, that should watch like
a nurse by our side, falls as fast asleep as we do.

Honeywood. To say truth, if we compare that part of life
which is to come, by that which we have past, the prospect
is hideous.

Croaker. Life, at the greatest and best, is but a froward
child, that must be humoured and coaxed a little till it
falls asleep, and then all the care is over.[1]

Honeywood. Very true, Sir, nothing can exceed the vanity
of our existence, but the folly of our pursuits. ' We wept
when we came into the world, and every day tells us why.

Croaker. Ah! my dear friend, it is a perfect satisfaction
to be miserable with you.   My son Leontine shan't lose the

---

[1] Sir William Temple concludes his essay 'Of Poetry' in almost
exactly the same words.   *Vide* ' Works,' Swift's edition, 1720, v. i.,
p. 249.—ED.

benefit of such fine conversation. I'll just step home for him. I am willing to show him so much seriousness in one scarce older than himself.—And what if I bring my last letter to the *Gazetteer*, on the increase and progress of earthquakes? It will amuse us, I promise you. I there prove how the late earthquake is coming round to pay us another visit—from London to Lisbon—from Lisbon to the Canary Islands—from the Canary Islands to Palmyra—from Palmyra to Constantinople, and so from Constantinople back to London again.   [*Exit.*

Honeywood. Poor Croaker! his situation deserves the utmost pity. I shall scarce recover my spirits these three days. Sure to live upon such terms, is worse than death itself. And yet, when I consider my own situation—a broken fortune, a hopeless passion, friends in distress, the wish, but not the power, to serve them——(*Pausing and sighing*).

Enter Butler.

Butler. More company below, Sir; Mrs. Croaker and Miss Richland; shall I show them up?—but they're showing up themselves.   [*Exit.*

Enter Mrs. Croaker and Miss Richland.

Miss Richland. You're always in such spirits.

Mrs. Croaker. We have just come, my dear Honeywood, from the auction. There was the old deaf dowager, as usual, bidding like a fury against herself. And then so curious in antiques! herself, the most genuine piece of antiquity in the whole collection.

Honeywood. Excuse me, ladies, if some uneasiness from friendship makes me unfit to share in this good humour: I know you'll pardon me.

Mrs. Croaker. I vow he seems as melancholy as if he had taken a dose of my husband this morning. Well, if Richland here can pardon you, I must.

Miss Richland. You would seem to insinuate, Madam, that I have particular reasons for being disposed to refuse it.

Mrs. Croaker. Whatever I insinuate, my dear, don't be so ready to wish an explanation.

Miss Richland. I own I should be sorry Mr. Honeywood's long friendship and mine should be misunderstood.

Honeywood. There's no answering for others, Madam; but I hope you'll never find me presuming to offer more than the most delicate friendship may readily allow.

Miss Richland. And I shall be prouder of such a tribute from you, than the most passionate professions from others.

Honeywood. My own sentiments, Madam: friendship is a disinterested commerce between equals; love, an abject intercourse between tyrants and slaves.

Miss Richland. And, without a compliment, I know none more disinterested, or more capable of friendship, than Mr. Honeywood.

Mrs. Croaker. And, indeed, I know nobody that has more friends, at least among the ladies. Miss Fruzz, Miss Oddbody, and Miss Winterbottom, praise him in all companies. As for Miss Biddy Bundle, she's his professed admirer.

Miss Richland. Indeed! an admirer!—I did not know, Sir, you were such a favourite there. But is she, seriously, so handsome? Is she the mighty thing talked of?

Honeywood. The town, Madam, seldom begins to praise a lady's beauty, till she's beginning to lose it. (*Smiling.*)

Mrs. Croaker. But she's resolved never to lose it, it seems. For as her natural face decays, her skill improves in making the artificial one. Well, nothing diverts me more than one of those fine, old, dressy things, who thinks to conceal her age by everywhere exposing her person; sticking herself up in the front of a side-box; trailing through a minuet at Almack's; and then, in the public gardens—looking, for all the world, like one of the painted ruins of the place.

Honeywood. Every age has its admirers, ladies. While you, perhaps, are trading among the warmer climates of youth, there ought to be some to carry on a useful commerce in the frozen latitudes beyond fifty.

Miss Richland. But, then, the mortifications they must suffer, before they can be fitted out for traffic. I have seen one of them fret a whole morning at her hairdresser, when all the fault was her face.

Honeywood. And yet, I'll engage, has carried that face at last to a very good market. This good-natured town, Madam, has husbands, like spectacles, to fit every age, from fifteen to fourscore.

Mrs. Croaker. Well, you're a dear good-natured creature. But you know you're engaged with us this morning upon a strolling party. I want to show Olivia the town, and the things : I believe I shall have business for you the whole day.

Honeywood. I am sorry, Madam, I have an appointment with Mr. Croaker, which it is impossible to put off.

Mrs. Croaker. What ! with my husband ! then I'm resolved to take no refusal. Nay, I protest you must. You know I never laugh so much as with you.

Honeywood. Why, if I must, I must. I'll swear you have put me into such spirits. Well, do you find jest, and I'll find laugh, I promise you. We'll wait for the chariot in the next room. [*Exeunt.*

Enter Leontine and Olivia.

Leontine. There they go, thoughtless and happy. My dearest Olivia, what would I give to see you capable of sharing in their amusements, and as cheerful as they are !

Olivia. How, my Leontine, how can I be cheerful, when I have so many terrors to oppress me ? The fear of being detected by this family, and the apprehensions of a censuring world, when I must be detected——

Leontine. The world, my love ! what can it say ? At worst it can only say, that, being compelled by a mercenary guardian to embrace a life you disliked, you formed a resolution of flying with the man of your choice ; that you confided in his honour, and took refuge in my father's house,—the only one where yours could remain without censure.

Olivia. But consider, Leontine, your disobedience and my indiscretion ; your being sent to France to bring home a sister, and, instead of a sister, bringing home——

Leontine. One dearer than a thousand sisters. One that I am convinced will be equally dear to the rest of the family, when she comes to be known.

Olivia. And that, I fear, will shortly be.

Leontine. Impossible, till we ourselves think proper to make the discovery. My sister, you know, has been with her aunt, at Lyons, since she was a child, and you find every creature in the family takes you for her.

Olivia. But mayn't she write? mayn't her aunt write?

Leontine. Her aunt scarce ever writes, and all my sister's letters are directed to me.

Olivia. But won't your refusing Miss Richland, for whom you know the old gentleman intends you, create a suspicion?

Leontine. There, there's my master stroke. I have resolved not to refuse her; nay, an hour hence I have consented to go with my father to make her an offer of my heart and fortune.

Olivia. Your heart and fortune!

Leontine. Don't be alarm'd, my dearest. Can Olivia think so meanly of my honour, or my love, as to suppose I could ever hope for happiness from any but her? No, my Olivia, neither the force, nor, permit me to add, the delicacy of my passion, leave any room to suspect me. I only offer Miss Richland a heart I am convinced she will refuse; as I am confident, that, without knowing it, her affections are fixed upon Mr. Honeywood.

Olivia. Mr. Honeywood! You'll excuse my apprehensions; but when your merits come to be put in the balance——

Leontine. You view them with too much partiality. However, by making this offer, I show a seeming compliance with my father's command; and perhaps, upon her refusal, I may have his consent to choose for myself.

Olivia. Well, I submit. And yet, my Leontine, I own, I shall envy her even your pretended addresses. I consider every look, every expression of your esteem, as due only to me. This is folly perhaps: I allow it; but it is natural to suppose, that merit which has made an impression on one's own heart may be powerful over that of another.

Leontine. Don't, my life's treasure, don't let us make imaginary evils, when you know we have so many real ones to encounter. At worst, you know, if Miss Richland

should consent, or my father refuse his pardon, it can but
end in a trip to Scotland; and——

Enter Croaker.

Croaker. Where have you been, boy? I have been
seeking you. My friend Honeywood here has been saying
such comfortable things! Ah! he's an example indeed.
Where is he? I left him here.

Leontine. Sir, I believe you may see him, and hear him
too, in the next room : he's preparing to go out with the
ladies.

Croaker. Good gracious! can I believe my eyes or my
ears? I'm struck dumb with his vivacity, and stunned
with the loudness of his laugh. Was there ever such a
transformation! (*A laugh behind the scenes : Croaker mimics
it.*) Ha! ha! ha! there it goes : a plague take their bal-
derdash! yet I could expect nothing less, when my precious
cious wife was of the party. On my conscience, I believe
she could spread a horse-laugh through the pews of a
tabernacle.

Leontine. Since you find so many objections to a wife,
Sir, how can you be so earnest in recommending one to
me?

Croaker. I have told you, and tell you again, boy, that
Miss Richland's fortune must not go out of the family;
one may find comfort in the money, whatever one does in
the wife.

Leontine. But, Sir, though in obedience to your desire,
I am ready to marry her, it may be possible she has no
inclination to me.

Croaker. I'll tell you once for all how it stands. A good
part of Miss Richland's large fortune consists in a claim
upon government, which my good friend, Mr. Lofty,
assures me the treasury will allow. One half of this she
is to forfeit, by her father's will, in case she refuses to
marry you. So, if she rejects you, we seize half her fortune; if she accepts you, we seize the whole, and a fine
girl into the bargain.

Leontine. But, Sir, if you will but listen to reason——

Croaker. Come, then, produce your reasons. I tell you,

I'm fixed, determined—so now produce your reasons.
When I am determined, I always listen to reason, because
it can then do no harm.

Leontine. You have alleged that a mutual choice was the
first requisite in matrimonial happiness.

Croaker. Well, and you have both of you a mutual choice.
She has her choice,—to marry you or lose half her fortune ;
and you have your choice,—to marry her, or pack out of
doors without any fortune at all.

Leontine. An only son, Sir, might expect more indul-
gence.

Croaker. An only father, Sir, might expect more obedience. Besides, has not your sister here, that never disobliged me in her life, as good a right as you? He's a
sad dog, Livy, my dear, and would take all from you.
But he shan't : I tell you he shan't ; for you shall have
your share.

Olivia. Dear Sir, I wish you'd be convinced, that I can
never be happy in any addition to my fortune which is
taken from his.

Croaker. Well, well, it's a good child, so say no more ;
but come with me, and we shall see something that will
give us a great deal of pleasure, I promise you :—old
Ruggins, the currycomb maker, lying in state : I am told
he makes a very handsome corpse, and becomes his coffin
prodigiously. He was an intimate friend of mine, and
these are friendly things we ought to do for each other.

[*Exeunt.*

ACT II.

SCENE.—CROAKER'S HOUSE.

Miss Richland, Garnet.

Miss Richland. Olivia not his sister? Olivia not Leontine's sister ? You amaze me !

Garnet. No more his sister than I am ; I had it all from
his own servant ; I can get anything from that quarter.

Miss Richland. But how ? Tell me again, Garnet.

Garnet. Why, Madam, as I told you before, instead of

going to Lyons to bring home his sister, who has been
there with her aunt these ten years, he never went farther
than Paris: there he saw and fell in love with this young
lady—by the by, of a prodigious family.

Miss Richland. And brought her home to my guardian
as his daughter?

Garnet. Yes, and his daughter she will be. If he don't
consent to their marriage, they talk of trying what a Scotch
parson can do.

Miss Richland. Well, I own they have deceived me.
And so demurely as Olivia carried it too!—Would you
believe it, Garnet, I told her all my secrets; and yet the
sly cheat concealed all this from me?

Garnet. And, upon my word, Madam, I don't much
blame her: she was loth to trust one with her secrets that
was so very bad at keeping her own.

Miss Richland. But, to add to their deceit, the young
gentleman, it seems, pretends to make me serious proposals. My guardian and he are to be here presently, to
open the affair in form. You know I am to lose half my
fortune if I refuse him.

Garnet. Yet, what can you do? For being, as you are,
in love with Mr. Honeywood, Madam——

Miss Richland. How! idiot, what do you mean? In love
with Mr. Honeywood! Is this to provoke me?

Garnet. That is, Madam, in friendship with him: I
meant nothing more than friendship, as I hope to be
married—nothing more.

Miss Richland. Well, no more of this! As to my guardian
and his son, they shall find me prepared to receive them:
I'm resolved to accept their proposal with seeming pleasure, to mortify them by compliance, and so throw the
refusal at last upon them.

Garnet. Delicious! and that will secure your whole
fortune to yourself. Well, who could have thought so
innocent a face could cover so much 'cuteness!

Miss Richland. Why, girl, I only oppose my prudence to
their cunning, and practise a lesson they have taught me
against themselves.

Garnet. Then you're likely not long to want employment,
for here they come, and in close conference.

Enter Croaker and Leontine.

Leontine. Excuse me, Sir, if I seem to hesitate upon the point of putting to the lady so important a question.

Croaker. Lord! good Sir, moderate your fears; you're so plaguy shy, that one would think you had changed sexes. I tell you we must have the half or the whole. Come, let me see with what spirit you begin. Well, why don't you? Eh! What? Well then, I must, it seems.— Miss Richland, my dear, I believe you guess at our business; an affair which my son here comes to open, that nearly concerns your happiness.

Miss Richland. Sir, I should be ungrateful not to be pleased with anything that comes recommended by you.

Croaker. How, boy, could you desire a finer opening? Why don't you begin, I say? (*To Leontine.*)

Leontine. 'Tis true, Madam,—my father, Madam,—has some intentions—hem—of explaining an affair,—which— himself can best explain, Madam.

Croaker. Yes, my dear; it comes entirely from my son; it's all a request of his own, Madam. And I will permit him to make the best of it.

Leontine. The whole affair is only this, Madam: my father has a proposal to make, which he insists none but himself shall deliver.

Croaker. My mind misgives me, the fellow will never be brought on. (*Aside.*) In short, Madam, you see before you one that loves you—one whose whole happiness is all in you.

Miss Richland. I never had any doubts of your regard, Sir; and I hope you can have none of my duty.

Croaker. That's not the thing, my little sweeting; my love! no, no, another-guess lover than I: there he stands, Madam; his very looks declare the force of his passion— Call up a look, you dog! (*Aside.*) But then, had you seen him, as I have, weeping, speaking soliloquies and blank verse, sometimes melancholy, and sometimes absent——

Miss Richland. I fear, Sir, he's absent now; or such a declaration would have come most properly from himself.

Croaker. Himself, Madam! he would die before he could make such a confession; and if he had not a channel for his passion through me, it would ere now have drowned his understanding.

Miss Richland. I must grant, Sir, there are attractions in modest diffidence above the force of words. A silent address is the genuine eloquence of sincerity.

Croaker. Madam, he has forgot to speak any other language; silence is become his mother-tongue.

Miss Richland. And it must be confessed, Sir, it speaks very powerfully in his favour. And yet I shall be thought too forward in making such a confession; shan't I, Mr. Leontine?

Leontine. Confusion! my reserve will undo me. But, if modesty attracts her, impudence may disgust her. I'll try. (*Aside.*) Don't imagine from my silence, Madam, that I want a due sense of the honour and happiness intended me. My father, Madam, tells me your humble servant is not totally indifferent to you. He admires you: I adore you; and when we come together, upon my soul, I believe we shall be the happiest couple in all St. James's.

Miss Richland. If I could flatter myself you thought as you speak, Sir——

Leontine. Doubt my sincerity, Madam? By your dear self I swear! Ask the brave if they desire glory; ask cowards if they covet safety——

Croaker. Well, well, no more questions about it.

Leontine. Ask the sick if they long for health; ask misers if they love money; ask——

Croaker. Ask a fool if he can talk nonsense! What's come over the boy? What signifies asking, when there's not a soul to give you an answer? If you would ask to the purpose, ask this lady's consent to make you happy.

Miss Richland. Why, indeed, Sir, his uncommon ardour almost compels me—forces me to comply.—And yet I'm afraid he'll despise a conquest gained with too much ease; won't you, Mr. Leontine?

Leontine. Confusion! (*Aside.*) Oh, by no means, Madam, by no means. And yet, Madam, you talked of force. There is nothing I would avoid so much as compulsion in

a thing of this kind.   No, Madam, I will still be generous,
and leave you at liberty to refuse.

Croaker. But I tell you, Sir, the lady is not at liberty.
It's a match.   You see she says nothing.   Silence gives
consent.

Leontine. But, Sir, she talked of force.   Consider, Sir,
the cruelty of constraining her inclinations.

Croaker. But I say there's no cruelty.   Don't you know,
blockhead, that girls have always a round-about way of
saying yes before company?   So get you both gone together
into the next room, and hang him that interrupts the
tender explanation.   Get you gone, I say; I'll not hear a
word.

Leontine. But, Sir, I must beg leave to insist——

Croaker. Get off, you puppy, or I'll beg leave to insist
upon knocking you down.   Stupid whelp!   But I don't
wonder : the boy takes entirely after his mother.

[*Exeunt Miss Richland and Leontine.*

Enter Mrs. Croaker.

Mrs. Croaker. Mr. Croaker, I bring you something, my
dear, that I believe will make you smile.

Croaker. I'll hold you a guinea of that, my dear.

Mrs. Croaker. A letter ; and as I knew the hand, I ventured to open it.

Croaker. And how can you expect your breaking open
my letters should give me pleasure?

Mrs. Croaker. Pooh ! it's from your sister at Lyons, and
contains good news : read it.

Croaker. What a Frenchified cover is here ! That sister
of mine has some good qualities, but I could never teach
her to fold a letter.

Mrs. Croaker. Fold a fiddlestick ! Read what it contains.

Croaker, (reading.)

" DEAR NICK,—An English gentleman, of large fortune,
has for some time made private, though honourable, proposals to your daughter Olivia.   They love each other
tenderly, and I find she has consented, without letting any
of the family know, to crown his addresses.   As such good

offers don't come every day, your own good sense, his large fortune, and family considerations, will induce you to forgive her.   Yours ever,

"RACHAEL CROAKER."

My daughter Olivia privately contracted to a man of large fortune! This is good news indeed. My heart never foretold me of this.   And yet, how slily the little baggage has carried it since she came home.   Not a word on't to the old ones for the world.   Yet I thought I saw something she wanted to conceal.

Mrs. Croaker. Well, if they have concealed their amour, they shan't conceal their wedding; that shall be public, I'm resolved.

Croaker. I tell thee, woman, the wedding is the most foolish part of the ceremony.   I can never get this woman to think of the more serious part of the nuptial engagement.

Mrs. Croaker. What! would you have me think of their funeral? But come, tell me, my dear, don't you owe more to me than you care to confess?—Would you have ever been known to Mr. Lofty, who has undertaken Miss Richland's claim at the Treasury, but for me?   Who was it first made him an acquaintance at Lady Shabbaroon's rout? Who got him to promise us his interest?   Is not he a back-stairs favourite—one that can do what he pleases with those that do what they please?   Isn't he an acquaintance that all your groaning and lamentations could never have got us?

Croaker. He is a man of importance, I grant you.   And yet what amazes me is, that, while he is giving away places to all the world, he can't get one for himself.

Mrs. Croaker. That, perhaps, may be owing to his nicety. Great men are not easily satisfied.

Enter French Servant.

Servant. An expresse from Monsieur Lofty. He vil be vait upon your honours instammant. He be only giving four five instruction, read two tree memorial, call upon von ambassadeur. He vil be vid you in one tree minutes.

Mrs. Croaker. You see now, my dear. What an extensive department! Well, friend, let your master know that we are extremely honoured by this honour. Was there anything ever in a higher style of breeding? All messages among the great are now done by express.

[*Exit French servant.*

Croaker. To be sure, no man does little things with more solemnity, or claims more respect, than he. But he's in the right on't. In our bad world, respect is given where respect is claimed.

Mrs. Croaker. Never mind the world, my dear; you were never in a pleasanter place in your life. Let us now think of receiving him with proper respect, (*a loud rapping at the door,*) and there he is, by the thundering rap.

Croaker. Ay, verily, there he is! as close upon the heels of his own express, as an endorsement upon the back of a bill. Well, I'll leave you to receive him, whilst I go to chide my little Olivia for intending to steal a marriage without mine or her aunt's consent. I must seem to be angry, or she too may begin to despise my authority.

[*Exit.*

Enter Lofty, speaking to his Servant.

Lofty. And if the Venetian ambassador, or that teasing creature the Marquis, shall call, I'm not at home. Dam'me, I'll be pack-horse to none of them.—My dear Madam, I have just snatched a moment—And if the expresses to his Grace be ready, let them be sent off; they're of importance.—Madam, I ask ten thousand pardons.

Mrs. Croaker. Sir, this honour——

Lofty. And, Dubardieu! if the person calls about the commission, let him know that it is made out. As for Lord Cumbercourt's stale request, it can keep cold: you understand me.—Madam, I ask ten thousand pardons.

Mrs. Croaker. Sir, this honour——

Lofty. And, Dubardieu! if the man comes from the Cornish borough, you must do him; you must do him, I say. —Madam, I ask ten thousand pardons.—And if the Russian—ambassador calls; but he will scarce call to-day, I believe.—And now, Madam, I have just got time to express

my happiness in having the honour of being permitted to
profess myself your most obedient humble servant.

Mrs. Croaker. Sir, the happiness and honour are all
mine; and yet, I'm only robbing the public while I detain
you.

Lofty. Sink the public, Madam, when the fair are to be
attended. Ah, could all my hours be so charmingly devoted! Sincerely, don't you pity us poor creatures in
affairs? Thus it is eternally; solicited for places here,
teased for pensions there, and courted everywhere. I know
you pity me. Yes, I see you do.

Mrs. Croaker. Excuse me, Sir, "Toils of empires pleasures are," as Waller says.

Lofty. Waller—Waller; is he of the House?

Mrs. Croaker. The modern poet of that name, Sir.

Lofty. Oh, a modern! We men of business despise the
moderns; and as for the ancients, we have no time to read
them. Poetry is a pretty thing enough for our wives and
daughters; but not for us. Why now, here I stand that
know nothing of books. I say, Madam, I know nothing of
books; and yet, I believe, upon a land-carriage fishery, a
stamp act, or a jag-hire, I can talk my two hours without
feeling the want of them.

Mrs. Croaker. The world is no stranger to Mr. Lofty's
eminence in every capacity.

Lofty. I vow to gad, Madam, you make me blush. I'm
nothing, nothing, nothing in the world; a mere obscure
gentleman. To be sure, indeed, one or two of the present
ministers are pleased to represent me as a formidable man.
I know they are pleased to bespatter me at all their little
dirty levees. Yet, upon my soul, I wonder what they see in
me to treat me so! Measures, not men, have always been my
mark; and I vow, by all that's honourable, my resentment
has never done the men, as mere men, any manner of harm
—that is, as mere men.

Mrs. Croaker. What importance, and yet what modesty!

Lofty. Oh, if you talk of modesty, Madam, there, I own,
I'm accessible to praise: modesty is my foible: it was so
the Duke of Brentford used to say of me. "I love Jack
Lofty," he used to say, "no man has a finer knowledge of
things; quite a man of information; and when he speaks

upon his legs, by the Lord, he's prodigious—he scouts them! and yet all men have their faults: too much modesty is his," says his Grace.

Mrs. Croaker. And yet, I dare say, you don't want assurance when you come to solicit for your friends.

Lofty. Oh, there, indeed, I'm in bronze. Apropos! I have just been mentioning Miss Richland's case to a certain personage; we must name no names. When I ask, I'm not to be put off, Madam. No, no, I take my friend by the button. "A fine girl, Sir; great justice in her case—A friend of mine—Borough interest. Business must be done, Mr. Secretary. I say, Mr. Secretary, her business must be done, Sir." That's my way, Madam.

Mrs. Croaker. Bless me! you said all this to the Secretary of State, did you?

Lofty. I did not say the Secretary, did I? Well, curse it, since you have found me out, I will not deny it :—it was to the Secretary.

Mrs. Croaker. This was going to the fountain-head at once, not applying to the understrappers, as Mr. Honeywood would have had us.

Lofty. Honeywood! he! he! He was, indeed, a fine solicitor. I suppose you have heard what has just happened to him?

Mrs. Croaker. Poor dear man! no accident, I hope?

Lofty. Undone, Madam, that's all. His creditors have taken him into custody—a prisoner in his own house.

Mrs. Croaker. A prisoner in his own house! How? At this very time? I'm quite unhappy for him.

Lofty. Why, so am I. The man, to be sure, was immensely good-natured. But then, I could never find that he had any thing in him.

Mrs. Croaker. His manner, to be sure, was excessive harmless; some, indeed, thought it a little dull. For my part, I always concealed my opinion.

Lofty. It can't be concealed, Madam; the man was dull—dull as the last new comedy! a poor impracticable creature! I tried once or twice to know if he was fit for business; but he had scarce talents to be groom-porter to an orange-barrow.

Mrs. Croaker. How differently does Miss Richland think

of him! For, I believe, with all his faults, she loves him.

Lofty. Loves him! Does she? You should cure her of that by all means. Let me see; what if she were sent to him this instant, in his present doleful situation? My life for it, that works her cure. Distress is a perfect antidote to love. Suppose we join her in the next room? Miss Richland is a fine girl, has a fine fortune, and must not be thrown away. Upon my honour, Madam, I have a regard for Miss Richland; and, rather than she should be thrown away, I should think it no indignity to marry her myself.

[*Exeunt.*

Enter Olivia and Leontine.

Leontine. And yet, trust me, Olivia, I had every reason to expect Miss Richland's refusal, as I did every thing in my power to deserve it. Her indelicacy surprises me!

Olivia. Sure, Leontine, there's nothing so indelicate in being sensible of your merit. If so, I fear I shall be the most guilty thing alive.

Leontine. But you mistake, my dear. The same attention I used to advance my merit with you, I practised to lessen it with her. What more could I do?

Olivia. Let us now rather consider what's to be done. We have both dissembled too long. I have always been ashamed—I am now quite weary of it. Sure I could never have undergone so much for any other but you.

Leontine. And you shall find my gratitude equal to your kindest compliance. Though our friends should totally forsake us, Olivia, we can draw upon content for the deficiencies of fortune.

Olivia. Then why should we defer our scheme of humble happiness, when it is now in our power? I may be the favourite of your father, it is true; but can it ever be thought, that his present kindness to a supposed child will continue to a known deceiver?

Leontine. I have many reasons to believe it will. As his attachments are but few, they are lasting. His own marriage was a private one, as ours may be. Besides, I have sounded him already at a distance, and find all his answers exactly to our wish. Nay, by an expression or two that dropped from him, I am induced to think he knows of this affair.

Olivia. Indeed! But that would be a happiness too great to be expected.

Leontine. However it be, I'm certain you have power over him; and am persuaded, if you informed him of our situation, that he would be disposed to pardon it.

Olivia. You had equal expectations, Leontine, from your last scheme with Miss Richland, which you find has succeeded most wretchedly.

Leontine. And that's the best reason for trying another.

Olivia. If it must be so, I submit.

Leontine. As we could wish, he comes this way. Now, my dearest Olivia, be resolute. I'll just retire within hearing, to come in at a proper time, either to share your danger, or confirm your victory.   [*Exit.*

Enter Croaker.

Croaker. Yes, I must forgive her; and yet not too easily .neither. It will be proper to keep up the decorums of resentment a little, if it be only to impress her with an idea of my authority.

Olivia. How I tremble to approach him!—Might I presume, Sir—If I interrupt you—

Croaker. No, child, where I have an affection, it is not a little thing can interrupt me. Affection gets over little things.

Olivia. Sir, you're too kind. I'm sensible how ill I deserve this partiality; yet, Heaven knows, there is nothing I would not do to gain it.

Croaker. And you have but too well succeeded, you little hussy, you. With those endearing ways of yours, on my conscience, I could be brought to forgive any thing, unless it were a very great offence indeed.

Olivia. But mine is such an offence—When you know my guilt—Yes, you shall know it, though I feel the greatest pain in the confession.

Croaker. Why, then, if it be so very great a pain, you may spare yourself the trouble; for I know every syllable of the matter before you begin.

Olivia. Indeed ! then I'm undone.

Croaker. Ay, Miss, you wanted to steal a match, without letting me know it, did you ? But I'm not worth being consulted, I suppose, when there's to be a marriage in my own family. No, I'm to have no hand in the disposal of my own children. No, I'm nobody. I'm to be a mere article of family lumber ; a piece of cracked china, to be stuck up in a corner.

Olivia. Dear Sir, nothing but the dread of your authority could induce us to conceal it from you.

Croaker. No, no, my consequence is no more ; I'm as little minded as a dead Russian in winter, just stuck up with a pipe in its mouth till there comes a thaw.—It goes to my heart to vex her. (*Aside.*)

Olivia. I was prepared, Sir, for your anger, and despaired of pardon, even while I presumed to ask it. But your severity shall never abate my affection, as my punishment is but justice.

Croaker. And yet you should not despair neither, Livy. We ought to hope all for the best.

Olivia. And do you permit me to hope, Sir ? Can I ever expect to be forgiven ? But hope has too long deceived me.

Croaker. Why then, child, it shan't deceive you now, for I forgive you this very moment. I forgive you all ; and now you are indeed my daughter !

Olivia. Oh, transport ! this kindness overpowers me.

Croaker. I was always against severity to our children. We have been young and giddy ourselves, and we can't expect boys and girls to be old before their time.

Olivia. What generosity ! But can you forget the many falsehoods, the dissimulation——

Croaker. You did indeed dissemble, you urchin you ; but where's the girl that won't dissemble for a husband ? My wife and I had never been married, if we had not dissembled a little beforehand.

Olivia. It shall be my future care never to put such generosity to a second trial. And as for the partner of my offence and folly, from his native honour, and the just sense he has of his duty, I can answer for him that——

Enter Leontine.

Leontine. Permit him thus to answer for himself. (*Kneeling.*)   Thus, Sir, let me speak my gratitude for this unmerited forgiveness.   Yes, Sir, this even exceeds all your former tenderness: I now can boast the most indulgent of fathers.   The life he gave, compared to this, was but a trifling blessing.

Croaker. And, good Sir, who sent for you, with that fine tragedy face, and flourishing manner? I don't know what we have to do with your gratitude upon this occasion.

Leontine. How, Sir! Is it possible to be silent, when so much obliged? Would you refuse me the pleasure of being grateful? of adding my thanks to my Olivia's? of sharing in the transports that you have thus occasioned?

Croaker. Lord, Sir, we can be happy enough without your coming in to make up the party. I don't know what's the matter with the boy all this day; he has got into such a rhodomontade manner all this morning!

Leontine. But, Sir, I that have so large a part in the benefit, is it not my duty to show my joy? Is the being admitted to your favour so slight an obligation? Is the happiness of marrying my Olivia so small a blessing?

Croaker. Marrying Olivia! marrying Olivia! marrying his own sister! Sure the boy is out of his senses. His own sister!

Leontine. My sister!

Olivia. Sister! how have I been mistaken! (*Aside.*)

Leontine. Some curs'd mistake in all this, I find.
(*Aside.*)

Croaker. What does the booby mean? or has he any meaning? Eh, what do you mean, you blockhead, you?

Leontine. Mean, Sir?—why, Sir—only when my sister is to be married, that I have the pleasure of marrying her, Sir,—that is, of giving her away, Sir—I have made a point of it.

Croaker. Oh, is that all? Give her away. You have made a point of it? Then you had as good make a point

of first giving away yourself, as I'm going to prepare the
writings between you and Miss Richland this very minute.
What a fuss is here about nothing! Why, what's the
matter now? I thought I had made you at least as happy
as you could wish.

Olivia. Oh, yes, Sir; very happy.

Croaker. Do you foresee anything, child? You look as
if you did. I think if anything was to be foreseen, I have
as sharp a look-out as another; and yet I foresee nothing.
[*Exit.*

Leontine and Olivia.

Olivia. What can it mean?

Leontine. He knows something, and yet, for my life, I
can't tell what.

Olivia. It can't be the connection between us, I'm pretty
certain.

Leontine. Whatever it be, my dearest, I'm resolved to
put it out of fortune's power to repeat our mortification.
I'll haste and prepare for our journey to Scotland this
very evening. My friend Honeywood has promised me
his advice and assistance. I'll go to him and repose our
distresses on his friendly bosom; and I know so much of
his honest heart, that if he can't relieve our uneasinesses,
he will at least share them. [*Exeunt.*

ACT III.

SCENE.—YOUNG HONEYWOOD'S HOUSE.

Bailiff, Honeywood, Follower.

Bailiff. Looky, Sir, I have arrested as good men as you
in my time—no disparagement of you neither—men that
would go forty guineas on a game of cribbage. I challenge
the town to show a man in more genteeler practice than
myself.

Honeywood. Without all question, Mr. —— I forget
your name, Sir.

Bailiff. How can you forget what you never knew? he! he! he!

Honeywood. May I beg leave to ask your name?

Bailiff. Yes, you may.

Honeywood. Then pray, Sir, what is your name?

Bailiff. That I didn't promise to tell you.—He! he! he! —A joke breaks no bones, as we say among us that practise the law.

Honeywood. You may have reason for keeping it a secret perhaps?

Bailiff. The law does nothing without reason. I'm ashamed to tell my name to no man, Sir. If you can show cause, as why, upon a special capus, that I should prove my name—But, come, Timothy Twitch is my name. And, now you know my name, what have you to say to that?

Honeywood. Nothing in the world, good Mr. Twitch, but that I have a favour to ask, that's all.

Bailiff. Ay, favours are more easily asked than granted, as we say among us that practise the law. I have taken an oath against granting favours. Would you have me perjure myself?

Honeywood. But my request will come recommended in so strong a manner, as, I believe, you'll have no scruple. (*Pulling out his purse.*) The thing is only this: I believe I shall be able to discharge this trifle in two or three days at farthest; but as I would not have the affair known for the world, I have thoughts of keeping you, and your good friend here, about me, till the debt is discharged; for which I shall be properly grateful.

Bailiff. Oh! that's another maxum, and altogether within my oath. For certain, if an honest man is to get any thing by a thing, there's no reason why all things should not be done in civility.

Honeywood. Doubtless, all trades must live, Mr. Twitch; and yours is a necessary one. (*Gives him money.*)

Bailiff. Oh! your honour; I hope your honour takes nothing amiss as I does, as I does nothing but my duty in so doing. I'm sure no man can say I ever give a gentleman, that was a gentleman, ill usage. If I saw that a gentleman was a gentleman, I have taken money not to see him for ten weeks together.

Honeywood. Tenderness is a virtue, Mr. Twitch.

Bailiff. Ay, Sir, it's a perfect treasure. I love to see a gentleman with a tender heart. I don't know, but I think I have a tender heart myself. If all that I have lost by my heart was put together, it would make a—but no matter for that.

Honeywood. Don't account it lost, Mr. Twitch. The ingratitude of the world can never deprive us of the conscious happiness of having acted with humanity ourselves.

Bailiff. Humanity, Sir, is a jewel. It's better than gold. I love humanity. People may say, that we in our way have no humanity; but I'll show you my humanity this moment. There's my follower here, little Flanigan, with a wife and four children—a guinea or two would be more to him, than twice as much to another. Now, as I can't show him any humanity myself, I must beg leave you'll do it for me.

Honeywood. I assure you, Mr. Twitch, yours is a most powerful recommendation. (*Giving money to the follower.*)

Bailiff. Sir, you're a gentleman. I see you know what to do with your money. But, to business: we are to be with you here as your friends, I suppose. But set in case company comes. Little Flanigan here, to be sure, has a good face—a very good face; but then, he is a little seedy, as we say among us that practise the law,—not well in clothes. Smoke the pocket-holes.

Honeywood. Well, that shall be remedied without delay.

Enter Servant.

Servant. Sir, Miss Richland is below.

Honeywood. How unlucky! Detain her a moment. We must improve, my good friend, little Mr. Flanigan's appearance first. Here, let Mr. Flanigan have a suit of my clothes—quick—the brown and silver—Do you hear?

Servant. That your honour gave away to the begging gentleman that makes verses, because it was as good as new.

Honeywood. The white and gold then.

Servant. That, your honour, I made bold to sell, because it was good for nothing.

Honeywood. Well, the first that comes to hand then—the blue and gold. I believe Mr. Flanigan will look best in blue. [*Exit Flanigan.*

Bailiff. Rabbit me! but little Flanigan will look well in any thing. Ah, if your honour knew that bit of flesh as well as I do, you'd be perfectly in love with him. There's not a prettier scout in the four counties after a shy-cock than he : scents like a hound—sticks like a weasel. He was master of the ceremonies to the black Queen of Morocco, when I took him to follow me. (*Re-enter Flanigan.*) Heh! ecod, I think he looks so well, that I don't care if I have a suit from the same place for myself.

Honeywood. Well, well, I hear the lady coming. Dear Mr. Twitch, I beg you'll give your friend directions not to speak. As for yourself, I know you will say nothing without being directed.

Bailiff. Never you fear me ; I'll show the lady that I have something to say for myself as well as another. One man has one way of talking, and another man has another, that's all the difference between them.

Enter Miss Richland and her Maid.

Miss Richland. You'll be surprised, Sir, with this visit. But, you know, I'm yet to thank you for choosing my little library.

Honeywood. Thanks, Madam, are unnecessary ; as it was I that was obliged by your commands. Chairs here. Two of my very good friends, Mr. Twitch and Mr. Flanigan. Pray, gentlemen, sit without ceremony.

Miss Richland. Who can these odd-looking men be! I fear it is as I was informed. It must be so. (*Aside.*)

Bailiff. (*After a pause.*) Pretty weather ; very pretty weather for the time of the year, Madam.

Follower. Very good circuit weather in the country.

Honeywood. You officers are generally favourites among the ladies. My friends, Madam, have been upon very disagreeable duty, I assure you. The fair should, in some measure, recompense the toils of the brave.

Miss Richland. Our officers do indeed deserve every

favour. The gentlemen are in the marine service, I presume, Sir?

Honeywood. Why, Madam, they do—occasionally serve
in the Fleet, Madam : a dangerous service!

Miss Richland. I'm told so. And I own it has often
surprised me, that while we have had so many instances
of bravery there, we have had so few of wit at home to
praise it.

Honeywood. I grant, Madam, that our poets have not
written as our sailors [1] have fought ; but they have done
all they could, and Hawke or Amherst could do no
more.

Miss Richland. I'm quite displeased when I see a fine
subject spoiled by a dull writer.

Honeywood. We should not be so severe against dull
writers, Madam. It is ten to one but the dullest writer
exceeds the most rigid French critic who presumes to
despise him.

Follower. Damn the French, the parle vous, and all that
belongs to them!

Miss Richland. Sir!

Honeywood. Ha, ha, ha! honest Mr. Flanigan. A true
English officer, Madam ; he's not contented with beating
the French, but he will scold them too.

Miss Richland. Yet, Mr. Honeywood, this does not convince me but that severity in criticism is necessary. It
was our first adopting the severity of French taste, that
has brought them in turn to taste us.

Bailiff. Taste us! by the Lord, Madam, they devour
us. Give Mounseers but a taste, and I'll be damn'd but
they come in for a bellyful.

Miss Richland. Very extraordinary this!

Follower. But very true. What makes the bread rising?
the parle vous that devour us. What makes the mutton
fivepence a pound? the parle vous that eat it up. What
makes the beer threepence-halfpenny a pot?——

Honeywood. Ah! the vulgar rogues; all will be out.
(*Aside.*) Right, gentlemen, very right, upon my word, and
quite to the purpose. They draw a parallel, Madam, be-

---

[1] The earliest editions have "soldiers."—ED.

tween the mental taste and that of our senses. We are injured as much by French severity in the one, as by French rapacity in the other. That's their meaning.

Miss Richland. Though I don't see the force of the parallel, yet I'll own, that we should sometimes pardon books, as we do our friends, that have now and then agreeable absurdities to recommend them.

Bailiff. That's all my eye. The King only can pardon, as the law says: for, set in case——

Honeywood. I'm quite of your opinion, Sir. I see the whole drift of your argument. Yes, certainly, our presuming to pardon any work, is arrogating a power that belongs to another. If all have power to condemn, what writer can be free?

Bailiff. By his habus corpus. His habus corpus can set him free at any time: for, set in case——

Honeywood. I'm obliged to you, Sir, for the hint. If, Madam, as my friend observes, our laws are so careful of a gentleman's person, sure we ought to be equally careful of his dearer part, his fame.

Follower. Ay, but if so be a man's nabb'd, you know——

Honeywood. Mr. Flanigan, if you spoke for ever, you could not improve the last observation. For my own part, I think it conclusive.

Bailiff. As for the matter of that, mayhap——

Honeywood. Nay, Sir, give me leave, in this instance, to be positive. For where is the necessity of censuring works without genius, which must shortly sink of themselves? what is it, but aiming our unnecessary blow against a victim already under the hands of justice?

Bailiff. Justice! Oh, by the elevens! if you talk about justice, I think I am at home there: for, in a course of law——

Honeywood. My dear Mr. Twitch, I discern what you'd be at perfectly; and I believe the lady must be sensible of the art with which it is introduced. I suppose you perceive the meaning, Madam, of his course of law?

Miss Richland. I protest, Sir, I do not. I perceive only that you answer one gentleman before he has finished, and the other before he has well begun.

Bailiff. Madam, you are a gentlewoman, and I will make the matter out. This here question is about severity, and justice, and pardon, and the like of they. Now, to explain the thing——

Honeywood. Oh! curse your explanations! (*Aside.*)

Enter Servant.

Servant. Mr. Leontine, Sir, below, desires to speak with you upon earnest business.

Honeywood. That's lucky. (*Aside.*) Dear Madam, you'll excuse me and my good friends here, for a few minutes. There are books, Madam, to amuse you. Come, gentlemen, you know I make no ceremony with such friends. After you, Sir. Excuse me. Well, if I must. But I know your natural politeness.

Bailiff. Before and behind, you know.

Follower. Ay, ay, before and behind, before and behind.
          [*Exeunt Honeywood, Bailiff, and Follower.*

Miss Richland. What can all this mean, Garnet?

Garnet. Mean, Madam! why, what should it mean, but what Mr. Lofty sent you here to see? These people he calls officers, are officers sure enough : sheriff's officers—bailiffs, Madam.

Miss Richland. Ay, it is certainly so. Well, though his perplexities are far from giving me pleasure, yet I own there's something very ridiculous in them, and a just punishment for his dissimulation.

Garnet. And so they are : but I wonder, Madam, that the lawyer you just employed to pay his debts, and set him free, has not done it by this time. He ought at least to have been here before now. But lawyers are always more ready to get a man into troubles than out of them.

Enter Sir William Honeywood.

Sir William. For Miss Richland to undertake setting him free, I own, was quite unexpected. It has totally unhinged my schemes to reclaim him. Yet it gives me pleasure to find, that among a number of worthless friendships, he has made one acquisition of real value ; for there

must be some softer passion on her side, that prompts this
generosity. Ha! here before me: I'll endeavour to sound
her affections.—Madam, as I am the person that have had
some demands upon the gentleman of this house, I hope
you'll excuse me, if, before I enlarged him, I wanted to see
yourself.

Miss Richland. The precaution was very unnecessary,
Sir. I suppose your wants were only such as my agent
had power to satisfy.

Sir William. Partly, Madam. But I was also willing
you should be fully apprised of the character of the gentleman you intended to serve.

Miss Richland. It must come, Sir, with a very ill grace
from you. To censure it, after what you have done, would
look like malice; and to speak favourably of a character
you have oppressed, would be impeaching your own. And
sure, his tenderness, his humanity, his universal friendship, may atone for many faults.

Sir William. That friendship, Madam, which is exerted
in too wide a sphere, becomes totally useless. Our bounty,
like a drop of water, disappears when diffused too widely.
They who pretend most to this universal benevolence,
are either deceivers or dupes,—men who desire to cover
their private ill-nature, by a pretended regard for all,
or men who, reasoning themselves into false feelings,
are more earnest in pursuit of splendid, than of useful
virtues.

Miss Richland. I am surprised, Sir, to hear one, who has
probably been a gainer by the folly of others, so severe in
his censure of it.

Sir William. Whatever I may have gained by folly,
Madam, you see I am willing to prevent your losing by it.

Miss Richland. Your cares for me, Sir, are unnecessary.
I always suspect those services which are denied where they
are wanted, and offered, perhaps, in hopes of a refusal. No,
Sir, my directions have been given, and I insist upon their
being complied with.

Sir William. Thou amiable woman! I can no longer
contain the expressions of my gratitude—my pleasure.
You see before you one who has been equally careful of his
interest; one, who has for some time been a concealed

spectator of his follies, and only punished in hopes to re-claim them,—his uncle!

Miss Richland. Sir William Honeywood! You amaze me. How shall I conceal my confusion? I fear, Sir, you'll think I have been too forward in my services. I confess I——

Sir William. Don't make any apologies, Madam. I only find myself unable to repay the obligation. And yet, I have been trying my interest of late to serve you. Having learnt, Madam, that you had some demands upon Government, I have, though unasked, been your solicitor there.

Miss Richland. Sir, I'm infinitely obliged to your inten-tions. But my guardian has employed another gentleman, who assures him of success.

Sir William. Who, the important little man that visits here? Trust me, Madam, he's quite contemptible among men in power, and utterly unable to serve you. Mr. Lofty's promises are much better known to people of fashion than his person, I assure you.

Miss Richland. How have we been deceived! As sure as can be, here he comes.

Sir William. Does he? Remember I'm to continue un-known. My return to England has not as yet been made public. With what impudence he enters!

Enter Lofty.

Lofty. Let the chariot—let my chariot drive off: I'll visit to his Grace's in a chair. Miss Richland here before me! Punctual, as usual, to the calls of humanity. I'm very sorry, Madam, things of this kind should happen, especially to a man I have shown every where, and carried amongst us as a particular acquaintance.

Miss Richland. I find, Sir, you have the art of making the misfortunes of others your own.

Lofty. My dear Madam, what can a private man like me do? One man can't do every thing; and then, I do so much in this way every day. Let me see—something con-siderable might be done for him by subscription; it could not fail if I carried the list. I'll undertake to set down a brace of dukes, two dozen lords, and half the lower House, at my own peril.

Sir William. And, after all, it's more than probable, Sir, he might reject the offer of such powerful patronage.

Lofty. Then, Madam, what can we do? You know I never make promises. In truth, I once or twice tried to do something with him in the way of business; but, as I often told his uncle, Sir William Honeywood, the man was utterly impracticable.

Sir William. His uncle! then that gentleman, I suppose, is a particular friend of yours?

Lofty. Meaning me, Sir?—Yes, Madam, as I often said, " My dear Sir William, you are sensible I would do any thing, as far as my poor interest goes, to serve your family : but what can be done? there's no procuring first-rate places for ninth-rate abilities."

Miss Richland. I have heard of Sir William Honeywood ; he's abroad in employment : he confided in your judgment, I suppose?

Lofty. Why, yes, Madam, I believe Sir William had some reason to confide in my judgment—one little reason, perhaps.

Miss Richland. Pray, Sir, what was it?

Lofty. Why, Madam—but let it go no farther,—it was I procured him his place.

Sir William. Did you, Sir?

Lofty. Either you or I, Sir.

Miss Richland. This, Mr. Lofty, was very kind indeed.

Lofty. I did love him, to be sure ; he had some amusing qualities ; no man was fitter to be a toast-master to a club, or had a better head.

Miss Richland. A better head?

Lofty. Ay, at a bottle. To be sure he was as dull as a choice spirit ; but hang it, he was grateful, very grateful ; and gratitude hides a multitude of faults.

Sir William. He might have reason, perhaps. His place is pretty considerable, I'm told.

Lofty. A trifle, a mere trifle among us men of business. The truth is, he wanted dignity to fill up a greater.

Sir William. Dignity of person do you mean, Sir? I'm told he's much about my size and figure, Sir.

Lofty. Ay, tall enough for a marching regiment; but then he wanted a something—a consequence of form—a kind of a—I believe the lady perceives my meaning.

Miss Richland. Oh, perfectly! you courtiers can do any thing, I see.

Lofty. My dear Madam, all this is but a mere exchange; we do greater things for one another every day. Why, as thus, now: Let me suppose you the first lord of the Treasury; you have an employment in you that I want—. I have a place in me that you want; do me here, do you there: interest of both sides, few words, flat, done and done, and it's over.

Sir William. A thought strikes me. (*Aside.*) Now you mention Sir William Honeywood, Madam; and as he seems, Sir, an acquaintance of yours, you'll be glad to hear he is arrived from Italy: I had it from a friend who knows him as well as he does me, and you may depend on my information.

Lofty. (*Aside.*) The devil he is! If I had known that, we should not have been quite so well acquainted.

Sir William. He is certainly returned; and as this gentleman is a friend of yours, he can be of signal service to us, by introducing me to him: there are some papers relative to your affairs that require despatch, and his inspection.

Miss Richland. This gentleman, Mr. Lofty, is a person employed in my affairs: I know you'll serve us?

Lofty. My dear Madam, I live but to serve you. Sir William shall even wait upon him, if you think proper to command it.

Sir William. That would be quite unnecessary.

Lofty. Well, we must introduce you then. Call upon me—let me see—ay, in two days.

Sir William. Now, or the opportunity will be lost for ever.

Lofty. Well, if it must be now, now let it be; but, damn it, that's unfortunate. My Lord Grig's curs'd Pensacola business comes on this very hour, and I'm engaged to attend—another time——

Sir William. A short letter to Sir William will do.

Lofty. You shall have it; yet, in my opinion, a letter is

a very bad way of going to work; face to face, that's my way.

Sir William. The letter, Sir, will do quite as well.

Lofty. Zounds! Sir, do you pretend to direct me? direct me in the business of office? Do you know me, Sir? Who am I?

Miss Richland. Dear Mr. Lofty, this request is not so much his as mine; if my commands—but you despise my power.

Lofty. Delicate creature! your commands could even control a debate at midnight: to a power so constitutional, I am all obedience and tranquillity. He shall have a letter: where is my secretary? Dubardieu! And yet, I protest, I don't like this way of doing business. I think if I spoke first to Sir William—But you will have it so.

[*Exit with Miss Richland.*

Sir William. (*Alone.*) Ha! ha! ha! This, too, is one of my nephew's hopeful associates. O vanity! thou constant deceiver, how do all thy efforts to exalt serve but to sink us! Thy false colourings, like those employed to heighten beauty, only seem to mend that bloom which they contribute to destroy. I'm not displeased at this interview: exposing this fellow's impudence to the contempt it deserves may be of use to my design; at least, if he can reflect, it will be of use to himself.

Enter Jarvis.

How now, Jarvis, where's your master, my nephew?

Jarvis. At his wit's end, I believe: he's scarce gotten out of one scrape, but he's running his head into another.

Sir William. How so?

Jarvis. The house has but just been cleared of the bailiffs, and now he's again engaging, tooth and nail, in assisting old Croaker's son to patch up a clandestine match with the young lady that passes in the house for his sister.

Sir William. Ever busy to serve others.

Jarvis. Ay, any body but himself. The young couple, it seems, are just setting out for Scotland; and he supplies them with money for the journey.

Sir William. Money! how is he able to supply others, who has scarce any for himself?

Jarvis. Why, there it is: he has no money, that's true; but then, as he never said *No* to any request in his life, he has given them a bill, drawn by a friend of his upon a merchant in the city, which I am to get changed; for you must know that I am to go with them to Scotland myself.

Sir William. How!

Jarvis. It seems the young gentleman is obliged to take a different road from his mistress, as he is to call upon an uncle of his that lives out of the way, in order to prepare a place for their reception when they return; so they have borrowed me from my master, as the properest person to attend the young lady down.

Sir William. To the land of matrimony! A pleasant journey, Jarvis.

Jarvis. Ay, but I'm only to have all the fatigues on't.

Sir William. Well, it may be shorter, and less fatiguing, than you imagine. I know but too much of the young lady's family and connections, whom I have seen abroad. I have also discovered that Miss Richland is not indifferent to my thoughtless nephew; and will endeavour, though I fear in vain, to establish that connection. But, come, the letter I wait for must be almost finished; I'll let you farther into my intentions in the next room. [*Exeunt.*

ACT IV.

SCENE.—CROAKER'S HOUSE.

Enter Lofty.

Lofty. Well, sure the devil's in me of late, for running my head into such defiles, as nothing but a genius like my own could draw me from. I was formerly contented to husband out my places and pensions with some degree of frugality; but, curse it, of late I have given away the whole Court Register in less time than they could print the title page; yet, hang it, why scruple a lie or two to come at a

fine girl, when I every day tell a thousand for nothing.
Ha! Honeywood here before me. Could Miss Richland
have set him at liberty?

Enter Honeywood.

Mr. Honeywood, I'm glad to see you abroad again. I find
my concurrence was not necessary in your unfortunate
affairs. I had put things in a train to do your business;
but it is not for me to say what I intended doing.

Honeywood. It was unfortunate, indeed, Sir. But what
adds to my uneasiness is, that while you seem to be
acquainted with my misfortune, I myself continue still a
stranger to my benefactor.

Lofty. How! not know the friend that served you?

Honeywood. Can't guess at the person.

Lofty. Inquire.

Honeywood. I have; but all I can learn is, that he
chooses to remain concealed, and that all inquiry must be
fruitless.

Lofty. Must be fruitless?

Honeywood. Absolutely fruitless.

Lofty. Sure of that?

Honeywood. Very sure.

Lofty. Then I'll be damn'd if you shall ever know it
from me.

Honeywood. How, Sir?

Lofty. I suppose now, Mr. Honeywood, you think my
rent-roll very considerable, and that I have vast sums of
money to throw away? I know you do. The world, to be
sure, says such things of me.

Honeywood. The world, by what I learn, is no stranger
to your generosity. But where does this tend?

Lofty. To nothing—nothing in the world. The town,
to be sure, when it makes such a thing as me the subject
of conversation, has asserted, that I never yet patronized
a man of merit.

Honeywood. I have heard instances to the contrary, even
from yourself.

Lofty. Yes, Honeywood; and there are instances to the
contrary, that you shall never hear from myself.

Honeywood. Ha! dear Sir, permit me to ask you but one question.

Lofty. Sir, ask me no questions; I say, Sir, ask me no questions; I'll be damn'd if I answer them.

Honeywood. I will ask no farther. My friend! my benefactor! it is, it must be here, that I am indebted for freedom—for honour. Yes, thou worthiest of men, from the beginning I suspected it, but was afraid to return thanks; which if undeserved, might seem reproaches.

Lofty. I protest I do not understand all this, Mr. Honeywood: you treat me very cavalierly. I do assure you, Sir—Blood! Sir, can't a man be permitted to enjoy the luxury of his own feelings without all this parade?

Honeywood. Nay, do not attempt to conceal an action that adds to your honour. Your looks, your air, your manner, all confess it.

Lofty. Confess it, Sir! torture itself, Sir, shall never bring me to confess it. Mr. Honeywood, I have admitted you upon terms of friendship. Don't let us fall out; make me happy, and let this be buried in oblivion. You know I hate ostentation; you know I do. Come, come, Honeywood, you know I always loved to be a friend, and not a patron. I beg this may make no kind of distance between us. Come, come, you and I must be more familiar—indeed we must.

Honeywood. Heavens! Can I ever repay such friendship? Is there any way? Thou best of men, can I ever return the obligation?

Lofty. A bagatelle, a mere bagatelle! But I see your heart is labouring to be grateful. You shall be grateful. It would be cruel to disappoint you.

Honeywood. How? teach me the manner. Is there any way?

Lofty. From this moment you're mine. Yes, my friend, you shall know it—I'm in love.

Honeywood. And can I assist you?

Lofty. Nobody so well.

Honeywood. In what manner? I'm all impatience.

Lofty. You shall make love for me.

Honeywood. And to whom shall I speak in your favour?

Lofty. To a lady with whom you have great interest, I assure you : Miss Richland.

Honeywood. Miss Richland !

Lofty. Yes, Miss Richland. She has struck the blow, up to the hilt in my bosom, by Jupiter !

Honeywood. Heavens ! was ever any thing more unfortunate ? It is too much to be endured.

Lofty. Unfortunate, indeed ! And yet I can endure it, till you have opened the affair to her for me. Between ourselves, I think she likes me. I'm not apt to boast, but I think she does.

Honeywood. Indeed ! But, do you know the person you apply to ?

Lofty. Yes, I know you are her friend and mine : that's enough. To you, therefore, I commit the success of my passion. I'll say no more, let friendship do the rest. I have only to add, that if at any time my little interest can be of service—but, hang it, I'll make no promises : you know my interest is yours at any time. No apologies, my friend, I'll not be answered ; it shall be so.   [*Exit.*

Honeywood. Open, generous, unsuspecting man ! He little thinks that I love her too ; and with such an ardent passion ! But then it was ever but a vain and hopeless one ; my torment, my persecution ! What shall I do ? Love, friendship ; a hopeless passion, a deserving friend ! Love that has been my tormentor ; a friend, that has perhaps distressed himself to serve me. It shall be so. Yes, I will discard the fondling hope from my bosom, and exert all my influence in his favour. And yet to see her in the possession of another !—Insupportable ! But then to betray a generous, trusting friend !—Worse, worse ! Yes, I'm resolved. Let me but be the instrument of their happiness, and then quit a country, where I must for ever despair of finding my own.   [*Exit.*

Enter Olivia, and Garnet, who carries a milliner's box.

Olivia. Dear me, I wish this journey were over. No news of Jarvis yet ? I believe the old peevish creature delays purely to vex me.

Garnet. Why, to be sure, Madam, I did hear him say, a

little snubbing before marriage would teach you to bear it the better afterwards.

Olivia. To be gone a full hour, though he had only to get a bill changed in the city! How provoking!

Garnet. I'll lay my life, Mr. Leontine, that had twice as much to do, is setting off by this time from his inn; and here you are left behind.

Olivia. Well, let us be prepared for his coming, however. Are you sure you have omitted nothing, Garnet?

Garnet. Not a stick, Madam; all's here. Yet I wish you could take the white and silver to be married in. It's the worst luck in the world in anything but white. I knew one Bett Stubbs, of our town, that was married in red; and, as sure as eggs is eggs, the bridegroom and she had a miff before morning.

Olivia. No matter; I'm all impatience till we are out of the house.

Garnet. Bless me, Madam, I had almost forgot the wedding ring! The sweet little thing. I don't think it would go on my little finger. And what if I put in a gentleman's nightcap, in case of necessity, Madam?—But here's Jarvis.

Enter Jarvis.

Olivia. O Jarvis, are you come at last! We have been ready this half hour. Now let's be going. Let us fly!

Jarvis. Ay, to Jericho; for we shall have no going to Scotland this bout, I fancy.

Olivia. How! what's the matter?

Jarvis. Money, money is the matter, Madam. We have got no money. What the plague do you send me of your fool's errand for? My master's bill upon the city is not worth a rush. Here it is; Mrs. Garnet may pin up her hair with it.

Olivia. Undone! How could Honeywood serve us so! What shall we do? Can't we go without it?

Jarvis. Go to Scotland without money! To Scotland without money! Lord, how some people understand geography! We might as well set sail for Patagonia upon a cork-jacket.

Olivia. Such a disappointment! What a base, insincere

man was your master, to serve us in this manner! Is this his good-nature?

Jarvis. Nay, don't talk ill of my master, Madam. I won't bear to hear any body talk ill of him but myself.

Garnet. Bless us! now I think on't, Madam, you need not be under any uneasiness: I saw Mr. Leontine receive forty guineas from his father just before he set out, and he can't yet have left the inn. A short letter will reach him there.

Olivia. Well remembered, Garnet; I'll write immediately. How's this! Bless me, my hand trembles so, I can't write a word. Do you write, Garnet; and, upon second thought, it will be better from you.

Garnet. Truly, Madam, I write and indite but poorly. I never was 'cute at my learning. But I'll do what I can to please you. Let me see. All out of my own head, I suppose?

Olivia. Whatever you please.

Garnet (*Writing.*) "Muster Croaker"—Twenty guineas, Madam?

Olivia. Ay, twenty will do.

Garnet. "At the bar of the Talbot till called for.—Expedition—Will be blown up—All of a flame—Quick, dispatch—Cupid, the little god of love."—I conclude it, Madam, with Cupid: I love to see a love-letter end like poetry.

Olivia. Well, well, what you please, any thing. But how shall we send it? I can trust none of the servants of this family.

Garnet. Odso, Madam, Mr. Honeywood's butler is in the next room: he's a dear, sweet man; he'll do anything for me.

Jarvis. He! the dog, he'll certainly commit some blunder. He's drunk and sober ten times a-day.

Olivia. No matter. Fly, Garnet: any body we can trust will do. [*Exit Garnet.*] Well, Jarvis, now we can have nothing more to interrupt us. You may take up the things, and carry them on to the inn. Have you no hands, Jarvis?

Jarvis. Soft and fair, young lady. You that are going to be married think things can never be done too fast; but

we, that are old, and know what we are about, must elope
methodically, Madam.

Olivia. Well, sure, if my indiscretions were to be done
over again——

Jarvis. My life for it, you would do them ten times
over.

Olivia. Why will you talk so? If you knew how unhappy they make me——

Jarvis. Very unhappy, no doubt: I was once just as
unhappy when I was going to be married myself. I'll
tell you a story about that——

Olivia. A story! when I am all impatience to be away.
Was there ever such a dilatory creature!——

Jarvis. Well, Madam, if we must march, why we will
march; that's all. Though, odds-bobs, we have still forgot one thing we should never travel without,—a case of
good razors, and a box of shaving-powder. But no
matter, I believe we shall be pretty well shaved by the
way. (*Going.*)

Enter Garnet.

Garnet. Undone, undone, Madam! Ah, Mr. Jarvis, you
said right enough. As sure as death, Mr. Honeywood's
rogue of a drunken butler dropped the letter before he
went ten yards from the door. There's old Croaker has
just picked it up, and is this moment reading it to himself
in the hall.

Olivia. Unfortunate! we shall be discovered.

Garnet. No, Madam; don't be uneasy: he can make
neither head nor tail of it. To be sure he looks as if he
was broke loose from Bedlam about it, but he can't find
what it means for all that. O lud, he is coming this way
all in the horrors!

Olivia. Then let us leave the house this instant, for
fear he should ask farther questions. In the meantime,
Garnet, do you write and send off just such another.

[*Exeunt.*

Enter Croaker.

Croaker. Death and destruction! Are all the horrors
of air, fire, and water, to be levelled only at me? Am I

only to be singled out for gunpowder-plots, combustibles, and conflagration? Here it is — an incendiary letter dropped at my door. "To Muster Croaker, these with speed." Ay, ay, plain enough - the direction: all in the genuine incendiary spelling, and as cramp as the devil. "With speed." Oh, confound your speed! But let me read it once more. (*Reads.*) "Muster Croaker, as sone as yoew see this, leve twenty gunnes at the bar of the Talboot tell caled for, or yoew and yower experetion will be al blown up." Ah, but too plain! Blood and gunpowder in every line of it. Blown up! murderous dog! All blown up! Heavens! what have I and my poor family done, to be all blown up? (*Reads.*) "Our pockets are low, and money we must have." Ay, there's the reason; they'll blow us up, because they have got low pockets. (*Reads.*) "It is but a short time you have to consider; for if this takes wind, the house will quickly be all of a flame." Inhuman monsters! blow us up, and then burn us! The earthquake at Lisbon was but a bonfire to it. (*Reads.*) "Make quick dispatch, and so no more at present. But may Cupid, the little god of Love, go with you wherever you go." The little god of love! Cupid, the little god of love, go with me!—Go you to the devil, you and your little Cupid together. I'm so frightened, I scarce know whether I sit, stand, or go. Perhaps this moment I'm treading on lighted matches, blazing brimstone, and barrels of gunpowder. They are preparing to blow me up into the clouds. Murder! We shall be all burnt in our beds; we shall be all burnt in our beds![1]

Enter Miss Richland.

Miss Richland. Lord, Sir, what's the matter?

Croaker. Murder's the matter. We shall be all blown up in our beds before morning.

Miss Richland. I hope not, Sir.

---

[1] It was in the reading of this letter that Shuter made the great hit of the piece. Boswell says ('Life of Johnson,' i., 250, iii., 38, Bohn's edition) that Goldsmith admitted he had taken the character of Croaker from Johnson's Suspirius in the 'Rambler;' but he may have taken it from his own desponding philosopher in the 'Citizen of the World,' No. XCII.—ED.

Croaker. What signifies what you hope, Madam, when I have a certificate of it here in my hand ? Will nothing alarm my family ? Sleeping and eating—sleeping and eating is the only work from morning till night in my house. My insensible crew could sleep though rocked by an earthquake, and fry beef-steaks at a volcano.

Miss Richland. But, Sir, you have alarmed them so often already ; we have nothing but earthquakes, famines, plagues, and mad dogs, from year's end to year's end. You remember, Sir, it is not above a month ago, you assured us of a conspiracy among the bakers to poison us in our bread ; and so kept the whole family a week upon potatoes.

Croaker. And potatoes were too good for them. But why do I stand talking here with a girl, when I should be facing the enemy without? Here, John, Nicodemus, search the house. Look into the cellars, to see if there be any combustibles below; and above, in the apartments, that no matches be· thrown in at the windows. Let all the fires be put out, and let the engine be drawn out in the yard, to play upon the house in case of necessity.

[Exit.

Miss Richland. (*Alone.*) What can he mean by all this? Yet why should I enquire, when he alarms us in this manner almost every day. But Honeywood has desired an interview with me in private. What can he mean? or rather, what means this palpitation at his approach? It is the first time he ever showed any thing in his conduct that seemed particular. Sure he cannot mean to—but he's here.

Enter Honeywood.

Honeywood. I presumed to solicit this interview, Madam, before I left town, to be permitted——

Miss Richland. Indeed!—leaving town, Sir?

Honeywood. Yes, Madam ; perhaps the kingdom. I have presumed, I say, to desire the favour of this interview, in order to disclose something which our long friendship prompts. And yet my fears——

Miss Richland. His fears! what are his fears to mine! (*Aside.*) We have, indeed, been long acquainted, Sir ;

very long. If I remember, our first meeting was at the French ambassador's. Do you recollect how you were pleased to rally me upon my complexion there?

Honeywood. Perfectly, Madam: I presumed to reprove you for painting; but your warmer blushes soon convinced the company that the colouring was all from nature.

Miss Richland. And yet you only meant it, in your good-natured way, to make me pay a compliment to myself. In the same manner, you danced that night with the most awkward woman in company, because you saw nobody else would take her out.

Honeywood. Yes; and was rewarded the next night, by dancing with the finest woman in company, whom every body wished to take out.

Miss Richland. Well, sir, if you thought so then, I fear your judgment has since corrected the errors of a first impression. We generally show to most advantage at first. Our sex are like poor tradesmen, that put all their best goods to be seen at the windows.

Honeywood. The first impression, Madam, did indeed deceive me. I expected to find a woman with all the faults of conscious flattered beauty: I expected to find her vain and insolent. But every day has since taught me, that it is possible to possess sense without pride, and beauty without affectation.

Miss Richland. This, Sir, is a style very unusual with Mr. Honeywood; and I should be glad to know why he thus attempts to increase that vanity which his own lessons have taught me to despise.

Honeywood. I ask pardon, Madam. Yet, from our long friendship, I presumed I might have some right to offer, without offence, what you may refuse without offending.

Miss Richland. Sir! I beg you'd reflect: though I fear, I shall scarce have any power to refuse a request of yours, yet you may be precipitate: consider, Sir.

Honeywood. I own my rashness; but as I plead the cause of friendship, of one who loves—don't be alarmed, Madam—who loves you with the most ardent passion, whose whole happiness is placed in you——

Miss Richland. I fear, Sir, I shall never find whom you mean, by this description of him.

Honeywood. Ah, Madam, it but too plainly points
him out; though he should be too humble himself to
urge his pretensions, or you too modest to understand
them.

Miss Richland. Well, it would be affectation any longer
to pretend ignorance; and I will own, Sir, I have long
been prejudiced in his favour. It was but natural to wish
to make his heart mine, as he seemed himself ignorant of
its value.

Honeywood. I see she always loved him. (*Aside.*) I
find, Madam, you're already sensible of his worth, his
passion. How happy is my friend to be the favourite of
one with such sense to distinguish merit, and such beauty
to reward it!

Miss Richland. Your friend, Sir! What friend?

Honeywood. My best friend—my friend Mr. Lofty,
Madam.

Miss Richland. He, Sir!

Honeywood. Yes, he, Madam. He is, indeed, what your
warmest wishes might have formed him; and to his other
qualities he adds that of the most passionate regard for
you.

Miss Richland. Amazement!—No more of this, I beg
you, Sir.

Honeywood. I see your confusion, Madam, and know how
to interpret it. And, since I so plainly read the language
of your heart, shall I make my friend happy, by communicating your sentiments?

Miss Richland. By no means.

Honeywood. Excuse me, I must; I know you desire it.

Miss Richland. Mr. Honeywood, let me tell you, that you
wrong my sentiments and yourself. When I first applied
to your friendship, I expected advice and assistance; but
now, Sir, I see that it is in vain to expect happiness from
him, who has been so bad an economist of his own; and
that I must disclaim his friendship who ceases to be a
friend to himself.   [*Exit.*

Honeywood. How is this! She has confessed she loved
him, and yet she seemed to part in displeasure. Can I
have done any thing to reproach myself with? No; I
believe not: yet, after all, these things should not be done

by a third person: I should have spared her confusion.
My friendship carried me a little too far.

Enter Croaker, with the letter in his hand, and Mrs. Croaker.

Mrs. Croaker. Ha! ha! ha! And so, my dear, it's your
supreme wish that I should be quite wretched upon this
occasion? Ha! ha!

Croaker (Mimicking.) Ha! ha! ha! And so, my dear,
it's your supreme pleasure to give me no better consolation?

Mrs. Croaker. Positively, my dear: what is this incendiary stuff and trumpery to me? Our house may travel
through the air like the house of Loretto, for aught I care,
if I am to be miserable in it.

Croaker. Would to Heaven it were converted into a
house of correction for your benefit. Have we not every
thing to alarm us? Perhaps this very moment the tragedy
is beginning!

Mrs. Croaker. Then let us reserve our distress till the
rising of the curtain, or give them the money they want,
and have done with them.

Croaker. Give them my money!—And pray, what right
have they to my money?

Mrs. Croaker. And pray, what right, then, have you to
my good-humour?

Croaker. And so your good-humour advises me to part
with my money? Why, then, to tell your good-humour a
piece of my mind, I'd sooner part with my wife. Here's
Mr. Honeywood, see what he'll say to it. My dear Honeywood, look at this incendiary letter dropped at my door.
It will freeze you with terror; and yet lovey here can read
it—can read it, and laugh.

Mrs. Croaker. Yes, and so will Mr. Honeywood.

Croaker. If he does, I'll suffer to be hanged the next
minute in the rogue's place, that's all.

Mrs. Croaker. Speak, Mr. Honeywood; is there any
thing more foolish than my husband's fright upon this
occasion?

Honeywood. It would not become me to decide, Madam;
but, doubtless, the greatness of his terrors now will but
invite them to renew their villainy another time.

Mrs. Croaker. I told you, he'd be of my opinion.

Croaker. How, Sir! Do you maintain that I should lie down under such an injury, and show, neither by my fears[1] nor complaints, that I have something of the spirit of a man in me?

Honeywood. Pardon me, Sir. You ought to make the loudest complaints, if you desire redress. The surest way to have redress, is to be earnest in the pursuit of it.

Croaker. Ay, whose opinion is he of now?

Mrs. Croaker. But don't you think that laughing off our fears is the best way?

Honeywood. What is the best, Madam, few can say; but I'll maintain it to be a very wise way.

Croaker. But we're talking of the best. Surely the best way is to face the enemy in the field, and not wait till he plunders us in our very bed-chamber.

Honeywood. Why, Sir, as to the best, that—that's a very wise way too.

Mrs. Croaker. But can any thing be more absurd, than to double our distresses by our apprehensions, and put it in the power of every low fellow, that can scrawl ten words of wretched spelling, to torment us?

Honeywood. Without doubt, nothing more absurd.

Croaker. How! would it not be more absurd to despise the rattle till we are bit by the snake?

Honeywood. Without doubt, perfectly absurd.

Croaker. Then you are of my opinion?

Honeywood. Entirely.

Mrs. Croaker. And you reject mine?

Honeywood. Heavens forbid, Madam! No: sure no reasoning can be more just than yours. We ought certainly to despise malice if we cannot oppose it, and not make the incendiary's pen as fatal to our repose as the highwayman's pistol.

Mrs. Croaker. Oh, then you think I'm quite right?

Honeywood. Perfectly right.

Croaker. A plague of plagues, we can't be both right. I ought to be sorry, or I ought to be glad. My hat must be on my head, or my hat must be off.

---

[1] The earliest editions have "tears or complaints."—ED.

Mrs. Croaker. Certainly, in two opposite opinions, if one be perfectly reasonable, the other can't be perfectly right.

Honeywood. And why may not both be right, Madam? Mr. Croaker in earnestly seeking redress, and you in waiting the event with good humour? Pray, let me see the letter again. I have it. This letter requires twenty guineas to be left at the bar of the Talbot Inn. If it be indeed an incendiary letter, what if you and I, sir, go there; and when the writer comes to be paid his expected booty, seize him?

Croaker. My dear friend, it's the very thing—the very thing. While I walk by the door, you shall plant yourself in ambush near the bar; burst out upon the miscreant like a masked battery; extort a confession at once, and so hang him up by surprise.

Honeywood. Yes; but I would not choose to exercise too much severity. It is my maxim, Sir, that crimes generally punish themselves.

Croaker. Well, but we may upbraid him a little, I suppose? (*Ironically.*)

Honeywood. Ay, but not punish him too rigidly.

Croaker. Well, well, leave that to my own benevolence.

Honeywood. Well, I do; but remember that universal benevolence is the first law of nature.

[*Exeunt Honeywood and Mrs. Croaker.*

Croaker. Yes; and my universal benevolence will hang the dog, if he had as many necks as a hydra.

ACT V.

SCENE—AN INN.

Enter Olivia and Jarvis.

Olivia. Well, we have got safe to the inn, however. Now, if the post-chaise were ready——

Jarvis. The horses are just finishing their oats; and, as they are not going to be married, they choose to take their own time.

Olivia. You are for ever giving wrong motives to my impatience.

Jarvis. Be as impatient as you will, the horses must take their own time; besides, you don't consider we have got no answer from our fellow-traveller yet. If we hear nothing from Mr. Leontine, we have only one way left us.

Olivia. What way?

Jarvis. The way home again.

Olivia. Not so. I have made a resolution to go, and nothing shall induce me to break it.

Jarvis. Ay; resolutions are well kept, when they jump with inclination. However, I'll go hasten things without. And I'll call, too, at the bar to see if any thing should be left for us there. Don't be in such a plaguy hurry, Madam, and we shall go the faster, I promise you.

[*Exit Jarvis.*

Enter Landlady.

Landlady. What! Solomon, why don't you move? Pipes and tobacco for the Lamb there. Will nobody answer? To the Dolphin; quick. The Angel has been outrageous this half hour. Did your ladyship call, Madam?

Olivia. No, Madam.

Landlady. I find as you're for Scotland, Madam—But that's no business of mine; married, or not married, I ask no questions. To be sure we had a sweet little couple set off from this two days ago for the same place. The gentleman, for a tailor, was, to be sure, as fine a spoken tailor as ever blew froth from a full pot. And the young lady so bashful, it was near half an hour before we could get her to finish a pint of rasberry between us.

Olivia. But this gentleman and I are not going to be married, I assure you.

Landlady. May be not. That's no business of mine. For certain, Scotch marriages seldom turn out well. There was, of my own knowledge, Miss Macfag, that married her father's footman. Alack-a-day, she and her hus-

band soon parted, and now keep separate cellars in
Hedge-Lane.[1]

Olivia (Aside.) A very pretty picture of what lies before
me!

Enter Leontine.

Leontine. My dear Olivia, my anxiety, till you were out
of danger, was too great to be resisted. I could not help
coming to see you set out, though it exposes us to a discovery.

Olivia. May every thing you do prove as fortunate. Indeed, Leontine, we have been most cruelly disappointed.
Mr. Honeywood's bill upon the city has, it seems, been
protested, and we have been utterly at a loss how to
proceed.

Leontine. How! an offer of his own too! Sure he could
not mean to deceive us?

Olivia. Depend upon his sincerity; he only mistook the
desire for the power of serving us. But let us think no
more of it. I believe the post-chaise is ready by this.

Landlady. Not quite yet; and begging your ladyship's
pardon, I don't think your ladyship quite ready for the
post-chaise. The north road is a cold place, Madam. I
have a drop in the house of as pretty rasberry as ever was
tipt over tongue. Just a thimble-full to keep the wind off
your stomach. To be sure, the last couple we had here,
they said it was a perfect nosegay. Ecod, I sent them
both away as good-natured—Up went the blinds, round
went the wheels, and "Drive away post-boy!" was the
word.

Enter Croaker.

Croaker. Well, while my friend Honeywood is upon the
post of danger at the bar, it must be my business to have
an eye about me here. I think I know an incendiary's
look; for wherever the devil makes a purchase, he never
fails to set his mark. Ha! who have we here? My son
and daughter! What can they be doing here?

[1] This view of runaway marriages was afterwards amusingly amplified by the author in the essay 'A Register of Scotch Marriages;' see
additional essays in v. iv.--ED.

Landlady. I tell you, Madam, it will do you good; I think I know by this time what's good for the north road. It's a raw night, Madam.—Sir——

Leontine. Not a drop more, good Madam. I should now take it as a greater favour, if you hasten the horses, for I am afraid to be seen myself.

Landlady. That shall be done. Wha, Solomon! are you all dead there? Wha, Solomon, I say!

[*Exit, bawling.*

Olivia. Well, I dread lest an expedition begun in fear, should end in repentance. Every moment we stay increases our danger, and adds to my apprehensions.

Leontine. There's no danger, trust me, my dear; there can be none. If Honeywood has acted with honour, and kept my father, as he promised, in employment till we are out of danger nothing can interrupt our journey.

Olivia. I have no doubt of Mr. Honeywood's sincerity, and even his desires to serve us. My fears are from your father's suspicions. A mind so disposed to be alarmed without a cause, will be but too ready when there's a reason.

Leontine. Why, let him, when we are out of his power. But believe me, Olivia, you have no great reason to dread his resentment. His repining temper, as it does no manner of injury to himself, so will it never do harm to others. He only frets to keep himself employed, and scolds for his private amusement.

Olivia. I don't know that; but I'm sure, on some occasions, it makes him look most shockingly.

Croaker. (*Discovering himself.*) How does he look now? —How does he look now?

Olivia. Ah!

Leontine. Undone!

Croaker. How do I look now? Sir, I am your very humble servant. Madam, I am yours! What! you are going off, are you? Then, first, if you please, take a word or two from me with you before you go. Tell me first where you are going; and when you have told me that, perhaps I shall know as little as I did before.

Leontine. If that be so, our answer might but increase your displeasure, without adding to your information.

Croaker. I want no information from you, puppy : and you too, good Madam, what answer have you got ?   Eh ! (*A cry without,* " *Stop him.*")   I think I heard a noise. My friend Honeywood, without—has he seized the incendiary ?   Ah, no, for now I hear no more on't.

Leontine. Honeywood without !   Then, Sir, it was Mr. Honeywood that directed you hither ?

Croaker. No, Sir, it was Mr. Honeywood conducted me hither.

Leontine. Is it possible ?

Croaker. Possible !   Why, he's in the house now, Sir ; more anxious about me than my own son, Sir.

Leontine. Then, Sir, he's a villain.

Croaker. How, sirrah !   a villain, because he takes most care of your father ?   I'll not bear it.   I tell you, I'll not bear it.   Honeywood is a friend to the family, and I'll have him treated as such.

Leontine. I shall study to repay his friendship as it deserves.

Croaker. Ah, rogue, if you knew how earnestly he entered into my griefs, and pointed out the means to detect them, you would love him as I do.   (*A cry without,* " *Stop him.*")   Fire and fury ! they have seized the incendiary : they have the villain, the incendiary in view.   Stop him ! stop an incendiary ! a murderer ! stop him !   [*Exit.*

Olivia. Oh, my terrors !   What can this new tumult mean ?

Leontine. Some new mark, I suppose, of Mr. Honeywood's sincerity.   But we shall have satisfaction : he shall give me instant satisfaction.

Olivia. It must not be, my Leontine, if you value my esteem or my happiness.   Whatever be our fate, let us not add guilt to our misfortunes : consider that our innocence will shortly be all that we have left us.   You must forgive him.

Leontine. Forgive him !   Has he not in every instance betrayed us ?   Forced me to borrow money from him, which appears a mere trick to delay us ; promised to keep my father engaged till we were out of danger, and here brought him to the very scene of our escape !

Olivia. Don't be precipitate.   We may yet be mistaken.

*Enter Postboy, dragging in Jarvis ; Honeywood entering
soon after.*

Postboy. Ay, master, we have him fast enough. Here
is the incendiary dog. I'm entitled to the reward; I'll
take my oath I saw him ask for the money at the bar, and
then run for it.

Honeywood. Come, bring him along. Let us see him.
Let him learn to blush for his crimes. (*Discovering his
mistake.*) Death ! what's here ? Jarvis, Leontine, Olivia !
What can all this mean ?

Jarvis. Why, I'll tell you what it means : that I was an
old fool, and that you are my master—that's all.

Honeywood. Confusion !

Leontine. Yes, Sir, I find you have kept your word with
me. After such baseness, I wonder how you can venture
to see the man you have injured.

Honeywood. My dear Leontine, by my life, my honour——

Leontine. Peace, peace, for shame ; and do not continue
to aggravate baseness by hypocrisy. I know you, Sir, I
know you.

Honeywood. Why won't you hear me ! By all that's
just, I knew not——

Leontine. Hear you, Sir ! to what purpose ? I now see
through all your low arts ; your ever complying with
every opinion ; your never refusing any request ; your
friendship, as common as a prostitute's favours, and as
fallacious ; all these, Sir, have long been contemptible to
the world, and are now perfectly so to me.

Honeywood. Ha ! contemptible to the world ! That
reaches me. (*Aside.*)

Leontine. All the seeming sincerity of your professions,
I now find were only allurements to betray ; and all your
seeming regret for their consequences, only calculated to
cover the cowardice of your heart. Draw, villain !

Enter Croaker, out of breath.

Croaker. Where is the villain ? Where is the incendiary ? (*Seizing the Postboy.*) Hold him fast, the dog ;

he has the gallows in his face. Come, you dog, confess;
confess all, and hang yourself.

Postboy. Zounds! master, what do you throttle me for?

Croaker. (*Beating him.*) Dog, do you resist? do you
resist?

Postboy. Zounds! master, I'm not he; there's the man
that we thought was the rogue, and turns out to be one of
the company.

Croaker. How!

Honeywood. Mr. Croaker, we have all been under a
strange mistake here; I find there is nobody guilty; it
was all an error—entirely an error of our own.

Croaker. And I say, Sir, that you're in an error; for
there's guilt and double guilt, a plot, a damned jesuitical,
pestilential plot, and I must have proof of it.

Honeywood. Do but hear me.

Croaker. What! you intend to bring 'em off, I suppose!
I'll hear nothing.

Honeywood. Madam, you seem at least calm enough to
hear reason.

Olivia. Excuse me.

Honeywood. Good Jarvis, let me then explain it to you.

Jarvis. What signifies explanations when the thing is
done?

Honeywood. Will nobody hear me? Was there ever
such a set, so blinded by passion and prejudice? (*To the
Postboy.*) My good friend, I believe you'll be surprised
when I assure you——

Postboy. Sure me nothing—I'm sure of nothing but a
good beating.

Croaker. Come then you, Madam; if you ever hope for
any favour or forgiveness, tell me sincerely all you know
of this affair.

Olivia. Unhappily, Sir, I'm but too much the cause of
your suspicions: You see before you, Sir, one that, with
false pretences, has stept into your family to betray it;
not your daughter——

Croaker. Not my daughter!

Olivia. Not your daughter—but a mean deceiver—who
—support me, I cannot——

Honeywood. Help! she's going; give her air.

Croaker. Ay, ay, take the young woman to the air; I would not hurt a hair of her head, whosesoever daughter she may be—not so bad as that neither.

[Exeunt all but Croaker.

Yes, yes, all's out; I now see the whole affair. My son is either married, or going to be so, to this lady, whom he imposed upon me as his sister. Ay, certainly so; and yet • I don't find it afflicts me so much as one might think. There's the advantage of fretting away our misfortunes beforehand,—we never feel them when they come.

Enter Miss Richland and Sir William.

Sir William. But how do you know, Madam, that my nephew intends setting off from this place?

Miss Richland. My maid assured me he was come to this inn, and my own knowledge of his intending to leave the kingdom suggested the rest. But what do I see? my guardian here before us! Who, my dear Sir, could have expected meeting you here? To what accident do we owe this pleasure?

Croaker. To a fool, I believe.

Miss Richland. But to what purpose did you come?

Croaker. To play the fool.

Miss Richland. But with whom?

Croaker. With greater fools than myself.

Miss Richland. Explain.

Croaker. Why, Mr. Honeywood brought me here, to do nothing now I am here; and my son is going to be married, to I don't know who, that is here. So now you are as wise as I am.

Miss Richland. Married! to whom, Sir?

Croaker. To Olivia, my daughter, as I took her to be; but who the devil she is, or whose daughter she is, I know no more than the man in the moon.

Sir William. Then, Sir, I can inform you; and, though a stranger, yet you shall find me a friend to your family. It will be enough, at present, to assure you, that both in point of birth and fortune, the young lady is at least your son's equal. Being left by her father, Sir James Woodville——

Croaker. Sir James Woodville! What, of the west?

Sir William. Being left by him, I say, to the care of a mercenary wretch, whose only aim was to secure her fortune to himself, she was sent to France, under pretence of education, and there every art was tried to fix her for life in a convent, contrary to her inclinations. Of this I was informed upon my arrival at Paris; and, as I had been once her father's friend, I did all in my power to frustrate her guardian's base intentions. I had even meditated to rescue her from his authority, when your son stept iu with more pleasing violence, gave her liberty, and you a daughter.

Croaker. But I intend to have a daughter of my own choosing, Sir. A young lady, Sir, whose fortune, by my interest with those that have interest, will be double what my son has a right to expect. Do you know Mr. Lofty, Sir?

Sir William. Yes, Sir; and know that you are deceived in him. But step this way, and I'll convince you. (*Croaker and Sir William seem to confer.*)

Enter Honeywood.

Honeywood. Obstinate man, still to persist in his outrage! Insulted by him, despised by all, I now begin to grow contemptible even to myself. How have I sunk, by too great an assiduity to please! How have I overtaxed all my abilities, lest the approbation of a single fool should escape me! But all is now over: I have survived my reputation, my fortune, my friendships, and nothing remains henceforward for me but solitude and repentance.

Miss Richland. Is it true, Mr. Honeywood, that you are setting off, without taking leave of your friends? The report is, that you are quitting England. Can it be?

Honeywood. Yes, Madam; and though I am so unhappy as to have fallen under your displeasure, yet, thank Heaven! I leave you to happiness—to one who loves you, and deserves your love—to one who has power to procure you affluence, and generosity to improve your enjoyment of it.

Miss Richland. And are you sure, Sir, that the gentleman you mean is what you describe him?

Honeywood. I have the best assurances of it,—his serving me. He does indeed deserve the highest happiness, and that is in your power to confer. As for me, weak and wavering as I have been, obliged by all, and incapable of serving any, what happiness can I find but in solitude? what hope, but in being forgotten?

Miss Richland. A thousand! to live among friends that esteem you, whose happiness it will be to be permitted to oblige you.

Honeywood. No, Madam, my resolution is fixed. Inferiority among strangers is easy; but among those that once were equals, insupportable. Nay, to show you how far my resolution can go, I can now speak with calmness of my former follies, my vanity, my dissipation, my weakness. I will even confess, that, among the number of my other presumptions, I had the insolence to think of loving you. Yes, Madam, while I was pleading the passion of another, my heart was tortured with its own. But it is over; it was unworthy our friendship, and let it be forgotten.

Miss Richland. You amaze me!

Honeywood. But you'll forgive it, I know you will; since the confession should not have come from me even now, but to convince you of the sincerity of my intention of— never mentioning it more. (*Going.*)

Miss Richland. Stay, Sir, one moment—Ha! he here——

Enter Lofty.

Lofty. Is the coast clear? None but friends? I have followed you here with a trifling piece of intelligence; but it goes no farther; things are not yet ripe for a discovery. I have spirits working at a certain board; your affair at the Treasury will be done in less than—a thousand years. Mum!

Miss Richland. Sooner, Sir, I should hope.

Lofty. Why, yes, I believe it may, if it falls into proper hands, that know where to push and where to parry; that know how the land lies—eh, Honeywood?

Miss Richland. It has fallen into yours.

Lofty. Well, to keep you no longer in suspense, your thing is done. It is done, I say—that's all. I have just had assurances from Lord Neverout, that the claim has been examined, and found admissible. *Quietus* is the word, Madam.

Honeywood. But how? his lordship has been at New-market these ten days.

Lofty. Indeed! Then Sir Gilbert Goose must have been most damnably mistaken. I had it of him.

Miss Richland. He! why, Sir Gilbert and his family have been in the country this month.

Lofty. This month! it must certainly be so—Sir Gilbert's letter did come to me from Newmarket, so that he must have met his lordship there; and so it came about. I have his letter about me; I'll read it to you. (*Taking out a large bundle.*) That's from Paoli, of Corsica, that from the Marquis of Squilachi.—Have you a mind to see a letter from Count Poniatowski, now King of Poland? Honest Pon!—(*Searching.*) O, Sir, what, are you here too? I'll tell you what, honest friend, if you have not absolutely de-livered my letter to Sir William Honeywood, you may return it. The thing will do without him.

Sir William. Sir, I have delivered it; and must inform you, it was received with the most mortifying contempt.

Croaker. Contempt! Mr. Lofty, what can that mean?

Lofty. Let him go on, let him go on, I say. You'll find it come to something presently.

Sir William. Yes, Sir; I believe you'll be amazed. After waiting some time in the antichamber—after being surveyed with insolent curiosity by the passing servants, I was at last assured, that Sir William Honeywood knew no such person, and I must certainly have been imposed upon.

Lofty. Good! let me die! very good! Ha! ha! ha!

Croaker. Now, for my life, I can't find out half the good-ness of it.

Lofty. You can't? Ha! ha!

Croaker. No, for the soul of me: I think it was as con-founded a bad answer as ever was sent from one private gentleman to another.

Lofty. And so you can't find out the force of the message? Why, I was in the house at that very time. Ha! ha! It was I that sent that very answer to my own letter. Ha! ha!

Croaker. Indeed! How? why?

Lofty. In one word, things between Sir William and me must be behind the curtain. A party has many eyes. He sides with Lord Buzzard; I side with Sir Gilbert Goose. So that unriddles the mystery.

Croaker. And so it does, indeed; and all my suspicions are over.

Lofty. Your suspicions! What, then, you have been suspecting, you have been suspecting, have you? Mr. Croaker, you and I were friends—we are friends no longer. Never talk to me. It's over; I say, it's over.

Croaker. As I hope for your favour, I did not mean to offend. It escaped me. Don't be discomposed.

Lofty. Zounds! Sir, but I am discomposed, and will be discomposed. To be treated thus! Who am I? Was it for this I have been dreaded both by ins and outs? Have I been libelled in the *Gazetteer*, and praised in the *St. James's?* have I been chaired at Wildman's, and a speaker at Merchant-Tailors' Hall, have I had my hand to addresses, and my head in the print-shops,—and talk to me of suspects?

Croaker. My dear Sir, be pacified. What can you have but asking pardon?

Lofty. Sir, I will not be pacified—Suspects! Who am I? To be used thus! Have I paid court to men in favour to serve my friends, the lords of the Treasury, Sir William Honeywood, and the rest of the gang, and talk to me of suspects! Who am I, I say, who am I?

Sir William. Since, Sir, you are so pressing for an answer, I'll tell you who you are:—A gentleman as well acquainted with politics as with men in power; as well acquainted with persons of fashion as with modesty; with lords of the Treasury as with truth; and, with all, as you are with Sir William Honeywood. I am Sir William Honeywood. (*Discovering his ensigns of the Bath.*)

Croaker. Sir William Honeywood!

Honeywood. Astonishment! my uncle! (*Aside.*)

Lofty. So, then, my confounded genius has been all this time only leading me up to the garret, in order to fling me out of the window.

Croaker. What, Mr. Importance, and are these your works? Suspect you! You, who have been dreaded by the ins and outs; you, who have had your hand to addresses, and your head stuck up in print-shops. If you were served right, you should have your head stuck up in the pillory.

Lofty. Ay, stick it where you will; for, by the lord, it cuts but a very poor figure where it sticks at present.

Sir William. Well, Mr. Croaker, I hope you now see how incapable this gentleman is of serving you, and how little Miss Richland has to expect from his influence.

Croaker. Ay, Sir, too well I see it; and I can't but say I have had some boding of it these ten days. So I'm resolved, since my son has placed his affections on a lady of moderate fortune, to be satisfied with his choice, and not run the hazard of another Mr. Lofty in helping him to a better.

Sir William. I approve your resolution; and here they come, to receive a confirmation of your pardon and consent.

Enter Mrs. Croaker, Jarvis, Leontine, and Olivia.

Mrs. Croaker. Where's my husband? Come, come, lovey, you must forgive them. Jarvis here has been to tell me the whole affair; and I say, you must forgive them. Our own was a stolen match, you know, my dear; and we never had any reason to repent of it.

Croaker. I wish we could both say so. However, this gentleman, Sir William Honeywood, has been beforehand with you in obtaining their pardon. So, if the two poor fools have a mind to marry, I think we can tack them together without crossing the Tweed for it. (*Joining their hands.*)

Leontine. How blest, and unexpected! What, what can we say to such goodness? But our future obedience shall be the best reply. And as for this gentleman, to whom we owe——

Sir William. Excuse me, Sir, if I interrupt your thanks, as I have here an interest that calls me. (*Turning to Honeywood.*) Yes, Sir, you are surprised to see me; and I own that a desire of correcting your follies led me hither. I saw, with indignation, the errors of a mind that only sought applause from 'others; that easiness of disposition which, though inclined to the right, had not courage to condemn the wrong. I saw, with regret, those splendid errors, that still took name from some neighbouring duty; your charity, that was but injustice; your benevolence, that was but weakness; and your friendship, but credulity. I saw, with regret, great talents and extensive learning only employed to add sprightliness to error, and increase your perplexities. I saw your mind with a thousand natural charms; but the greatness of its beauty served only to heighten my pity for its prostitution.

Honeywood. Cease to upbraid me, Sir: I have for some time but too strongly felt the justice of your reproaches. But there is one way still left me. Yes, Sir, I have determined this very hour to quit for ever a place where I have made myself the voluntary slave of all, and to seek among strangers that fortitude which may give strength to the mind, and marshal all its dissipated virtues.[1] Yet, ere I depart, permit me to solicit favour for this gentleman, who, notwithstanding what has happened, has laid me under the most signal obligations. Mr. Lofty ——

Lofty. Mr. Honeywood, I'm resolved upon a reformation as well as you. I now begin to find that the man who first invented the art of speaking truth, was a much cunninger fellow than I thought him. And to prove that I design to speak truth for the future, I must now assure you, that you owe your late enlargement to another; as, upon my soul, I had no hand in the matter. So now, if any of the company has a mind for preferment, he may take my place: I'm determined to resign.   [*Exit.*

Honeywood. How have I been deceived!

Sir William. No, Sir, you have been óbliged to a kinder,

---

[1] Some think the idea of the character of Honeywood, and also the play's name, were suggested by the career of Mr. S——, called the " good-natured man," who figures as the lover of the unfortunate game-stress, Fanny Braddock, in Goldsmith's Life of Beau Nash.—ED.

fairer friend, for that favour,—to Miss Richland. Would she complete our joy, and make the man she has honoured by her friendship happy in her love, I should then forget all, and be as blest as the welfare of my dearest kinsman can make me.

Miss Richland. After what is past, it would be but affectation to pretend to indifference. Yes, I will own an attachment, which I find was more than friendship. And if my entreaties cannot alter his resolution to quit the country, I will even try—if my hand has not power to detain him. (*Giving her hand.*)

Honeywood. Heavens! how can I have deserved all this? How express my happiness—my gratitude? A moment like this overpays an age of apprehension.

Croaker. Well, now I see content in every face; but Heaven send we be all better this day three months!

Sir William. Henceforth, nephew, learn to respect yourself. He who seeks only for applause from without, has all his happiness in another's keeping.

Honeywood. Yes, Sir, I now too plainly perceive my errors: my vanity, in attempting to please all by fearing to offend any: my meanness, in approving folly, lest fools should disapprove. Henceforth, therefore, it shall be my study to reserve my pity for real distress; my friendship for true merit; and my love for her who first taught me what it is to be happy.   [*Exeunt omnes.*

EPILOGUE;[1]

SPOKEN BY MRS. BULKLEY.

As puffing quacks some caitiff wretch procure
To swear the pill, or drop, has wrought a cure;
Thus, on the stage, our play-wrights still depend
For Epilogues and Prologues on some friend,

[1] The author, in expectation of an Epilogue from a friend at Oxford, deferred writing one himself till the very last hour. What is here offered, owes all its success to the graceful manner of the actress who spoke it.—GOLDSMITH.

Who knows each art of coaxing up the town,
And makes full many a bitter pill go down.
Conscious of this, our bard has gone about,
And teased each rhyming friend to help him out.
An Epilogue! things can't go on without it!
It could not fail, would you but set about it.
"Young man," cries one, (a bard laid up in clover,)
"Alas! young man, my writing days are over!
Let boys play tricks, and kick the straw, not I;
Your brother Doctor, there, perhaps, may try."
"What I, dear Sir?" the Doctor interposes,
"What, plant my thistle, Sir, among his roses!
No, no, I've other contests to maintain;
To-night I head our troops at Warwick-Lane.[1]
Go ask your manager"—"Who, me! Your pardon;
Those things are not our forte at Covent Garden."
Our author's friends, thus placed at happy distance,
Give him good words indeed, but no assistance.
As some unhappy wight, at some new play,
At the pit door stands elbowing a way,
While oft, with many a smile, and many a shrug,
He eyes the centre, where his friends sit snug;
His simpering friends, with pleasure in their eyes,
Sink as he sinks, and as he rises rise:
He nods, they nod; he cringes, they grimace;
But not a soul will budge to give him place.
Since, then, unhelp'd, our bard must now conform
" To 'bide the pelting of this pitt'less storm,"
Blame where you must, be candid where you can,
And be each critic the *Good-Natured Man.*[2]

[1] Where was the College of Physicians at that time. A vignette
view of the building adorns vol. ii. of Dr. William Munk's ' Roll of the
Royal College of Physicians.' Perhaps Goldsmith's " brother Doctor "
was Dr., afterwards Sir George, Baker, who, Dr. Munk records, filled
in succession many important offices in the College of Physicians, and to
whom Goldsmith addressed his ' Reply to an Invitation to Dinner:' see
Poems, p. 93.—ED.

[2] In the earliest editions the last line ran:—

" And view with favour, the ' Good-Natur'd Man.' "

Mr. Piozzi has told the following story of Goldsmith's demeanour after
the first performance of this his first play :—" Returning home one day
from dining at the chaplain's table, he [Dr. Johnson] told me, that Dr.

Goldsmith had given a very comical and unnecessarily exact recital there of his own feelings when his play was hissed; telling the company how he went indeed to the Literary Club at night, and chatted gaily among his friends as if nothing had happened amiss; that to impress them still more forcibly with an idea of his magnanimity, he even sung his favourite song about '*an old woman tossed in a blanket seventeen times as high as the moon;*' but '*all this while I was suffering horrid tortures,*' said he, '*and verily believe that if I had put a bit into my mouth it would have strangled me on the spot, I was so excessively ill; but I made more noise than usual to cover all that; and so they never perceived my not eating, nor I believe at all imagined to themselves the anguish of my heart; but when all were gone except Johnson here, I burst out a-crying, and even swore by —— that I would never write again.*' ' All which, Doctor,' says Mr. Johnson, amazed at his odd frankness, ' I thought had been a secret between you and me; and I am sure I would not have said any thing about it for the world.' " See Piozzi's ' Anecdotes of Dr. Johnson,' 1786, p. 245.—ED.

THE BAILIFFS' SCENE (Act III.: see also Goldsmith's Preface to the play.) It seems that this scene, the one hissed, and in consequence omitted after the first representation, though printed in the earliest editions of the play, was restored to the stage in 1773—soon after the production of ' She Stoops to Conquer.' Genest records that on May 3, 1773, the performance being for the benefit of Mrs. Green, the original Mrs. Hardcastle, ' The Good-Natured Man ' was given with, " by particular desire," the bailiffs' scene " restored." Upon this occasion Morris and Quick were the bailiffs, and Lee Lewes played Lofty for the " first time."—ED.

SHE STOOPS TO CONQUER;

OR,

THE MISTAKES OF A NIGHT.

A COMEDY.[1]

[DEDICATION.]

Dr.

TO SAMUEL JOHNSON, LL.D.

DEAR SIR,—By inscribing this slight performance to you, I do not mean so much to compliment you as myself. It may do me some honour to inform the public, that I have lived many years in intimacy with you. It may serve the interests of mankind also to inform them, that the greatest wit may be found in a character, without impairing the most unaffected piety.

I have, particularly, reason to thank you for your partiality to this performance. The undertaking a comedy, not merely sentimental, was very dangerous; and Mr. Colman, who saw this piece in its various stages, always thought it so.[2] However, I ventured to trust it to the public; and, though it was necessarily delayed till late in the season, I have every reason to be grateful.

I am, dear Sir,

Your most sincere friend

And admirer,

OLIVER GOLDSMITH.

[1] 'She Stoops to Conquer' was represented for the first time, March 15, 1773. It was very successful, and became a stock play. The author's friends had some difficulty in fixing upon a name for it: Goldsmith himself originally entitled it 'The Old House a New Inn.'—B. See Goldsmith's essay on 'Sentimental and Laughing Comedy,' in vol. i., also note at p. 218.—ED.

[2] On March 4, eleven days before the first performance of this comedy, Dr. Johnson wrote to the Rev. Mr. White:—"Goldsmith has a new comedy in rehearsal at Covent Garden, to which the manager [the elder Colman] predicts ill success. I hope he will be mistaken. I think it deserves a very kind reception."—BOSWELL'S *Johnson* (Bohn's edition), vol. iii., p. 244.—ED.

DRAMATIS PERSONÆ.

[THE CAST OF THE CHARACTERS AT COVENT GARDEN
IN 1773.]

MEN.

Sir Charles Marlow	MR. GARDNER.
Young Marlow (his son) . . .	MR. LEWES.[1]
Hardcastle	MR. SHUTER.
Hastings	MR. DUBELLAMY.
Tony Lumpkin	MR. QUICK.[2]
Diggory	MR. SAUNDERS.

WOMEN.

Mrs. Hardcastle	MRS. GREEN.
Miss Hardcastle	MRS. BULKLEY.[3]
Miss Neville	MRS. KNIVETON.
Maid	MISS WILLEMS.

Landlord, Servants, &c. &c.

[1] Lee Lewes, also famous as harlequin. He took the part of Young Marlow on its being refused by " Gentleman" Smith. Goldsmith testified to the success of the young actor by writing an epilogue for his benefit performance : see it in the Poems. Lee Lewes also travelled with an entertainment of the ' Mathews at Home ' order, and published his ' Memoirs ' in four volumes. The latter work, curiously enough, makes no mention of Goldsmith. Sir Walter Scott gives several anecdotes of our author purporting to be from these ' Memoirs.' These anecdotes, however, are not in Lewes's Memoirs,' but in Cooke's anecdotes, published in the *European Magazine*, vol. xxiv., p. 17, &c.—ED.

[2] The character of Tony Lumpkin first made this actor famous. Similarly, as in Lee Lewes's case, Quick took his part on its refusal by the actor who should have taken it—Woodward, who spoke the Prologue. For more concerning John Quick, see our introductory note to ' The Grumbler,' p. 295.—ED.

[3] Mrs. Bulkley was also the original Miss Richland in ' The Good-Natured Man.' See Goldsmith's note on this actress at p. 213; also see the notes to the epilogues at the end of the present play, pp. 289-90.—ED.

SHE STOOPS TO CONQUER;

OR,

THE MISTAKES OF A NIGHT.

PROLOGUE.

BY DAVID GARRICK, ESQ.

*Enter Mr. Woodward, dressed in black, and holding a
handkerchief to his eyes.*

Excuse me, Sirs, I pray—I can't yet speak—
I'm crying now—and have been all the week.
"'Tis not alone this mourning suit," good masters:
"I've that within" for which there are no plasters!
Pray, would you know the reason why I'm crying?
The Comic Muse, long sick, is now a-dying!
And if she goes, my tears will never stop;
For, as a player, I can't squeeze out one drop:
I am undone, that's all—shall lose my bread—
I'd rather—but that's nothing—lose my head.
When the sweet maid is laid upon the bier,
Shuter and I shall be chief mourners here.
To her a mawkish drab of spurious breed,
Who deals in Sentimentals, will succeed![1]

---

[1] In Reed and Jones's edition of Baker's 'Biographia Dramatica,'
1812 (vol. iii., p. 263), it is remarked :—"When this piece was originally
brought forward, the taste of the nation had sickened with a preposterous
love for what was termed sentimental comedy ; that is a dramatic composition, in which the ordinary business of life, which in a free country
like Great Britain, produces such a diversity of character, was to be
superseded by an unnatural affectation of polished dialogue, in which the
usages and singularities of the multitude were to be nearly, if not alto-

Poor Ned and I are dead to all intents ;
We can as soon speak Greek as Sentiments !
Both nervous grown, to keep our spirits up,
We now and then take down a hearty cup.
What shall we do ?   If Comedy forsake us,
They'll turn us out, and no one else will take us !
But why can't I be moral ?   Let me try :—
My heart thus pressing—fix'd my face and eye—
With a sententious look that nothing means,
(Faces are blocks in sentimental scenes,)·
Thus I begin :—" All is not gold that glitters,
" Pleasures seem sweet, but prove a glass of bitters.
" When Ign'rance enters, Folly is at hand :
" Learning is better far than house and land.
" Let not your virtue trip : who trips may stumble,
" And Virtue is not Virtue, if she tumble."

I give it up—morals won't do for me ;
To make you laugh, I must play tragedy.
One hope remains :—hearing the maid was ill,
A Doctor comes this night to show his skill :
To cheer her heart, and give your muscles motion,
He, in Five Draughts prepar'd, presents a potion—
A kind of magic charm—for, be assur'd,
If you will swallow it, the maid is cur'd :
But desp'rate the Doctor's and her case is,
If you reject the dose, and make wry faces !
This truth he boasts, will boast it while he lives,
No pois'nous drugs are mix'd in what he gives.
Should he succeed, you'll give him his degree ;
If not, within he will receive no fee !
The College, *you*, must his pretensions back,
Pronounce him Regular, or dub him Quack.

gether rejected. This false taste was borrowed from France ; where
it was the practice then, more than at the present day, to keep what
they were pleased to term the higher order of comedy, in a material
sense unconnected with the unshackled ebullitions of nature ; Kelly and
others were enforcing this principle with ardour, when Oliver Goldsmith
planted the standard of Thalia on the boards of Covent Garden Theatre."
—Ed.

ACT I.

SCENE I.—A CHAMBER IN AN OLD-FASHIONED HOUSE.

Enter Mrs. Hardcastle and Mr. Hardcastle.

Mrs. Hardcastle. I vow, Mr. Hardcastle, you're very particular. Is there a creature in the whole country, but ourselves, that does not take a trip to town now and then, to rub off the rust a little? There's the two Miss Hoggs, and our neighbour Mrs. Grigsby, go to take a month's polishing every winter.

Hardcastle. Ay, and bring back vanity and affectation to last them the whole year. I wonder why London cannot keep its own fools at home. In my time, the follies of the town crept slowly among us, but now they travel faster than a stage-coach. Its fopperies come down not only as inside pasengers, but in the very basket.

Mrs. Hardcastle. Ay, *your* times were fine times, indeed; you have been telling us of them for many a long year. Here we live in an old rumbling mansion, that looks for all the world like an inn, but that we never see company. Our best visitors are old Mrs. Oddfish, the curate's wife, and little Cripplegate, the lame dancing-master; and all our entertainment your old stories of Prince Eugene and the Duke of Marlborough. I hate such old-fashioned trumpery.

Hardcastle. And I love it. I love everything that's old: old friends, old times, old manners, old books, old wine; and, I believe, Dorothy, (*taking her hand*), you'll own I have been pretty fond of an old wife.

Mrs. Hardcastle. Lord, Mr. Hardcastle, you're for ever at your Dorothy's and your old wives. You may be a Darby, but I'll be no Joan, I promise you. I'm not so old as you'd make me, by more than one good year. Add twenty to twenty, and make money of that.

Hardcastle. Let me see; twenty added to twenty, makes just fifty and seven.

Mrs. Hardcastle. It's false, Mr. Hardcastle: I was but twenty when I was brought to bed of Tony, that I had by

Mr. Lumpkin, my first husband; and he's not come to years of discretion yet.

Hardcastle. Nor ever will, I dare answer for him. Ay, you have taught *him* finely!

Mrs. Hardcastle. No matter; Tony Lumpkin has a good fortune. My son is not to live by his learning. I don't think a boy wants much learning to spend fifteen hundred a-year.

Hardcastle. Learning, quotha! a mere composition of tricks and mischief.

Mrs. Hardcastle. Humour, my dear; nothing but humour. Come, Mr. Hardcastle, you must allow the boy a little humour.

Hardcastle. I'd sooner allow him a horse-pond. If burning the footman's shoes, frightening the maids, and worrying the kittens be humour, he has it. It was but yesterday he fastened my wig to the back of my chair, and when I went to make a bow, I popt my bald head in Mrs. Frizzle's face.

Mrs. Hardcastle. And am I to blame? The poor boy was always too sickly to do any good. A school would be his death. When he comes to be a little stronger, who knows what a year or two's Latin may do for him?

Hardcastle. Latin for him! A cat and fiddle. No, no; the alehouse and the stable are the only schools he'll ever go to.

Mrs. Hardcastle. Well, we must not snub the poor boy now, for I believe we shan't have him long among us. Any body that looks in his face may see he's consumptive.

Hardcastle. Ay, if growing too fat be one of the symptoms.

Mrs. Hardcastle. He coughs sometimes.

Hardcastle. Yes, when his liquor goes the wrong way.

Mrs. Hardcastle. I'm actually afraid of his lungs.

Hardcastle. And truly so am I; for he sometimes whoops like a speaking-trumpet—(*Tony hallooing behind the scenes.*) —Oh, there he goes—a very consumptive figure, truly!

Enter Tony, crossing the Stage.

Mrs. Hardcastle. Tony, where are you going, my charmer? Won't you give papa and I a little of your company, lovey?

Tony. I'm in haste, mother, I cannot stay.

Mrs. Hardcastle. You shan't venture out this raw evening, my dear: you look most shockingly.

Tony. I can't stay, I tell you. The Three Pigeons expects me down every moment. There's some fun going forward.

Hardcastle. Ay, the alehouse, the old place; I thought so.

Mrs. Hardcastle. A low, paltry set of fellows.

Tony. Not so low, neither. There's Dick Muggins, the exciseman, Jack Slang, the horse-doctor, little Aminadab, that grinds the music-box, and Tom Twist, that spins the pewter platter.

Mrs. Hardcastle. Pray, my dear, disappoint them for one night at least.

Tony. As for disappointing *them*, I should not so much mind; but I can't abide to disappoint *myself*.

Mrs. Hardcastle. (*Detaining him.*) You shan't go.

Tony. I will, I tell you.

Mrs. Hardcastle. I say you shan't.

Tony. We'll see which is the strongest, you or I.

[*Exit, hauling her out.*

Hardcastle. (*Alone.*) Ay, there goes a pair that only spoil each other. But is not the whole age in a combination to drive sense and discretion out of doors? There's my pretty darling, Kate; the fashions of the times have almost infected her too. By living a year or two in town, she is as fond of gauze and French frippery as the best of them.

Enter Miss Hardcastle.

Hardcastle. Blessings on my pretty innocence! Drest out as usual, my Kate. Goodness! What a quantity of superfluous silk hast thou got about thee, girl! I could never teach the fools of this age, that the indigent world could be clothed out of the trimmings of the vain.

Miss Hardcastle. You know our agreement, Sir. You allow me the morning to receive and pay visits, and to dress in my own manner; and in the evening I put on my house-wife's dress to please you.

Hardcastle. Well, remember I insist on the terms of our agreement; and, by the by, I believe I shall have occasion to try your obedience this very evening.

Miss Hardcastle. I protest, Sir, I don't comprehend your meaning.

Hardcastle. Then, to be plain with you, Kate, I expect the young gentleman I have chosen to be your husband from town this very day. I have his father's letter, in which he informs me his son is set out, and that he intends to follow himself shortly after.

Miss Hardcastle. Indeed! I wish I had known some-thing of this before. Bless me, how shall I behave? It's a thousand to one I shan't like him. Our meeting will be so formal, and so like a thing of business, that I shall find no room for friendship or esteem.

Hardcastle. Depend upon it, child, I'll never control your choice; but Mr. Marlow, whom I have pitched upon, is the son of my old friend, Sir Charles Marlow, of whom you have heard me talk so often. The young gentleman has been bred a scholar, and is designed for an employ-ment in the service of his country. I am told he's a man of an excellent understanding.

Miss Hardcastle. Is he.

Hardcastle. Very generous.

Miss Hardcastle. I believe I shall like him.

Hardcastle. Young and brave.

Miss Hardcastle. I'm sure I shall like him.

Hardcastle. And very handsome.

Miss Hardcastle. My dear papa, say no more, (*kissing his hand*) he's mine—I'll have him.

Hardcastle. And, to crown all, Kate, he's one of the most bashful and reserved young fellows in all the world.

Miss Hardcastle. Eh! You have frozen me to death again. That word *reserved* has undone all the rest of his accomplishments. A reserved lover, it is said, always makes a suspicious husband.

Hardcastle. On the contrary, modesty seldom resides in

a breast that is not enriched with nobler virtues. It was
the very feature in his character that first struck me.

Miss Hardcastle. He must have more striking features
to catch me, I promise you. However, if he be so young,
so handsome, and so every thing, as you mention, I believe
he'll do still. I think I'll have him.

Hardcastle. Ay, Kate, but there is still an obstacle. It's
more than an even wager he may not have you.

. *Miss Hardcastle.* My dear papa, why will you mortify
one so?—Well, if he refuses, instead of breaking my heart
at his indifference, I'll only break my glass for its flattery,
set my cap to some newer fashion, and look out for some
less difficult admirer.   ,

Hardcastle. Bravely resolved! In the meantime I'll go
prepare the servants for his reception: as we seldom see
company, they want as much training as a company of
recruits the first day's muster.   [*Exit.*

Miss Hardcastle. (*Alone.*) Lud, this news of papa's puts
me all in a flutter. Young, handsome; these he put last,
but I put them foremost. Sensible, good-natured; I like
all that. But then, reserved and sheepish; that's much
against him. Yet can't he be cured of his timidity, by
being taught to be proud of his wife? Yes; and can't I—
But I vow I'm disposing of the husband, before I have
secured the lover.

Enter Miss Neville.

Miss Hardcastle. I'm glad you're come, Neville, my dear.
Tell me, Constance, how do I look this evening? Is there
any thing whimsical about me? Is it one of my well-
looking days, child? Am I in face to-day?

Miss Neville. Perfectly, my dear. Yet, now I look again
—bless me!—sure no accident has happened among the
canary birds or the gold fishes. Has your brother or
the cat been meddling? or has the last novel been too
moving?

Miss Hardcastle. No; nothing of all this. I have been
threatened—I can scarce get it out—I have been threatened
with a lover.

Miss Neville. And his name——

Miss Hardcastle. Is Marlow.

Miss Neville. Indeed!

Miss Hardcastle. The son of Sir Charles Marlow.

Miss Neville. As I live, the most intimate friend of Mr. Hastings, *my* admirer. They are never asunder. I believe you must have seen him when we lived in town.

Miss Hardcastle. Never.

Miss Neville. He's a very singular character, I assure you. Among women of reputation and virtue, he is the modestest man alive; but his acquaintance give him a very different character among creatures of another stamp —you understand me.

Miss Hardcastle. An odd character, indeed. I shall never be able to manage him. What shall I do? Pshaw! think no more of him, but trust to occurrences for success. But how goes on your own affair, my dear? has my mother been courting you for my brother Tony, as usual?

Miss Neville. I have just come from one of our agreeable *tête-à-têtes.* She has been saying a hundred tender things, and setting off her pretty monster as the very pink of perfection.

Miss Hardcastle. And her partiality is such, that she actually thinks him so. A fortune like yours is no small temptation. Besides, as she has the sole management of it, I'm not surprised to see her unwilling to let it go out of the family.

Miss Neville. A fortune like mine, which chiefly consists in jewels, is no such mighty temptation. But, at any rate, if my dear Hastings be but constant, I make no doubt to be too hard for her at last. However, I let her suppose that I am in love with her son, and she never once dreams that my affections are fixed upon another.

Miss Hardcastle. My good brother holds out stoutly. I could almost love him for hating you so.

Miss Neville. It is a good-natured creature at bottom, and I'm sure would wish to see me married to any body but himself. But my aunt's bell rings for our afternoon's walk round the improvements. *Allons!* Courage is necessary, as our affairs are critical.

Miss Hardcastle. "Would it were bed-time, and all were well!" [*Exeunt.*

SCENE II.—AN ALEHOUSE ROOM.

Several shabby fellows with punch and tobacco: Tony at the head of the table, a little higher than the rest: a mallet in his hand.

Omnes. Hurrea! hurrea! hurrea! bravo!

First Fellow. Now, gentlemen, silence for a song. The Squire is going to knock himself down for a song.

Omnes. Ay, a song, a song!

Tony. Then I'll sing you, gentlemen, a song I made upon this alehouse, The Three Pigeons.[1]

SONG.

> Let schoolmasters puzzle their brain,
>   With grammar, and nonsense, and learning;
> Good liquor, I stoutly maintain,
>   Gives *genus* a better discerning.
> Let them brag of their heathenish gods,
>   Their Lethes, their Styxes, and Stygians,
> Their *quis*, and their *quæs*, and their *quods*,
>   They're all but a parcel of pigeons.
>   Toroddle, toroddle, toroll.

> When methodist preachers come down,
>   A-preaching that drinking is sinful,
> I'll wager the rascals a crown,
>   They always preach best with a skinful.
> But when you come down with your pence,
>   For a slice of their scurvy religion,
> I'll leave it to all men of sense,
>   But you, my good friend, are the pigeon.
>   Toroddle, toroddle, toroll.

[1] *The Three Pigeons.*—Newell, p. 80, quotes Mangin as saying that Goldsmith, while a youth at Lissoy, spent too much time of an evening at "The Pidgeons," the alehouse of that village, where he was very popular, &c.; and this, together with Newell's and other accounts of visits to the "Three Jolly Pigeons" inn of the same place, as the original of the "Three Pigeons" of this comedy, has induced the belief that Goldsmith took the name of Tony Lumpkin's alehouse from the Lissoy inn. It seems, however, that the latter was not called the "Three Pigeons," and that the inn which took its place after Goldsmith's death —though not quite on the old site—and was by Captain Hogan "made up" to tally with the inn described in the 'Deserted Village' (see Appendix to the Poems), was called the "Three Jolly Pigeons" from the inn in this comedy. See also the note at p. 228.—ED,

> Then come, put the jorum about,
>   And let us be merry and clever,
> Our hearts and our liquors are stout,
>   Here's the Three Jolly Pigeons for ever.
> Let some cry up woodcock or hare,
>   Your bustards, your ducks, and your widgeons;
> But of all the [gay [1]] birds in the air,
>   Here's a health to the Three Jolly Pigeons,
>   Toroddle, toroddle, toroll.

Omnes. Bravo, bravo!

First Fellow. The Squire has got spunk in him.

Second Fellow. I loves to hear him sing, bekeays he never gives us nothing that's *low*.

Third Fellow. Oh, damn anything that's *low*, I cannot bear it.

Fourth Fellow. The genteel thing is the genteel thing at any time: if so be that a gentleman bees in a concatenation accordingly.

Third Fellow. I like the maxum of it, Master Muggins. What though I am obligated to dance a bear, a man may be a gentleman for all that. May this be my poison, if my bear ever dances but to the very genteelest of tunes; "Water Parted," or the minuet in "Ariadne."

Second Fellow. What a pity it is the Squire is not come to his own. It would be well for all the publicans within ten miles round of him.

Tony. Ecod, and so it would, Master Slang. I'd then show what it was to keep choice of company.

Second Fellow. Oh, he takes after his own father for that. To be sure, old Squire Lumpkin was the finest gentleman I ever set my eyes on. For winding the straight horn, or beating a thicket for a hare, or a wench, he never had his fellow. It was a saying in the place, that he kept the best horses, dogs, and girls in the whole county.

Tony. Ecod, and when I'm of age, I'll be no bastard, I promise you. I have been thinking of Bet Bouncer and the miller's gray mare to begin with. But come, my boys, drink about and be merry, for you pay no reckoning. Well, Stingo, what's the matter?

---

[1] The word "gay" appears in some editions, but is not in the earliest. —ED.

Enter Landlord.

Landlord. There be two gentlemen in a post-chaise at the door. They have lost their way upo' the forest; and they are talking something about Mr. Hardcastle.

Tony. As sure as can be, one of them must be the gentleman that's coming down to court my sister. Do they seem to be Londoners?

Landlord. I believe they may. They look woundily like Frenchmen.

Tony. Then desire them to step this way, and I'll set them right in a twinkling. (*Exit Landlord.*) Gentlemen, as they mayn't be good enough company for you, step down for a moment, and I'll be with you in the squeezing of a lemon.   [*Exeunt mob.*

Tony. (*Alone.*) Father-in-law has been calling me whelp, and hound, this half-year. Now, if I pleased, I could be so revenged upon the old grumbletonian. But then I'm afraid—Afraid of what? I shall soon be worth fifteen hundred a-year, and let him frighten me out of *that* if he can.

Enter Landlord, conducting Marlow and Hastings.

Marlow. What a tedious, uncomfortable day have we had of it! We were told it was but forty miles across the country, and we have come about three score.[1]

Hastings. And all, Marlow, from that unaccountable reserve of yours, that would not let us inquire more frequently on the way.

Marlow. I own, Hastings, I am unwilling to lay myself under an obligation to every one I meet, and often stand the chance of an unmannerly answer.

Hastings. At present, however, we are not likely to receive any answer.

Tony. No offence, gentlemen. But I'm told you have been inquiring for one Mr. Hardcastle in these parts. Do you know what part of the country you are in?

---

[1] In 1882 Dr. Pearson read a paper before the Cambridge Antiquarian Society to show that the inn called the "Three Pigeons," at the cross roads between Thame and Abingdon, was probably the scene of Tony Lumpkin's revels.—ED.

Hastings. Not in the least, Sir, but should thank you for information.

Tony. Nor the way you came?

Hastings. No, Sir; but if you can inform us——

Tony. Why, gentlemen, if you know neither the road you are going, nor where you are, nor the road you came, the first thing I have to inform you is, that—you have lost your way.

Marlow. We wanted no ghost to tell us that.

Tony. Pray, gentlemen, may I be so bold as to ask the place from whence you came?

Marlow. That's not necessary towards directing us where we are to go.

Tony. No offence; but question for question is all fair, you know. Pray, gentlemen, is not this same Hardcastle a cross-grained, old-fashioned, whimsical fellow, with an ugly face, a daughter, and a pretty son?

Hastings. We have not seen the gentleman; but he has the family you mention.

Tony. The daughter, a tall, trapesing, trolloping, talkative maypole; the son, a pretty, well-bred, agreeable youth, that every body is fond of?

Marlow. Our information differs in this. The daughter is said to be well-bred, and beautiful; the son an awkward booby, reared up and spoiled at his mother's apron-string.

Tony. He-he-hem!—Then, gentlemen, all I have to tell you is, that you won't reach Mr. Hardcastle's house this night, I believe.

Hastings. Unfortunate!

Tony. It's a damned long, dark, boggy, dirty, dangerous way. Stingo, tell the gentlemen the way to Mr. Hardcastle's; (*winking upon the Landlord,*) Mr. Hardcastle's, of Quagmire Marsh—you understand me.

Landlord. Master Hardcastle's! Lock-a-daisy, my masters, you're come a deadly deal wrong! When you came to the bottom of the hill, you should have crossed down Squash-lane. ·

Marlow. Cross down Squash-lane!

Landlord. Then you were to keep straight forward, till you came to four roads.

Marlow. Come to where four roads meet?

Tony. Ay; but you must be sure to take only one of them.

Marlow. O Sir, you're facetious.

Tony. Then keeping to the right, you are to go sideways, till you come upon Crack-skull common : there you must look sharp for the track of the wheel, and go forward till you come to farmer Murrain's barn. Coming to the farmer's barn, you are to turn to the right, and then to the left, and then to the right about again, till you find out the old mill——

Marlow. Zounds, man! we could as soon find out the longitude!

Hastings. What's to be done, Marlow?

Marlow. This house promises but a poor reception; though perhaps the landlord can accommodate us.

Landlord. Alack, master, we have but one spare bed in the whole house.

Tony. And to my knowledge, that's taken up by three lodgers already. (*After a pause in which the rest seem disconcerted.*) I have hit it : don't you think, Stingo, our landlady could accommodate the gentlemen by the fireside, with—three chairs and a bolster?

Hastings. I hate sleeping by the fire-side.

Marlow. And I detest your three chairs and a bolster.

Tony. You do, do you?—Then, let me see,—what if you go on a mile further, to the Buck's Head—the old Buck's Head on the hill, one of the best inns in the whole county?

Hastings. O ho! so we have escaped an adventure for this night, however.

Landlord. (*Apart to Tony.*) Sure, you ben't sending them to your father's as an inn, be you?

Tony. Mum, you fool you. Let them find that out. (*To them.*) You have only to keep on straight forward, till you come to a large old house by the road side. You'll see a pair of large horns over the door. That's the sign. Drive up the yard, and call stoutly about you.

Hastings. Sir, we are obliged to you. The servants can't miss the way?

Tony. No, no : But I tell you, though, the landlord is rich, and going to leave off business; so he wants to be thought a gentleman, saving your presence, he! he! he! He'll be for giving you his company; and, ecod, if you mind him, he'll persuade you that his mother was an alderman, and his aunt a justice of peace.

Landlord. A troublesome old blade, to be sure; but a keeps as good wines and beds as any in the whole country.

Marlow. Well, if he supplies us with these, we shall want no farther connection.   We are to turn to the right, did you say?

Tony. No, no; straight forward.   I'll just step myself, and show you a piece of the way. (*To the Landlord.*) Mum!

Landlord. Ah, bless your heart, for a sweet, pleasant ——damned, mischievous, son of a whore.   [*Exeunt.*

ACT II.

SCENE I.—MR. HARDCASTLE'S HOUSE.

Enter Hardcastle, followed by three or four awkward Servants.

Hardcastle. Well, I hope you are perfect in the table exercise I have been teaching you these three days.   You all know your posts and your places, and can show that you have been used to good company, without ever stirring from home?

Omnes. Ay, ay.

Hardcastle. When company comes, you are not to pop out and stare, and then run in again, like frighted rabbits in a warren.

Omnes. No, no.

Hardcastle. You, Diggory, whom I have taken from the barn, are to make a show at the side-table; and you, Roger, whom I have advanced from the plough, are to place yourself behind my chair.   But you're not to stand so, with your hands in your pockets.   Take your hands from your pockets, Roger—and from your head, you block-head you.   See how Diggory carries his hands.   They're a little too stiff, indeed, but that's no great matter.

Diggory. Ay, mind how I hold them.   I learned to hold
my hands this way, when I was upon drill for the militia.
And so being upon drill——

Hardcastle. You must not be so talkative, Diggory.
You must be all attention to the guests.   You must hear
us talk, and not think of talking; you must see us drink,
and not think of drinking; you must see us eat, and not
think of eating.

Diggory. By the laws, your worship, that's perfectly un-
possible.   Whenever Diggory sees yeating going forward
ecod, he's always wishing for a mouthful himself.

Hardcastle. Blockhead! is not a bellyful in the kitchen
as good as a bellyful in the parlour?   Stay your stomach
with that reflection.

Diggory. Ecod, I thank your worship, I'll make a shift
to stay my stomach with a slice of cold beef in the pantry.

Hardcastle. Diggory, you are too talkative.   Then, if I
happen to say a good thing, or tell a good story, at table,
you must not all burst out a-laughing, as if you made part
of the company.

Diggory. Then, ecod, your worship must not tell the
story of Ould Grouse in the gun-room: I can't help laughing at that—he! he! he!—for the soul of me.   We have
laughed at that these twenty years—ha! ha! ha!

Hardcastle. Ha! ha! ha!   The story is a good one.
Well, honest Diggory, you may laugh at that; but still
remember to be attentive.   Suppose one of the company
should call for a glass of wine, how will you behave?   A
glass of wine, Sir, if you please, (*To Diggory*)—Eh, why
don't you move?

Diggory. Ecod, your worship, I never have courage till
I see the eatables and drinkables brought upo' the table,
and then I'm as bauld as a lion.

Hardcastle. What, will nobody move?

First Servant. I'm not to leave this pleace.

Second Servant. I'm sure it's no pleace of mine.

Third Servant. Nor mine, for sartain.

Diggory. Wauns, and I'm sure it canna be mine.

Hardcastle. You numskulls! and so, while, like your
betters, you are quarrelling for places, the guests must
be starved!   O you dunces! I find I must begin all over

again——But don't I hear a coach drive into the yard?
To your posts, you blockheads. I'll go in the meantime,
and give my old friend's son a hearty reception at the
gate.   [*Exit Hardcastle.*

Diggory. By the elevens! my place is quite gone out of
my head.

Roger. I know that my pleace is to be everywhere.

First Servant. Where the devil is mine?

Second Servant. My pleace is to be no where at all; and
so I'se go about my business.

[*Exeunt Servants, running about, as if frighted,
different ways.*

*Enter Servant, with candles, showing in Marlow and
Hastings.*

Servant. Welcome, gentlemen, very welcome! This way.

Hastings. After the disappointments of the day, welcome
once more, Charles, to the comforts of a clean room and a
good fire. Upon my word, a very well-looking house:
antique, but creditable.

Marlow. The usual fate of a large mansion. Having
first ruined the master by good house-keeping, it at last
comes to levy contributions as an inn.

Hastings. As you say, we passengers are to be taxed to
pay all these fineries. I have often seen a good sideboard,
or a marble chimney-piece, though not actually put in the
bill, inflame a reckoning confoundedly.

Marlow. Travellers, George, must pay in all places.
The only difference is, that in good' inns you pay dearly
for luxuries; in bad inns you are fleeced and starved.

Hastings. You have lived pretty much among them. In
truth, I have been often surprised, that you, who have seen
so much of the world, with your natural good sense, and
your many opportunities, could never yet acquire a requisite share of assurance.

Marlow. The Englishman's malady. But tell me, George,
where could I have learned that assurance you talk of?
My life has been chiefly spent in a college, or an inn, in
seclusion from that lovely part of the creation that chiefly
teach men confidence. I don't know that I was ever

familiarly acquainted with a single modest woman, except my mother—But among females of another class, you know——

Hastings. Ay, among them you are impudent enough, of all conscience.

Marlow. They are of *us*, you know.

Hastings. But in the company of women of reputation, I never saw such an idiot—such a trembler; you look for all the world as if you wanted an opportunity of stealing out of the room.

Marlow. Why, man, that's because I *do* want to steal out of the room. Faith, I have often formed a resolution to break the ice, and rattle away at any rate. But, I don't know how, a single glance from a pair of fine eyes has totally overset my resolution. An impudent fellow may counterfeit modesty, but I'll be hanged if a modest man can ever counterfeit impudence.

Hastings. If you could but say half the fine things to them, that I have heard you lavish upon the bar-maid of an inn, or even a college bed-maker——

Marlow. Why, George, I can't say fine things to them—they freeze, they petrify me. They may talk of a comet, or a burning mountain, or some such bagatelle; but to me, a modest woman, drest out in all her finery, is the most tremendous object of the whole creation.

Hastings. Ha! ha! ha! At this rate, man, how can you ever expect to marry?

Marlow. Never; unless, as among kings and princes, my bride were to be courted by proxy. If, indeed, like an Eastern bridegroom, one were to be introduced to a wife he never saw before, it might be endured. But to go through all the terrors of a formal courtship, together with the episode of aunts, grandmothers, and cousins, and at last to blurt out the broad, staring question of, "Madam, will you marry me?" No, no, that's a strain much above me, I assure you.

Hastings. I pity you. But how do you intend behaving to the lady you are come down to visit, at the request of your father?

Marlow. As I behave to all other ladies: bow very low; answer yes, or no, to all her demands. But for the rest,

I don't think I shall venture to look in her face, till I see my father's again.

Hastings. I'm surprised that one who is so warm a friend, can be so cool a lover.

Marlow. To be explicit, my dear Hastings, my chief inducement down was to be instrumental in forwarding your happiness, not my own. Miss Neville loves you, the family don't know you; as my friend, you are sure of a reception, and let honour do the rest.

Hastings. My dear Marlow! But I'll suppress the emotion. Were I a wretch, meanly seeking to carry off a fortune, you should be the last man in the world I would apply to for assistance. But Miss Neville's person is all I ask, and that is mine, both from her deceased father's consent, and her own inclination.

Marlow. Happy man! You have talents and art to captivate any woman. I'm doomed to adore the sex, and yet to converse with the only part of it I despise. This stammer in my address, and this awkward unprepossessing[1] visage of mine, can never permit me to soar above the reach of a milliner's 'prentice, or one of the duchesses of Drury-lane. Pshaw! this fellow here to interrupt us.

Enter Hardcastle.

Hardcastle. Gentlemen, once more you are heartily welcome. Which is Mr. Marlow? Sir, you are heartily welcome. It's not my way, you see, to receive my friends with my back to the fire. I like to give them a hearty reception in the old style at my gate. I like to see their horses and trunks taken care of.

Marlow. (Aside.) He has got our names from the servants already. *(To him.)* We approve your caution and hospitality, Sir. *(To Hastings.)* I have been thinking, George, of changing our travelling dresses in the morning. I am grown confoundedly ashamed of mine.

Hardcastle. I beg, Mr. Marlow, you'll use no ceremony in this house.

Hastings. I fancy, Charles, you're right: the first blow

---

[1] " Prepossessing " in the early editions.—Ed.

is half the battle. I intend opening the campaign with the white and gold.

Hardcastle. Mr. Marlow—Mr. Hastings—gentlemen—pray be under no restraint in this house. This is Liberty-hall, gentlemen. You may do just as you please here.

Marlow. Yet, George, if we open the campaign too fiercely at first, we may want ammunition before it is over. I think to reserve the embroidery to secure a retreat.

Hardcastle. Your talking of a retreat, Mr. Marlow, puts me in mind of the Duke of Marlborough, when we went to besiege Denain. He first summoned the garrison——

Marlow. Don't you think the *ventre d'or* waistcoat will do with the plain brown?

Hardcastle. He first summoned the garrison, which might consist of about five thousand men——

Hastings. I think not : brown and yellow mix but very poorly.

Hardcastle. I say, gentlemen, as I was telling you, he summoned the garrison, which might consist of about five thousand men——

Marlow. The girls like finery.

Hardcastle. Which might consist of about five thousand men, well appointed with stores, ammunition, and other implements of war. Now, says the Duke of Marlborough to George Brooks, that stood next to him—You must have heard of George Brooks—I'll pawn my dukedom, says he, but I take that garrison without spilling a drop of blood. So——

Marlow. What, my good friend, if you gave us a glass of punch in the meantime? it would help us to carry on the siege with vigour.

Hardcastle. Punch, Sir ! (*Aside.*) This is the most unaccountable kind of modesty I ever met with.

Marlow. Yes, Sir, punch. A glass of warm punch, after our journey, will be comfortable. This is Liberty-hall, you know.

[*Enter Roger with a cup.*]

Hardcastle. Here's a cup, Sir.

Marlow. (*Aside.*) So this fellow, in his Liberty-hall, will only let us have just what he pleases.

Hardcastle. (*Taking the cup.*) I hope you'll find it to your a mind. I have prepared it with my own hands, and e believe you'll own the ingredients are tolerable. Will you be so good as to pledge me, Sir? Here, Mr. Marlow, here is to our better acquaintance. (*Drinks.*)

Marlow. (*Aside.*) A very impudent fellow this! but he's a character, and I'll humour him a little. Sir, my service to you. (*Drinks.*)

Hastings. (*Aside.*) I see this fellow wants to give us his company, and forgets that he's an inn-keeper, before he has learned to be a gentleman.

Marlow. From the excellence of your cup, my old friend, I suppose you have a good deal of business in this part of the country. Warm work, now and then, at elections, I suppose?

Hardcastle. No, Sir, I have long given that work over. Since our betters have hit upon the expedient of electing each other, there is no business " for us that sell ale."

Hastings. So, then, you have no turn for politics, I find.

Hardcastle. Not in the least. There was a time, indeed, I fretted myself about the mistakes of government, like other people; but finding myself every day grow more angry, and the government growing no better, I left it to mend itself. Since that, I no more trouble my head about Hyder Ally, or Ally Cawn, than about Ally Croaker. Sir, my service to you.

Hastings. So that with eating above stairs, and drinking below, with receiving your friends within, and amusing them without, you lead a good, pleasant, bustling life of it.

Hardcastle. I do stir about a great deal, that's certain. Half the differences of the parish are adjusted in this very parlour.

Marlow. (*After drinking.*) And you have an argument in your cup, old gentleman, better than any in West-minster-hall.

Hardcastle. Ay, young gentleman, that, and a little philosophy.

Marlow. (*Aside.*) Well, this is the first time I ever heard of an innkeeper's philosophy!

Hastings. So, then, like an experienced general, you

is j..ck them on every quarter. If you find their reason
tuanageable, you attack it with your philosophy; if you
find they have no reason, you attack them with this.
Here's your health, my philosopher. (*Drinks.*)

Hardcastle. Good, very good, thank you; ha! ha!
Your generalship puts me in mind of Prince Eugene, when
he fought the Turks, at the battle of Belgrade. You shall
hear—

Marlow. Instead of the battle of Belgrade, I believe it's
almost time to talk about supper. What has your philosophy got in the house for supper?

Hardcastle. For supper, Sir! (*Aside.*) Was ever such
a request to a man in his own house!

Marlow. Yes, Sir, supper, Sir; I begin to feel an appetite. I shall make devilish work to-night in the larder, I
promise you.

Hardcastle. (*Aside.*) Such a brazen dog sure never my
eyes beheld! (*To him.*) Why, really, Sir, as for supper,
I can't well tell. My Dorothy and the cookmaid settle
these things between them. I leave these kind of things
entirely to them.

Marlow. You do, do you?

Hardcastle. Entirely. By the bye, I believe they are in
actual consultation upon what's for supper this moment in
the kitchen.

Marlow. Then I beg they'll admit me as one of their
privy-council. It's a way I have got. When I travel I
always choose to regulate my own supper. Let the cook
be called. No offence, I hope, Sir?

Hardcastle. O no, Sir, none in the least; yet I don't
know how—our Bridget, the cook-maid, is not very com-
municative upon these occasions. Should we send for her,
she might scold us all out of the house.

Hastings. Let's see the list of the larder, then. I ask
it as a favour. I always match my appetite to my bill of
fare.

Marlow. (*To Hardcastle, who looks at them with surprise.*)
Sir, he's very right, and it's my way too.

Hardcastle. Sir, you have a right to command here.
Here, Roger, bring us the bill of fare for to-night's supper:
I believe it's drawn out.—Your manner, Mr. Hastings,

puts me in mind of my uncle, Colonel Wallop. It was a saying of his, that no man was sure of his supper till he had eaten it.

[Enter Roger.]

Hastings. (*Aside.*) All upon the high ropes! His uncle a colonel! we shall soon hear of his mother being a justice of peace. But let's hear the bill of fare.

Marlow. (*Perusing.*) What's here? For the first course; for the second course; for the desert. The devil, Sir, do you think we have brought down the whole Joiners' Company, or the Corporation of Bedford, to eat up such a supper? Two or three little things, clean and comfortable, will do.

Hastings. But, let's hear it.

Marlow. (*Reading.*) "For the first course:—At the top, a pig, and pruin sauce."

Hastings. Damn your pig! I say.

Marlow. And damn your pruin sauce! say I.

Hardcastle. And yet, gentlemen, to men that are hungry pig with pruin sauce is very good eating.

Marlow. "At the bottom a calf's tongue and brains."

Hastings. Let your brains be knocked out, my good Sir; I don't like them.

Marlow. Or you may clap them on a plate by themselves. I do.

Hardcastle. (*Aside.*) Their impudence confounds me! (*To them.*) Gentlemen, you are my guests, make what alterations you please. Is there any thing else you wish to retrench or alter, gentlemen?

Marlow. "Item: A pork pie; a boiled rabbit and sausages; a Florentine; a shaking pudding, and a dish of tiff—taff—taffety cream!"

Hastings. Confound your made dishes; I shall be as much at a loss in this house as at a green and yellow dinner at the French ambassador's table. I'm for plain eating.

Hardcastle. I'm sorry, gentlemen, that I have nothing you like; but if there be any thing you have a particular fancy to——

Marlow. Why, really, Sir, your bill of fare is so exquisite,

that any one part of it is full as good as another. Send
us what you please. So much for supper. And now to
see that our beds are aired, and properly taken care of.

Hardcastle. I entreat you'll leave all that to me. You
shall not stir a step.

Marlow. Leave that to you! I protest, Sir, you must
excuse me ; I always look to these things myself.

Hardcastle. I must insist, Sir, you'll make yourself easy
on that head.

Marlow. You see I'm resolved on it. (*Aside.*) A very
troublesome fellow this, as ever I met with.

Hardcastle. Well, Sir, I'm resolved at least to attend
you. (*Aside.*) This may be modern modesty, but I never
saw any thing look so like old-fashioned impudence.

[*Exeunt Marlow and Hardcastle..*

Hastings. (*Alone.*) So I find this fellow's civilities begin
to grow troublesome. But who can be angry at those assiduities which are meant to please him?—Ha! what do I
see? Miss Neville, by all that's happy!

Enter Miss Neville.

Miss Neville. My dear Hastings! To what unexpected
good fortune—to what accident, am I to ascribe this happy
meeting ?

Hastings. Rather let me ask the same question, as I
could never have hoped to meet my dearest Constance at
an inn.

Miss Neville. An inn! sure you mistake : my aunt, my
guardian, lives here. What could induce you to think this
house an inn?

Hastings. My friend, Mr. Marlow, with whom I came
down, and I, have been sent here as to an inn, I assure
you. A young fellow whom we accidentally met at a house
hard by, directed us hither.

Miss Neville. Certainly it must be one of my hopeful
cousin's tricks, of whom you have heard me talk so often ;
ha! ha! ha!

Hastings. He whom your aunt intends for you? he of
whom I have such just apprehensions ?

Miss Neville. You have nothing to fear from him, I

assure you.   You'd adore him if you knew how heartily he despises me.   My aunt knows it too, and has undertaken to court me for him, and actually begins to think she has made a conquest.

Hastings. Thou dear dissembler ! You must know, my Constance, I have just seized this happy opportunity of my friend's visit here to get admittance into the family. The horses that carried us down are now fatigued with their journey, but they'll soon be refreshed ; and, then, if my dearest girl will trust in her faithful Hastings, we shall soon be landed in France, where even among slaves the laws of marriage are respected.[1]

Miss Neville. I have often told you, that though ready to obey you, I yet should leave my little fortune behind with reluctance.   The greatest part of it was left me by my uncle, the India Director, and chiefly consists in jewels. I have been for some time persuading my aunt to let me wear them.   I fancy I'm very near succeeding.   The instant they are put into my possession, you shall find me ready to make them and myself yours.

Hastings. Perish the baubles !   Your person is all I desire.   In the meantime, my friend Marlow must not be let into his mistake.   I know the strange reserve of his temper is such, that if abruptly informed of it, he would instantly quit the house, before our plan was ripe for execution.

Miss Neville. But how shall we keep him in the deception ?—Miss Hardcastle is just returned from walking—

---

[1] Prior says of this passage :—" The Duke of Gloucester, for whom, in consequence of the Royal Marriage Act, some public sympathy existed, was present the first night of representation, whether from previous intimation of a passage in the play does not appear.· But when Hastings uttered the speech to Miss Neville—' we shall soon be landed in France, where even among slaves the laws of marriage are respected,' it was instantly applied to his Royal Highness by the audience, and several rounds of applause testified to their feeling for his situation. —*Life of Goldsmith*, ii., 393. The Royal Marriage Act—levelled at the Royal Dukes, the brothers of George III.—was passed in 1772. Goldsmith was advised to cut out this passage, which, it was thought, might prevent a "royal command" for the play.   The author, however, stood by his text ; and, as it turned out, the King and Queen "commanded" a performance for May 5th—its tenth night,—and again the next season, for Nov. 10th.—ED.

What if we still continue to deceive him?——This, this
way——   [*They confer.*

Enter Marlow.

Marlow. The assiduities of these good people tease me
beyond bearing. My host seems to think it ill manners to
leave me alone, and so he claps not only himself but his
old-fashioned wife on my back. They talk of coming
to sup with us too; and then, I suppose, we are to run
the gauntlet through all the rest of the family.—What
have we got here?

Hastings. My dear Charles! Let me congratulate you—
The most fortunate accident!—Who do you think is just
alighted?

Marlow. Cannot guess.

Hastings. Our mistresses, boy, Miss Hardcastle and
Miss Neville. Give me leave to introduce Miss Constance
Neville to your acquaintance. Happening to dine in the
neighbourhood, they called, on their return, to take fresh
horses here. Miss Hardcastle has just stept into the
next room, and will be back in an instant. Wasn't it
lucky? eh!

Marlow. (*Aside.*) I have been mortified enough of all
conscience, and here comes something to complete my embarrassment.

Hastings. Well, but wasn't it the most fortunate thing
in the world?

Marlow. Oh, yes. Very fortunate—a most joyful encounter—But our dresses, George, you know, are in disorder—What if we should postpone the happiness till to-
morrow?—To-morrow at her own house—It will be every
bit as convenient—and rather more respectful—To-morrow
let it be. (*Offering to go.*)

Miss Neville. By no means, Sir. Your ceremony will
displease her. The disorder of your dress will show the
ardour of your impatience. Besides, she knows you are
in the house, and will permit you to see her.

Marlow. Oh, the devil! How shall I support it?—Hem!
hem! Hastings, you must not go. You are to assist me,
you know. I shall be confoundedly ridiculous. Yet hang
it! I'll take courage. Hem!

Hastings. Pshaw, man! It's but the first plunge, and all's over. She's but a woman, you know.

Marlow. And of all women, she that I dread most to ✓ encounter!

Enter Miss Hardcastle, as returned from walking,
a bonnet, &c.

Hastings. (*Introducing them.*) Miss Hardcastle, Mr. Marlow. I'm proud of bringing two persons of such merit together, that only want to know, to esteem each other.

Miss Hardcastle. (*Aside.*) Now for meeting my modest gentleman with a demure face, and quite in his own manner. (*After a pause, in which he appears very uneasy and disconcerted.*) I'm glad of your safe arrival, Sir—I'm told you had some accidents by the way.

Marlow. Only a few, Madam. Yes, we had some. Yes, Madam, a good many accidents; but should be sorry—Madam—or rather glad, of any accidents—that are so agreeably concluded. Hem!

Hastings. (*To him.*) You never spoke better in your whole life. Keep it up, and I'll insure you the victory.

Miss Hardcastle. I'm afraid you flatter, Sir. You that have seen so much of the finest company, can find little entertainment in an obscure corner of the country.

Marlow. (*Gathering courage.*) I have lived, indeed, in the world, Madam; but I have kept very little company. I have been but an observer upon life, Madam, while others ✓ were enjoying it.

Miss Neville. But that, I am told, is the way to enjoy it at last.

Hastings. (*To him.*) Cicero never spoke better. Once more, and you are confirmed in assurance for ever.

Marlow. (*To him.*) Hem! stand by me, then; and when I'm down, throw in a word or two to set me up again.

Miss Hardcastle. An observer, like you, upon life, were, I fear, disagreeably employed, since you must have had much more to censure than to approve.

Marlow. Pardon me, Madam. I was always willing to be amused. The folly of most people is rather an object of mirth than uneasiness.

Hastings. (*To him.*) Bravo, bravo. Never spoke so well in your whole life. Well, Miss Hardcastle, I see that you and Mr. Marlow are going to be very good company. I believe our being here will but embarrass the interview—

Marlow. Not in the least, Mr. Hastings. We like your company of all things. (*To him.*) Zounds! George, sure you won't go? how can you leave us?

Hastings. Our presence will but spoil conversation, so we'll retire to the next room. (*To him.*) You don't consider, man, that we are to manage a little *tête-à-tête* of our own. [*Exeunt.*

Miss Hardcastle. (*After a pause.*) But you have not been wholly an observer, I presume, Sir: the ladies, I should hope, have employed some part of your addresses.

Marlow. (*Relapsing into timidity.*) Pardon me, Madam, I —I—I—as yet, have studied—only—to—deserve them.

Miss Hardcastle. And that, some say, is the very worst way to obtain them.

Marlow. Perhaps so, Madam. But I love to converse only with the more grave and sensible part of the sex— But I'm afraid I grow tiresome.

Miss Hardcastle. Not at all, Sir; there is nothing I like so much as grave conversation myself; I could hear it for ever. Indeed I have often been surprised how a man of sentiment could ever admire those light airy pleasures, where nothing reaches the heart.

Marlow. It's——a disease——of the mind, Madam. In the variety of tastes there must be some, who, wanting a relish——for——um—a—um.

Miss Hardcastle. I understand you, Sir. There must be some, who, wanting a relish for refined pleasures, pretend to despise what they are incapable of tasting.

Marlow. My meaning, Madam; but infinitely better expressed. And I can't help observing——a——

Miss Hardcastle. (*Aside.*) Who could ever suppose this fellow impudent upon some occasions! (*To him.*) You were going to observe, Sir——

Marlow. I was observing, Madam—I protest, Madam, I forget what I was going to observe.

Miss Hardcastle. (*Aside.*) I vow, and so do I. (*To him.*)

You were observing, Sir, that in this age of hypocrisy—
something about hypocrisy, Sir.

Marlow. Yes, Madam. In this age of hypocrisy, there
are few, who, upon strict inquiry, do not—a—a—a——

Miss Hardcastle. I understand you perfectly, Sir.

Marlow. (*Aside.*) Egad! and that's more than I do
myself.

Miss Hardcastle. You mean that in this hypocritical age,
there are few that do not condemn in public what they
practise in private, and think they pay every debt to virtue
when they praise it.

Marlow. True, Madam; those who have most virtue in
their mouths, have least of it in their bosoms. But I'm
sure I tire you, Madam.

Miss Hardcastle. Not in the least, Sir; there's something
so agreeable and spirited in your manner, such life and
force—Pray, Sir, go on.

Marlow. Yes, Madam, I was saying——that there are
some occasions—when a total want of courage, Madam,
destroys all the——and puts us——upon—a—a—a——

Miss Hardcastle. I agree with you entirely: a want of
courage upon some occasions, assumes the appearance of
ignorance, and betrays us when we most want to excel. I
beg you'll proceed.

Marlow. Yes, Madam. Morally speaking, Madam—But
I see Miss Neville expecting us in the next room. I would
not intrude for the world.

Miss Hardcastle. I protest, Sir, I never was more agree-
ably entertained in all my life. Pray go on.

Marlow. Yes, Madam, I was——But she beckons us to
join her. Madam, shall I do myself the honour to attend
you?

Miss Hardcastle. Well, then, I'll follow.

Marlow. (*Aside.*) This pretty smooth dialogue has done
for me. [*Exit.*

Miss Hardcastle. (*Alone.*) Ha! ha! ha! Was there ever
such a sober, sentimental interview! I'm certain he scarce
looked in my face the whole time. Yet the fellow, but for
his unaccountable bashfulness, is pretty well too. He has
good sense; but then so buried in his fears, that it fatigues
one more than ignorance. If I could teach him a little

confidence, it would be doing somebody that I know of a
piece of service. But who is that somebody? That, faith,
is a question I can scarce answer.   [*Exit.*

*Enter Tony and Miss Neville, followed by Mrs. Hardcastle
and Hastings.*

Tony. What do you follow me for, cousin Con? I wonder you're not ashamed to be so very engaging.

Miss Neville. I hope, cousin, one may speak to one's own
relations, and not be to blame.

Tony. Ay, but I know what sort of a relation you want
to make me though; but it won't do. I tell you, cousin
Con, it won't do; so I beg you'll keep your distance—I
want no nearer relationship.

          [*She follows, coquetting him to the back scene.*

Mrs. Hardcastle. Well, I vow, Mr. Hastings, you are very
entertaining. There's nothing in the world I love to talk
of so much as London, and the fashions; though I was
never there myself.

Hastings. Never there! You amaze me! From your air
and manner, I concluded you had been bred all your life
either at Ranelagh, St. James's, or Tower Wharf.

Mrs. Hardcastle. Oh, Sir, you're only pleased to say so.
We country persons can have no manner at all. I'm in
love with the town, and that serves to raise me above some
of our neighbouring rustics; but who can have a manner,
that has never seen the Pantheon, the Grotto Gardens,
the Borough, and such places where the nobility chiefly
resort? All I can do is to enjoy London at second-hand.
I take care to know every *tête-à-tête* from the *Scandalous
Magazine,* and have all the fashions, as they come out, in
a letter from the two Miss Rickets of Crooked Lane. Pray,
how do you like this head, Mr. Hastings?

Hastings. Extremely elegant and *dégagée,* upon my word,
Madam. Your friseur is a Frenchman, I suppose?

Mrs. Hardcastle. I protest,—I dressed it myself from a
print in the *Ladies' Memorandum-book* for the last year.

Hastings. Indeed! Such a head in a side-box at the
play-house, would draw as many gazers as my Lady
Mayoress at a city ball.

Mrs. Hardcastle. I vow, since inoculation began, there is no such thing to be seen as a plain woman ; so one must dress a little particular, or one may escape in the crowd.

Hastings. But that can never be your case, Madam, in any dress.   (*Bowing.*)

Mrs. Hardcastle. Yet, what signifies my dressing, when I have such a piece of antiquity by my side as Mr. Hardcastle : all I can say will never argue down a single button from his clothes.   I have often wanted him to throw off his great flaxen wig, and where he was bald, to plaster it over, like my Lord Pately, with powder.

Hastings. You are right, Madam ; for, as among the ladies there are none ugly, so among the men there are none old.

Mrs. Hardcastle. But what do you think his answer was ? Why, with his usual Gothic vivacity, he said I only wanted him to throw off his wig to convert it into a *tête* for my own wearing.

Hastings. Intolerable ! At your age you may wear what you please, and it must become you.

Mrs. Hardcastle. Pray, Mr. Hastings, what do you take to be the most fashionable age about town ?

Hastings. Some time ago, forty was all the mode ; but I'm told the ladies intend to bring up fifty for the ensuing winter.

Mrs. Hardcastle. Seriously ?   Then I shall be too young for the fashion.

Hastings. No lady begins now to put on jewels till she's past forty.   For instance, miss there, in a polite circle, would be considered as a child—a mere maker of samplers.

Mrs. Hardcastle. And yet, Mrs. Niece thinks herself as much a woman, and is as fond of jewels, as the oldest of us all.

Hastings. Your niece, is she ?   And that young gentleman—a brother of yours, I should presume ?

Mrs. Hardcastle. My son, Sir.   They are contracted to each other.   Observe their little sports.   They fall in and out ten times a-day, as if they were man and wife already. (*To them.*) Well, Tony, child, what soft things are you saying to your cousin Constance this evening ?

Tony. I have been saying no soft things; but that it's very hard to be followed about so. Ecod! I've not a place in the house now that's left to myself, but the stable.

Mrs. Hardcastle. Never mind him, Con, my dear, he's in another story behind your back.

Miss Neville. There's something generous in my cousin's manner. He falls out before faces, to be forgiven in private.

Tony. That's a damned, confounded—crack.

Mrs. Hardcastle. Ah! he's a sly one. Don't you think they're like each other about the mouth, Mr. Hastings? The Blenkinsop mouth to a T. They're of a size too. Back to back, my pretties, that Mr. Hastings may see you. Come, Tony.

Tony. You had as good not make me, I tell you.
                                        (*Measuring.*)

Miss Neville. O lud! he has almost cracked my head.

Mrs. Hardcastle. Oh, the monster! For shame, Tony. You a man, and behave so!

Tony. If I'm a man, let me have my fortin. Ecod! I'll not be made a fool of no longer.

Mrs. Hardcastle. Is this, ungrateful boy, all that I'm to get for the pains I have taken in your education? I that have rocked you in your cradle, and fed that pretty mouth with a spoon! Did not I work that waistcoat to make you genteel? Did not I prescribe for you every day, and weep while the receipt was operating?

Tony. Ecod! you had reason to weep, for you have been dosing me ever since I was born. I have gone through every receipt in the *Complete Housewife* ten times over; and you have thoughts of coursing me through *Quincy* next spring. But, ecod! I tell you, I'll not be made a fool of no longer.

Mrs. Hardcastle. Wasn't it all for your good, viper? Wasn't it all for your good?

Tony. I wish you'd let me and my good alone, then. Snubbing this way when I'm in spirits! If I'm to have any good, let it come of itself; not to keep dinging it, dinging it into one so.

Mrs. Hardcastle. That's false; I never see you when you're in spirits. No, Tony, you then go to the alehouse or kennel. I'm never to be delighted with your agreeable wild notes, unfeeling monster!

Tony. Ecod! mamma, your own notes are the wildest of the two.

Mrs. Hardcastle. Was ever the like? But I see he wants to break my heart; I see he does.

Hastings. Dear Madam, permit me to lecture the young gentleman a little. I'm certain I can persuade him to his duty.

Mrs. Hardcastle. Well, I must retire. Come, Constance, my love. You see, Mr. Hastings, the wretchedness of my situation: was ever poor woman so plagued with a dear sweet, pretty, provoking, undutiful boy!

[*Exeunt Mrs. Hardcastle and Miss Neville.*

Tony. (*Singing.*)

> There was a young man riding by,
> And fain would have his will.
>   Rang do didlo dee.—

Don't mind her. Let her cry. It's the comfort of her heart. I have seen her and sister cry over a book for an hour together; and they said they liked the book the better the more it made them cry.

Hastings. Then you're no friend to the ladies, I find, my pretty young gentleman?

Tony. That's as I find 'um.

Hastings. Not to her of your mother's choosing, I dare answer? And yet she appears to me a pretty, well tempered girl.

· *Tony.* That's because you don't know her as well as I. Ecod! I know every inch about her; and there's not a more bitter cantankerous toad in all Christendom.

Hastings. (*Aside.*) Pretty encouragement this for a lover!

Tony. I have seen her since the height of that. She has as many tricks as a hare in a thicket, or a colt the first day's breaking.

Hastings. To me she appears sensible and silent.

Tony. Ay, before company. But when she's with her playmates, she's as loud as a hog in a gate.

Hastings. But there is a meek modesty about her that charms me.

Tony. Yes, but curb her never so little, she kicks up, and you're flung in a ditch.

Hastings. Well, but you must allow her a little beauty. —Yes, you must allow her some beauty.

Tony. Bandbox! She's all a made-up thing, mun. Ah! could you but see Bet Bouncer of these parts, you might then talk of beauty. Ecod! she has two eyes as black as sloes, and cheeks as broad and red as a pulpit cushion. She'd make two of she.

Hastings. Well, what say you to a friend that would take this bitter bargain off your hands?

Tony. Anon!

Hastings. Would you thank him that would take Miss Neville, and leave you to happiness and your dear Betsy?

Tony. Ay; but where is there such a friend, for who would take her?

Hastings. I am he. If you but assist me, I'll engage to whip her off to France, and you shall never hear more of her.

Tony. Assist you! Ecod I will, to the last drop of my blood. I'll clap a pair of horses to your chaise that shall trundle you off in a twinkling, and may be get you a part of her fortin beside, in jewels, that you little dream of.

Hastings. My dear Squire, this looks like a lad of spirit.

Tony. Come along, then, and you shall see more of my spirit before you have done with me. (*Singing.*)

> We are the boys
> That fears no noise
> Where the thundering cannons roar.

[*Exeunt.*

ACT III.

[SCENE.—A ROOM IN MR. HARDCASTLE'S HOUSE.]

Enter Hardcastle.

Hardcastle. What could my old friend Sir Charles mean by recommending his son as the modestest young man in town? To me he appears the most impudent piece of brass that ever spoke with a tongue. He has taken possession of the easy chair by the fire-side already. He took off his boots in the parlour, and desired me to see them taken care of. I'm desirous to know how his impudence affects my daughter. She will certainly be shocked at it.

Enter Miss Hardcastle, plainly dressed.

Hardcastle. Well, my Kate, I see you have changed your dress, as I bid you; and yet, I believe, there was no great occasion.

Miss Hardcastle. I find such a pleasure, Sir, in obeying your commands, that I take care to observe them without ever debating their propriety.

Hardcastle. And yet, Kate, I sometimes give you some cause, particularly when I recommended my *modest* gentleman to you as a lover to-day.

Miss Hardcastle. You taught me to expect something extraordinary, and I find the original exceeds the description.

Hardcastle. I was never so surprised in my life! He has quite confounded all my faculties.

Miss Hardcastle. I never saw any thing like it; and a man of the world too!

Hardcastle. Ay, he learned it all abroad—what a fool was I, to think a young man could learn modesty by travelling. He might as soon learn wit at a masquerade.

Miss Hardcastle. It seems all natural to him.

Hardcastle. A good deal assisted by bad company and a French dancing-master.

Miss Hardcastle. Sure you mistake, papa. A French

dancing-master could never have taught him that timid look—that awkward address—that bashful manner.

Hardcastle. Whose look? whose manner, child?

Miss Hardcastle. Mr. Marlow's: his *mauvaise honte*, his timidity, struck me at the first sight.

Hardcastle. Then your first sight deceived you; for I think him one of the most brazen first sights that ever astonished my senses.

Miss Hardcastle. Sure, Sir, you rally! I never saw any one so modest.

Hardcastle. And can you be serious? I never saw such a bouncing, swaggering puppy since I was born. Bully Dawson was but a fool to him.

Miss Hardcastle. Surprising! He met me with a respectful bow, a stammering voice, and a look fixed on the ground.

Hardcastle. He met me with a loud voice, a lordly air, and a familiarity that made my blood freeze again.

Miss Hardcastle. He treated me with diffidence and respect; censured the manners of the age; admired the prudence of girls that never laughed; tired me with apologies for being tiresome; then left the room with a bow, and "Madam, I would not for the world detain you."

Hardcastle. He spoke to me as if he knew me all his life before; asked twenty questions, and never waited for an answer; interrupted my best remarks with some silly pun; and when I was in my best story of the Duke of Marlborough and Prince Eugene, he asked if I had not a good hand at making punch! Yes, Kate, he asked your father if he was a maker of punch!

Miss Hardcastle. One of us must certainly be mistaken.

Hardcastle. If he be what he has shown himself, I'm determined he shall never have my consent.

Miss Hardcastle. And if he be the sullen thing I take him, he shall never have mine.

Hardcastle. In one thing, then, we are agreed,—to reject him.

Miss Hardcastle. Yes—but upon conditions. For if you should find him less impudent, and I more presuming; if you find him more respectful, and I more importunate—

I don't know—the fellow is well enough, for a man—
Certainly we don't meet many such at a horse-race in the
country.

Hardcastle. If we should find him so—— But that's
impossible. The first appearance has done my business.
I'm seldom deceived in that.

Miss Hardcastle. And yet there may be many good qualities under that first appearance.

Hardcastle. Ay, when a girl finds a fellow's outside to
her taste, she then sets about guessing the rest of his
furniture. With her, a smooth face stands for good sense,
and a genteel figure for every virtue.

Miss Hardcastle. I hope, Sir, a conversation begun with
a compliment to my good sense, won't end with a sneer at
my understanding !

Hardcastle. Pardon me, Kate. But if young Mr. Brazen
can find the art of reconciling contradictions, he may please
us both, perhaps.

Miss Hardcastle. And as one of us must be mistaken,
what if we go to make farther discoveries ?

Hardcastle. Agreed. But, depend on't, I'm in the
right.

Miss Hardcastle. And, depend on't, I'm not much in the
wrong.   [*Exeunt.*

Enter Tony, running in with a casket.

Tony. Ecod ! I have got them. Here they are. My
cousin Con's necklaces, bobs and all. My mother shan't
cheat the poor souls out of their fortin neither. O my
genus, is that you ?

Enter Hastings.

Hastings. My dear friend, how have you managed with
your mother ? I hope you have amused her with pretending love for your cousin, and that you are willing to
be reconciled at last ? Our horses will be refreshed in a
short time, and we shall soon be ready to set off.

Tony. And here's something to bear your charges by
the way—(*giving the casket*)—your sweetheart's jewels.
Keep them ; and hang those, I say, that would rob you of
one of them.

Hastings. But how have you procured them from your mother?

Tony. Ask me no questions, and I'll tell you no fibs. I procured them by the rule of thumb. If I had not a key to every drawer in mother's bureau, how could I go to the alehouse so often as I do? An honest man may rob himself of his own at any time.

Hastings. Thousands do it every day. But, to be plain with you, Miss Neville is endeavouring to procure them from her aunt this very instant. If she succeeds, it will be the most delicate way, at least, of obtaining them.

Tony. Well, keep them, till you know how it will be. But I know how it will be well enough;—she'd as soon part with the only sound tooth in her head.

Hastings. But I dread the effects of her resentment, when she finds she has lost them.

Tony. Never you mind her resentment, leave *me* to manage that. I don't value her resentment the bounce of a cracker. Zounds! here they are. Morrice! Prance!

[*Exit Hastings.*

Enter Mrs. Hardcastle and Miss Neville.

Mrs. Hardcastle. Indeed, Constance, you amaze me. Such a girl as you want jewels! It will be time enough for jewels, my dear, twenty years hence, when your beauty begins to want repairs.

Miss Neville. But what will repair beauty at forty, will certainly improve it at twenty, Madam.

Mrs. Hardcastle. Yours, my dear, can admit of none. That natural blush is beyond a thousand ornaments. Besides, child, jewels are quite out at present. Don't you see half the ladies of our acquaintance, my Lady Kill-day-light, and Mrs. Crump, and the rest of them, carry their jewels to town, and bring nothing but paste and marcasites back.

Miss Neville. But who knows, Madam, but somebody that shall be nameless would like me best with all my little finery about me?

Mrs. Hardcastle. Consult your glass, my dear, and then see if, with such a pair of eyes, you want any better sparklers. What do you think, Tony, my dear? Does your cousin Con want any jewels, in your eyes, to set off her beauty?

Tony. That's as thereafter may be.

Miss Neville. My dear aunt, if you knew how it would oblige me.

Mrs. Hardcastle. A parcel of old-fashioned rose and table-cut things. They would make you look like the court of King Solomon at a puppet-show. Besides, I believe, I can't readily come at them. They may be missing for aught I know to the contrary.

Tony. (*Apart to Mrs. Hardcastle.*) Then why don't you tell her so at once, as she's so longing for them? Tell her they're lost; it's the only way to quiet her. Say they're lost, and call me to bear witness.

Mrs. Hardcastle. (*Apart to Tony.*) You know, my dear, I'm only keeping them for you. So if I say they're gone, you'll bear me witness, will you? He! he! he!

Tony. Never fear me. Ecod! I'll say I saw them taken out with my own eyes.

Miss Neville. I desire them but for a day, Madam—just to be permitted to show them as relics, and then they may be locked up again.

Mrs. Hardcastle. To be plain with you, my dear Constance; if I could find them you should have them. They're missing, I assure you. Lost, for aught I know; but we must have patience wherever they are.

Miss Neville. I'll not believe it; this is but a shallow pretence to deny me. I know they are too valuable to be so slightly kept, and as you are to answer for the loss——

Mrs. Hardcastle. Don't be alarmed, Constance. If they be lost, I must restore an equivalent. But my son knows they are missing, and not to be found.

Tony. That I can bear witness to. They are missing, and not to be found; I'll take my oath on't.

Mrs. Hardcastle. You must learn resignation, my dear; for though we lose our fortune, yet we should not lose our patience. See me, how calm I am.

Miss Neville. Ay, people are generally calm at the misfortunes of others.

Mrs. Hardcastle. Now, I wonder a girl of your good

sense should waste a thought upon such trumpery. We
shall soon find them; and in the meantime you shall
make use of my garnets till your jewels be found.

Miss Neville. I detest garnets.

Mrs. Hardcastle. The most becoming things in the world
to set off a clear complexion. You have often seen how
well they look upon me. You shall have them.   [*Exit.*

Miss Neville. I dislike them of all things. You shan't
stir.—Was ever any thing so provoking, to mislay my
own jewels, and force me to wear her trumpery.

Tony. Don't be a fool. If she gives you the garnets,
take what you can get. The jewels are your own already.
I have stolen them out of her bureau, and she does not
know it. Fly to your spark; he'll tell you more of the
matter. Leave me to manage her.

Miss Neville. My dear cousin!

Tony. Vanish. She's here, and has missed them already.
[*Exit Miss Neville.*] Zounds! how she fidgets and spits
about like a catherine wheel!

Enter Mrs. Hardcastle.

Mrs. Hardcastle. Confusion! thieves! robbers! We are
cheated, plundered, broke open, undone.

Tony. What's the matter, what's the matter, mamma?
I hope nothing has happened to any of the good family?

Mrs. Hardcastle. We are robbed! My bureau has been
broken open, the jewels taken out, and I'm undone.

Tony. Oh! is that all? Ha! ha! ha! By the laws, I
never saw it better acted in my life. Ecod, I thought you
was ruined in earnest, ha! ha! ha!

Mrs. Hardcastle. Why, boy, I *am* ruined in earnest. My
bureau has been broken open, and all taken away.

Tony. Stick to that, ha! ha! ha! stick to that. I'll
bear witness, you know! call me to bear witness.

Mrs. Hardcastle. I tell you, Tony, by all that's precious,
the jewels are gone, and I shall be ruined for ever.

Tony. Sure I know they are gone, and I am to say so.

Mrs. Hardcastle. My dearest Tony, but hear me. They're
gone, I say.

Tony. By the laws, mamma, you make me for to laugh,
ha! ha! I know who took them well enough, ha! ha! ha!

Mrs. Hardcastle. Was there ever such a blockhead, that can't tell the difference between jest and earnest! I tell you I'm not in jest, booby.

Tony. That's right, that's right; you must be in a bitter passion, and then nobody will suspect either of us. I'll bear witness that they are gone.

Mrs. Hardcastle. Was there ever such a cross-grained brute, that won't hear me! Can you bear witness that you're no better than a fool? Was ever poor woman so beset with fools on one hand, and thieves on the other!

Tony. I can bear witness to that.

Mrs. Hardcastle. Bear witness again, you blockhead, you, and I'll turn you out of the room directly. My poor niece, what will become of her! Do you laugh, you unfeeling brute, as if you enjoyed my distress?

Tony. I can bear witness to that.

Mrs. Hardcastle. Do you insult me, monster? I'll teach you to vex your mother, I will!

Tony. I can bear witness to that. (*He runs off, she follows him.*)

Enter Miss Hardcastle and Maid.

Miss Hardcastle. What an unaccountable creature is that brother of mine, to send them to the house as an inn, ha! ha! I don't wonder at his impudence.

Maid. But what is more, Madam, the young gentleman, as you passed by in your present dress, asked me if you were the bar-maid? He mistook you for the bar-maid, Madam!

Miss Hardcastle. Did he? Then, as I live, I'm resolved to keep up the delusion. Tell me, Pimple, how do you like my present dress? Don't you think I look something like Cherry in the *Beaux' Stratagem?*

Maid. It's the dress, Madam, that every lady wears in the country, but when she visits or receives company.

Miss Hardcastle. And are you sure he does not remember my face or person?

Maid. Certain of it.

Miss Hardcastle. I vow I thought so; for though we spoke for some time together, yet his fears were such that

he never once looked up during the interview. Indeed, if
he had, my bonnet would have kept him from seeing me.

Maid. But what do you hope from keeping him in his
mistake?

Miss Hardcastle. In the first place, I shall be *seen*, and
that is no small advantage to a girl who brings her face
to market.   Then I shall perhaps make an acquaintance,
and that's no small victory gained over one who never
addresses any but the wildest of her sex.   But my chief
aim is to take my gentleman off his guard, and, like an
invisible champion of romance, examine the giant's force
before I offer to combat.

Maid. But are you sure you can act your part, and disguise your voice so that he may mistake that, as he has
already mistaken your person?

Miss Hardcastle. Never fear me. I think I have got the
true bar cant—Did your honour call?—Attend the Lion
there.—Pipes and tobacco for the Angel.—The Lamb has
been outrageous this half hour.

Maid. It will do, Madam. But he's here. [*Exit Maid.*

Enter Marlow.

Marlow. What a bawling in every part of the house! I
have scarce a moment's repose. If I go to the best room,
there I find my host and his story; if I fly to the gallery,
there we have my hostess with her curtsey down to the
ground. I have at last got a moment to myself, and now
for recollection.   [*Walks and muses.*

Miss Hardcastle. Did you call, Sir?   Did your honour
call?

Marlow. (*Musing.*) As for Miss Hardcastle, she's too
grave and sentimental for me.

Miss Hardcastle. Did your honour call?

[*She still places herself before him, he turning away.*

Marlow. No, child, (*Musing.*) Besides, from the glimpse
I had of her, I think she squints.

Miss Hardcastle. I'm sure, Sir, I heard the bell ring.

Marlow. No, no, (*Musing.*) I have pleased my father,
however, by coming down, and I'll to-morrow please
myself by returning. (*Taking out his tablets and perusing.*)

Miss Hardcastle. Perhaps the other gentleman called, Sir?

Marlow. I tell you, no.

Miss Hardcastle. I should be glad to know, Sir: we have such a parcel of servants.

Marlow. No, no, I tell you, (*Looks full in her face.*) Yes, child, I think I did call. I wanted—I wanted—I vow, ♥ child, you are vastly handsome.

Miss Hardcastle. O la, Sir, you'll make one ashamed.

Marlow. Never saw a more sprightly malicious eye. Yes, yes, my dear, I did call. Have you got any of your —a—what d' ye call it, in the house?

Miss Hardcastle. No, Sir, we have been out of that these ten days.

Marlow. One may call in this house, I find, to very little purpose. Suppose I should call for a taste, just by way of trial, of the nectar of your lips, perhaps I might be disappointed in that too.

Miss Hardcastle. Nectar! nectar! That's a liquor there's no call for in these parts. French, I suppose. We keep no French wines here, Sir.

Marlow. Of true English growth, I assure you.

Miss Hardcastle. Then it's odd I should not know it. We brew all sorts of wines in this house, and I have lived here these eighteen years.

Marlow. Eighteen years! Why, one would think, child, you kept the bar before you were born. How old are you?

Miss Hardcastle. Oh, Sir, I must not tell my age. They say women and music should never be dated.

Marlow. To guess at this distance, you can't be much above forty. (*Approaching.*) Yet nearer, I don't think so much. (*Approaching.*) By coming close to some women, they look younger still; but when we come very close indeed—(*Attempting to kiss her.*)

Miss Hardcastle. Pray, Sir, keep your distance. One would think you wanted to know one's age as they do horses, by mark of mouth.

Marlow. I protest, child, you use me extremely ill. If you keep me at this distance, how is it possible you and I can ever be acquainted?

Miss Hardcastle. And who wants to be acquainted with you? I want no such acquaintance, not I. I'm sure you did not treat Miss Hardcastle, that was here awhile ago, in this obstropalous manner. I'll warrant me, before her you looked dashed, and kept bowing to the ground, and talked, for all the world, as if you were before a justice of peace.

Marlow. (*Aside.*) Egad, she has hit it, sure enough! (*To her.*) In awe of her, child? Ha! ha! ha! A mere awkward, squinting thing! No, no. I find you don't know me. I laughed and rallied her a little; but I was unwilling to be too severe. No, I could not be too severe, curse me?

Miss Hardcastle. Oh, then, Sir, you are a favourite, I find, among the ladies?

Marlow. Yes, my dear, a great favourite. And yet, hang me, I don't see what they find in me to follow. At the Ladies' Club in town I'm called their agreeable Rattle. Rattle, my child, is not my real name, but one I'm known by. My name is Solomons; Mr. Solomons, my dear, at your service. (*Offering to salute her.*)

Miss Hardcastle. Hold, Sir; you are introducing me to your club, not to yourself. And you're so great a favourite there, you say?

Marlow. Yes, my dear. There's Mrs. Mantrap, Lady Betty Blackleg, the Countess of Sligo, Mrs. Langhorns, old Miss Biddy Buckskin,[1] and your humble servant, keep up the spirit of the place.

Miss Hardcastle. Then it's a very merry place, I suppose?

[1] Horace Walpole, writing to Lady Ossory, March 27, 1773, says this name was originally Rachael Buckskin, and now meant for Miss Lloyd:—"Miss Loyd is in the new play by the name of Rachael Buckskin, though he has altered it in the printed copies. Somebody wrote for her a very sensible reproof to him [Goldsmith], only it ended in an indecent *grossièreté*. However, the fool took it seriously, and wrote a most dull and scurrilous answer; but, luckily for him, Mr. Beauclerk and Mr. Garrick intercepted it."—See Walpole's 'Letters.' The club satirized was a club for ladies and gentlemen, which Walpole, in another letter to Lady Ossory (Dec. 14, 1771), speaks of as "our Albemarle Street Club." Walpole was a member. He said of Goldsmith's comedy generally that it was "wretched" and "low," though he confessed that it "makes you laugh very much."—ED.

Marlow. Yes, as merry as cards, suppers, wine, and old women can make us.

Miss Hardcastle. And their agreeable Rattle, ha! ha! ha!

Marlow. (*Aside.*) Egad! I don't quite like this chit. She looks knowing, methinks. You laugh, child!

Miss Hardcastle. I can't but laugh to think what time they all have for minding their work, or their family.

Marlow. (*Aside.*) All's well; she don't laugh at me. (*To her.*) Do *you* ever work, child?

Miss Hardcastle. Ay, sure. There's not a screen or a quilt in the whole house but what can bear witness to that.

Marlow. Odso! then you must show me your embroidery. I embroider and draw patterns myself a little. If you want a judge of your work, you must apply to me. (*Seizing her hand.*)

Miss Hardcastle. Ay, but the colours don't look well by candle-light. You shall see all in the morning. (*Struggling.*)

Marlow. And why not now, my angel? Such beauty fires beyond the power of resistance.—Pshaw! the father here! My old luck: I never nicked seven that I did not throw ames ace three times following.[1]   [*Exit Marlow.*

Enter Hardcastle, who stands in surprise.

Hardcastle. So, Madam. So I find this is your modest lover. This is your humble admirer, that kept his eyes fixed on the ground, and only adored at humble distance. Kate, Kate, art thou not ashamed to deceive your father so?

Miss Hardcastle. Never trust me, dear papa, but he's still the modest man I first took him for; you'll be convinced of it as well as I.

Hardcastle. By the hand of my body, I believe his impudence is infectious! Didn't I see him seize your hand? Didn't I see him haul you about like a milk-maid? And now you talk of his respect and his modesty, forsooth!

---

[1] Ames ace, or ambs ace, is two aces thrown at the same time on two dice. As seven is the main, to throw ames ace thrice running, when the player nicks, that is, hazards his money on seven, is singularly bad luck.—B.

Miss Hardcastle. But if I shortly convince you of his modesty, that he has only the faults that will pass off with time, and the virtues that will improve with age, I hope you'll forgive him.

Hardcastle. The girl would actually make one run mad! I tell you I'll not be convinced. I am convinced. He has scarce been three hours in the house, and he has already encroached on all my prerogatives. You may like his impudence, and call it modesty; but my son-in-law, Madam, must have very different qualifications.

Miss Hardcastle. Sir, I ask but this night to convince you.

Hardcastle. You shall not have half the time, for I have thoughts of turning him out this very hour.

Miss Hardcastle. Give me that hour, then, and I hope to satisfy you.

Hardcastle. Well, an hour let it be then. But I'll have no trifling with your father. All fair and open, do you mind me?

Miss Hardcastle. I hope, Sir, you have ever found me to that I considered your commands as my pride; for your kindness is such, that my duty, as yet, has been inclination.

[*Exeunt.*

ACT IV.

[SCENE—A ROOM IN MR. HARDCASTLE'S HOUSE.]

Enter Hastings and Miss Neville.

Hastings. You surprise me: Sir Charles Marlow expected here this night! Where have you had your information?

Miss Neville. You may depend upon it. I just saw his letter to Mr. Hardcastle, in which he tells him he intends setting out a few hours after his son.

Hastings. Then, my Constance, all must be completed before he arrives. He knows me; and should he find me here, would discover my name, and, perhaps, my designs, to the rest of the family.

Miss Neville. The jewels, I hope, are safe?

Hastings. Yes, yes. I have sent them to Marlow, who keeps the keys of our baggage. In the meantime, I'll go to prepare matters for our elopement. I have had the Squire's promise of a fresh pair of horses; and if I should not see him again, will write him further directions.

[Exit.

Miss Neville. Well, success attend you! In the meantime, I'll go amuse my aunt with the old pretence of a violent passion for my cousin.   *[Exit.*

Enter Marlow, followed by a Servant.

Marlow. I wonder what Hastings could mean by sending me so valuable a thing as a casket to keep for him, when he knows the only place I have is the seat of a post-coach at an inn door. Have you deposited the casket with the landlady, as I ordered you? Have you put it into her own hands?

Servant. Yes, your honour.

Marlow. She said she'd keep it safe, did she?

Servant. Yes; she said she'd keep it safe enough. She asked me how I came by it; and she said she had a great mind to make me give an account of myself.

[Exit Servant.

Marlow. Ha! ha! ha! They're safe, however. What an unaccountable set of beings have we got amongst! This little bar-maid, though, runs in my head most strangely, and drives out the absurdities of all the rest of the family. She's mine, she must be mine, or I'm greatly mistaken.

Enter Hastings.

Hastings. Bless me! I quite forgot to tell her that I intended to prepare at the bottom of the garden. Marlow here, and in spirits too!

Marlow. Give me joy, George! Crown me: shadow me with laurels! Well, George, after all, we modest fellows don't want for success among the women.

Hastings. Some women, you mean. But what success has your honour's modesty been crowned with now, that it grows so insolent upon us?

Marlow. Didn't you see the tempting, brisk, lovely little thing, that runs about the house with a bunch of keys to its girdle?

Hastings. Well! and what then?

Marlow. She's mine, you rogue, you. Such fire, such motion, such eyes, such lips—but, egad! she would not let me kiss them though.

Hastings. But are you so sure, so very sure of her?

Marlow. Why, man, she talked of showing me her work above stairs, and I am to approve[1] the pattern.

Hastings. But how can *you*, Charles, go about to rob a woman of her honour?

Marlow. Pshaw! pshaw! We all know the honour of the bar-maid of an inn. I don't intend to rob her, take my word for it; there's nothing in this house I shan't honestly pay for.

Hastings. I believe the girl has virtue.

Marlow. And if she has, I should be the last man in the world that would attempt to corrupt it.

Hastings. You have taken care, I hope, of the casket I sent you to lock up. It's in safety?

Marlow. Yes, yes; it's safe enough. I have taken care of it. But how could you think the seat of a post-coach at an inn-door a place of safety? Ah! numskull! I have taken better precautions for you than you did for yourself. —I have——

Hastings. What?

Marlow. I have sent it to the landlady to keep for you.

Hastings. To the landlady!

Marlow. The landlady.

Hastings. You did?

Marlow. I did. She's to be answerable for its forthcoming, you know.

Hastings. Yes, she'll bring it forth, with a witness.

Marlow. Wasn't I right? I believe you'll allow that I acted prudently upon this occasion?

Hastings. (*Aside.*) He must not see my uneasiness.

Marlow. You seem a little disconcerted though, me-thinks. Sure nothing has happened?

[1] The early editions have "improve." Bp. Percy's edition has "approve." —ED.

Hastings. No, nothing. Never was in better spirits in all my life. And so you left it with the landlady, who, no doubt, very readily undertook the charge ?

Marlow. Rather too readily; for she not only kept the casket, but, through her great precaution, was going to keep the messenger too. Ha! ha! ha!

Hastings. He! he! he! They're safe, however.

Marlow. As a guinea in a miser's purse.

Hastings. (*Aside.*) So now all hopes of fortune are at an end, and we must set off without it. (*To him.*) Well, Charles, I'll leave you to your meditations on the pretty bar-maid, and, he! he! he! may you be as successful for yourself as you have been for me!   [*Exit.*

Marlow. Thank ye, George: I ask no more. Ha! ha! ha!

Enter Hardcastle.

Hardcastle. I no longer know my own house. It's turned all topsy-turvy. His servants have got drunk already. I'll bear it no longer; and yet, from my respect for his father, I'll be calm. (*To him.*) Mr. Marlow, your servant. I'm your very humble servant. (*Bowing low.*)

Marlow. Sir, your humble servant. (*Aside.*) What's to be the wonder now ?

Hardcastle. I believe, Sir, you must be sensible, Sir, that no man alive ought to be more welcome than your father's son, Sir. I hope you think so ?

Marlow. I do, from my soul, Sir. I don't want much entreaty. I generally make my father's son welcome wherever he goes.

Hardcastle. I believe you do, from my soul, Sir. But though I say nothing to your own conduct, that of your servants is insufferable. Their manner of drinking is setting a very bad example in this house, I assure you.

Marlow. I protest, my very good Sir, that is no fault of mine. If they don't drink as they ought, *they* are to blame. I ordered them not to spare the cellar. I did, I assure you. (*To the side scene.*) Here, let one of my servants come up. (*To Hardcastle.*) My positive directions were, that, as I did not drink myself, they should make up for my deficiencies below.

Hardcastle. Then they had your orders for what they do! I'm satisfied!

✓   *Marlow.* They had, I assure you. You shall hear from one of themselves.

Enter Servant, drunk.

Marlow. You, Jeremy! Come forward, sirrah! What were my orders? Were you not told to drink freely, and call for what you thought fit, for the good of the house?

Hardcastle. (*Aside.*) I begin to lose my patience!

Jeremy. Please your honour, liberty and Fleet-Street for ever! Though I'm but a servant, I'm as good as another man. I'll drink for no man before supper, Sir, dammy! Good liquor will sit upon a good supper, but a good supper will not sit upon——hiccup——upon my conscience, Sir.
[*Exit.*

Marlow. You see, my old friend, the fellow is as drunk as he can possibly be. I don't know what you'd have more, unless you'd have the poor devil soused in a beer-barrel.

Hardcastle. Zounds, he'll drive me distracted, if I contain myself any longer! Mr. Marlow: Sir; I have submitted to your insolence for more than four hours, and I see no likelihood of its coming to an end. I'm now resolved to be master here, Sir, and I desire that you and your drunken pack may leave my house directly.

✓   *Marlow.* Leave your house!—Sure you jest, my good friend? What! when I'm doing what I can to please you?

Hardcastle. I tell you, Sir, you don't please me; so I desire you'll leave my house.

Marlow. Sure you cannot be serious? at this time o' night, and such a night! You only mean to banter me.

Hardcastle. I tell you, Sir, I'm serious! And now that my passions are roused, I say this house is mine, Sir; this house is mine, and I command you to leave it directly!

Marlow. Ha! ha! ha! A puddle in a storm. I shan't stir a step, I assure you. (*In a serious tone.*) This your house, fellow! It's my house. This is my house. Mine while I choose to stay. What right have you to bid me leave this house, Sir? I never met with such impudence, curse me; never in my whole life before.

Hardcastle. Nor I, confound me if ever I did ! To come
to my house, to call for what he likes, to turn me out of
my own chair, to insult the family, to order his servants
to get drunk, and then to tell me, " This house is mine,
Sir !" By all that's impudent, it makes me laugh. Ha !
ha ! ha ! Pray, Sir, (*bantering*) as you take the house, what
think you of taking the rest of the furniture ? There's a
pair of silver candlesticks, and there's a fire-screen, and
here's a pair of brazen-nosed bellows, perhaps you may
take a fancy to them ?

Marlow. Bring me your bill, Sir; bring me your bill,
and let's make no more words about it.

Hardcastle. There are a set of prints, too. What think
you of the *Rake's Progress*, for your own apartment ?

Marlow. Bring me your bill, I say; and I'll leave you
and your infernal house directly.

Hardcastle. Then there's a mahogany table that you may
see your own face in.

Marlow. My bill, I say.

Hardcastle. I had forgot the great chair, for your own
particular slumbers, after a hearty meal.

Marlow. Zounds ! bring me my bill, I say, and let's hear
no more on't.

Hardcastle. Young man, young man, from your father's
letter to me, I was taught to expect a well-bred, modest
man as a visitor here, but now I find him no better than
a coxcomb and a bully ; but he will be down here presently, and shall hear more of it.   *[Exit.*

Marlow. How's this ! Sure I have not mistaken the
house. Every thing looks like an inn; the servants cry,
" coming "; the attendance is awkward; the bar-maid, too,
to attend us. But she's here, and will farther inform me.
Whither so fast, child ? A word with you.

Enter Miss Hardcastle.

Miss Hardcastle. Let it be short then. I'm in a hurry.
(*Aside.*) I believe he begins to find out his mistake. But
it's too soon quite to undeceive him.

Marlow. Pray, child, answer me one question. What
are you, and what may your business in this house be ?

Miss Hardcastle. A relation of the family, Sir.

Marlow. What, a poor relation?

Miss Hardcastle. Yes, Sir; a poor relation, appointed to keep the keys, and to see that the guests want nothing in my power to give them.

Marlow. That is, you act as the bar-maid of this inn.

Miss Hardcastle. Inn! O law!——What brought that into your head? One of the best families in the county keep an inn!—Ha! ha! ha! old Mr. Hardcastle's house an inn!

Marlow. Mr. Hardcastle's house! Is this Mr. Hardcastle's house, child?

Miss Hardcastle. Ay, sure. Whose else should it be?

Marlow. So then, all's out, and I have been damnably imposed on. Oh, confound my stupid head, I shall be laughed at over the whole town! I shall be stuck up in caricatura in all the print-shops—The *Dullissimo-Maccaroni.* To mistake this house of all others for an inn, and my father's old friend for an inn-keeper! What a swaggering puppy must he take me for! What a silly puppy do I find myself! There, again, may I be hang'd, my dear, but I mistook you for the bar-maid.

Miss Hardcastle. Dear me! dear me! I'm sure there's nothing in my behaviour to put me upon a level with one of that stamp.

Marlow. Nothing, my dear, nothing. But I was in for a list of blunders, and could not help making you a subscriber. My stupidity saw every thing the wrong way. I mistook your assiduity for assurance, and your simplicity for allurement. But it's over—this house I no more show my face in.

Miss Hardcastle. I hope, Sir, I have done nothing to disoblige you. I'm sure I should be sorry to affront any gentleman who has been so polite, and said so many civil things to me. I'm sure I should be sorry (*pretending to cry*) if he left the family upon my account. I'm sure I should be sorry people said any thing amiss, since I have no fortune but my character.

Marlow. (*Aside.*) By Heaven! she weeps. This is the first mark of tenderness I ever had from a modest woman, and it touches me. (*To her.*) Excuse me, my lovely girl;

you are the only part of the family I leave with reluctance. But, to be plain with you, the difference of our birth, fortune, and education, make an honourable connection impossible; and I can never harbour a thought of seducing simplicity that trusted in my honour, of bringing ruin upon one, whose only fault was being too lovely.

Miss Hardcastle. (*Aside.*) Generous man ! I now begin to admire him. (*To him.*) But I am sure my family is as good as Miss Hardcastle's; and though I'm poor, that's no great misfortune to a contented mind ; and until this moment, I never thought that it was bad to want fortune.

Marlow. And why now, my pretty simplicity ?

Miss Hardcastle. Because it puts me at a distance from one, that if I had a thousand pounds, I would give it all to.

Marlow. (*Aside.*) This simplicity bewitches me so, that if I stay I'm undone. I must make one bold effort, and leave her. (*To her.*) Your partiality in my favour, my dear, touches me most sensibly; and were I to live for my- self alone, I could easily fix my choice. But I owe too much to the opinion of the world, too much to the authority of a father ; so that—I can scarcely speak it—it affects me.— Farewell. [*Exit.*

Miss Hardcastle. I never knew half his merit till now. He shall not go, if I have power or art to detain him. I'll still preserve the character in which I stoop'd to conquer, but will undeceive my papa, who, perhaps, may laugh him out of his resolution. [*Exit.*

Enter Tony and Miss Neville.

Tony. Ay, you may steal for yourselves the next time. I have done my duty. She has got the jewels again, that's a sure thing ; but she believes it was all a mistake of the servants.

Miss Neville. But, my dear cousin, sure you won't forsake us in this distress ? If she in the least suspects that I am going off, I shall certainly be locked up, or sent to my aunt Pedigree's, which is ten times worse.

Tony. To be sure, aunts of all kinds are damned bad ings. But what can I do ? I have got you a pair of

horses that will fly like Whistle-jacket; and I'm sure
you can't say but I have courted you nicely before her face.
Here she comes. We must court a bit or two more, for
fear she should suspect us.

(They retire, and seem to fondle.)

Enter Mrs. Hardcastle.

Mrs. Hardcastle. Well, I was greatly fluttered, to be
sure. But my son tells me it was all a mistake of the
servants. I shan't be easy, however, till they are fairly
married, and then let her keep her own fortune. But
what do I see? fondling together, as I'm alive. I never
saw Tony so sprightly before. Ah! have I caught you,
my pretty doves? What, billing, exchanging stolen
glances and broken murmurs? Ah!

Tony. As for murmurs, mother, we grumble a little now
and then, to be sure; but there's no love lost between us.

Mrs. Hardcastle. A mere sprinkling, Tony, upon the
flame, only to make it burn brighter.

Miss Neville. Cousin Tony promises to give us more of
his company at home. Indeed, he shan't leave us any more.
It won't leave us, cousin Tony, will it?

Tony. O! it's a pretty creature. No, I'd sooner leave
my horse in a pound, than leave you when you smile upon
one so. Your laugh makes you so becoming.

Miss Neville. Agreeable cousin! Who can help admiring
that natural humour, that pleasant, broad, red, thoughtless, *(patting his cheek)*—ah! it's a bold face!

Mrs. Hardcastle. Pretty innocence!

Tony. I'm sure I always loved cousin Con's hazel eyes,
and her pretty long fingers, that she twists this way and
that over the haspicholls, like a parcel of bobbins.

Mrs. Hardcastle. Ah! he would charm the bird from the
tree. I was never so happy before. My boy takes after
his father, poor Mr. Lumpkin, exactly. The jewels, my
dear Con, shall be yours incontinently. You shall have
them. Isn't he a sweet boy, my dear? You shall be
married to-morrow, and we'll put off the rest of his education, like Dr. Drowsy's sermons, to a fitter opportunity.

Enter Diggory.

Diggory. Where's the Squire? I have got a letter for your worship.

Tony. Give it to my mamma. She reads all my letters first.

Diggory. I had orders to deliver it into your own hands.

Tony. Who does it come from?

Diggory. Your worship mun ask that o' the letter itself.

Tony. I could wish to know though, (*turning the letter, and gazing on it.*)

Miss Neville. (*Aside.*) Undone! undone! A letter to him from Hastings: I know the hand. If my aunt sees it, we are ruined for ever. I'll keep her employed a little, if I can. (*To Mrs. Hardcastle.*) But I have not told you, Madam, of my cousin's smart answer just now to Mr. Marlow. We so laugh'd—You must know, Madam—This way a little, for he must not hear us. (*They confer.*)

Tony. (*Still gazing.*) A damn'd cramp piece of penmanship, as ever I saw in my life. I can read your print hand very well; but here there are such handles, and shanks, and dashes, that one can scarce tell the head from the tail. "To Anthony Lumpkin, Esquire." It's very odd, I can read the outside of my letters, where my own name is, well enough. But when I come to open it, it's all——buzz. That's hard—very hard; for the inside of the letter is always the cream of the correspondence.

Mrs. Hardcastle. Ha! ha! ha! Very well, very well. And so my son was too hard for the philosopher?

Miss Neville. Yes, Madam; but you must hear the rest, Madam. A little more this way, or he may hear us. You'll hear how he puzzled him again.

Mrs. Hardcastle. He seems strangely puzzled now himself, methinks.

Tony (*Still gazing.*) A damned up and down hand, as if it was disguised in liquor. (*Reading.*) "Dear sir,"—Ay, that's that. Then there's an M, and a T, and an S, but whether the next be an izzard or an R, confound me, I cannot tell![1]

---

[1] There is a portrait of Quick in this scene, by De Wilde. It shows Tony dressed in the ordinary indoor costume of a country gentleman.

Mrs. Hardcastle. What's that, my dear ; can I give you any assistance ?

Miss Neville. Pray, aunt, let me read it. Nobody reads a cramp hand better than I. (*Twitching the letter from him.*) Do you know who it is from ?

Tony. Can't tell, except from Dick Ginger, the feeder.

Miss Neville. Ay, so it is, (*pretending to read.*) Dear Squire, hoping that you're in health, as I am at this present. The gentlemen of the Shake-bag Club has cut the gentlemen of the Goose Green quite out of feather. The odds——um——odd battle—um—long fighting—um—here, here, it's all about cocks and fighting ; it's of no consequence—here, put it up, put it up. (*Thrusting the crumpled letter upon him.*)

Tony. But I tell you, miss, it's of all the consequence in the world. I would not lose the rest of it for a guinea. Here, mother, do you make it out. Of no consequence !

[*Giving Mrs. Hardcastle the letter.*

Mrs. Hardcastle. How's this ! (*reads,*) " Dear Squire, I'm now waiting for Miss Neville, with a postchaise and pair, at the bottom of the garden, but I find my horses yet unable to perform the journey. I expect you'll assist us with a pair of fresh horses, as you promised. Despatch is necessary, as the hag "—ay, the hag—" your mother, will otherwise suspect us. Yours, Hastings." Grant me patience : I shall run distracted ! My rage chokes me !

Miss Neville. I hope, Madam, you'll suspend your resentment for a few moments, and not impute to me any impertinence, or sinister design, that belongs to another.

Mrs. Hardcastle. (*Curtsying very low.*) Fine spoken, Madam, you are most miraculously polite and engaging, and quite the very pink of courtesy and circumspection, Madam. (*Changing her tone.*) And you, you great ill-fashioned oaf, with scarce sense enough to keep your mouth shut,—were you, too, joined against me ? But I'll defeat all your plots in a moment. As for you, Madam, since you have got a pair of fresh horses ready, it would be cruel to disappoint them. So, if you please, instead of running away with your spark, prepare, this very moment, to run off with *me*.

Mr. Buckstone and Mr. Lionel Brough, the two most famous Tonys of our time, dressed the character in hunting costume throughout.—ED.

Your old aunt Pedigree will keep you secure, I'll warrant me. You too, Sir, may mount your horse, and guard us upon the way.—Here, Thomas, Roger, Diggory!—I'll show you, that I wish you better than you do yourselves.

[Exit.

Miss Neville. So now I'm completely ruined.

Tony. Ay, that's a sure thing.

Miss Neville. What better could be expected, from being connected with such a stupid fool—and after all the nods and signs I made him.

Tony. By the laws, miss, it was your own cleverness, and not my stupidity, that did your business! You were so nice and so busy with your Shake-bags and Goose-Greens, that I thought you could never be making believe.

Enter Hastings.

Hastings. So, Sir, I find by my servant, that you have shown my letter, and betrayed us. Was this well done, young gentleman?

Tony. Here's another! Ask miss, there, who betrayed you. Ecod! it was her doing, not mine.

Enter Marlow.

Marlow. So, I have been finely used here among you. Rendered contemptible, driven into ill manners, despised, insulted, laughed at.

Tony. Here's another! We shall have old Bedlam broke loose presently.

Miss Neville. And there, Sir, is the gentleman to whom we all owe every obligation.

Marlow. What can I say to him? a mere boy, an idiot, whose ignorance and age are a protection.

Hastings. A poor contemptible booby, that would but disgrace correction.

Miss Neville. Yet with cunning and malice enough to make himself merry with all our embarrassments.

Hastings. An insensible cub.

Marlow. Replete with tricks and mischief.

Tony. Baw! damme, but I'll fight you both, one after the other,——with baskets.

II.   T

Marlow. As for him, he's below resentment. But your conduct, Mr. Hastings, requires an explanation : You knew of my mistakes, yet would not undeceive me.

Hastings. Tortured as I am with my own disappointments, is this a time for explanations ? It is not friendly, Mr. Marlow.

Marlow. But, Sir——

Miss Neville. Mr. Marlow, we never kept on your mistake, till it was too late to undeceive you. Be pacified.

Enter Servant.

Servant. My mistress desires you'll get ready immediately, Madam. The horses are putting to. Your hat and things are in the next room. We are to go thirty miles before morning.   [*Exit Servant.*

Miss Neville. Well, well, I'll come presently.

Marlow. (*To Hastings.*) Was it well done, Sir, to assist in rendering me ridiculous ?—To hang me out for the scorn of all my acquaintance? Depend upon it, Sir, I shall expect an explanation.

Hastings. Was it well done, Sir, if you're upon that subject, to deliver what I entrusted to yourself, to the care of another, Sir.

Miss Neville. Mr. Hastings ! Mr. Marlow ! Why will you increase my distress by this groundless dispute ? I implore—I intreat you——

Enter Servant.

Servant. Your cloak, Madam. My mistress is impatient.   [*Exit Servant.*

Miss Neville. I come. Pray, be pacified. If I leave you thus, I shall die with apprehension.

Enter Servant.

Servant. Your fan, muff, and gloves, Madam. The horses are waiting.   [*Exit Servant.*

Miss Neville. O, Mr. Marlow ! if you knew what a scene of constraint and ill-nature lies before me, I am sure would convert your resentment into pity !

Marlow. I'm so distracted with a variety of passions, that I don't know what I do. Forgive me, Madam. George, forgive me. You know my hasty temper, and should not exasperate it.

Hastings. The torture of my situation is my only excuse.

Miss Neville. Well, my dear Hastings, if you have that esteem for me that I think—that I am sure you have, your constancy for three years will but increase the happiness of our future connection. If——

Mrs. Hardcastle. (*Within.*) Miss Neville! Constance! why Constance, I say!

Miss Neville. I'm coming! Well, constancy; remember, constancy is the word.   [*Exit.*

Hastings. My heart! how can I support this? To be so near happiness, and such happiness!

Marlow. (*To Tony.*) You see now, young gentleman, the effects of your folly. What might be amusement to you, is here disappointment, and even distress.

Tony. (*From a reverie.*) Ecod, I have hit it: it's here! Your hands. Yours, and yours, my poor Sulky. My boots there, ho!—Meet me, two hours hence, at the bottom of the garden; and if you don't find Tony Lumpkin a more good-natured fellow than you thought for, I'll give you leave to take my best horse, and Bet Bouncer into the bargain. Come along. My boots, ho!   [*Exeunt.*

ACT V.

SCENE CONTINUES.

Enter Hastings and Servant.

Hastings. You saw the old lady and Miss Neville drive off, you say?

Servant. Yes, your honour. They went off in a post-coach, and the young squire went on horseback. They're thirty miles off by this time.

Hastings. Then all my hopes are over!

Servant. Yes, Sir. Old Sir Charles is arrived. He and

the old gentleman of the house have been laughing at Mr.
Marlow's mistake this half hour. They are coming this
way.   *[Exit.*

Hastings. Then I must not be seen. So now to my
fruitless appointment at the bottom of the garden. This
is about the time.   *[Exit.*

Enter Sir Charles Marlow and Hardcastle.

Hardcastle. Ha! ha! ha! The peremptory tone in
which he sent forth his sublime commands!

Sir Charles. And the reserve with which I suppose he
treated all your advances.

Hardcastle. And yet he might have seen something in
me above a common inn-keeper, too.

Sir Charles. Yes, Dick, but he mistook you for an uncommon inn-keeper; ha! ha! ha!

Hardcastle. Well, I'm in too good spirits to think of
any thing but joy. Yes, my dear friend, this union of our
families will make our personal friendships hereditary;
and though my daughter's fortune is but small——

Sir Charles. Why, Dick, will you talk of fortune to me?
My son is possessed of more than a competence already,
and can want nothing but a good and virtuous girl to share
his happiness and increase it. If they like each other, as
you say they do——

Hardcastle. *If,* man! I tell you they *do* like each other.
My daughter as good as told me so.

Sir Charles. But girls are apt to flatter themselves, you
know.

Hardcastle. I saw him grasp her hand in the warmest
manner myself; and here he comes to put you out of your
ifs, I warrant him.

Enter Marlow.

Marlow. I come, Sir, once more, to ask pardon for my
strange conduct. I can scarce reflect on my insolence
without confusion.

Hardcastle. Tut, boy, a trifle. You take it too gravely.
An hour or two's laughing with my daughter, will set all
to rights again. She'll never like you the worse for it.

Marlow. Sir, I shall be always proud of her approbation.

Hardcastle. Approbation is but a cold word, Mr. Marlow; if I am not deceived, you have something more than
approbation thereabouts. You take me?

Marlow. Really, Sir, I have not that happiness.

Hardcastle. Come, boy, I'm an old fellow, and know
what's what as well as you that are younger. I know what
has past between you; but, mum!

Marlow. Sure, Sir, nothing has past between us but the
most profound respect on my side, and the most distant
reserve on hers. You don't think, Sir, that my impudence
has been past upon all the rest of the family?

Hardcastle. Impudence! No, I don't say that—not
quite impudence—though girls like to be played with, and
rumpled a little, too, sometimes. But she has told no
tales, I assure you.

Marlow. I never gave her the slightest cause.

Hardcastle. Well, well, I like modesty in its place well
enough; but this is over-acting, young gentleman. You
may be open. Your father and I will like you the better
for it.

Marlow. May I die, Sir, if I ever——

Hardcastle. I tell you, she don't dislike you; and as
I'm sure you like her——

Marlow. Dear Sir—I protest, Sir——

Hardcastle. I see no reason why you should not be
joined as fast as the parson can tie you.

Marlow. But hear me, Sir——

Hardcastle. Your father approves the match, I admire
it; every moment's delay will be doing mischief, so——

Marlow. But why won't you hear me? By all that's
just and true, I never gave Miss Hardcastle the slightest
mark of my attachment, or even the most distant hint to
suspect me of affection. We had but one interview, and
that was formal, modest, and uninteresting.

Hardcastle. (*Aside.*) This fellow's formal, modest impudence is beyond bearing.

Sir Charles. And you never grasped her hand, or made
any protestations?

Marlow. As Heaven is my witness! I came down in

obedience to your commands; I saw the lady without
emotion, and parted without reluctance. I hope you'll
exact no further proofs of my duty, nor prevent me from
leaving a house in which I suffer so many mortifications.

[*Exit.*

Sir Charles. I'm astonished at the air of sincerity with
which he parted.

Hardcastle. And I'm astonished at the deliberate intrepidity of his assurance.

Sir Charles. I dare pledge my life and honour upon his
truth.

Hardcastle. Here comes my daughter, and I would stake
my happiness upon her veracity.

Enter Miss Hardcastle.

Hardcastle. Kate, come hither, child. Answer us sincerely, and without reserve. Has Mr. Marlow made you
any professions of love and affection?

Miss Hardcastle. The question is very abrupt, Sir!
But since you require unreserved sincerity—I think he
has.

Hardcastle. (*To Sir Charles.*) You see.

Sir Charles. And pray, Madam, have you and my son
had more than one interview?

Miss Hardcastle. Yes, Sir, several.

Hardcastle (*To Sir Charles.*) You see.

Sir Charles. But did he profess any attachment?

Miss Hardcastle. A lasting one.

Sir Charles. Did he talk of love?

Miss Hardcastle. Much, Sir.

Sir Charles. Amazing! And all this formally?

Miss Hardcastle. Formally.

Hardcastle. Now, my friend, I hope you are satisfied.

Sir Charles. And how did he behave, Madam?

Miss Hardcastle. As most profest admirers do: said
some civil things of my face; talked much of his want of
merit, and the greatness of mine; mentioned his heart,
gave a short tragedy speech, and ended with pretended
rapture.

Sir Charles. Now I'm perfectly convinced, indeed. I

know his conversation among women to be modest and submissive. This forward, canting, ranting manner by no means describes him, and, I am confident he never sat for the picture.

Miss Hardcastle. Then, what, Sir, if I should convince you to your face of my sincerity? If you and my papa, in about half an hour, will place yourselves behind that screen, you shall hear him declare his passion to me in person.

Sir Charles. Agreed. And if I find him what you describe, all my happiness in him must have an end. [*Exit.*

Miss Hardcastle. And if you don't find him what I describe, I fear my happiness must never have a beginning.

[*Exeunt.*

SCENE CHANGES TO THE BACK OF THE GARDEN.

Enter Hastings.

Hastings. What an idiot am I to wait here for a fellow who probably takes a delight in mortifying me. He never intended to be punctual, and I'll wait no longer. What do I see? It is he! and perhaps with news of my Constance.

Enter Tony, booted and spattered.

Hastings. My honest Squire! I now find you a man of your word. This looks like friendship.

Tony. Ay, I'm your friend, and the best friend you have in the world, if you knew but all. This riding by night, by the bye, is cursedly tiresome. It has shook me worse than the basket of a stage-coach.

Hastings. But how? Where did you leave your fellow-travellers? Are they in safety? Are they housed?

Tony. Five and twenty miles in two hours and a half is no such bad driving. The poor beasts have smoked for it: rabbit me! but I'd rather ride forty miles after a fox, than ten with such *varment.*

Hastings. Well, but where have you left the ladies? I die with impatience.

Tony. Left them! Why, where should I leave them but where I found them?

Hastings. This is a riddle.

Tony. Riddle me this, then. What's that goes round the house, and round the house, and never touches the house?

Hastings. I'm still astray.

Tony. Why, that's it, mon. I have led them astray. By jingo, there's not a pond or a slough within five miles of the place but they can tell the taste of.

Hastings. Ha! ha! ha! I understand: you took them in a round, while they supposed themselves going forward; and so you have at last brought them home again.

Tony. You shall hear. I first took them down Feather-bed Lane, where we stuck fast in the mud. I then rattled them crack over the stones of Up-and-down Hill. I then introduced them to the gibbet on Heavy-tree Heath; and from that, with a circumbendibus, I fairly lodged them in the horse-pond at the bottom of the garden.

Hastings. But no accident, I hope?

Tony. No, no; only mother is confoundedly frightened. She thinks herself forty miles off. She's sick of the journey; and the cattle can scarce crawl. So, if your own horses be ready, you may whip off with cousin, and I'll be bound that no soul here can budge a foot to follow you.

Hastings. My dear friend, how can I be grateful?

Tony. Ay, now it's dear friend! noble Squire! Just now, it was all idiot, cub, and run me through the guts. Damn *your* way of fighting, I say. After we take a knock in this part of the country, we kiss and be friends. But if you had run me through the guts, then I should be dead, and you might go kiss the hangman.

Hastings. The rebuke is just. But I must hasten to relieve Miss Neville. If you keep the old lady employed, I promise to take care of the young one.   [*Exit Hastings.*

Tony. Never fear me. Here she comes. Vanish! She's got from the pond, and draggled up to the waist like a mermaid.

Enter Mrs. Hardcastle.

Mrs. Hardcastle. Oh, Tony, I'm killed! Shook! battered to death! I shall never survive it. That last jolt, that laid us against the quickset hedge, has done my business.

Tony. Alack, mamma! it was all your own fault. You would be for running away by night, without knowing one inch of the way.

Mrs. Hardcastle. I wish we were at home again. I never met so many accidents in so short a journey. Drenched in the mud, overturned in a ditch, stuck fast in a slough, jolted to a jelly, and at last to lose our way! Whereabouts do you think we are, Tony?

Tony. By my guess, we should be upon Crackskull Common, about forty miles from home.

Mrs. Hardcastle. O lud! O lud! the most notorious spot in all the country! We only want a robbery to make a complete night on't.

Tony. Don't be afraid, mamma; don't be afraid. Two of the five that kept here are hanged, and the other three may not find us. Don't be afraid.—Is that a man that's galloping behind us? No, it's only a tree.—Don't be afraid.

Mrs. Hardcastle. The fright will certainly kill me.

Tony. Do you see any thing like a black hat moving behind the thicket?

Mrs. Hardcastle. Oh, death!

Tony. No; it's only a cow. Don't be afraid, mamma; don't be afraid.

Mrs. Hardcastle. As I'm alive, Tony, I see a man coming towards us. Ah! I'm sure on't. If he perceives us, we are undone.

Tony. (*Aside.*) Father-in-law, by all that's unlucky, come to take one of his night walks. (*To her.*) Ah! it's a highwayman with pistols as long as my arm. A damn'd ill-looking fellow!

Mrs. Hardcastle. Good Heaven defend us! He approaches.

Tony. Do you hide yourself in that thicket, and leave me to manage him. If there be any danger, I'll cough, and cry hem. When I cough, be sure to keep close.

[*Mrs. Hardcastle hides behind a tree in the back scene.*

Enter Hardcastle.

Hardcastle. I'm mistaken, or I heard voices of people in want of help. Oh, Tony, is that you? I did not expect you so soon back. Are your mother and her charge in safety?

Tony. Very safe, Sir, at my aunt Pedigree's. Hem.

Mrs. Hardcastle. (*From behind.*) Ah, death! I find there's danger.

Hardcastle. Forty miles in three hours; sure that's too much, my youngster.

Tony. Stout horses and willing minds make short journeys, as they say. Hem.

Mrs. Hardcastle. (*From behind.*) Sure, he'll do the dear boy no harm.

Hardcastle. But I heard a voice here; I should be glad to know from whence it came.

Tony. It was I, Sir, talking to myself, Sir. I was saying that forty miles in four hours was very good going. Hem. As to be sure it was. Hem. I have got a sort of cold by being out in the air. We'll go in, if you please. Hem.

Hardcastle. But if you talked to yourself, you did not answer yourself. I'm certain I heard two voices, and am resolved (*raising his voice*) to find the other out.

Mrs. Hardcastle. (*From behind.*) Oh! he's coming to find me out. Oh!

Tony. What need you go, Sir, if I tell you? Hem. I'll lay down my life for the truth—hem—I'll tell you all, Sir. (*Detaining him.*)

Hardcastle. I tell you I will not be detained. I insist on seeing. It's in vain to expect I'll believe you.

Mrs. Hardcastle. (*Running forward from behind.*) O lud! he'll murder my poor boy, my darling! Here, good gentleman, whet your rage upon me. Take my money, my life, but spare that young gentleman; spare my child, if you have any mercy!

Hardcastle. My wife, as I'm a Christian. From whence can she come? or what does she mean?

Mrs. Hardcastle. (*Kneeling.*) Take compassion on us, good Mr. Highwayman. Take our money, our watches, all we have, but spare our lives. We will never bring you to justice ; indeed we won't, good Mr. Highwayman.

Hardcastle. I believe the woman's out of her senses. What, Dorothy, don't you know me?

Mrs. Hardcastle. Mr. Hardcastle, as I'm alive ! My fears blinded me. But who, my dear, could ████ expected to meet you here, in this frightful place ████ ████ home ? What has brought you to follow us ████

Hardcastle. Sure, Dorothy, you ██ ████ your wits ? So far from home, when you are ████ yards of your own door ! (*To him.*) This is ████ old tricks, you graceless rogue, you. (*To h*████ ou know the gate and the mulberry-tree ? an██ ████ emember the horse-pond, my dear?

Mrs. Hardcastle. Ye██ ████ ember the horse-pond as long as I live ; I ████ ██t my death in it. (*To Tony.*) And is it ████ graceless varlet, I owe all this ? I'll teach ████ e your mother—I will.

Tony. Ecod, ████ ne parish says you have spoiled ✓ me, and so y██ ████ he fruits on't.

Mrs. H█ ████ poil you, I will.

               [*Follows him off the stage.*

Ha█ ████ e's morality, however, in his reply.

                         [*Exit.*

Enter Hastings and Miss Neville.

Hastings. My dear Constance, why will you deliberate th██ █ If we delay a moment, all is lost for ever. Pluck ██ ██tle resolution, and we shall soon be out of the reach ██ █alignity.

██*Neville.* I find it impossible. My spirits are so ██ith the agitations I have suffered, that I am unable ██ any new danger. Two or three years patience will ██ crown us with happiness.

██*ings.* Such a tedious delay is worse than incon-██ Let us fly, my charmer ! Let us date our happi-██om this very moment. Perish fortune ! Love and ██t will increase what we possess beyond a monarch's ██e. Let me prevail !

██*ss Neville.* No, Mr. Hastings, no. Prudence once ██ore comes to my relief, and I will obey its dictates. In

the moment of passion, fortune may be despised, but it
ever produces a lasting repentance. I'm resolved to apply
to Mr. Hardcastle's compassion and justice for redress.

Hastings. But though he had the will, he has not the
power, to relieve.you.

Miss Nevill ─── t he has influence, and upon that I am
resolved to rel

Hastings ─── o hopes. But since you persist, I
must relucta ─── ou.   [*Exeunt.*

─── HANGES.

[SCENE III.—A R ─── HARDCASTLE'S HOUSE.]

Enter Sir Charles ─── *Miss Hardcastle.*

Sir Charles. What a sit ─── in! If what you say
appears, I shall then find a ─── If what he says be
true, I shall then lose one that ─── s, I most wished
for a daughter.

Miss Hardcastle. I am proud o ─── tion; and
to show I merit it, if you place yo ─── irected,
you shall hear his explicit declaration. ─── es.

Sir Charles. I'll to your father, and ─── him to the
appointment.   ·   [*Exit Sir Charles.*

Enter Marlow.

Marlow. Though prepared for setting out, I co ─── ce
more to take leave; nor did I, till this moment, k ───
pain I feel in the separation.

Miss Hardcastle. (*In her own natural manner.*) I
these sufferings cannot be very great, Sir, which
so easily remove. A day or two longer, perhaps
lessen your uneasiness, by showing the little value
you now think proper to regret.

Marlow. (*Aside.*) This girl every moment in
upon me. (*To her.*) It must not be, Madam;
already trifled too long with my heart. My very
begins to submit to my passion. The disparity of
tion and fortune, the anger of a parent, and the con
of my equals, begin to lose their weight; and no

can restore me to myself but this painful effort of resolution.

Miss Hardcastle. Then go, Sir: I'll urge nothing more
to detain you. Though my family be as good as hers you
came down to visit, and my education, I hope, not inferior, what are these advantages without equal affluence?
I must remain contented with the slight approbation of
imputed merit; I must have only the mockery of your
addresses, while all your serious aims are fixed on fortune.

Enter Hardcastle and Sir Charles Marlow, from behind.

Sir Charles. Here, behind this screen.

Hardcastle. Ay, ay; make no noise. I'll engage my Kate
covers him with confusion at last.

Marlow. By heavens! Madam, fortune was ever my
smallest consideration. Your beauty at first caught my
eye; for who could see that without emotion? But every
moment that I converse with you steals in some new
grace, heightens the picture, and gives it stronger expression. What at first seemed rustic plainness, now appears
refined simplicity; what seemed forward assurance, now
strikes me as the result of courageous innocence and conscious virtue.

Sir Charles. What can it mean? He amazes me!

Hardcastle. I told you how it would be. Hush!

Marlow. I am now determined to stay, Madam, and I
have too good an opinion of my father's discernment,
when he sees you, to doubt his approbation.

Miss Hardcastle. No, Mr. Marlow, I will not, cannot
detain you. Do you think I could suffer a connection in
which there is the smallest room for repentance? Do
you think I would take the mean advantage of a transient
passion to load you with confusion? Do you think I
could ever relish that happiness which was acquired by
lessening yours?

Marlow. By all that's good, I can have no happiness
but what's in your power to grant me! Nor shall I ever
feel repentance, but in not having seen your merits before.
I will stay, even contrary to your wishes; and though you
should persist to shun me, I will make my respectful assiduities atone for the levity of my past conduct.

Miss Hardcastle. Sir, I must entreat you'll desist. As our acquaintance began, so let it end, in indifference. I might have given an hour or two to levity; but seriously, Mr. Marlow, do you think I could ever submit to a connection where *I* must appear mercenary, and *you* imprudent? Do you think I could ever catch at the confident addresses of a secure admirer?

Marlow. (*Kneeling.*) Does this look like security? Does this look like confidence? No, Madam, every moment that shows me your merit, only serves to increase my diffidence and confusion. Here let me continue——

— *Sir Charles.* I can hold it no longer. Charles, Charles, how hast thou deceived me! Is this your indifference, your uninteresting conversation?

Hardcastle. Your cold contempt; your formal interview! What have you to say now?

Marlow. That I'm all amazement! What can it mean?

Hardcastle. It means that you can say and unsay things at pleasure: that you can address a lady in private, and deny it in public: that you have one story for us, and another for my daughter.

Marlow. Daughter!—this lady your daughter?

Hardcastle. Yes, Sir, my only daughter—my Kate; whose else should she be?

Marlow. Oh, the devil!

Miss Hardcastle. Yes, Sir, that very identical tall squinting lady you were pleased to take me for; (*curtsying*) she that you addressed as the mild, modest, sentimental man of gravity, and the bold, forward, agreeable Rattle of the Ladies' club. Ha! ha! ha!

Marlow. Zounds! there's no bearing this; it's worse than death!

Miss Hardcastle. In which of your characters, Sir, will you give us leave to address you? As the faltering gentleman, with looks on the ground, that speaks just to be heard, and hates hypocrisy; or the loud confident creature, that keeps it up with Mrs. Mantrap, and old Miss Biddy Buckskin till three in the morning?—Ha! ha! ha!

Marlow. O, curse on my noisy head! I never attempted to be impudent yet that I was not taken down! I must be gone.

Hardcastle. By the hand of my body, but you shall not.
I see it was all a mistake, and I am rejoiced to find it.
You shall not, Sir, I tell you. I know she'll forgive you.
Won't you forgive him, Kate? We'll all forgive you.
Take courage, man.

[*They retire, she tormenting him, to the back scene.*

Enter Mrs. Hardcastle and Tony.

Mrs. Hardcastle. So, so, they're gone off. Let them go,
I care not.

Hardcastle. Who gone?

Mrs. Hardcastle. My dutiful niece and her gentleman,
Mr. Hastings, from town. He who came down with our
modest visitor here.

Sir Charles. Who, my honest George Hastings? As
worthy a fellow as lives, and the girl could not have made
a more prudent choice.

Hardcastle. Then, by the hand of my body, I'm proud
of the connection.

Mrs. Hardcastle. Well, if he has taken away the lady, he
has not taken her fortune; that remains in this family to
console us for her loss.

Hardcastle. Sure, Dorothy, you would not be so mercenary?

Mrs. Hardcastle. Ay, that's my affair, not yours.

Hardcastle. But, you know, if your son, when of age,
refuses to marry his cousin, her whole fortune is then at
her own disposal.

Mrs. Hardcastle. Ay, but he's not of age, and she has
not thought proper to wait for his refusal.

Enter Hastings and Miss Neville.

Mrs. Hardcastle. (*Aside.*) What, returned so soon! I
begin not to like it.

Hastings. (*To Hardcastle.*) For my late attempt to fly off
with your niece, let my present confusion be my punishment. We are now come back, to appeal from your justice
to your humanity. By her father's consent I first paid
her my addresses, and our passions were first founded in
duty.

Miss Neville. Since his death, I have been obliged to stoop to dissimulation to avoid oppression. In an hour of levity, I was ready even to give up my fortune to secure my choice: but I am now recovered from the delusion, and hope from your tenderness what is denied me from a nearer connection.

Mrs. Hardcastle. Pshaw, pshaw! this is all but the whining end of a modern novel.

Hardcastle. Be it what it will, I'm glad they're come back to reclaim their due. Come hither, Tony, boy. Do you refuse this lady's hand, whom I now offer you?

Tony. What signifies my refusing? You know I can't refuse her till I'm of age, father.

Hardcastle. While I thought concealing your age, boy, was likely to conduce to your improvement, I concurred with your mother's desire to keep it secret. But since I find she turns it to a wrong use, I must now declare you have been of age these three months.

Tony. Of age! Am I of age, father?

Hardcastle. Above three months.

Tony. Then you'll see the first use I'll make of my liberty. (*Taking Miss Neville's hand.*) Witness all men by these presents, that I, Anthony Lumpkin, esquire, of BLANK place, refuse you, Constantia Neville, spinster, of no place at all, for my true and lawful wife. So Constance Neville may marry whom she pleases, and Tony Lumpkin is his own man again.[1]

Sir Charles. O brave Squire!

Hastings. My worthy friend!

Mrs. Hardcastle. My undutiful offspring!

Marlow. Joy, my dear George, I give you joy sincerely! And, could I prevail upon my little tyrant here to be less arbitrary, I should be the happiest man alive—if you would return me the favour.

Hastings. (*To Miss Hardcastle.*) Come, Madam, you are

---

[1] A common stage reading of this passage:—" So Constantia Neville may go to the devil," &c., has no warrant in the originals. If Quick, tempted by the rhyme, interpolated this reading, and so gave the "tradition" to later actors, the fact would almost excuse the charges of vulgarity which were brought against the piece by Horace Walpole and others.—ED.

now driven to the very last scene of all your contrivances.
I know you like him, I'm sure he loves you, and you must
and shall have him.

Hardcastle. (*Joining their hands.*) And I say so too.
And, Mr. Marlow, if she makes as good a wife as she has
a daughter, I don't believe you'll ever repent your bargain. So now to supper. To-morrow we shall gather all
the poor of the parish about us, and the Mistakes of the
Night shall be crowned with a merry morning. So, boy,
take her; and, as you have been mistaken in the mistress,
my wish is, that you may never be mistaken in the wife.

[*Exeunt omnes.*

EPILOGUE,

BY DR. GOLDSMITH.

SPOKEN BY MRS. BULKLEY, IN THE CHARACTER OF MISS HARDCASTLE.[1]

WELL, having stoop'd to conquer with success,
And gain'd a husband without aid from dress,
Still, as a bar-maid, I could wish it too,
As I have conquer'd him to conquer you:
And let me say, for all your resolution,
That pretty bar-maids have done execution.
Our life is all a play, compos'd to please;
"We have our exits and our entrances."
The first act shows the simple country maid,
Harmless and young, of ev'ry thing afraid;
Blushes when hired, and, with unmeaning action,
"I hopes as how to give you satisfaction."
Her second act displays a livelier scene,—
Th' unblushing bar-maid of a country inn,
Who whisks about the house, at market caters,
Talks loud, coquets the guests, and scolds the waiters.

---

[1] The original Miss Hardcastle first figured on the stage as Miss
Wilford. Then she played as Mrs. Bulkley; and later as Mrs. Barres
ford. She died in 1792. See also note to the following epilogue.—ED.

Next the scene shifts to town, and there she soars,
The chop-house toast of ogling *connoisseurs*:
On 'squires and cits she there displays her arts,
And on the gridiron broils her lovers' hearts—
And, as she smiles, her triumphs to complete,
Ev'n Common-councilmen forget to eat.
The fourth act shows her wedded to the Squire,
And madam now begins to hold it higher;
Pretends to taste, at operas cries *caro!*
And quits her *Nancy Dawson*[1] for *Che Faro*:
Doats upon dancing, and, in all her pride,
Swims round the room, the Heinel[2] of Cheapside;
Ogles and leers, with artificial skill,
Till, having lost in age the power to kill,
She sits all night at cards, and ogles at spadille.
Such, through our lives, the eventful history—
The fifth and last act still remains for me:
The bar-maid now for your protection prays,
Turns female barrister, and pleads for Bayes.[3]

EPILOGUE,

TO BE SPOKEN IN THE CHARACTER OF TONY LUMPKIN.

By J. CRADOCK, Esq.[4]

WELL—now all's ended—and my comrades gone,
Pray what becomes of mother's nonly son?
A hopeful blade!—in town I'll fix my station,
And try to make a bluster in the nation:
As for my cousin Neville, I renounce her—
Off, in a crack, I'll carry big Bet Bouncer!

---

[1] See the Mrs. Bulkley Epilogue, and its note, in the Poems.—ED.
[2] See p. 112, and note.—ED.
[3] Some editors print "bays." The early editions have "Bayes." Of course bays is meant, but no doubt there is the double meaning which includes *Bayes*, the character in the Duke of Buckingham's 'Rehearsal,' whose name, as Mr. Bolton Corney says, had become synonymous with *dramatist*, and had been so used by Garrick and Colman.—ED.
[4] This came too late to be spoken.—*Note in original.* Joseph Cradock, author of 'Zobeide,' &c., see Poems, p. 95. In Goldsmith's letter to

Why should not I in the great world appear?
I soon shall have a thousand pounds a-year!
No matter what a man may here inherit,
In London—'gad, they've some regard to spirit.
I see the horses prancing up the streets,
And big Bet Bouncer bobs to all she meets;
Then hoiks to jigs and pastimes ev'ry night—
Not to the plays—they say it an't polite:
To Sadler's-Wells, perhaps, or operas go,
And once, by chance, to the roratorio.
Thus here and there, for ever up and down,
We'll set the fashions, too, to half the town;
And then at auctions—money ne'er regard—
Buy pictures, like the great, ten pounds a-yard:
Zounds! we shall make these London gentry say,
We know what's damn'd genteel as well as they!

Cradock, acknowledging the receipt of this epilogue (see Letters in vol. i.), our author simply says that "it could not be used," but "should be printed." Cradock, in his 'Memoirs,' says it was not meant for publication. Cradock also tells a curious story of having revised, or "altered," 'She Stoops to Conquer' for Goldsmith, "in Leicestershire." See the notes to Goldsmith's letters to Cradock in vol. i. In one of these letters Goldsmith tells of some of his troublesome "stage adventures" in connection with the production of 'She Stoops to Conquer.' For two other epilogues intended for this play, see the Poems. Also for a song intended to have been sung by Miss Hardcastle, see p. 110. At this last reference it is shown that Mrs. Bulkley, the original Miss Hardcastle, could not sing. There is a story that the part was meant for Mrs. Abington (the original Lady Teazle, 1777), who could sing. The story, however, is doubtful; and, as it is told by Mr. Forster, partly on the authority of Northcote, it seems certainly wrong. See the following Appendix.—ED.

APPENDIX

TO THIS EDITION OF 'SHE STOOPS TO CONQUER.'

MRS. ABINGTON AND THE PART OF MISS HARDCASTLE.

THE story to the effect that the part of Miss Hardcastle was refused by Mrs. Abington (as mentioned in the note above), seems to need refutation, seeing that it affects both the celebrated actress who is alleged to have made the refusal and the popular actress, Mrs. Bulkley, who really played the part. The story in the first place looks doubtful from the fact that no mention is made of it by Boswell and most of the rest of the numerous gossippers who have retailed so much about Goldsmith's play. Only Northcote, the biographer of Reynolds, tells it, and that some forty years after the play's production. But Mr. Forster, having adopted Northcote's story, and added to it, there seems some chance of its taking root as a popular error. Hence the necessity, as it seems to us, of the following attempted refutation. Mr. Forster says ('Life of Goldsmith,' 1854, vol. ii. p. 369), "Mortification still attended Goldsmith there [at Covent Garden Theatre]. The actors and actresses had taken their tone from the manager. Gentleman Smith threw up Young Marlow; Woodward refused Tony Lumpkin; Mrs. Abington (and this was the greatest blow of all) declined Miss Hard-castle; and in the teeth of his own misgivings, Colman could not contest with theirs. So alarming was the defection, to some of Goldsmith's friends, that they urged the postponement of the comedy. 'No,' he said, giving to his necessity the braver look of independence, 'I'd rather my play were damned by bad players, than merely saved by good acting.'" This, so far as Mrs. Abington is concerned, is founded upon Northcote's 'Life of Sir J. Reynolds,' 1818, vol. i. p. 128, where it is stated that:—"She [Mrs. Abington], however, much offended Goldsmith, at last, by refusing to take the part which he had written on purpose for her, in his comedy of 'She Stoops to Conquer,' which character was, of necessity, performed by another actress, to Goldsmith's great mortification, on the first night's representation." The statement of the refusal, &c., must be wrong, because Mrs. Abington was not of the Covent Garden company at the time, but was, instead, of the rival house, Drury Lane. Of course Goldsmith originally may have had an eye to Mrs. Abington as an impersonator of his Miss Hardcastle; but, after having given up his comedy to Colman for production at Colman's theatre, and waited some months for its production there (see Goldsmith's correspondence with both Colman and Garrick upon the subject in the Letters at the end of our vol. i.), he could hardly have expected Mrs. Abington would play in it. Mr. Forster has further embellished his version of the story by adding that Goldsmith "freely talked in Gerrard-street of the part he had 'written on purpose for Mrs. Abington'"; but Mr. Forster has not stated where he got the item showing how Goldsmith "freely talked," &c. It is not with the other statement in North-cote. Goldsmith published in his 'Good-Natured Man' a note praising Mrs. Bulkley for her delivery of the Epilogue to this play (see the Epilogue), and we may assume, therefore, that he was at least fairly well satisfied with the way in which this actress had played his first stage heroine, Miss Richland.—ED.

SCENE

FROM

THE GRUMBLER,

A FARCE:

PLAYED AT COVENT GARDEN THEATRE, MAY 8TH, 1773.

DRAMATIS PERSONÆ.

Sourby (the Grumbler)	MR. QUICK.
Octavio (his Son)	MR. DAVIS.
Wentworth (Brother-in-law to Sourby) .	MR. OWENSON.
Dancing Master (called Signior Capriole in the Bills)	MR. KING.
Scamper (Servant)	MR. SAUNDERS.
Clarissa (in love with Octavio) . .	MISS HELME.
Jenny (her Maid)	MISS PEARCE.

SCENE

FROM

THE GRUMBLER.

['The Grumbler' was produced specially for the comedian Quick's benefit. Quick, who had played the Postboy in Goldsmith's 'Good-Natured Man,' made a great stride both for himself and his author in his rendering of Tony Lumpkin in 'She Stoops to Conquer;' and as an acknowledgment of his success in this character, Goldsmith, it seems, produced and presented him with 'The Grumbler.' The farce, however, is merely an adaptation of Sir C. Sedley's 'Grumbler,' a piece in three acts, produced in 1702, which was evidently taken from the French of the then popular D. A. Brueys' (1640-1723) comedy 'Le Grondeur.' It was never printed, and appears to have been acted only upon the occasion of Quick's benefit, May 8, 1773. The scene now given was first printed in Prior's edition of Goldsmith's Works, 1837, from the Licenser's copy, now in the possession of Mr. John Payne Collier. One may imagine a first-rate actor making something of the scene of the forced dance, but, apart from this, there seems nothing likely to prove very attractive in the little piece. Prior summarizes the plot thus :— "Sourby, an ill-tempered, discontented man, is the torment of his family, neighbours, and servants. In the opening of the piece his son is on the point of being married to Clarissa, the consent of Sourby being chiefly obtained by the lady, who believes he has a design upon her himself, relinquishing her naturally mild character for that of a termagant. The character thus assumed agrees however so well with his own, that, in defiance of previous arrangements, he determines to marry her himself, a design favoured by her fortune being in his power. No other remedy occurs to the lovers to avoid his tyranny than further deception : the lady therefore assumes the character of an extravagant, giddy woman of fashion, who is determined to have 'habits, feasts, fiddles, hautboys, masquerades, concerts, and especially a ball for fifteen days after their nuptials.' Above all, her intended husband must learn to dance ; and she will admit of no excuse on the plea of years." Then comes the following scene.—ED.]

*Enter Scamper (Sourby's servant) to Sourby, and his
intended wife's maid Jenny.*

Scamper. Sir, a gentleman would speak with you.

Jenny. Good! Here comes Scamper; he'll manage
you, I'll warrant me. (*Aside.*)

Sourby. Who is it?

Scamper. He says his name is Monsieur Ri—Ri—Stay,
Sir, I'll go and ask him again.

Sourby. (*Pulling him by the ears.*) Take that, sirrah, by
the way.

Scamper. Ahi! Ahi!   [*Exit.*

Jenny. Sir, you have torn off his hair, so that he must
now have a wig: you have pulled his ears off; but there
are none of them to be had for money.

Sourby. I'll teach him—'Tis certainly Mr. Rigaut, my
notary; I know who it is, let him come in. Could he find
no time but this to bring me money? Plague take the
blockhead!

Enter Dancing-Master and his Fiddler.

Sourby. This is not my man. Who are you, with your
compliments?

Dancing Master. (*Bowing often.*) I am called Rigaudon,
Sir, at your service.

Sourby. (*To Jenny.*) Have not I seen that face somewhere before?

Jenny. There are a thousand people like one another.

Sourby. Well, Mr. Rigaudon, what is your business?

Dancing Master. To give you this letter from Madame
Clarissa.

Sourby. Give it to me—I would fain know who taught
Clarissa to fold a letter thus. What contains it?

Jenny. (*Aside, while he unfolds the letter.*) A lover, I believe, never complained of that before.

Sourby. (*Reads.*) "Everybody says I am to marry the
most brutal of men. I would disabuse them; and for
that reason you and I must begin the ball to-night." She
is mad!

Dancing Master. Go on, pray, Sir.

Sourby. (*Reads.*) " You told me you cannot dance; but I have sent you the first man in the world." (*Sourby looks at him from head to foot.*)

Dancing Master. Oh Lord, Sir.

Sourby. (*Reads.*) " Who will teach you in less than an hour enough to serve your purpose." I learn to dance!

Dancing Master. Finish, if you please.

Sourby. " And if you love me, you will learn the Allemande." The Allemande! I, the Allemande! Mr. the first man in the world, do you know you are in some danger here?

Dancing Master. Come, Sir, in a quarter of an hour, you shall dance to a miracle!

Sourby. Mr. Rigaudon, do you know I will send you out of the window if I call my servants?

Dancing Master. (*Bidding his man play.*) Come, brisk, this little prelude will put you in humour; you must be held by the hand; or have you some steps of your own?

Sourby. Unless you put up that d—d fiddle, I'll beat it about your ears.

Dancing Master. Zounds, Sir! if you are thereabouts, you shall dance presently—I say presently.

Sourby. Shall I dance, villain?

Dancing Master. Yes. By the heavens above shall you dance. I have orders from Clarissa to make you dance. She has paid me, and dance you shall; first, let him go out. [*He draws his sword, and puts it under his arm.*

Sourby. Ah! I'm dead. What a madman has this woman sent me!

Jenny. I see I must interpose. Stay you there, Sir; let me speak to him; Sir, pray do us the favour to go and tell the lady, that it's disagreeable to my master.

Dancing Master. I will have him dance.

Sourby. The rascal! the rascal!

Jenny. Consider, if you please, my master is a grave man.

Dancing Master. I'll have him dance.

Jenny. You may stand in need of him.

Sourby. (*Taking her aside.*) Yes, tell him that when he will, without costing him a farthing, I'll bleed and purge him his bellyfull.

Dancing Master. I have nothing to do with that; I'll have him dance, or have his blood.

Sourby. The rascal! (*muttering.*)

Jenny. Sir, I can't work upon him; the madman will not hear reason; some harm will happen—we are alone.

Sourby. 'Tis very true.

Jenny. Look on him; he has an ill look.

Sourby. He has so (*trembling*).

Dancing Master. Make haste, I say, make haste.

Sourby. Help! neighbours! murder!

Jenny. Aye, you may cry for help; do you know that all your neighbours would be glad to see you robbed and your throat cut? Believe me, Sir, two Allemande steps may save your life.

Sourby. But if it should come to be known, I should be taken for a fool.

Jenny. Love excuses all follies; and I have heard say that when Hercules was in love, he spun for Queen Omphale.

Sourby. Yes, Hercules spun, but Hercules did not dance the Allemande.

Jenny. Well, you must tell him so; the gentleman will teach you another.

Dancing Master. Will you have a minuet, Sir?

Sourby. A minuet; no.

Dancing Master. The loure.

Sourby. The loure; no.

Dancing Master. The passay!

Sourby. The passay; no.

Dancing Master. What then? the trocanny, the tricotez, the rigadon? Come, choose, choose.

Sourby. No, no, no, I like none of these.

Dancing Master. You would have a grave, serious dance, perhaps?

Sourby. Yes, a serious one, if there be any—but a very serious dance.

Dancing Master. Well, the courante, the hornpipe, the brocane, the saraband?

Sourby. No, no, no!

Dancing Master. What the devil then will you have? But make haste, or—death!

Sourby. Come on then, since it must be so; I'll learn a few steps of the—the——

Dancing Master. What of the—the——

Sourby. I know not what.

Dancing Master. You mock me, Sir; you shall dance the Allemande, since Clarissa will have it so, or——

[*He leads him about, the fiddle playing the Allemande.*

Sourby. I shall be laughed at by the whole town if it should be known. I am determined, for this frolic, to deprive Clarissa of that invaluable blessing, the possession of my person.

Dancing Master. Come, come, Sir, move, move. (*Teaching him.*)

Sourby. Cockatrice!

Dancing Master. One, two, three! (*Teaching.*)

Sourby. A d—d, infernal——

Enter Wentworth.

Oh! brother, you are come in good time to free me from this cursed bondage.

Wentworth. How! for shame, brother, at your age to be thus foolish.

Sourby. As I hope for mercy—

Wentworth. For shame, for shame—practising at sixty what should have been finished at six?

Dancing Master. He's not the only grown gentleman I have had in hand.

Wentworth. Brother, brother, you'll be the mockery of the whole city.

Sourby. Eternal babbler! hear me; this curs'd, confounded villain will make me dance perforce.

Wentworth. Perforce!

Sourby. Yes; by order, he says, of Clarissa; but since I now find she is unworthy, I give her up—renounce her for ever.

[Prior sums up the rest of the play thus:—" The young couple enter immediately after this declaration, and finding no farther obstruction to their union, the piece

finishes with the consent of the Grumbler, ' in the hope,'
as he says, ' that they are possessed of mutual requi-
sites to be the plague of each other.' "—ED.']

¹ John Quick, of whom this piece may be said to constitute a memorial, died in 1831, aged 83.   He retired from the stage in 1798, having
acquired a fortune of £10,000.   He lived during his later years at
Hornsey (afterwards Will's) Row, Islington, and for many years was
wont to preside at convivial meetings held at the Old King's Head,
opposite Islington Church.   Beside Tony Lumpkin, he was famous in
Isaac Mendoza, Bob Acres, and such characters.   Genest says he had
not much variety, but his oddity of appearance and voice made people
laugh.   Boaden speaks of him as "the favourite comedian of his late
majesty " (George III.).   With 'Quick's Whim,' a pamphlet, of about
the year 1795, purporting to give the "Jokes and Stories" uttered by
the comedian, he, probably, had little or nothing to do, otherwise this
collection might have contained something about Goldsmith.—ED.

THE BEE:

BEING

ESSAYS

ON THE

MOST INTERESTING SUBJECTS.

Floriferis ut Apes in saltibus omnia libant,
Omnia Nos itidem.

['The Bee' was a weekly periodical; but it ran for only eight weeks, from Oct. 6 to Nov. 24, 1759. The following advertisement announcing its appearance is from the *London Chronicle*:—

"Saturday next, October the 6th, will be published (to be continued weekly, price three-pence), neatly printed in crown octavo, and on good paper, containing two sheets, or thirty-two pages, stitched in blue covers, Number I. of a new periodical paper, entitled—

"THE BEE. Consisting of a variety of Essays on the Amusements, Follies, and Vices in fashion: particularly the most recent Topics of Conversation: Remarks on Theatrical Exhibitions: Memoirs of Modern Literature, &c., &c. Printed for J. Wilkie, at the Bible in St. Paul's Church Yard.

"*₊* The Publisher begs leave to inform the public, that every twelve numbers will make a handsome pocket volume, at the end of which shall be given an emblematical frontispiece, title, and table of contents. Letters to the author of the Bee, directed to J. Wilkie, as above (post-paid), will be duly regarded."

Goldsmith, it is supposed, supplied the entire contents. Wilkie, the publisher, was also the publisher of the *Lady's Magazine*, to which Goldsmith was likewise a contributor, if not, for a time, editor. In December, 1759, the eight numbers of 'The Bee' were issued in a 12mo volume. We here print the entire work, excepting only the poetical pieces, which appear in our edition of the Poems. Our text is that of the original so far as regards most of the pieces. Goldsmith republished eight of the pieces in his 'Essays' in 1765 and 1766, and these we have omitted from our edition of the 'Essays' in order that they may appear here under their original heading. In doing this, however, we have thought that Goldsmith's *latest* form of these twice given pieces would be most acceptable. The text of the eight pieces in question, consequently, is for the most part that of the 'Essays' issue. The principal differences as between the first and the 'Essays' issue are indicated in the notes.—ED.]

THE BEE.

CONTENTS.

THE BEE.

No. I.—SATURDAY, OCTOBER 6, 1759.

INTRODUCTION.[1]

THERE is not, perhaps, a more whimsically dismal figure in nature, than a man of real modesty, who assumes an air of impudence—who, while his heart beats with anxiety, studies ease, and affects good-humour. In this situation, however, a periodical writer often finds himself, upon his first attempt to address the public in form. All his power of pleasing is damped by solicitude, and his cheerfulness dashed with apprehension. Impressed with the terrors of the tribunal before which he is going to appear, his natural humour turns to pertness, and for real wit he is obliged to substitute vivacity. His first publication draws a crowd; they part dissatisfied; and the author, never more to be indulged a favourable hearing, is left to condemn the indelicacy of his own address, or their want of discernment.

For my part, as I was never distinguished for address, and have often even blundered in making my bow, such bodings as these had like to have totally repressed my ambition. I was at a loss whether to give the public specious promises, or give none; whether to be merry or sad on this solemn occasion. If I should decline all merit, it was too probable the hasty reader might have taken me at my word. If, on the other hand, like labourers in the Magazine trade, I had, with modest impudence, humbly presumed to promise an epitome of all the good things that

---

[1] Afterwards this appeared, slightly altered, as the first of the ' Essays,' 1765.—ED.

ever were said or written, this might have disgusted those readers I most desire to please. Had I been merry, I might have been censured as *vastly low ;*[1] and had I been sorrowful, I might have been left to mourn in solitude and silence: in short, whichever way I turned, nothing presented but prospects of terror, despair, chandlers' shops, and waste paper.[2]

In this debate between fear and ambition, my publisher,[3] happening to arrive, interrupted for a while my anxiety. Perceiving my embarrassment about making my first appearance, he instantly offered his assistance and advice. " You must know, Sir," says he, " that the republic of letters is at present divided into three classes. One writer, for instance, excels at a plan, or a title-page, another works away the body of the book, and a third is a dab at an index. Thus a Magazine is not the result of any single man's industry, but goes through as many hands as a new pin, before it is fit for the public. I fancy, Sir," continues he, " I can provide an eminent hand, and upon moderate terms, to draw up a promising plan to smooth up our readers a little, and pay them as Colonel Charteris paid his seraglio, at the rate of three halfpence in hand, and three shillings more in promises."[4]

He was proceeding in his advice, which, however, I thought proper to decline, by assuring him, that as I intended to pursue no fixed method, so it was impossible to form any regular plan ; determined never to be tedious in order to be logical, wherever pleasure presented, I was resolved to follow. Like the Bee, which I had taken for the title of my paper, I would rove from flower to flower, with seeming inattention, but concealed choice, expatiate over

---

[1] Goldsmith had to combat this imputation again upon the production of his ' She Stoops to Conquer,' 1773.—Ed.

[2] This paragraph, from " Had I been merry," &c., did not appear in the ' Essays' issue.—Ed.

[3] The word is " bookseller " in the ' Essays.'—Ed.

[4] Colonel Charteris.—" A man infamous for all manner of vices," says Pope, ' Moral Essays,' iii. His profligacy brought him to condemnation to the gallows. He, however, was imprisoned in Newgate and heavily fined instead of hanged. He died in Scotland in 1732. Hogarth is said to have figured him in the first plate of his ' Harlot's Progress.'—Ed.

all the beauties of the season, and make my industry my amusement.

This reply may also serve as an apology to the reader, who expects, before he sits down, a bill of his future entertainment. It would be improper to pall his curiosity by lessening his surprise, or anticipate any pleasure I am able to procure him, by saying what shall come next. Thus much, however, he may be assured of, that neither war nor scandal shall make any part of it. Homer finely imagines his deity turning away with horror from the prospect of a field of battle, and seeking tranquillity among a nation noted for peace and simplicity. Happy, could any effort of mine, but for a moment, repress that savage pleasure some men find in the daily accounts of human misery! How gladly would I lead them from scenes of blood and altercation, to prospects of innocence and ease, where every breeze breathes health, and every sound is but the echo of tranquillity.[1]

But whatever the merit of his intentions may be, every writer is now convinced that he must be chiefly indebted to good fortune for finding readers willing to allow him any degree of reputation. It has been remarked, that almost every character which has excited either attention or praise, has owed part of its success to merit, and part to a happy concurrence of circumstances in its favour. Had Cæsar or Cromwell exchanged countries, the one might have been a sergeant, and the other an exciseman. So it is with wit, which generally succeeds more from being happily addressed, than from its native poignancy.[2] A *bon mot*, for instance, that might be relished at White's, may lose all its flavour when delivered at the Cat and Bagpipes in St. Giles's.[2] A jest calculated to spread at a gaming table, may be received with a perfect neutrality of face, should it happen to drop in a mackerel boat. We have all seen dunces triumph in some companies, where men of real humour were disregarded by a general combination in favour of stupidity. To drive the observation as far as it will go, should the labours of a writer who designs his performances for readers of a more refined appe-

---

[1] See also p. 364.—Ed.   [2]—[2] Omitted in the 'Essays.'—Ed.

tite, fall into the hands of a devourer of compilations, what can he expect but contempt and confusion? If his merits are to be determined by judges who estimate the value of a book from its bulk, or its frontispiece, every rival must acquire an easy superiority, who, with persuasive eloquence, promises four extraordinary pages of letter-press, or three beautiful prints, curiously coloured from nature.

But to proceed: Though I cannot promise as much entertainment, or as much elegance, as others have done, yet the reader may be assured, he shall have as much of both as I can. He shall, at least, find me alive while I study his entertainment; for I solemnly assure him, I was never yet possessed of the secret at once of writing and sleeping.

During the course of this paper, therefore, all the wit and learning I have are heartily at his service; which, if, after so candid a confession, he should, notwithstanding, still find intolerably dull, low, or sad stuff, this, I protest, is more than I know. I have a clear conscience, and am entirely out of the secret.

Yet I would not have him, upon the perusal of a single paper, pronounce me incorrigible; he may try a second, which, as there is a studied difference in subject and style, may be more suited to his taste; if this also fails, I must refer him to a third, or even to a fourth, in case of extremity. If he should still continue refractory, and find me dull to the last, I must inform him, with Bayes,[1] in the 'Rehearsal,' that I think him a very odd kind of a fellow, and desire no more of his acquaintance.

It is with such reflections as these I endeavour to fortify myself against the future contempt or neglect of some readers, and am prepared for their dislike by mutual recrimination. If such should impute dealing neither in battles nor scandal to me as a fault, instead of acquiescing in their censure, I must beg leave to tell them a story.—

A traveller, in his way to Italy, happening to pass at the foot of the Alps, found himself at last in a country where the inhabitants had each a large excrescence depending

---

[1] See the first Epilogue to 'She Stoops to Conquer,' p. 290.—ED.

from the chin, like the pouch of a monkey. This deformity, as it was endemic, and the people little used to
strangers, it had been the custom, time immemorial, to
look upon as the greatest ornament of the human visage.
Ladies grew toasts from the size of their chins, and none
were regarded as pretty fellows, but such whose faces were
broadest at the bottom.—It was Sunday; a country church
was at hand, and our traveller was willing to perform the
duties of the day. Upon his first appearance at the church
door, the eyes of all were naturally fixed upon the stranger;
but what was their amazement, when they found that he
actually wanted that emblem of beauty, a pursed chin!
This was a defect that not a single creature had sufficient
gravity (though they were noted for being grave) to withstand. Stifled bursts of laughter, winks, and whispers,
circulated from visage to visage, and the prismatic figure
of the stranger's face was a fund of infinite gaiety; even
the parson, equally remarkable for his gravity and chin,
could hardly refrain joining in the good humour. Our
traveller could no longer patiently continue an object for
deformity to point at. "Good folks," said he, "I perceive
that I am the unfortunate cause of all this good humour.
It is true, I may have faults in abundance, but I shall
never be induced to reckon my want of a swelled face
among the number." [1]

ON A BEAUTIFUL YOUTH STRUCK BLIND WITH LIGHTNING.

Imitated from the Spanish. [2]

Sure 'twas by Providence design'd,
 Rather in pity than in hate,
That he should be, like Cupid, blind,
 To save him from Narcissus' fate.

---

[1] In the 'Essays' issue the conclusion is—"I perceive that I am a
very ridiculous figure here, but I assure you I am reckoned no way
deformed at home." The swelled-face affliction is of course the *goître*
of the Alpine villages.—Ed.

[2] Re-published in the Poems.—Ed.

ANOTHER; IN THE SAME SPIRIT.

LUMINE Acon dextro capta est Leonida sinistro,
Et poterat forma vincere uterque Deos.
Parve puer, lumen quod habes concede puellæ;
Sic tu cæcus amor, sic erit illa Venus.

REMARKS ON OUR THEATRES.

OUR theatres are now opened, and all Grub Street[1] is preparing its advice to the managers. We shall undoubtedly hear learned disquisitions on the structure of one actor's legs, and another's eyebrows. We shall be told much of enunciations, tones, and attitudes; and shall have our lightest pleasures commented upon by didactic dullness. We shall, it is feared, be told that Garrick is a fine actor; but then as a manager, so avaricious! That Palmer is a most surprising genius, and Holland likely to do well in a particular cast of character. We shall have them giving Shuter[2] instructions to amuse us by rule, and deploring over the ruins of desolated Majesty at Covent Garden. As I love to be advising too—for advice is easily given, and bears a show of wisdom and superiority—I must be permitted to offer a few observations upon our theatres and actors, without, on this trivial occasion, throwing my thoughts into the formality of method.

There is something in the deportment of all our players infinitely more stiff and formal than among the actors of other nations. Their action sits uneasy upon them; for as the English use very little gesture in ordinary conversation, our English bred actors are obliged to supply stage gestures by their imagination alone. A French comedian finds proper models of action in every company, and in

---

[1] Now Milton Street, Finsbury. In Goldsmith's time it was inhabited by the poor poets and newspaper writers.—ED.

[2] Afterwards the original Croaker in Goldsmith's ' Good-Natured Man.'—ED.

every coffeehouse he enters. An Englishman is obliged
to take his models from the stage itself; he is obliged to
imitate nature from an imitation of nature. I know of no
set of men more likely to be improved by travelling than
those of the theatrical profession. The inhabitants of the
Continent are less reserved than here; they may be seen
through upon a first acquaintance: such are the proper
models to draw from; they are at once striking, and are
found in great abundance.

Though it would be inexcusable in a comedian to add
any thing of his own to the poet's dialogue, yet, as to
action, he is entirely at liberty. By this he may show the
fertility of his genius, the poignancy of his humour, and
the exactness of his judgment; we scarce see a coxcomb
or a fool in common life, that has not some peculiar oddity
in his action. These peculiarities it is not in the power of
words to represent, and depend solely upon the actor.
They give a relish to the humour of the poet, and make
the appearance of nature more illusive. The Italians, it
is true, mask some characters, and endeavour to preserve
the peculiar humour by the make of the mask; but I
have seen others still preserve a great fund of humour in
the face without a mask; one actor, particularly, by a
squint which he threw into some characters of low life,
assumed a look of infinite solidity. This, though upon
reflection we might condemn, yet immediately, upon representation, we could not avoid being pleased with.

To illustrate what I have been saying by the plays I have
of late gone to see : In 'The Miser,' which was played a few
nights ago at Covent Garden, Lovegold appears through
the whole in circumstances of exaggerated avarice; all the
player's action, therefore, should conspire with the poet's
design, and represent him as an epitome of penury. The
French comedian, in this character, in the midst of one of
his most violent passions, while he appears in an ungovernable rage, feels the demon of avarice still upon
him, and stoops down to pick up a pin, which he quilts
into the flap of his coat-pocket with great assiduity. Two
candles are lighted up for his wedding; he flies and turns
one of them into the socket: it is, however, lighted up
again; he then steals to it, and privately crams it into

his pocket. The 'Mock Doctor'[1] was lately played at the other house. Here again the comedian had an opportunity of heightening the ridicule by action. The French player sits in a chair with a high back, and then begins to show away by talking nonsense, which he would have thought Latin by those whom he knows do not understand a syllable of the matter. At last he grows enthusiastic, enjoys the admiration of the company, tosses his legs and arms about, and, in the midst of his raptures and vociferation, he and the chair fall back together. All this appears dull enough in the recital, but the gravity of Cato could not stand it in the representation. In short, there is hardly a character in comedy to which a player of any real humour might not add strokes of vivacity that could not fail of applause. But, instead of this, we too often see our fine gentlemen do nothing, through a whole part, but strut and open their snuff-box; our pretty fellows sit indecently with their legs across, and our clowns pull up their breeches. These, if once, or even twice, repeated, might do well enough; but to see them served up in every scene, argues the actor almost as barren as the character he would expose.

The magnificence of our theatres is far superior to any others in Europe, where plays only are acted. The great care our performers take in painting for a part, their exactness in all the minutiæ of dress, and other little scenical proprieties, have been taken notice of by Riccoboni,[2] a gentleman of Italy, who travelled Europe with no other design but to remark upon the stage; but there are several apparent improprieties still continued, or lately come into fashion. As, for instance, spreading a carpet punctually at the beginning of the death scene, in order to prevent our actors from spoiling their clothes; this immediately apprises us of the tragedy to follow; for laying the cloth is not a more sure indication of dinner, than laying the carpet of bloody work at Drury-Lane. Our little pages, also, with unmeaning faces, that bear up the train of a

---

[1] Both 'The Miser' and 'The Mock Doctor' were by Fielding, from Molière.—ED.

[2] Riccoboni was also a comedian. He published a book on the 'Theatres of Europe,' 1741.—ED.

weeping princess, and our awkward lords in waiting, take off much from her distress. Mutes of every kind divide our attention, and lessen our sensibility; but here it is entirely ridiculous, as we see them seriously employed in doing nothing. If we must have dirty-shirted guards upon the theatres, they should be taught to keep their eyes fixed on the actors, and not roll them round upon the audience, as if they were ogling the boxes.

Beauty, methinks, seems a requisite qualification in an actress. This seems scrupulously observed elsewhere, and, for my part, I could wish to see it observed at home. I can never conceive a hero dying for love of a lady totally destitute of beauty. I must think the part unnatural; for I cannot bear to hear him call that face angelic, where even paint cannot hide its wrinkles. I must condemn him of stupidity; and the person whom I can accuse for want of taste, will seldom become the object of my affections or admiration. But if this be a defect, what must be the entire perversion of scenical decorum, when, for instance, we see an actress that might act the Wapping Landlady without a bolster, pining in the character of Jane Shore, and, while unwieldy with fat, endeavouring to convince the audience that she is dying with hunger!

For the future, then, I could wish that the parts of the young or beautiful were given to performers of suitable figures; for I must own, I could rather see the stage filled with agreeable objects, though they might sometimes bungle a little, than see it crowded with withered or mis-shapen figures, be their emphasis, as I think it is called, ever so proper. The first may have the awkward appearance of new-raised troops; but in viewing the last, I cannot avoid the mortification of fancying myself placed in a hospital of invalids.

THE STORY OF ALCANDER AND SEPTIMIUS.

Translated from a Byzantine Historian.[1]

ATHENS, long after the decline of the Roman empire, still continued the seat of learning, politeness, and wisdom. Theodoric, the Ostrogoth, repaired the schools which barbarity was suffering to fall into decay, and continued those pensions to men of learning, which avaricious governors had monopolized.

In this city, and about this period, Alcander and Septimius were fellow students together. The one the most subtile reasoner of all the Lyceum; the other the most eloquent speaker in the Academic grove. Mutual admiration soon begot a friendship. Their fortunes were nearly equal, and they were natives of the two most celebrated cities in the world; for Alcander was of Athens, Septimius came from Rome.

In this state of harmony they lived for some time together, when Alcander, after passing the first part of his youth in the indolence of philosophy, thought at length of entering into the busy world; and, as a step previous to this, placed his affections on Hypatia, a lady of exquisite beauty. The day of their intended nuptials was fixed; the previous ceremonies were performed; and nothing now remained but her being conducted in triumph to the apartment of the intended bridegroom.

Alcander's exultation in his own happiness, or being unable to enjoy any satisfaction without making his friend Septimius a partner, prevailed upon him to introduce Hypatia to his fellow student; which he did with all the gaiety of a man who found himself equally happy in friendship and love. But this was an interview fatal to the future peace of both; for Septimius no sooner saw her, but he was smitten with an involuntary passion; and

---

[1] No. II. in the 'Essays.' As stated in our introductory note concerning the re-printed pieces, the text here given is that of the six years later published 'Essays.' The present story is a rendering of the original of Boccaccio's Titus and Gisippus—the Eighth Novel of the Tenth Day in the 'Decameron.'—ED.

though he used every effort to suppress desires at once so imprudent and unjust, the emotions of his mind in a short time became so strong, that they brought on a fever, which the physicians judged incurable.

During this illness, Alcander watched him with all the anxiety of fondness, and brought his mistress to join in those amiable offices of friendship. The sagacity of the physicians, by these means, soon discovered that the cause of their patient's disorder was love; and Alcander, being apprised of their discovery, at length extorted a confession from the reluctant dying lover.

It would but delay the narrative to describe the conflict between love and friendship in the breast of Alcander on this occasion; it is enough to say, that the Athenians were at that time arrived at such refinement in morals, that every virtue was carried to excess. In short, forgetful of his own felicity, he gave up his intended bride, in all her charms, to the young Roman. They were married privately by his connivance; and this unlooked-for change of fortune wrought as unexpected a change in the constitution of the now happy Septimius. In a few days he was perfectly recovered, and set out with his fair partner for Rome. Here, by an exertion of those talents which he was so eminently possessed of, Septimius in a few years arrived at the highest dignities of the state, and was constituted the city judge, or prætor.

In the meantime Alcander not only felt the pain of being separated from his friend and his mistress, but a prosecution was also commenced against him by the relations of Hypatia, for having basely given up his bride, as was suggested, for money. His innocence of the crime laid to his charge, and even his eloquence in his own defence, were not able to withstand the influence of a powerful party. He was cast and condemned to pay an enormous fine. However, being unable to raise so large a sum at the time appointed, his possessions were confiscated, he himself was stripped of the habit of freedom, exposed as a slave in the market-place, and sold to the highest bidder.

A merchant of Thrace becoming his purchaser, Alcander, with some other companions of distress, was carried into that region of desolation and sterility. His stated employment was to follow the herds of an imperious master; and his success in hunting was all that was allowed him to supply his precarious subsistence. Every morning waked him to a renewal of famine or toil, and every change of season served but to aggravate his unsheltered distress. After some years of bondage, however, an opportunity of escaping offered; he embraced it with ardour, so that travelling by night, and lodging in caverns by day, to shorten a long story, he at last arrived in Rome. The same day on which Alcander arrived, Septimius sat administering justice in the forum, whither our wanderer came, expecting to be instantly known, and publicly acknowledged by his former friend. Here he stood the whole day amongst the crowd, watching the eyes of the judge, and expecting to be taken notice of; but he was so much altered by a long succession of hardships, that he continued unnoted among the rest; and, in the evening, when he was going up to the prætor's chair, he was brutally repulsed by the attending lictors. The attention of the poor is generally driven from one ungrateful object to another; for night coming on, he now found himself under a necessity of seeking a place to lie in, and yet knew not where to apply. All emaciated and in rags as he was, none of the citizens would harbour so much wretchedness; and sleeping in the streets might be attended with interruption or danger: in short, he was obliged to take up his lodging in one of the tombs without the city, the usual retreat of guilt, poverty, and despair. In this mansion of horror, laying his head upon an inverted urn, he forgot his miseries for a while in sleep; and found, on his flinty couch, more ease than beds of down can supply to the guilty.

As he continued here, about midnight, two robbers came to make this their retreat; but happening to disagree about the division of their plunder, one of them stabbed the other to the heart, and left him weltering in blood at the entrance. In these circumstances he was found next morning dead at the mouth of the vault. This naturally induced a further enquiry; an alarm was spread; the cave was examined; and Alcander being found was immediately apprehended and accused of robbery and murder. The circumstances against him were strong, and the wretchedness of his appearance confirmed suspicion. Misfortune and he were now so long acquainted that he at last became regardless of life. He detested a world where he had found only ingratitude, falsehood, and cruelty; he was determined to make no defence; and thus, lowering with resolution, he was dragged, bound with cords, before the tribunal of Septimius. As the proofs were positive against him, and he offered nothing in his own vindication, the judge was proceeding to doom him to a most cruel and ignominious death, when the attention of the multitude was soon divided by another object. The robber who had been really guilty, was apprehended selling his plunder, and, struck with a panic, had confessed his crime. He was brought bound to the same tribunal, and acquitted every other person of any partnership in his guilt. Alcander's innocence, therefore, appeared, but the sullen rashness of his conduct remained a wonder to the surrounding multitude; but their astonishment was still farther increased when they saw their judge start from his tribunal to embrace the supposed criminal: Septimius recollected his friend and former benefactor, and hung upon his neck with tears of pity and of joy. Need the sequel be related? Alcander was acquitted; shared the friendship and honours of the principal citizens of Rome; lived afterwards in happiness and ease; and left it to be engraved on his tomb, that,—No circumstances are so desperate which Providence may not relieve.

A LETTER FROM MR. VOLTAIRE TO MR. D'ARGET, OF LAUSANNE.[1]

[Voltaire " retired from the World to Happiness" at Geneva.—Frederick the Great.]

You demand, my dear friend and companion of Pots-dam, in what manner Pyrrhus[2] and Cineas[3] have been reconciled. First, then, Pyrrhus turned my tragedy of ' Merope ' into an opera, which he sent me. Again, he was so kind as to offer me his key, which, however, will not serve to open Paradise ; and to this he added an offer of all his favours ; but I am too old to accept the favours of kings at present.[4] To one of his sisters, who has ever preserved a friendship for me, I am obliged for these marks of kindness. To her I owe the correspondence which is now and then renewed between the heroic, poetical, warlike, singular, brilliant, proud, modest king, and Cineas the Swiss, retired from the world to happiness.[5] Would you be so good as to pay us a short visit in this part of the world, I fancy we could spend the time agree-ably enough ; the world does not afford a finer prospect than that from one of my windows. Imagine a canal on one side, that lengthens out of sight, bordered by a hun-dred gardens ; on the other the vast Genevan lake, like a boundless mirror, reflects the mountains on the opposite side, that lift themselves above the clouds, in form of the most magnificent amphitheatre ; and then I am so suited. to a house, I feel no inconvenience, except from flies in the

[1] We give this and the other three translations from Voltaire in their original places in the ' Bee.' The editors have hitherto left them out. Their re-publication, besides adding to the completeness of the ' Bee,' may throw some additional light upon Goldsmith's ' Memoirs of Vol-taire,' which was written at about the same time.—ED.

[2] K. of Prussia.—GOLDSMITH.   [3] M. de Voltaire.—GOLDSMITH.

[4] The " key " was that of Voltaire's office of Chamberlain to the King of Prussia, which he had resigned on leaving Berlin in consequence of the quarrel about Maupertuis : see p. 322.—ED.

[5] See Carlyle's chapter on the Correspondence of Frederick the Great and Voltaire, ' History of Freidrich,' 1865, vol. v., p. 605.—ED.

midst of winter. Madame Dennis [1] has shown the elegance of her taste in the furniture. We live here much more comfortably than Pyrrhus, and I fancy fare better too, when we have a good appetite; without this neither Pyrrhus nor Cineas can be happy.

We acted a tragedy yesterday; if you choose to take a part, you have only to come to be fitted. In this manner we forget the quarrels of kings and men of letters, those frightful, these ridiculous! We have had a premature account of a battle between Marshal Richelieu and the Prince of Brunswick. I know not whether the Prince can succeed, for it is certain I have won fifty guineas from him at chess. However, it is possible to lose at chess, and win at a game where people play with thirty thousand bayonets.

I grant you that the King of Prussia may have some foibles, but no body understands the game he is playing better than he. He has infinite despatch, and his troops have been disciplined long before he came to command them. It is an easy matter to conceive how regular machines must behave, who have long been used to war, who see their sovereign at their head, who are personally known to him, and whom he exhorts with his hat in his hand to do their duty. Droll fellows these at a platoon, at handling their cartridges, and firing six or seven times in a minute. Yet with all this dexterity their master lately thought that all was lost. About three months ago he was disposed to die; he bid me adieu both in verse and prose; but he is now quite recovered. By his discipline and despatch he has gained two great battles in the space of a month. He flies to the French, turns back upon the Austrians, retakes Breslau, takes forty thousand prisoners of war, and makes epigrams. We shall see how this bloody tragedy, so pathetic, and yet so complicated, will end.

Happy they, who, with an eye to tranquillity, can behold these great events of the best of possible systems. As for the affair of the Abbé Prade, I have yet been able to receive no authentic information. Fame says he is

---

[1] Voltaire's niece.—ED.

hanged; but she knows not what she says. I should be sorry that all the king's readers should come to an unhappy end.

Your's, &c.
VOLTAIRE.

Jan. 8, 1758.[1]

A LETTER FROM A TRAVELLER.

[*On the Condition of the Poles.*]

(The sequel of this correspondence to be continued occasionally. I shall alter nothing either in the style or substance of these letters, and the reader may depend on their being genuine.)[2]

CRACOW, *August* 2, 1758.

MY DEAR WILL,—You see, by the date of my letter, that I am arrived in Poland. When will my wanderings be at an end? When will my restless disposition give me leave to enjoy the present hour? When at Lyons, I thought all happiness lay beyond the Alps; when in Italy, I found myself still in want of something, and expected to leave solicitude behind me by going into Romelia; and now you find me turning back, still expecting ease every where but where I am. It is now seven years since I saw the face of a single creature who cared a farthing whether I was dead or alive. Secluded from all the comforts of confidence, friendship, or society, I feel the solitude of a hermit, but not his ease.[3]

The Prince of * * * has taken me in his train, so that I am in no danger of starving for this bout. The Prince's governor is a rude ignorant pedant, and his tutor a battered rake; thus, between two such characters, you may imagine he is finely instructed. I made some attempts

---

[1] This letter is dated Lausanne in the *Panthéon Littéraire* edition of Voltaire's Correspondence.—ED.
[2] This is Goldsmith's own notification, and it duly appears here as in the original at the head of the Letter. Nevertheless, the letter is most likely fictitious. Some passages recall lines in the 'Traveller;' but it is thought that Goldsmith was never in Poland.—ED.
[3] Compare the 'Traveller,' ll. 23, &c.—ED.

to display all the little knowledge I had acquired by reading or observation; but I find myself regarded as an
ignorant intruder. The truth is, I shall never be able to
acquire a power of expressing myself with ease in any
language but my own; and, out of my own country, the
highest character I can ever acquire, is that of being a
philosophic vagabond.

When I consider myself in the country which was once
so formidable in war, and spread terror and desolation
over the whole Roman empire, I can hardly account for
the present wretchedness and pusillanimity of its inhabitants: a prey to every invader; their cities plundered
without an enemy; their magistrates seeking redress by
complaints, and not by vigour. Every thing conspires to
raise my compassion for their miseries, were not my
thoughts too busily engaged by my own. The whole
kingdom is in strange disorder: when our equipage, which
consists of the Prince and thirteen attendants, had arrived
at some towns, there were no conveniences to be found,
and we were obliged to have girls to conduct us to the
next. I have seen a woman travel thus on horseback before
us for thirty miles, and think herself highly paid, and
make twenty reverences, upon receiving, with ecstasy, about
two-pence for her trouble. In general, we were better
served by the women than the men, on those occasions.
The men seemed directed by a low sordid interest alone;
they seemed mere machines, and all their thoughts were
employed in the care of their horses. If we gently desired
them to make more speed, they took not the least notice;
kind language was what they had by no means been used
to. It was proper to speak to them in the tones of anger,
and sometimes it was even necessary to use blows, to excite
them to their duty. How different these from the common people of England, whom a blow might induce to
return the affront sevenfold. These poor people, however,
from being brought up to vile usage, lose all the respect
which they should have for themselves. They have contracted a habit of regarding constraint as the great rule
of their duty. When they were treated with mildness,
they no longer continued to perceive a superiority. They
fancied themselves our equals, and a continuance of our

humanity might probably have rendered them insolent; but the imperious tone, menaces, and blows, at once changed their sensations and their ideas; their ears and their shoulders taught their souls to shrink back into servitude, from which they had for some moments fancied themselves disengaged.

The enthusiasm of liberty an Englishman feels is never so strong, as when presented by such prospects as these. I must own, in all my indigence, it is one of my comforts, (perhaps, indeed, it is my only boast,) that I am of that happy country; though I scorn to starve there; though I do not choose to lead a life of wretched dependence, or be an object for my former acquaintance to point at. While you enjoy all the ease and elegance of prudence and virtue, your old friend wanders over the world, without a single anchor to hold by, or a friend, except you, to confide in.

Yours, &c.

A SHORT ACCOUNT OF THE LATE MR. MAUPERTUIS.

MR. MAUPERTUIS, lately deceased,[1] was the first to whom the English philosophers owed their being particularly admired by the rest of Europe. The romantic system of Des Cartes was adapted to the taste of the superficial and the indolent; the foreign universities had embraced it with ardour, and such are seldom convinced of their errors till all others give up such false opinions as untenable. The philosophy of Newton and the metaphysics of Locke appeared; but, like all new truths, they were at once received with opposition and contempt. The English, it is true, studied, understood, and, consequently, admired them; it was very different on the Continent. Fontenelle, who seemed to preside over the republic of letters, unwilling to acknowledge that all his life had been spent in erroneous philosophy, joined in the universal disapprobation, and the English philosophers seemed entirely unknown.

---

[1] Pierre Louis Moreau de Maupertuis, b. 1698, d. 1759.—B.

Maupertuis, however, made them his study ; he thought
he might oppose the physics of his country, and yet still
be a good citizen; he defended our countrymen, wrote in
their favour, and, at last, as he had truth on his side,
carried his cause. Almost all the learning of the English,
till very lately, was conveyed in the language of France.
The writings of Maupertuis spread the reputation of his
master, Newton, and, by a happy fortune, have united his
fame with that of our human prodigy.

The first of his performances, openly in vindication of
the Newtonian system, is his treatise, entitled, ' Sur la
figure des Astres,' if I remember right; a work at once
expressive of a deep geometrical knowledge, and the most
happy manner of delivering abstruse science with ease.
This met with violent opposition from a people, though
fond of novelty in everything else, yet, however, in matters
of science, attached to ancient opinions with bigotry. As
the old and obstinate fell away, the youth of France embraced the new opinions, and now seem more eager to
defend Newton than even his countrymen.

The oddity of character which great men are sometimes
remarkable for, Maupertuis was not entirely free from. If
we can believe Voltaire, he once attempted to castrate
himself; but whether this be true or no, it is certain he
was extremely whimsical. Though born to a large fortune,
when employed in mathematical inquiries, he disregarded
his person to such a degree, and loved retirement so much,
that he has been more than once put on the list of modest
beggars by the curates of Paris, when he retired to some
private quarter of the town, in order to enjoy his meditations without interruption. The character given of him
by one of Voltaire's antagonists, if it can be depended upon,
is much to his honour. "You," says this writer to Mr.
Voltaire, " you were entertained by the King of Prussia as a
buffoon, but Maupertuis as a philosopher." It is certain,
that the preference which this royal scholar gave to Maupertuis was the cause of Voltaire's disagreement with him.[1]

---

[1] Voltaire commenced hostilities, by openly espousing the cause of
Koenig, professor of philosophy at Franeker, against Maupertuis, on his
publishing his ' Discourse on the Laws of Motion.' Voltaire had, till

Voltaire could not bear to see a man, whose talents he had no great opinion of, preferred before him as president of the Royal Academy. His 'Micromegas' was designed to ridicule Maupertuis ; and, probably, it has brought more disgrace on the author than the subject. Whatever absurdities men of letters have indulged, and how fantastical soever the modes of science have been, their anger is still more subject to ridicule.

then, lived on terms of the most intimate friendship with Maupertuis.—B. Voltaire's hostility to Maupertuis caused the former's retirement from the court of Prussia. The 'Micromegas' satire was burnt at Berlin by order of Frederick the Great. Some further account of Maupertuis will be found in Goldsmith's ' Memoirs of Voltaire.' See also *ante*, p. 317. —ED.

THE BEE.

ON DRESS.[1] [ST. JAMES'S PARK.]

FOREIGNERS observe, that there are no ladies in the world more beautiful, or more ill-dressed, than those of England. Our countrywomen have been compared to those pictures, where the face is the work of a Raphael, but the draperies thrown out by some empty pretender, destitute of taste, and unacquainted with design.

If I were a poet, I might observe, on this occasion, that so much beauty, set off with all the advantages of dress, would be too powerful an antagonist for the opposite sex; and, therefore, it was wisely ordered that our ladies should want taste, lest their admirers should entirely want reason.

But to confess a truth, I do not find they have a greater aversion to fine clothes than the women of any other country whatsoever. I cannot fancy that a shop-keeper's wife in Cheapside has a greater tenderness for the fortune of her husband than a citizen's wife in Paris; or, that Miss in a boarding-school is more an economist in dress than Mademoiselle in a nunnery.

Although Paris may be accounted the soil in which almost every fashion takes its rise, its influence is never so general there as with us. They study there the happy method of uniting grace and fashion, and never excuse a woman for being awkwardly dressed, by saying her clothes are in the mode. A French woman is a perfect

---

[1] This re-appeared as Essay XV. in 1765.—ED.

architect in dress: she never, with Gothic ignorance, mixes the orders; she never tricks out a squabby Doric shape with Corinthian finery; or, to speak without metaphor, she conforms to a general fashion only when it happens not to be repugnant to private beauty.

The English ladies, on the contrary, seem to have no other standard of grace but the run of the town. If fashion gives the word, every distinction of beauty, complexion, or stature, ceases. Sweeping trains, Prussian bonnets, and trollopees,[1] as like each other as if cut from the same piece, level all to one standard. The Mall, the gardens, and playhouses, are filled with ladies in uniform; and their whole appearance shows as little variety or taste, as if their clothes were bespoke by the colonel of a marching regiment, or fancied by the artist who dresses the three battalions of guards.

But not only the ladies of every shape and complexion, but of every age too, are possessed of this unaccountable passion levelling all distinction in dress. A lady of no quality travels fast behind the lady of some quality, and a woman of sixty is as gaudy as her granddaughter. A friend of mind, a good-natured old man, amused me the other day, with an account of his journey to the Mall. It seems, in his walk thither, he, for some time, followed a lady who, as he thought by her dress, was a girl of fifteen. It was airy, elegant, and youthful. My old friend had called up all his poetry on this occasion, and fancied twenty Cupids prepared for execution in every folding of her white negligee. He had prepared his imagination for an angel's face; but what was his mortification to find that the imaginary goddess was no other than his cousin Hannah, some years older than himself![2]

But to give it in his own words :—" After the transports of our first salute," said he, " were over, I could not avoid

---

[1] Sir James Prior said, in 1837, that "trollopees" were "a kind of loose dress for the ladies." Perhaps it was a nick-name. The word trollop = slattern, or a woman loosely dressed, was in use earlier.—ED.

[2] In the ' Bee ' version this story is told as an experience of the writer, who, however, writes as an old man who " shall be sixty-two the twelfth of next November." [N.B. Goldsmith's birthday is now held as being the 10th of November. See note to our Life of Goldsmith, p. 2.]—ED.

running my eye over her whole appearance. Her gown was of cambric, cut short before, in order to discover a high-heeled shoe, which was buckled almost at the toe. Her cap consisted of a few bits of cambric, and flowers of painted paper stuck on one side of her head. Her bosom, that had felt no hand, but the hand of time, these twenty years, rose suing to be pressed. I could, indeed, have wished her more than a handkerchief of Paris net to shade her beauties; for, as Tasso says of the rosebud, 'Quanto si mostra men tanto è più bella,' a female breast is generally thought more beautiful as it is more sparingly discovered.

" As my cousin had not put on all this finery for nothing, she was at that time sallying out to the Park, when I had overtaken her. Perceiving, however, that I had on my best wig, she offered, if I would 'squire her there, to send home the footman. Though I trembled for our reception in public, yet I could not, with any civility, refuse; so, to be as gallant as possible, I took her hand in my arm, and thus we marched on together.

" When we made our entry at the Park, two antiquated figures, so polite and so tender, soon attracted the eyes of the company. As we made our way among crowds who were out to show their finery as well as we, wherever we came I perceived we brought good-humour with us. The polite could not forbear smiling, and the vulgar burst out into a horse-laugh at our grotesque figures. Cousin Hannah, who was perfectly conscious of the rectitude of her own appearance, attributed all this mirth to the oddity of mine; while I as cordially placed the whole to her account. Thus, from being two of the best-natured creatures alive, before we got half way up the Mall, we both began to grow peevish, and, like two mice on a string, endeavoured to revenge the impertinence of the spectators upon each other. 'I am amazed, cousin Jeffrey,' says Miss, 'that I can never get you to dress like a Christian. I knew we should have the eyes of the Park upon us, with your great wig, so frizzed, and yet so beggarly, and your monstrous muff. I hate those odious muffs!' I could have patiently borne a criticism on all the rest of my equipage; but as I had had always a peculiar veneration for my muff, I could not forbear being piqued a little ; and, throwing my eyes with a spiteful air on her bosom, ' I could heartily wish, Madam,' replied I, ' that for your sake my muff was cut into a tippet.' [1]

" As my cousin, by this time, was grown heartily ashamed of her gentleman-usher, and as I was never very fond of any kind of exhibition myself, it was mutually agreed to retire for a while to one of the seats, and from that retreat remark on others as freely as they had remarked on us.

" When seated, we continued silent for some time, employed in very different speculations. I regarded the whole company, now passing in review before me, as drawn out merely for my amusement. For my entertainment the beauty had all that morning been improving her charms; the beau had put on lace, and the young doctor a big wig, merely to please me. But quite different were the sentiments of cousin Hannah : she regarded every well-dressed woman as a victorious rival, hated every face that seemed dressed in good-humour, or wore the appearance of greater happiness than her own. I perceived her uneasiness, and attempted to lessen it, by observing that there was no company in the Park to-day. To this she readily assented ; ' and yet,' says she, ' it is full enough of scrubs of one kind or another.' My smiling at this observation gave her spirits to pursue the bent of her inclination, and now she began to exhibit her skill in secret history, as she found me disposed to listen. ' Observe,' says she to me, ' that old woman in tawdry silk, and dressed out beyond the fashion. That is Miss Biddy Evergreen. Miss Biddy, it seems, has money ; and as she considers that money was never so scarce as it is now, she seems resolved to keep

---

[1] *Muffs worn by Men.*—Pepys' ' Diary,' under date " 30th Nov., 1662 (Lord's day)," has :—" This day I first did weare a muffe, being my wife's last year's muffe ; and now I have bought her a new one this serves me very well."—*Bohn's edition*, 1858, i., 354. Later, Steele, in the *Tatler*, No. 34, 1709, and Addison, in the same paper, No. 155, 1710, show that the practice existed in those days ; while the following, from Horace Walpole's ' Letters,' is evidence that the fashion prevailed even five years after Goldsmith wrote this essay :—" I send you a decent smallish muff, that you may put in your pocket, and it costs but four shillings."—*Letter to George Montagu*, dated Christmas-Eve, 1764.— ED.

what she has to herself. She is ugly enough, you see; yet, I assure you, she has refused several offers to my own knowledge within this twelvemonth. Let me see, three gentlemen from Ireland who study the law; two waiting captains; a doctor; and a Scotch preacher, who had like to have carried her off. All her time is passed between sickness and finery. Thus, she spends the whole week in a close chamber, with no other company but her monkey, her apothecary, and cat; and comes dressed out to the Park every Sunday, to show her airs, to get new lovers, to catch a new cold, and to make new work for the doctor.

"'There goes Mrs. Roundabout,—I mean the fat lady in the lutestring trollopee. Between you and I, she is but a cutler's wife. See how she's dressed, as fine as hands and pins can make her, while her two marriageable daughters, like bunters, in stiff gowns, are now taking sixpenny worth of tea at the White Conduit House.[1] Odious puss! how she waddles along, with her train two yards behind her! She puts me in mind of my Lord Bantam's Indian sheep, which are obliged to have their monstrous tails trundled along in a go-cart. For all her airs, it goes to her husband's heart to see four yards of good lutestring wearing against the ground, like one of his knives on a grindstone. To speak my mind, cousin Jeffrey, I never liked those tails; for suppose a young fellow should be rude, and the lady should offer to step back in the fright, instead of retiring, she treads upon her train, and falls fairly on her back; and then, you know, cousin,—her clothes may be spoiled.

"'Ah! Miss Mazzard! I knew we should not miss her in the Park; she in the monstrous Prussian bonnet. Miss, though so very fine, was bred a milliner; and might have had some custom if she had minded her business; but the girl was fond of finery, and instead of dressing her customers, laid out all her goods in adorning herself. Every new gown she put on impaired her credit; she still, however, went on improving her appearance, and

---

[1] In Penton Street, Islington. The grounds were long since covered with houses. See 'Citizen of the World,' Letter CXXII.—ED.

lessening her little fortune, and is now, you see, become a belle and a bankrupt.'

" My cousin was proceeding in her remarks, which were interrupted by the approach of the very lady she had been so freely describing. Miss had perceived her at a distance, and approached to salute her. I found, by the warmth of the two ladies' protestations, that they had been long intimate esteemed friends and acquaintance. Both were so pleased at this happy rencounter, that they were resolved not to part for the day. So we all crossed the Park together, and I saw them into a hackney coach at [1] St. James's. [2] I could not, however, help observing, *That they are generally most ridiculous themselves, who are apt to see most ridicule in others.*" [2]

[AN ACCOUNT OF THE SWEDES, WITH] SOME PARTICULARS
RELATIVE TO CHARLES XII.

NOT COMMONLY KNOWN.

STOCKHOLM.

SIR,—I cannot resist your solicitations, though it is possible I shall be unable to satisfy your curiosity. The polite of every country seem to have but one character. A gentleman of Sweden differs but little, except in trifles, from one of any other country. It is among the vulgar we are to find those distinctions which characterize a people, and from them it is that I take my picture of the Swedes.

Though the Swedes, in general, appear to languish under oppression, which often renders others wicked, or of malignant dispositions, it has not, however, the same influence upon them, as they are faithful, civil, and incapable of atrocious crimes. Would you believe that in Sweden highway robberies are not so much as heard of? For my part, I have not in the whole country seen a gibbet

---

[1] The ' Bee ' version has " at the gate of St. James's."—ED.
[2]—[2] This last observation appears only in the ' Bee ' version.—ED.

or a gallows. They pay an infinite respect to their eccle-
siastics, whom they suppose to be the privy-councillors of
Providence; who, on their part, turn this credulity to their
own advantage, and manage their parishioners as they
please. In general, however, they seldom abuse their
sovereign authority. Hearkened to as oracles, regarded
as the dispensers of eternal rewards and punishments,
they readily influence their hearers into justice, and
make them practical philosophers without the pains of
study.

As to their persons, they are perfectly well made, and
the men particularly have a very engaging air. The
greatest part of the boys which I saw in the country had
very white hair. They were as beautiful as Cupids, and
there was something open and entirely happy in their
little chubby faces. The girls, on the contrary, have
neither such fair nor such even complexions, and their
features are much less delicate, which is a circumstance
different from that of almost every other country. Besides this, it is observed, that the women are generally
afflicted with the itch, for which Scania is particularly remarkable. I had an instance of this in one of the inns on
the road. The hostess was one of the most beautiful
women I have ever seen; she had so fine a complexion,
that I could not avoid admiring it. But what was my
surprise, when she opened her bosom in order to suckle
her child, to perceive that seat of delight all covered with
this disagreeable distemper. The careless manner in
which she exposed to our eyes so disgusting an object,
sufficiently testifies that they regard it as no very extraordinary malady, and seem to take no pains to conceal it.
Such are the remarks, which probably you may think
trifling enough, I have made in my journey to Stockholm;
which, to take it altogether, is a large, beautiful, and even
populous city.

The arsenal appears to me one of its greatest curiosities:
it is a handsome, spacious building, but, however, illy
stored with the implements of war. To recompense this
defect, they have almost filled it with trophies, and other
marks of their former military glory. I saw there several
chambers filled with Danish, Saxon, Polish, and Russian

standards. There was at least enough to suffice half-a-
dozen armies; but new standards are more easily made
than new armies can be enlisted. I saw, besides, some very
rich furniture, and some of the crown jewels, of great
value; but what principally engaged my attention, and
touched me with passing melancholy, were the bloody, yet
precious, spoils of the two greatest heroes the North ever
produced. What I mean are the clothes in which the
great Gustavus Adolphus, and the intrepid Charles XII.
died, by a fate not unusual to kings. The first, if I remember, is a sort of a buff waistcoat, made antique fashion,
very plain, and without the least ornaments; the second,
which was even more remarkable, consisted only of a coarse
blue cloth coat, a large hat of less value, a shirt of coarse
linen, large boots, and buff gloves made to cover a great
part of the arm. His saddle, his pistols, and his sword,
have nothing in them remarkable; the meanest soldier
was in this respect no way inferior to his gallant monarch.
I shall use this opportunity to give you some particulars
of the life of a man already so well known, which I had
from persons who knew him when a child, and who now,
by a fate not unusual to courtiers, spend a life of poverty
and retirement, and talk over in raptures all the actions
of their old victorious king, companion, and master.

Courage and inflexible constancy formed the basis of
this monarch's character. In his tenderest years he gave
instances of both. When he was yet scarce seven years
old, being at dinner with the queen his mother, intending
to give a bit of bread to a great dog he was fond of, this
hungry animal snapt too greedily at the morsel, and bit his
hand in a terrible manner. The wound bled copiously,
but our young hero, without offering to cry, or taking the
least notice of his misfortune, endeavoured to conceal what
had happened, lest his dog should be brought into trouble,
and wrapped his bloody hand in the napkin. The queen,
perceiving that he did not eat, asked him the reason. He
contented himself with replying, that he thanked her, he
was not hungry. They thought he was taken ill, and so
repeated their solicitations: but all was in vain, though
the poor child was already grown pale with the loss of
blood. An officer who attended at table at last perceived

it; for Charles would sooner have died than betrayed his dog, who, he knew, intended no injury.

At another time, when in the small-pox, and his case appeared dangerous, he grew one day very uneasy in his bed, and a gentleman who watched him, desirous of covering him up close, received from the patient a violent box on his ear. Some hours after, observing the prince more calm, he entreated to know how he had incurred his displeasure, or what he had done to have merited a blow. "A blow?" replied Charles, "I don't remember any thing of it: I remember, indeed, that I thought myself in the battle of Arbela, fighting for Darius, where I gave Alexander a blow which brought him to the ground."

What great effects might not these two qualities of courage and constancy have produced, had they at first received a just direction! Charles, with proper instructions, thus naturally disposed, would have been the delight and the glory of his age. Happy those princes, who are educated by men who are at once virtuous and wise, and have been for some time in the school of affliction; who weigh happiness against glory, and teach their royal pupils the real value of fame; who are ever showing the superior dignity of man to that of royalty—that a peasant who does his duty is a nobler character than a king of even middling reputation! Happy, I say, were princes, could such men be found to instruct them; but those to whom such an education is generally intrusted, are men who themselves have acted in a sphere too high to know mankind. Puffed up themselves with ideas of false grandeur, and measuring merit by adventitious circumstances of greatness, they generally communicate those fatal prejudices to their pupils, confirm their pride by adulation, or increase their ignorance by teaching them to despise that wisdom which is found among the poor.

But not to moralize when I only intend a story,—what is related of the journeys of this prince is no less astonishing. He has sometimes been on horseback for four-and-twenty hours successively, and thus traversed the greatest part of his kingdom. At last, none of his officers were found capable of following him; he thus consequently rode the greatest part of these journeys quite alone, without taking a moment's repose, and without any other subsistence but a bit of bread. In one of these rapid courses he underwent an adventure singular enough. Riding thus post one day, all alone, he had the misfortune to have his horse fall dead under him. This might have embarrassed an ordinary man, but it gave Charles no sort of uneasiness. Sure of finding another horse, but not equally so of meeting with a good saddle and pistols, he ungirds his horse, claps the whole equipage on his own back, and, thus accoutred, marches on to the next inn, which by good fortune was not far off. Entering the stable, he here found a horse entirely to his mind; so, without further ceremony, he clapped on his saddle and housing with great composure, and was just going to mount, when the gentleman who owned the horse was apprized of a stranger's going to steal his property out of the stable. Upon asking the king, whom he had never seen, bluntly, how he presumed to meddle with his horse, Charles coolly replied, squeezing in his lips, which was his usual custom, that he took the horse because he wanted one; "for you see," continued he, "if I have none, I shall be obliged to carry the saddle myself." This answer did not seem at all satisfactory to the gentleman, who instantly drew his sword. In this the king was not much behindhand with him, and to it they were going, when the guards by this time came up, and testified that surprise which was natural to see arms in the hand of a subject against his king. Imagine whether the gentleman was less surprised than they at his unpremeditated disobedience. His astonishment, however, was soon dissipated by the king, who, taking him by the hand, assured him he was a brave fellow, and himself would take care he should be provided for. This promise was afterwards fulfilled, and I have been assured the king made him a captain.

I am, Sir, &c.

HAPPINESS, IN A GREAT MEASURE, DEPENDENT ON CONSTITUTION.[1] [DICK WILDGOOSE, ETC.]

WHEN I reflect on the unambitious retirement in which I passed the earlier part of my life in the country, I cannot avoid feeling some pain in thinking that those happy days are never to return. In that retreat all nature seemed capable of affording pleasure: I then made no refinements on happiness, but could be pleased with the most awkward efforts of rustic mirth; thought cross-purposes the highest stretch of human wit; and questions and commands the most rational way of spending the evening. Happy could so charming an illusion still continue! I find that age and knowledge only contribute to sour our dispositions. My present enjoyments may be more refined, but they are infinitely less pleasing. The pleasure the best actor[2] gives can no way compare to that I have received from a country wag who imitated a quaker's sermon. The music of the finest singer[3] is dissonance to what I felt when our old dairymaid sung me into tears with 'Johnny Armstrong's Last Good Night,' or the cruelty of 'Barbara Allan.'[4]

Writers of every age have endeavoured to show that pleasure is in us, and not in the objects offered for our amusement. If the soul be happily disposed, every thing becomes capable of affording entertainment; and distress will almost want a name. Every occurrence passes in review like the figures of a procession: some may be awkward, others ill dressed; but none but a fool is for this enraged with the master of the ceremonies.

I remember to have once seen a slave in a fortification in Flanders, who appeared no way touched with his situa-

---

[1] Essay III. in the volume of 'Essays.'—ED.

[2] The 'Bee' issue has "Garrick" for "best actor."—ED.

[3] "Matei" appears in 'The Bee' in lieu of "finest singer." Colomba Mattei had retired from the stage three years when the 'Essays' were published.—ED.

[4] "If I go to the opera where Signora Columba pours out all the mazes of melody, I sit and sigh for Lishoy fireside, and Johnny Armstrong's 'Last Good Night' from Peggy Golden."—GOLDSMITH to Hodson, Dec. 27, 1757, vide Letters, v. i.—ED.

tion. He was maimed, deformed, and chained; obliged to toil from the appearance of day till nightfall, and condemned to this for life; yet with all these circumstances of apparent wretchedness, he sung, would have danced, but that he wanted a leg, and appeared the merriest, happiest man of all the garrison. What a practical philosopher was here! a happy constitution supplied philosophy, and though seemingly destitute of wisdom, he was really wise. No reading or study had contributed to disenchant the fairy-land around him. Every thing furnished him with an opportunity of mirth; and though some thought him, from his insensibility, a fool, he was such an idiot as philosophers should wish to imitate; [1] for all philosophy is only forcing the trade of happiness, when nature seems to deny the means.[1]

They who, like our slave, can place themselves on that side of the world in which every thing appears in a pleasing light, will find something in every occurrence to excite their good humour. The most calamitous events, either to themselves or others, can bring no new affliction: the whole world is to them a theatre, on which comedies only are acted. All the bustle of heroism, or the rants of ambition, serve only to heighten the absurdity of the scene, and make the humour more poignant. They feel, in short, as little anguish at their own distress, or the complaints of others, as the undertaker, though dressed in black, feels sorrow at a funeral.

Of all the men I ever read of, the famous Cardinal de Retz [2] possessed this happiness of temper in the highest degree. As he was a man of gallantry, and despised all that wore the pedantic appearance of philosophy, wherever pleasure was to be sold, he was generally foremost to raise the auction. Being a universal admirer of the fair sex, when he found one lady cruel, he generally fell in love with another, from whom he expected a more favourable reception: if she too rejected his addresses, he never thought of

---

[1]—[1] This is not in the 'Bee' version.—ED.

[2] Jean Francis Paul Gondi, Cardinal de Retz, after a life of turbulence, in the course of which he experienced many changes of fortune, died in retirement in 1679. Voltaire said of him, that in his youth he lived like Catiline, and like Atticus in his old age.—B.

retiring into deserts, or pining in hopeless distress. He persuaded himself, that instead of loving the lady, he only fancied he had loved her, and so all was well again. When fortune wore her angriest look, and he at last fell into the power of his most deadly enemy, Cardinal Mazarine, (being confined a close prisoner in the Castle of Valenciennes), he never attempted to support his distress by wisdom or philosophy, for he pretended to neither. He only laughed at himself and his persecutor, and seemed infinitely pleased at his new situation. In this mansion of distress, though secluded from his friends, though denied all the amusements, and even the conveniences of life, he still retained his good humour; laughed at all the little spite of his enemies; and carried the jest so far as to be revenged, by writing the life of his gaoler.

All that the wisdom of the proud can teach,[1] is to be stubborn or sullen under misfortunes. The Cardinal's example will instruct us to be merry in circumstances of the highest affliction. It matters not whether our good humour be construed by others into insensibility, or even idiotism; it is happiness to ourselves, and none but a fool would measure his satisfaction by what the world thinks of it: [2]for my own part I never pass by one of our prisons for debt, that I do not envy that felicity which is still going forward among those people, who forget the cares of the world by being shut out from its ambition.[2]

The happiest silly fellow[3] I ever knew, was of the number of those good-natured creatures that are said to do no harm to any but themselves. Whenever he fell into any misery, he usually called it " seeing life." If his head was broke by a chairman, or his pocket picked by a sharper, he comforted himself by imitating the Hibernian dialect of the one, or the more fashionable cant of the other. Nothing came amiss to him. His inattention to money matters had incensed his father to such a degree, that all

---

[1] The ' Bee' version reads :—" All that philosophy can teach," &c.—ED.

[2]—[2] This was added in the ' Essays.'—ED.

[3] " Dick Wildgoose " is the name given to this " happiest silly fellow " in the ' Bee.' Though the full name was cut out for the ' Essays,' " Dick " remained, as will be seen in the following lines.—ED.

the intercession of friends in his favour was fruitless.
The old gentleman was on his deathbed. The whole
family, and Dick among the number, gathered around
him. "I leave my second son, Andrew," said the expiring
miser, "my whole estate, and desire him to be frugal."
Andrew, in a sorrowful tone, as is usual on these occasions,
prayed heaven to prolong his life and health to enjoy it
himself.—"I recommend Simon, my third son, to the care
of his elder brother, and leave him beside four thousand
pounds."—"Ah, father!" cried Simon, (in great affliction
to be sure,) "may heaven give you life and health to enjoy
it yourself!" At last, turning to poor Dick, "As for you,
you have always been a sad dog—you'll never come to
good; you'll never be rich; I'll leave you a shilling to
buy a halter."—"Ah, father!" cries Dick, without any
emotion, "may heaven give you life and health to enjoy
it yourself!" This was all the trouble the loss of fortune
gave this thoughtless, imprudent creature. However, the
tenderness of an uncle recompensed the neglect of a father;
and my friend is now not only excessively good humoured,
but competently rich.

Yes, let the world cry out at a bankrupt who appears at
a ball; at an author who laughs at the public which pro-
nounces him a dunce; at a general who smiles at the reproach of the vulgar; or the lady who keeps her good
humour in spite of scandal: but such is the wisest behaviour that any of us can possibly assume: it is certainly
a better way to oppose calamity by dissipation, than to
take up the arms of reason or resolution to oppose it: by
the first method we forget our miseries; by the last we
only conceal them from others. By struggling with misfortunes, we are sure to receive some wounds in the conflict; but a sure method to come off victorious, is by
running away.[1]

[1] The following well-known lines have been attributed to Goldsmith—
notably by Mr. J. Yeowell, of Islington, in *Notes and Queries* (3rd series,
vol. iv., p. 61)—on account of their appearing, as a paraphrase of the
two lines in 'Hudibras' (pt. iii., cant. iii., ll. 243, 244), in 'The Art of
Poetry,' a book of Newbery's, re-edited by Goldsmith in 1762 :—

    For he who fights and runs away
    May live to fight another day ;

ON OUR THEATRES.

MADEMOISELLE CLAIRON,[1] a celebrated actress at Paris, seems to me the most perfect female figure I have ever seen upon any stage. Not perhaps that nature has been more liberal of personal beauty to her, than some to be seen upon our theatres at home. There are actresses here who have as much of what connoisseurs call statuary grace, by which is meant elegance unconnected with motion, as she; but they all fall infinitely short of her, when the soul comes to give expression to the limbs, and animates every feature.

Her first appearance is excessively engaging: she never comes in staring round upon the company, as if she intended to count the benefits of the house, or at least to see, as well as be seen. Her eyes are always, at first, intently fixed upon the persons of the drama, and she lifts them, by degrees, with enchanting diffidence, upon the spectators. Her first speech, or at least the first part of it, is delivered with scarcely any motion of the arm; her hands and her tongue never set out together; but the one prepares us for the other. She sometimes begins with a mute, eloquent attitude; but never goes forward all at once with hands, eyes, head, and voice. This observation, though it may appear of no importance, should certainly be adverted to; nor do I see any one performer (Garrick only excepted) among us, that is not, in this particular, apt to offend. By this simple beginning she gives herself

---

But he who is in battle slain
Can never rise and fight again.

The truth, however, is, that these four lines appeared in the 1746 edition of Newbery's 'Art of Poetry,' with which of course Goldsmith could not have had anything to do, he being then but eighteen years old, and still in Ireland. In 1750 the above four lines appeared as a quotation in Ray's 'History of the Rebellion,' p. 48.—ED.

[1] Garrick, whose authority in stage criticism ought to carry some weight, professed the highest admiration of the professional talents of this accomplished actress, the Siddons' of the French stage. Voltaire also celebrated her in a poetical epistle addressed to her in 1765.—B. She retired from the stage in 1765, and died 1803.—ED.

a power of rising in the passion of the scene. As she proceeds, every gesture, every look, acquires new violence, till at last, transported, she fills the whole vehemence of the part, and all the idea of the poet.

Her hands are not alternately stretched out, and then drawn in again, as with the singing women at Sadler's Wells:[1] they are employed with graceful variety, and every moment please with new and unexpected eloquence. Add to this, that their motion is generally from the shoulder; she never flourishes her hands while the upper part of her arm is motionless, nor has she the ridiculous appearance as if her elbows were pinned to her hips.

But, of all the cautions to be given our rising actresses, I would particularly recommend it to them never to take notice of the audience upon any occasion whatsoever; let the spectators applaud never so loudly, their praises should pass, except at the end of the epilogue, with seeming inattention. I can never pardon a lady on the stage, who, when she draws the admiration of the whole audience, turns about to make them a low curtsy for their applause. Such a figure no longer continues Belvidera, but at once drops into Mrs. Cibber.[2] Suppose a sober tradesman, who once a-year takes his shilling's worth at Drury Lane, in order to be delighted with the figure of a queen—the queen of Sheba, for instance, or any other queen—this honest man has no other idea of the great but from their superior pride and impertinence: suppose such a man placed among the spectators, the first figure that presents on the stage is the queen herself, curtsying and cringing to all the company, how can he fancy her the haughty favourite of King Solomon the Wise, who appears actually more submissive than the wife of his bosom? We are all tradesmen of a nicer relish in this respect, and such conduct must disgust every spectator who loves to have the illusion of nature strong upon him.

Yet, while I recommend to our actresses a skilful atten-

---

[1] See Cradock's Epilogue to 'She Stoops to Conquer,' p. 291.—Ed.

[2] The wife of Theophilus Cibber, the actor, and sister of Dr. Arne, the composer. She played leading parts with Garrick, and was called " the nightingale of the stage." Nevertheless, Dr. Johnson thought her overrated as an actress. She died in 1766.—Ed.

tion to gesture, I would not have them study it in the
looking-glass. This, without some precaution, will render
their action formal; by too great an intimacy with this,
they become stiff and affected. People seldom improve
when they have no other model but themselves to copy
after. I remember to have known a notable performer of
the other sex, who made great use of this flattering monitor,
and yet was one of the stiffest figures I ever saw. I am
told his apartment was hung round with looking-glass,
that he might see his person twenty times reflected upon
entering the room; and I will make bold to say, he saw
twenty very ugly fellows whenever he did so.[1]

A LETTER FROM MR. VOLTAIRE TO MR. TIRIOT.

[Voltaire's ' History.'—Toleration.—Geneva.—' La Pucelle,' &c.]

Monrion, near Lausanne,
March 26, 1757.

DEAR SIR,

Of all the praises you are pleased to bestow on
my trifling ' Essay on General History,'[2] I can acquiesce
only in those which you mention of my impartiality, of
my love of truth, and of my zeal for the happiness of
society. All my life has been spent in contributing to
spread a spirit of philosophy and toleration, and such a
spirit now seems to characterize the age. This glorious
spirit, which animates every enlightened mind, has begun
to diffuse itself in this country, where first my valetudi-
nary constitution, and now the charms of tranquillity,
keep me. It is no small example of the progress of human
reason, that my History has been printed at Geneva with

---

[1] Said to have been Thomas Sheridan, father of the author of the
' School for Scandal.'—ED.

[2] Goldsmith had previously, August, 1757, written an article on this
history in the *Monthly Review*: see it in the Criticisms, in our vol. iv.—
ED.

public approbation, in which I have characterized Calvin as a man of a disposition as much more villainous as his understanding was more enlightened than that of the rest of mankind. The death of Servetus appears still abominable. The Dutch blush when they recollect their cruelty to Barnevelt. I know not whether the English yet find any remorse for theirs to Byng. The attempt and the tortures of Damien[1] have been objected to me as incongruous with my character of the present age. Almost every man of any figure in the literary world has demanded, Is this the nation which you have described as superior to others in wisdom? To this I answer (as I well may) that some men are of characters very different from that of their country, or the times they live in. A poor madman, of the dregs of the people, is not a model from which to characterize his country. But, on the other hand, Chatel and Ravillac were possessed with an epidemic fury, the spirit of public fanaticism turned their heads; and even so far was the age infected, that I have by me an apology for the behaviour of John Chatel, printed during the trial of this unhappy, but deluded creature. It is quite otherwise at present; Damien's attempt has been looked upon with indignation not only by France, but by all Europe.

In the little romantic country in which I reside, lying along the banks of the Genevan lake, we turn with horror from enormities like these. We act here as they ought to act at Paris; we live with tranquillity; we cultivate learning without divisions or envy. Tavernier observes that the prospect of Lausanne, from · the Genevan lake, resembles that of Constantinople; but what pleases me more than a prospect is, the love for the arts which inspires the generality of its inhabitants.

You have not been deceived when it was told you that 'Zara,' the 'Prodigal Son,'[2] and other plays, have been represented here as well as they could have been in Paris; yet, let not this surprise you, they neither know, nor speak any other language here than that of France. Al-

---

[1] See 'The Traveller,' line last but two.—ED.
[2] Two of Voltaire's own plays, the first being a version of Shakespeare's 'Othello.'—ED.

most all the families are of French extraction; and we have as much taste here as in any part of the world.

We have not here that low ridiculous history of the war in 1741, which they have printed at Paris with my name; nor the pretended *Porte feuille*, where there are scarce three sentences of mine; nor that infamous rhapsody, intituled, ' The Maid of Orleans,' replete with lines the most low and stupid that ever escaped from ignorance, and with insolencies the most atrocious that ever impudence had courage to avow. We must own that there have lately been many enormities committed at Paris, with both the dagger and the pen. I console myself at being distant from my friends, in finding myself removed from such enormities as these; and I must pity that amiable country which can thus produce monsters.[1]

VOLTAIRE.[2]

[1] Notwithstanding Voltaire's denial, and even denunciation of it, as here, ' La Pucelle,' somewhat altered to be sure, continues to be given in the works of Voltaire.—ED.

[2] This letter is in the *Panthéon Littéraire* edition of Voltaire's correspondence, and is dated as here.—ED.

THE BEE.

ON THE USE OF LANGUAGE.[1]

[*The true use of Speech is to conceal our wants—Pity and Friendship—It is Better to be Poor than to seem Poor—The story of Jack Spindle.*]

IT is usually said by grammarians, that the use of language is to express our wants and desires; but men who know the world hold, and I think with some show of reason, that he who best knows how to keep his necessities private is the most likely person to have them redressed; and that the true use of speech is not so much to express our wants, as to conceal them.[2]

When we reflect on the manner in which mankind generally confer their favours, there appears something so attractive in riches, that the large heap generally collects from the smaller; and the poor find as much pleasure in increasing the enormous mass of the rich, as the miser,

[1] No. V. in the volume of ' Essays.'—ED.

[2] A slightly different rendering of this idea is usually attributed to Talleyrand. He, however, may not have got the idea from Goldsmith, as Washington Irving has suggested. The Frenchman may rather have borrowed from Voltaire, who, in his 'Le Chapon et la Poularde' (Dialogues, XIV.), has :—" Ils n'emploient les paroles que pour déguiser leurs pensées." This to be sure is dated later than the ' Bee,' namely, in 1763; but it is hardly likely Voltaire saw Goldsmith's earliest collection of essays before 1763. But, before that date, in 1725, Dr. Young, in his ' Love of Fame,' satire ii.,-l. 207, had written :—

" Where Nature's end of language is declin'd,
And men talk only to conceal the mind ; "

while Jeremy Taylor, South (Sermons), Lloyd, and Butler had even earlier used the same idea.—ED.

who owns it, sees happiness in its increase. Nor is there in this any thing repugnant to the laws of morality. Seneca himself allows, that in conferring benefits, the present should always be suited to the dignity of the receiver. Thus the rich receive large presents, and are thanked for accepting them; men of middling stations are obliged to be content with presents something less; while the beggar, who may be truly said to want indeed, is well paid if a farthing rewards his warmest solicitations.

Every man who has seen the world, and has had his ups and downs in life, as the expression is, must have frequently experienced the truth of this doctrine, and must know, that to have much, or to seem to have it, is the only way to have more. Ovid finely compares a man of broken fortune to a falling column; the lower it sinks, the greater is that weight it is obliged to sustain. Thus, when a man's circumstances are such that he has no occasion to borrow, he finds numbers willing to lend him; but should his wants be such that he sues for a trifle, it is two to one whether he may be trusted with the smallest sum. A certain young fellow[1] whom I knew, whenever he had occasion to ask his friend for a guinea, used to prelude his request as if he wanted two hundred; and talked so familiarly of large sums, that none could ever think he wanted a small one. The same gentleman, whenever he wanted credit for a suit of clothes, always made the proposal in a laced coat; for he found by experience, that if he appeared 'shabby on these occasions, his tailor[2] had taken an oath against trusting; or, what was every whit as bad, his foreman was out of the way, and should not be at home for some time.

There can be no inducements to reveal our wants, except to find pity, and by this means relief; but before a poor man opens his mind in such circumstances, he should first consider whether he is contented to lose the esteem of the person he solicits, and whether he is willing to give up friendship to excite compassion. Pity and friendship

---

[1] The 'Bee' reads "at George's." This was a coffee-house in the Strand, near Temple Bar. There is another allusion to it in the essay on "Public Rejoicings for Victory" in vol. i.—ED.

[2] The 'Bee' version has "Mr. Lynch."—ED.

are passions incompatible with each other; and it is impossible that both can reside in any breast for the smallest space, without impairing each other. Friendship is made up of esteem and pleasure; pity is composed of sorrow and contempt: the mind may for some time fluctuate between them, but it never can entertain both at once.

In fact, pity though it may often relieve, is but at best, a short-lived passion, and seldom affords distress more than transitory assistance; with some it scarce lasts from the first impulse till the hand can be put into the pocket; with others it may continue for twice that space; and on some of extraordinary sensibility I have seen it operate for half an hour together: but still, last as it may, it generally produces but beggarly effects; and where, from this motive, we give five farthings, from others we give pounds; whatever be our feelings from the first impulse of distress, when the same distress solicits a second time, we then feel with diminished sensibility; and, like the repetition of an echo, every stroke becomes weaker; till, at last, our sensations lose all mixture of sorrow, and degenerate into downright contempt.

These speculations bring to my mind the fate of a very good natured fellow, who is now no more. He [1] was bred in a compting-house, and his father dying just as he was out of his time, left him a handsome fortune, and many friends to advise with. The restraint in which my friend had been brought up had thrown a gloom upon his temper, which some regarded as prudence; and, from such considerations, he had every day repeated offers of friendship. Such as had money, were ready to offer him their assistance that way; and they who had daughters, frequently, in the warmth of affection, advised him to marry. My friend, however, was in good circumstances; he wanted neither money, friends, nor a wife, and therefore modestly declined their proposals.

Some errors, however, in the management of his affairs, and several losses in trade, soon brought him to a different way of thinking; and he at last considered that it was his best way to let his friends know that their offers were

---

[1] Jack Spindle is his name in the ' Bee.'—ED.

at length acceptable. His first address was to a scrivener, who had formerly made him frequent offers of money and friendship, at a time when, perhaps, he knew those offers would have been refused. As a man, therefore, confident of not being refused, he requested the use of a hundred guineas for a few days, as he just then had occasion for money. "And pray, Sir," replied the scrivener, "do you want all this money?"—"Want it, Sir," says the other, "if I did not want it, I should not have asked it." —"I am sorry for that," says the friend; "for those who want money when they borrow, will always want money when they should come to pay. To say the truth, Sir, money is money now; and I believe it is all sunk in the bottom of the sea, for my part; and he that has got a little, is a fool if he does not keep what he has got."

Not quite disconcerted by this refusal, our adventurer was resolved to apply to another, whom he knew was the very best friend he had in the world. The gentleman whom he now addressed, received his proposal with all the affability that could be expected from generous friendship. "Let me see,—you want a hundred guineas; and, pray, dear Jack, would not fifty answer?"—"If you have but fifty to spare, Sir, I must be contented."—"Fifty to spare! I do not say that, for I believe I have but twenty about me."—"Then I must borrow the other thirty from some other friend."—"And pray," replied the friend, "would it not be the best way to borrow the whole money from that other friend, and then one note will serve for all, you know? You know, my dear Sir, that you need make no ceremony with me at any time; you know I'm your friend, when you choose a bit of dinner or so—You, Tom, see the gentleman down. You won't forget to dine with us now and then? Your very humble servant."

Distressed, but not discouraged, at this treatment, he was at last resolved to find that assistance from love, which he could not have from friendship. A young lady,[1] a distant relation by the mother's side, had a fortune in her own hands; and, as she had already made all the ad-

---

[1] The author names the lady "Miss Jenny Dismal" in the 'Bee.'— ED.

vances that her sex's modesty would permit, he made his proposal with confidence. He soon, however, perceived, that *No bankrupt ever found the fair one kind.* She had lately fallen deeply in love with another, who had more money, and the whole neighbourhood thought it would be a match.[1]

Every day now began to strip my poor friend of his former finery: his clothes flew piece by piece to the pawnbroker's, and he seemed at length equipped in the genuine livery of misfortune.[2] But still he thought himself secure from actual necessity; the numberless invitations he had received to dine, even after his losses, were yet unanswered; he was, therefore, now resolved to accept of a dinner, because he wanted one; and in this manner he actually lived among his friends a whole week without being openly affronted. The last place I saw him in was at a reverend divine's.[3] He had, as he fancied, just nicked the time of dinner, for he came in as the cloth was laying. He took a chair without being desired, and talked for some time without being attended to. He assured the company, that nothing procured so good an appetite as a walk in the Park,[4] where he had been that morning. He went on, and praised the figure of the damask table-cloth; talked of a feast where he had been the day before, but that the venison was overdone. But all this procured him no invitation:[5] finding, therefore, the gentleman of the house insensible to all his fetches, he thought proper, at last, to retire, and mend his appetite by a second walk in the Park.

You then, O ye beggars of my acquaintance, whether in rags or lace—whether in Kent Street, or the Mall—whether at the Smyrna[6] or St. Giles's,—might I be permitted to advise as a friend, never seem to want the favour which you solicit. Apply to every passion but human pity for

---

[1] In the 'Bee' it is—"Miss Jenny and Master Billy Galloon were lately fallen deeply in love," &c.—ED.

[2] It is "genuine mourning of antiquity" in the 'Bee.'—ED.

[3] "The Rev. Dr. Gosling's" in the 'Bee.'—ED.

[4] It is "to White Conduit House" in the 'Bee.' See p. 328.—ED.

[5] The 'Bee' adds—"and he was not yet sufficiently hardened to stay without being asked."—ED.

[6] "The Smyrna" was a coffee-house in Pall-Mall.—ED.

redress. You may find permanent relief from vanity, from
self-interest, or from avarice, but from compassion—never.[1]
The very eloquence of a poor man is disgusting; and that
mouth which is opened even by wisdom,[2] is seldom expected to close without the horrors of a petition.

To ward off the gripe of poverty, you must pretend to be
a stranger to her, and she will at least use you with ceremony.[3] If you be caught dining upon a halfpenny por-
ringer of pease-soup and potatoes, praise the wholesome-
ness of your frugal repast. You may observe that Dr.
Cheyne has prescribed pease-broth for the gravel; hint
that you are not one of those who are always making a
deity of your belly. If, again, you are obliged to wear
flimsy stuff in the midst of winter, be the first to remark
that stuffs are very much worn at Paris; or, if there be
found some irreparable defects in any part of your
equipage, which cannot be concealed by all the arts of sitting cross-legged, coaxing, or darning, say that neither you
nor Samson Gideon [4] were ever very fond of dress. If you
be a philosopher, hint that Plato or Seneca are the tailors
you choose to employ; assure the company, that man
ought to be content with a bare covering, since what is
now so much his pride, was formerly his shame.[5]

In short, however caught, never give out; but ascribe
to the frugality of your disposition, what others might be
apt to attribute to the narrowness of your circumstances.[6]
To be poor, and to seem poor, is a certain method never to
rise: pride in the great is hateful; in the wise it is ridiculous; but beggarly pride is a rational vanity which I have
been taught to applaud and excuse.[7]

[1] The 'Bee' has "but seldom from compassion."—ED.

[2] The 'Bee' has "even for flattery."—ED.

[3] The 'Bee' also has—"Hear not my advice, but that of Offellus."—
ED.

[4] Sampson Gideon was a rich Jew broker of the time. His son was
made an Irish peer (Baron Eardley of Spalding).—ED.

[5] Here follows in the 'Bee'—"Horace will give you a Latin sentence
fit for the occasion.—

   "Toga defendere frigus quamvis crassa queat."

[6] The 'Bee' text adds—"and appear rather to be a miser than a
beggar."—ED.

[7] The 'Bee' version is—"beggarly pride is the only sort of vanity I
can excuse."—ED.

THE HISTORY OF HYPATIA.[1]

Man, when secluded from society, is not a more solitary being than the woman who leaves the duties of her own sex to invade the privileges of ours. She seems, in such circumstances, like one in banishment; she appears like a neutral being between the sexes; and, though she may have the admiration of both, she finds true happiness from neither.

Of all the ladies of antiquity, I have read of none who was ever more justly celebrated than the beautiful Hypatia, the daughter of Theon the philosopher. This most accomplished of women was born at Alexandria, in the reign of Theodosius the younger. Nature was never more lavish of its gifts than it had been to her, endued as she was with the most exalted understanding, and the happiest turn to science. Education completed what nature had begun, and made her the prodigy not only of her age, but the glory of her sex.

From her father she learned geometry and astronomy; she collected from the conversation and schools of the other philosophers, for which Alexandria was at that time famous, the principles of the rest of the sciences.

What cannot be conquered by natural penetration and a passion for study! The boundless knowledge which, at that period of time, was required to form the character of a philosopher no way discouraged her; she delivered herself up to the study of Aristotle and Plato, and soon not one in all Alexandria understood so perfectly as she all the difficulties of these two philosophers.

But not their systems alone, but those of every other sect, were quite familiar to her; and, to this knowledge, she added that of polite learning, and the art of oratory. All the learning which it was possible for the human mind to contain, being joined to a most enchanting eloquence, rendered this lady the wonder not only of the populace,

[1] The 'Bee' spells the name "Hypasia;" and in line 10 says she was "the daughter of Leon the philosopher."—Ed.

who easily admire, but of philosophers themselves, who
are seldom fond of admiration.

The city of Alexandria was every day crowded with
strangers, who came from all parts of Greece and Asia to
see and hear her. As for the charms of her person, they
might not probably have been mentioned, did she not join
to a beauty the most striking, a virtue that might repress
the most assuming; and though, in the whole capital,
famed for charms, there was not one who could equal her
in beauty, though in a city the resort of all the learning
then existing in the world, there was not one who could
equal her in knowledge; yet, with such accomplishments,
Hypatia was the most modest of her sex. Her reputation
for virtue was not less than her virtues; and, though in a
city divided between two factions, though visited by the
wits and the philosophers of the age, calumny never dared
to suspect her morals, or attempt her character. Both
the Christians and the Heathens who have transmitted
her history and her misfortunes, have but one voice, when
they speak of her beauty, her knowledge, and her virtue.
Nay, so much harmony reigns in their accounts of this
prodigy of perfection, that, in spite of the opposition of
their faith, we should never have been able to judge of
what religion was Hypatia, were we not informed, from
other circumstances, that she was a heathen. Providence
had taken so much pains in forming her, that we are
almost induced to complain of its not having endeavoured
to make her a Christian; but from this complaint we are
deterred by a thousand contrary observations, which lead
us to reverence its inscrutable mysteries.

This great reputation, of which she so justly was possessed, was, at last, however, the occasion of her ruin.

The person who then possessed the patriarchate of
Alexandria, was equally remarkable for his violence,
cruelty, and pride. Conducted by an ill-grounded zeal
for the Christian religion, or, perhaps, desirous of aug-
menting his authority in the city, he had long meditated
the banishment of the Jews. A difference arising between
them and the Christians, with respect to some public
games, seemed to him a proper juncture for putting his
ambitious designs into execution. He found no difficulty

in exciting the people, naturally disposed to revolt. The prefect who, at that time, commanded the city, interposed on this occasion, and thought it just to put one of the chief creatures of the patriarch to the torture, in order to discover the first promoter of the conspiracy. The patriarch, enraged at the injustice he thought offered to his character and dignity, and piqued at the protection which was offered to the Jews, sent for the chiefs of the synagogue, and enjoined them to renounce their designs, upon pain of incurring his highest displeasure.

The Jews, far from fearing his menaces, excited new tumults, in which several citizens had the misfortune to fall. The patriarch could no longer contain : at the head of a numerous body of Christians, he flew to the synagogues, which he demolished, and drove the Jews from a city, of which they had been possessed since the times of Alexander the Great. It may be easily imagined, that the prefect could not behold, without pain, his jurisdiction thus insulted, and the city deprived of a number of its most industrious inhabitants.

The affair was, therefore, brought before the emperor. The patriarch complained of the excesses of the Jews, and the prefect, of the outrages of the patriarch. At this very juncture, five hundred monks of Mount Nitria, imagining the life of their chief to be in danger, and that their religion was threatened in his fall, flew into the city with ungovernable rage, attacked the prefect in the streets, and, not content with loading him with reproaches, wounded him in several places.

The citizens had by this time notice of the fury of the monks; they therefore assembled in a body, put the monks to flight, seized on him who had been found throwing a stone, and delivered him to the prefect, who caused him to be put to death without farther delay.

The patriarch immediately ordered the dead body, which had been exposed to view, to be taken down, procured for it all the pomp and rites of burial, and went even so far as himself to pronounce the funeral oration, in which he classed a seditious monk among the martyrs. This conduct was by no means generally approved of; the most moderate even among the Christians perceived and blamed his indiscretion; but he was now too far advanced to retire. He had made several overtures towards a reconciliation with the prefect, which not succeeding, he bore all those an implacable hatred whom he imagined to have any hand in traversing his designs; but Hypatia was particularly destined to ruin. She could not find pardon, as she was known to have a most refined friendship for the prefect; wherefore the populace were incited against her. Peter, a reader of the principal church, one of those vile slaves by which men in power are too frequently attended—wretches ever ready to commit any crime which they hope may render them agreeable to their employer,— this fellow, I say, attended by a crowd of villains, waited for Hypatia, as she was returning from a visit, at her own door, seized her as she was going in, and dragged her to one of the churches called Cesarea, where, stripping her in a most inhuman manner, they exercised the most inhuman cruelties upon her, cut her into pieces, and burnt her remains to ashes. Such was the end of Hypatia, the glory of her own sex, and the astonishment of ours.[1]

ON JUSTICE AND GENEROSITY.[2]

LYSIPPUS is a man whose greatness of soul the whole world admires. His generosity is such that it prevents a demand, and saves the receiver the trouble and the confusion of a request. His liberality also does not oblige more by its greatness than by his inimitable grace in giving. Sometimes he even distributes his bounties to strangers, and has been known to do good offices to those who professed themselves his enemies. All the world are unanimous in the praise of his generosity; there is only one

---

[1] Hypatia was murdered A.D. 415. The Christian patriarch of Alexandria, here, and in most other accounts, held responsible for her death was St. Cyril. Gibbon's account is to the same effect: see his 'Decline and Fall,' Bohn's edition, 1854, vol. v., p. 213. Hypatia's story is also told in Canon Kingsley's beautiful work bearing her name.—ED.

[2] No. VI. in the 'Essays.'—ED.

sort of people who complain of his conduct,—Lysippus does not pay his debts.

It is no difficult matter to account for a conduct so seemingly incompatible with itself. There is greatness in being generous, and there is only simple justice in his satisfying his creditors. Generosity is the part of a soul raised above the vulgar. There is in it something of what we admire in heroes, and praise with a degree of rapture. Justice, on the contrary, is a mere mechanic virtue, only fit for tradesmen, and what is practised by every broker in 'Change Alley.[1]

. In paying his debts a man barely does his duty, and it is an action attended with no sort of glory. Should Lysippus satisfy his creditors, who would be at the pains of telling it to the world? Generosity is a virtue of a very different complexion. It is raised above duty, and, from its elevation, attracts the attention and the praises of us little mortals below.

In this manner do men generally reason upon justice and generosity. The first is despised, though a virtue essential to the good of society; and the other attracts our esteem, which too frequently proceeds from an impetuosity of temper, rather directed by vanity than reason. Lysippus is told that his banker asks a debt of forty pounds, and that a distressed acquaintance petitions for the same sum. He gives it without hesitating to the latter; for he demands as a favour what the former requires as a debt.

Mankind in general are not sufficiently acquainted with the import of the word *justice*: it is commonly believed to consist only in a performance of those duties to which the laws of society can oblige us. This, I allow, is sometimes the import of the word, and in this sense justice is distinguished from equity; but there is a justice still more extensive, and which can be shown to embrace all the virtues united.

Justice may be defined [as], that virtue which impels us to give to every person what is his due. In this extended sense of the word, it comprehends the practice of every

---

[1] Jonathan's Coffee House, the resort of the stock-brokers, stood here, and so originated the Stock Exchange of our day.—ED.

virtue which reason prescribes, or society should expect. Our duty to our Maker, to each other, and to ourselves, are fully answered, if we give them what we owe them. Thus justice, properly speaking, is the only virtue; and all the rest have their origin in it.

The qualities of candour, fortitude, charity, and generosity, for instance, are not, in their own nature, virtues; and if ever they deserve the title, it is owing only to justice, which impels and directs them. Without such a moderator, candour might become indiscretion, fortitude obstinacy, charity imprudence, and generosity mistaken profusion.

A disinterested action, if it be not conducted by justice, is at best indifferent in its nature, and not unfrequently even turns to vice. The expenses of society, of presents, of entertainments, and the other helps to cheerfulness, are actions merely indifferent, when not repugnant to a better method of disposing of our superfluities; but they become vicious when they obstruct or exhaust our abilities from a more virtuous disposition of our circumstances.

True generosity is a duty as indispensably necessary as those imposed upon us by law. It is a rule imposed upon us by reason, which should be the sovereign law of a rational being. But this generosity does not consist in obeying every impulse of humanity, in following blind passion for our guide, and impairing our circumstances by present benefactions, so as to render us incapable of future ones.

Misers are generally characterized as men without honour, or without humanity, who live only to accumulate, and to this passion sacrifice every other happiness. They have been described as madmen, who, in the midst of abundance, banish every pleasure, and make, from imaginary wants, real necessities. But few, very few, correspond to this exaggerated picture; and perhaps there is not one in whom all these circumstances are found united. Instead of this, we find the sober and the industrious branded by the vain and the idle with this odious appellation; men who, by frugality and labour, raise themselves above their equals, and contribute their share of industry to the common stock.

Whatever the vain or the ignorant may say, well were it for society had we more of these characters amongst us. In general, these close men are found at last the true benefactors of society. With an avaricious man we seldom lose in our dealings; but too frequently in our commerce with prodigality.

A French priest, whose name was Godinot, went for a long time by the name of the Griper. He refused to relieve the most apparent wretchedness, and, by a skilful management of his vineyard, had the good fortune to acquire immense sums of money. The inhabitants of Rheims, who were his fellow-citizens, detested him; and the populace, who seldom love a miser, wherever he went followed him with shouts of contempt. He still, however, continued his former simplicity of life, his amazing and unremitted frugality. He had long perceived the wants of the poor in the city, particularly in having no water but what they were obliged to buy at an advanced price; wherefore, that whole fortune which he had been amassing, he laid out in an aqueduct; by which he did the poor more useful and lasting service, than if he had distributed his whole income in charity every day at his door.[1]

Among men long conversant with books, we too frequently find those misplaced virtues of which I have been now complaining. We find the studious animated with a strong passion for the great virtues, as they are mistakenly called, and utterly forgetful of the ordinary ones. The declamations of philosophy are generally rather exhausted on those supererogatory duties, than on such as are indispensably necessary. A man, therefore, who has taken his ideas of mankind from study alone, generally comes into the world with a heart melting at every fictitious distress. Thus he is induced, by misplaced liberality, to put himself into the indigent circumstances of the person he relieves.

I shall conclude this paper with the advice of one of the ancients, to a young man whom he saw giving away all his substance to pretended distress. "It is possible

---

[1] The curious defence of misers here attempted Goldsmith repeats, in substance, in No. V., "On Political Frugality" (p. 378), and elsewhere. —ED.

that the person you relieve may be an honest man; and I know that you who relieve him are such. You see, then, by your generosity, you rob a man who is certainly deserving, to bestow it on one who may possibly be a rogue; and, while you are unjust in rewarding uncertain merit, you are doubly guilty by stripping yourself."[1]

ON WIT.

BY VOLTAIRE.[2]

WIT seems to be one of those undetermined sounds to which we affix scarce any precise idea. It is something more than judgment, genius, taste, talent, penetration, grace, delicacy, and yet it partakes somewhat of each. It may be properly defined ingenious reason. It is one of those general terms which always want another word to determine their signification; and when we hear such a work praised for being witty, such a man applauded for wit, it is but just to ask of what sort.

Thus Corneille with sublimity, and Boileau with exactness; Fontaine with simplicity, and Bruyere by being natural, are reckoned men of wit, yet each differs from the other; and still more from some philosophers who may be accounted witty men, and join sagacity to imagination.

They who despise the genius of Aristotle (instead of being contented with rejecting his Physics only, which cannot be good, as he had but few experiments to direct them) will be much surprised to find in his rhetoric the manner of saying things wittily. He informs us there, that the art does not consist in simply using the proper term, which offers to the imagination nothing new. We ought, says he, rather to employ a metaphor, or a figure, the sense of which must be clear, and the expression energetic.

---

[1] Goldsmith enforces the lesson of this paper in the letter to his brother Henry dated [Feb., 1759]: see Letters, in v. i.—ED.

[2] An abridgment of the article "*Esprit*" in Voltaire's 'Philosophical Dictionary.'—ED.

Of this he gives several examples, and, among others, the expression of Pericles, in talking of a battle in which the most beautiful of the youth of Athens were slain, "The year has been deprived of its spring." He adds, that the thought also should have the grace of novelty. The person who first, to express how pleasures were generally attended with pain, made use of the simile of roses being gathered among thorns, had wit. But it is otherwise with those who repeat it after him.

But a metaphor is not always the wittiest manner of expressing a thing with spirit, a great deal consists in an unexpected turn, in leaving us to understand without trouble, a part of the poet's meaning. This is so much the more pleasing, as it seems an indirect compliment to the reader, and shows his wit as well as that of the poet. Allusion, allegory, comparison, each furnishes an extensive field of ingenuity; history, fable, and the effects of nature, furnish matter to a well-regulated imagination, that can never be exhausted.

Let us then consider in what places wit should be admitted. It seems pretty manifest, that, in works of dignity, it should be used with caution, as it is only, at best, an ornament. The great art is in the proper timing this ornament. A fine thought, a just and elegant comparison, are faults, when reason only, or when passion should speak, and particularly where the subject is interesting. Using it in such circumstances as these, should not be called false wit (as Addison commonly expresses it); but wit displaced, and every misplaced beauty is rather a defect. This is a fault in which Virgil never transgresses, and with which Tasso may be sometimes reproached, all admirable as he is at other times. This error generally arises from an author's exuberance; filled with ideas of different kinds, he is desirous of showing himself when he ought only to exhibit his personages. The best method of knowing the true use to be made of wit is, by reading the small number of good works both in the learned languages and in our own.

False wit, as I have already hinted, is very different from displaced wit. This is not only a false thought, but is generally far-fetched also. A man of some wit, who

formerly abridged Homer in French verse, imagined he
added beauties to the old simple bard, in sometimes lend-
ing him embellishments. On the reconciling of Achilles
with Agamemnon, he thus flourishes it:

> " *Tout le camp s'ecria, dans une joie extrème :*
> *Que ne vaincra-t-il point? il s'est vaincu lui-même !* "

> " The shouting army cry'd with joy extreme,
> He sure must conquer, who himself can tame ! " [1]

His taming himself does by no means imply his conquering others; but this is not the absurdity alone, but in
making the army, as if by inspiration, join in a far-fetched
observation. If this shocks the reader of nice discernment, how much more so must all those forced expressions, cold yet stiffened allusions, and bloated nothings
displease, which are found in great plenty in works of
otherwise real merit. How can we bear to hear a mathe-
matician say, " If Saturn should happen to be removed,
the remotest of his satellites would probably take his
place, since great princes always keep their successors at
a distance." It is intolerable, when speaking of Hercules
understanding physics, to say that there was no resisting
a philosopher of his force. The desire of sparkling and
surprising is too frequently the cause of excesses of this
kind.

This trifling vanity has also produced the playing upon
words in every language, which is the worst sort of false
wit.

False taste is very different from false wit, as the latter
always proceeds from affectation, from an effort to go
wrong; on the contrary, the other is a habit of going
wrong without design, and following, as if by instinct,
some bad, though established model. The incoherent
exuberance of an Oriental imagination is a false taste, and
an improper example to imitate : however, they more frequently transgress in this respect, rather from a poverty
than a copiousness of real genius. Falling stars, splitting
mountains, rivers flowing to their sources, the sun and
moon dissolving, false and unnatural comparisons, and

---

[1] This beautifier of Homer was Antony Houdart de la Motte, 1672-
1731.—ED.

nature everywhere exaggerated, form the character of these writers; and this arises from their never, in these countries, being permitted to speak in public. True eloquence has never been cultivated there, and it is much easier to write in a turgid strain, than with ease and delicate simplicity.

In a word, false wit is entirely the opposite of the Eastern manner; the man of false wit desires to say in riddles, what others have spoken naturally. He desires to unite ideas the most incompatible, to divide those which nature has united. To catch unnatural similitudes, without discretion to unite pleasantry with what is serious, to mix great and little images together, and to confuse instead of satisfying the imagination.

But perspicuity is not the only part of style in which false wit is not conspicuous, we are at the same time too fond of embellishment. In our most applauded productions there is scarce a sentence which is not loaded with unnecessary ornament, which, though it may add grace to a period, generally disunites the force of a paragraph. The attention, as in Gothic architecture, is split upon a number of minute elegances, which, though each is separately pretty, diminish the force of the whole.

These are faults that seem to characterize the age; to these every author who would be admired must conform. With these faults he is sure of immediate applause, though frequently scarce allowed a reading. We have seen many a writer, of late, make his appearance with these qualifications, instead of merit; we have seen him read by a few, praised by all, and soon forgotten.

I have been often at a loss, whether to ascribe the decline of taste in a nation, to the reader or the writer. Perhaps both are in fault; the one satiated with varied instances of perfection, grows whimsical, desires something new, and mistakes change for improvement. The other, willing to avoid the character of an imitator, borrows peculiarities from affectation, and becomes original only in trifles. In short, it is as difficult now, among such a number of candidates, to catch the attention without these oddities of style, as to be remarkable in a crowd without some peculiarity in dress or behaviour.

But these are generally fleeting modes, which are introduced by the great, brought up to please for a day, soon
to be displaced by others which have the advantage of
being more new to recommend them. The literary republic, however, will never suffer real injury from such;
for whatever pleases from its novelty alone, can never
please long. Not from these, then, but from the com-
pilers and commentators of the day, is literature to expect
the mortal blow; from pedants who have no claim but
their industry for our applause; from laborious drones,
who write through folios, but do not think through a
page.

SOME PARTICULARS RELATING TO FATHER FREIJO.[1]

> " Primus mortales tollere contra
> Est oculos ausus, primusque assurgere contra."—LUCR.

THE Spanish nation has, for many centuries past, been
remarkable for the grossest ignorance in polite literature,
especially in point of natural philosophy—a science so
useful to mankind, that her neighbours have ever esteemed
it a matter of the greatest importance to endeavour, by
repeated experiments, to strike a light out of the chaos in
which truth seemed to be confounded. Their curiosity in
this respect was so indifferent, that though they had discovered new worlds, they were at a loss to explain the
phenomena of their own, and their pride so unaccountable, that they disdained to borrow from others that instruction which their natural indolence permitted them
not to acquire.

It gives me, however, a secret satisfaction to behold an
extraordinary genius now existing in that nation, whose
studious endeavours seem calculated to undeceive the
superstitious, and instruct the ignorant,—I mean the celebrated Padre Freijo. In unravelling the mysteries of
nature, and explaining physical experiments, he takes an

[1] See also the 'Enquiry into Polite Learning,' &c., in v. iii., chap. 6.
—ED.

opportunity of displaying the concurrence of second causes, in those very wonders which the vulgar ascribe to supernatural influence.

An example of this kind happened a few years ago in a small town of the kingdom of Valencia. Passing through at the hour of mass, he alighted from his mule, and proceeded to the parish church, which he found extremely crowded, and there appeared on the faces of the faithful a more than usual alacrity. The sun, it seems, which had been for some minutes under a cloud, had begun to shine on a large crucifix, that stood on the middle of the altar, studded with several precious stones. The reflection from these, and from the diamond eyes of some silver saints, so dazzled the multitude, that they unanimously cried out, "A miracle! a miracle!" whilst the priest at the altar, with seeming consternation, continued his heavenly conversation. Padre Freijo soon dissipated the charm, by tying his handkerchief round the head of one of the statues, for which he was arraigned by the Inquisition; whose flames, however, he has had the good fortune hitherto to escape.

THE BEE.

No. IV.—SATURDAY, OCTOBER 27, 1759.

MISCELLANEOUS.

[The ' Bee.'—On the Uncertainty of Literary Success, &c.]

WERE I to measure the merit of my present under-taking by its success, or the rapidity of its sale, I might be led to form conclusions by no means favourable to the pride of an author. Should I estimate my fame by its extent, every newspaper and every magazine would leave me far behind. Their fame is diffused in a very wide circle, that of some as far as Islington, and some yet farther still; while mine, I sincerely believe, has hardly travelled beyond the sound of Bow-bell; and while the works of others fly like unpinioned swans, I find my own move as heavily as a new-plucked goose.

Still, however, I have as much pride as they who have ten times as many readers. It is impossible to repeat all the agreeable delusions in which a disappointed author is apt to find comfort. I conclude, that what my reputation wants in extent, is made up by its solidity. *Minus juvat Gloria lata quam magna.* I have great satisfaction in considering the delicacy and discernment of those readers I have, and in ascribing my want of popularity to the ignorance or inattention of those I have not. All the world may forsake an author, but vanity will never forsake him.

Yet, notwithstanding so sincere a confession, I was once induced to show my indignation against the public, by discontinuing my endeavours to please; and was bravely resolved, like Raleigh, to vex them by burning my manuscript in a passion.[1] Upon recollection, however, I considered what set or body of people would be displeased at my rashness. The sun, after so sad an accident, might shine next morning as bright as usual; men might laugh and sing the next day, and transact business as before, and not a single creature feel any regret but myself.

I reflected upon the story of a minister, who, in the reign of Charles II., upon a certain occasion, resigned all his posts, and retired into the country in a fit of resentment. But, as he had not given the world entirely up with his ambition, he sent a messenger to town, to see how the courtiers would bear his resignation. Upon the messenger's return he was asked, whether there appeared any commotion at court? To which he replied, there were very great ones. " Ay," says the minister, " I knew my friends would make a bustle; all petitioning the king for my restoration, I presume? "—" No, Sir," replied the messenger, " they are only petitioning his majesty to be put in your place." In the same manner, should I retire in indignation, instead of having Apollo in mourning, or the Muses in a fit of the spleen; instead of having the learned world apostrophizing at my untimely decease,—perhaps all Grub Street[2] might laugh at my fall, and self-approving dignity might never be able to shield me from ridicule. In short, I am resolved to write on, if it were only to spite them. If the present generation will not hear my voice, hearken, O Posterity, to you I call, and from you I expect redress! What rapture will it not give to have the Scaligers, Daciers, and Warburtons of future times, commenting with admiration upon every line I now write, working away those ignorant creatures who offer to arraign my merit, with all the virulence of learned reproach.[3] Ay, my friends, let them feel it: call names, never spare them; they deserve it all, and ten times more. I have been told of a critic,[4]

---

[1] Aubrey says this is what Sir Walter Raleigh did with the second volume of his ' History of the World.'—ED.

[2] See *ante*, p. 309.—ED.

[3] A similar passage occurs in the author's letter to Robert Bryanton, dated Aug. 14, 1758 : see the Letters at the end of vol. i.—ED.

[4] Zoilus, "*the scourge of Homer*," is said to have been crucified by

who was crucified, at the command of another, to the reputation of Homer. That, no doubt, was more than
poetical justice, and I shall be perfectly content if those
who criticise me are only clapped in the pillory, kept fifteen
days upon bread and water, and obliged to run the gantlope [1] through Pater-noster Row. The truth is, I can expect happiness from Posterity either way. If I write ill,
happy in being forgotten; if well, happy in being remembered with respect.

Yet, considering things in a prudential light, perhaps I
was mistaken in designing my paper as an agreeable relaxation to the studious, or a help to conversation among
the gay; instead of addressing it to such, I should have
written down to the taste and apprehension of the many,
and sought for reputation on the broad road. [2] Literary
fame, I now find, like religious, generally begins among
the vulgar. As for the polite, they are so very polite as
never to applaud upon any account. One of these, with a
face screwed up into affectation, tells you, that fools may
admire, but men of sense only *approve*. [3] Thus, lest he
should rise in rapture at any thing new, he keeps down
every passion but pride and self-importance; approves
with phlegm, and the poor author is damned in the taking
a pinch of snuff. Another has written a book himself,
and being condemned for a dunce, he turns a sort of king's
evidence in criticism, and now becomes the terror of every
offender. A third, possessed of full-grown reputation,
shades off every beam of favour from those who endeavour to grow beneath him, and keeps down that merit,
which, but for his influence, might rise into equal
eminence. While others, still worse, peruse old books
for their amusement, and new books only to condemn;
so that the public seem heartily sick of all but the
business of the day, and read every thing now with as

---

order of Ptolemy Philadelphus, who was a great encourager of learning.
—B.
[1] We say *gauntlet* now, but Goldsmith's (*gantlope*) is the correct
word.—ED.   [2] See *ante*, p. 306.—ED.
[3]   " Yet let not each gay turn thy rapture move;
        For fools admire, but men of sense approve."
            POPE's *Essay on Criticism*, ll. 390-1.—ED.

little attention as they examine the faces of the passing crowd.

From these considerations, I was once determined to throw off all connections with taste, and fairly address my countrymen in the same engaging style and manner with other periodical pamphlets, much more in vogue than probably mine shall ever be. To effect this, I had thoughts of changing the title into that of the ROYAL BEE, the ANTIGALLICAN BEE, or the BEE'S MAGAZINE. I had laid in a proper stock of popular topics, such as encomiums on the King of Prussia, invectives against the Queen of Hungary and the French, the necessity of a militia, our undoubted sovereignty of the seas, reflections upon the present state of affairs, a dissertation upon liberty, some seasonable thoughts upon the intended bridge of Blackfriars, and an address to Britons; the history of an old woman, whose teeth grew three inches long, an ode upon our victories, a rebus, an acrostic upon Miss Peggy P., and a journal of the weather. All this, together with four extraordinary pages of *letter-press*, a beautiful map of England, and two prints curiously coloured from nature, I fancied might touch their very souls. I was actually beginning an address to the people, when my pride at last overcame my prudence, and determined me to endeavour to please by the goodness of my entertainment, rather than by the magnificence of my sign.

The Spectator, and many succeeding essayists, frequently inform us of the numerous compliments paid them in the course of their lucubrations—of the frequent encouragements they meet to inspire them with ardour, and increase their eagerness to please. I have received *my letters* as well as they; but, alas! not congratulatory ones—not assuring me of success and favour,—but pregnant with bodings that might shake even fortitude itself.

One gentleman assures me, he intends to throw away no more threepences in purchasing the BEE; and, what is still more dismal, he will not recommend me as a poor author wanting encouragement to his neighbourhood, which, it seems, is very numerous. Were my soul set upon threepences, what anxiety might not a denunciation produce! But such does not happen to be the present motive of publication: I write partly to show my good nature, and partly to show my vanity ; nor will I lay down the pen till I am satisfied one way or another.

Others have disliked the title and the motto of my paper ; point out a mistake in the one, and assure me the other has been consigned to dulness by anticipation. All this may be true; *but what is that to me?* Titles and mottoes to books are like escutcheons and dignities in the hands of a king : the wise sometimes condescend to accept of them; but none but a fool will imagine them of any real importance. We ought to depend upon intrinsic merit, and not the slender helps of title. *Nam quæ non fecimus ipsi, vix ea nostra voco.*

For my part, I am ever ready to mistrust a promising title, and have, at some expense, been instructed not to hearken to the voice of an advertisement, let it plead never so loudly, or never so long. A countryman coming one day to Smithfield, in order to take a slice of Bartholomew Fair, found a perfect show before every booth. The drummer, the fire-eater, the wire-walker, and the salt-box, were all employed to invite him in. "Just a-going ; the court of the King of Prussia in all his glory : pray, gentlemen, walk in and see." From people who generously gave so much away, the clown expected a monstrous bargain for his money when he got in. He steps up, pays his sixpence, the curtain is drawn ; when, too late, he finds that he had the best part of the show for nothing at the door.

A FLEMISH TRADITION.

[*The Story of Bidderman.*]

EVERY country has its traditions, which, either too minute, or not sufficiently authentic to receive historical sanction, are handed down among the vulgar, and serve at once to instruct and amuse them. Of this number, the adventures of Robin Hood, the hunting of Chevy Chase, and the bravery of Johnny Armstrong, among the English ;

of Kaul Dereg, among the Irish; and Creigton, among the Scots, are instances. Of all the traditions, however, I remember to have heard, I do not recollect any more remarkable than one still current in Flanders; a story generally the first the peasants tell their children, when they bid them behave like Bidderman the Wise. It is by no means, however, a model to be set before a polite people for imitation; since if, on the one hand, we perceive in it the steady influence of patriotism, we, on the other, find as strong a desire of revenge. But, to wa[i]ve introduction, let us to the story.

When the Saracens overran Europe with their armies, and penetrated as far even as Antwerp, Bidderman was lord of a city, which time has since swept into destruction. As the inhabitants of this country were divided under separate leaders, the Saracens found an easy conquest, and the city of Bidderman, among the rest, became a prey to the victors.

Thus dispossessed of his paternal city, our unfortunate governor was obliged to seek refuge from the neighbouring princes, who were as yet unsubdued, and he for some time lived in a state of wretched dependence among them.

Soon, however, his love to his native country brought him back to his own city, resolved to rescue it from the enemy, or fall in the attempt. Thus, in disguise, he went among the inhabitants, and endeavoured, but in vain, to excite them to a revolt. Former misfortunes lay so heavily on their minds, that they rather chose to suffer the most cruel bondage, than attempt to vindicate their former freedom.

As he was thus one day employed, whether by information or from suspicion is not known, he was apprehended by a Saracen soldier as a spy, and brought before the very tribunal at which he once presided. The account he gave of himself was by no means satisfactory. He could produce no friends to vindicate his character; wherefore, as the Saracens knew not their prisoner, and as they had no direct proofs against him, they were content with condemning him to be publicly whipt as a vagabond.

The execution of this sentence was accordingly performed with the utmost rigour. Bidderman was bound

to the post, the executioner seeming disposed to add to
the cruelty of the sentence, as he received no bribe for
lenity. Whenever Bidderman groaned under the scourge,
the other, redoubling his blows, cried out, "Does the
villain murmur?" If Bidderman entreated but a moment's
respite from torture, the other only repeated his former
exclamation, "Does the villain murmur?"

From this period, revenge, as well as patriotism, took
entire possession of his soul. His fury stooped so low as
to follow the executioner with unremitting resentment.
But, conceiving that the best method to attain these ends
was to acquire some eminence in the city, he laid himself
out to oblige its new masters, studied every art, and
practised every meanness, that serve to promote the needy,
or render the poor pleasing; and, by these means, in a
few years, he came to be of some note in the city, which
justly belonged entirely to him.

The executioner was, therefore, the first object of his
resentment, and he even practised the lowest fraud to
gratify the revenge he owed him. A piece of plate, which
Bidderman had previously stolen from the Saracen governor, he privately conveyed into the executioner's house,
and then gave information of the theft. They who are
any way acquainted with the rigour of the Arabian laws,
know that theft is punished with immediate death. The
proof was direct in this case; the executioner had nothing
to offer in his own defence, and he was therefore condemned to be beheaded upon a scaffold in the public
market-place. As there was no executioner in the city
but the very man who was now to suffer, Bidderman himself undertook this, to him, most agreeable office. The
criminal was conducted from the judgment seat, bound
with cords; the scaffold was erected, and he placed in
such a manner as he might lie most convenient for the
blow.

But his death alone was not sufficient to satisfy the
resentment of this extraordinary man, unless it was aggravated with every circumstance of cruelty. Wherefore,
coming up the scaffold, and disposing every thing in
readiness for the intended blow, with the sword in his
hand he approached the criminal, and, whispering in a low

voice, assured him that he himself was the person that had once been used with so much cruelty; that, to his knowledge, he died very innocently, for the plate had been stolen by himself, and privately conveyed into the house of the other.

"Oh, my countrymen!" cried the criminal, "do you hear what this man says?"—"Does the villain murmur?" replied Bidderman, and immediately, at one blow, severed his head from his body.

Still, however, he was not content, till he had ample vengeance of the governors of the city, who condemned him. To effect this, he hired a small house adjoining to the town wall, under which he every day dug, and carried out the earth in a basket. In this unremitting labour he continued several years, every day digging a little, and carrying the earth unsuspected away. By this means, he at last made a secret communication from the country into the city, and only wanted the appearance of an enemy in order to betray it. This opportunity at length offered: the French army came into the neighbourhood, but had no thoughts of sitting down before a town which they considered as impregnable. Bidderman, however, soon altered their resolutions, and, upon communicating his plan to the general, he embraced it with ardour. Through the private passage above mentioned, he introduced a large body of the most resolute soldiers, who soon opened the gates for the rest, and the whole army rushing in, put every Saracen that was found to the sword.

THE SAGACITY OF SOME INSECTS [THE SPIDER].

TO THE AUTHOR OF THE BEE.

SIR,—Animals, in general, are sagacious, in proportion as they cultivate society. The elephant and the beaver show the greatest signs of this when united; but when man intrudes into their communities, they lose all their spirit of industry, and testify but a very small share of that sagacity, for which, when in a social state, they are so remarkable.

Among insects, the labours of the bee and the ant have employed the attention and admiration of the naturalist; but their whole sagacity is lost upon separation, and a single bee or ant seems destitute of every degree of industry, is the most stupid insect imaginable, languishes for a time in solitude, and soon dies.

Of all the solitary insects I have ever remarked, the spider is the most sagacious; and its actions, to me, who have attentively considered them, seem almost to exceed belief. This insect is formed by nature for a state of war, not only upon other insects, but upon each other. For this state nature seems perfectly well to have formed it. Its head and breast are covered with a strong natural coat of mail, which is impenetrable to the attempts of every other insect, and its belly is enveloped in a soft pliant skin, which eludes the sting even of a wasp. Its legs are terminated by strong claws, not unlike those of a lobster, and their vast length, like spears, serves to keep every assailant at a distance.

Not worse furnished for observation than for an attack or a defence, it has several eyes, large, transparent, and covered with a horny substance, which, however, does not impede its vision. Besides this, it is furnished with a forceps above the mouth, which serves to kill or secure the prey already caught in its claws or its net.

Such are the implements of war with which the body is immediately furnished; but its net to entangle the enemy seems what it chiefly trusts to, and what it takes most pains to render as complete as possible. Nature has furnished the body of this little creature with a glutinous liquid, which, proceeding from the anus, it spins into thread, coarser or finer as it chooses to contract or dilate its sphincter. In order to fix its thread, when it begins to weave it emits a small drop of its liquid against the wall, which, hardening by degrees, serves to hold the thread very firmly. Then receding from the first point, as it recedes the thread lengthens; and, when the spider has come to the place where the other end of the thread should be fixed, gathering up with its claws the thread which would otherwise be too slack, it is stretched tightly, and fixed in the same manner to the wall as before.

In this manner, it spins and fixes several threads parallel to each other, which, so to speak, serve as the warp to the intended web. To form the woof, it spins in the same manner its thread, transversely fixing one end to the first thread that was spun, and which is always the strongest of the whole web, and the other to the wall. All these threads, being newly spun, are glutinous, and therefore stick to each other wherever they happen to touch; and, in those parts of the web most exposed to be torn, our natural artist strengthens them, by doubling the threads sometimes six-fold.

Thus far naturalists have gone in the description of this animal; what follows, is the result of my own observation upon that species of the insect called a house spider.[1] I perceived, about four years ago, a large spider in one corner of my room, making its web; and, though the maid frequently levelled her fatal broom against the labours of the little animal, I had the good fortune then to prevent its destruction; and, I may say, it more than paid me by the entertainment it afforded.

In three days the web was, with incredible diligence, completed; nor could I avoid thinking, that the insect seemed to exult in its new abode. It frequently traversed it round, examined the strength of every part of it, retired into its hole, and came out very frequently. The first enemy, however, it had to encounter, was another and a much larger spider, which, having no web of its own, and having probably exhausted all its stock in former labours of this kind, came to invade the property of its neighbour. Soon, then, a terrible encounter ensued, in which the invader seemed to have the victory, and the laborious spider was obliged to take refuge in its hole. Upon this I perceived the victor using every art to draw the enemy

[1] Goldsmith's residence at this period was on the first floor of the house, No. 12, Green-Arbour Court, between the Old Bailey and what was at that time Fleet Market. In these apartments, little indebted, as we may believe, to the labours of the house-maid, he is said to have observed the habits and predatory life of the spider, and drawn up this paper.—PRIOR. See also ' Life,' p. 18.—ED.

from his strong-hold. He seemed to go off, but quickly returned; and when he found all arts vain, began to demolish the new web without mercy. This brought on another battle, and, contrary to my expectations, the laborious spider became conqueror, and fairly killed his antagonist.

Now, then, in peaceable possession of what was justly its own, it waited three days with the utmost patience, repairing the breaches of its web, and taking no sustenance that I could perceive. At last, however, a large blue fly fell into the snare, and struggled hard to get loose. The spider gave it leave to entangle itself as much as possible, but it seemed to be too strong for the cobweb. I must own I was greatly surprised when I saw the spider immediately sally out, and in less than a minute weave a new net round its captive, by which the motion of its wings was stopped; and when it was fairly hampered in this manner, it was seized, and dragged into the hole.

In this manner it lived, in a precarious state; and nature seemed to have fitted it for such a life, for upon a single fly it subsisted for more than a week. I once put a wasp into the net; but when the spider came out in order to seize it as usual, upon perceiving what kind of an enemy it had to deal with, it instantly broke all the bands that held it fast, and contributed all that lay in its power to disengage so formidable an antagonist. When the wasp was at liberty, I expected the spider would have set about repairing the breaches that were made in its net, but those it seems were irreparable; wherefore the cobweb was now entirely forsaken, and a new one begun, which was completed in the usual time.

I had now a mind to try how many cobwebs a single spider could furnish; wherefore I destroyed this, and the insect set about another. When I destroyed the other also, its whole stock seemed entirely exhausted, and it could spin no more. The arts it made use of to support itself, now deprived of its great means of subsistence, were indeed surprising. I have seen it roll up its legs like a ball, and lie motionless for hours together, but cautiously watching all the time; when a fly happened to approach sufficiently near, it would dart out all at once, and often seize its prey.

Of this life, however, it soon began to grow weary, and resolved to invade the possession of some other spider, since it could not make a web of its own. It formed an attack upon a neighbouring fortification with great vigour, and at first was as vigorously repulsed. Not daunted, however, with one defeat, in this manner it continued to lay siege to another's web for three days, and at length, having killed the defendant, actually took possession. When smaller flies happen to fall into the snare, the spider does not sally out at once, but very patiently waits till it is sure of them; for, upon his immediately approaching, the terror of his appearance might give the captive strength sufficient to get loose: the manner then is to wait patiently, till, by ineffectual and impotent struggles, the captive has wasted all its strength, and then he becomes a certain and an easy conquest.

The insect I am now describing lived three years;[1] every year it changed its skin, and got a new set of legs. I have sometimes plucked off a leg, which grew again in two or three days. At first it dreaded my approach to its web, but at last it became so familiar as to take a fly out of my hand, and, upon my touching any part of the web, would immediately leave its hole, prepared either for a defence or an attack.

To complete this description, it may be observed, that the male spiders are much less than the female, and that the latter are oviparous. When they come to lay, they spread a part of their web under the eggs, and then roll them up carefully, as we roll up things in a cloth, and thus hatch them in their hole. If disturbed in their holes, they never attempt to escape without carrying this young brood in their forceps away with them, and thus frequently are sacrificed to their parental[2] affection.

As soon as ever the young ones leave their artificial cover-

---

[1] Goldsmith is supposed to have lived in Green-Arbour Court from some time in 1758 to near the end of 1760, when he removed into Wine Office Court: see 'Life.'—ED.

[2] The original and some later editions give the word as "paternal." —ED.

ing, they begin to spin, and almost sensibly seem to grow bigger. If they have the good fortune, when even but a day old, to catch a fly, they fall-to with good appetites; but they live sometimes three or four days without any sort of sustenance, and yet still continue to grow larger, so as every day to double their former size. As they grow old, however, they do not still continue to increase, but their legs only continue to grow longer; and when a spider becomes entirely stiff with age, and unable to seize its prey, it dies at length of hunger.

THE CHARACTERISTICS OF GREATNESS.

In every duty, in every science in which we would wish to arrive at perfection, we should propose for the object of our pursuit some certain station even beyond our abilities —some imaginary excellence, which may amuse and serve to animate our enquiry. In deviating from others, in following an unbeaten road, though we perhaps may never arrive at the wished-for object, yet it is possible we may meet several discoveries by the way; and the certainty of small advantages, even while we travel with security, is not so amusing as the hopes of great rewards, which inspire the adventurer. *Evenit nonnunquam*, says Quintilian, *ut aliquid grande inveniat qui semper quærit quod nimium est.*

This enterprising spirit is, however, by no means the character of the present age: every person who should now leave received opinions, who should attempt to be more than a commentator upon philosophy, or an imitator in polite learning, might be regarded as a chimerical projector. Hundreds would be ready not only to point out his errors, but to load him with reproach. Our probable opinions are now regarded as certainties; the difficulties hitherto undiscovered as utterly inscrutable; and the writers of the last age inimitable, and therefore the properest models of imitation.

One might be almost induced to deplore the philosophic

spirit of the age, which, in proportion as it enlightens the mind, increases its timidity, and represses the vigour of every undertaking. Men are now content with being prudently in the right; which, though not the way to make new acquisitions, it must be owned, is the best method of securing what we have. Yet this is certain, that the writer who never deviates, who never hazards a new thought, or a new expression, though his friends may compliment him upon his sagacity, though criticism lifts her feeble voice in his praise, will seldom arrive at any degree of perfection. The way to acquire lasting esteem, is not by the fewness of a writer's faults, but the greatness of his beauties; and our noblest works are generally most replete with both.

An author who would be sublime, often runs his thought into burlesque: yet I can readily pardon his mistaking ten times for once succeeding. True genius walks along a line; and perhaps our greatest pleasure is in seeing it so often near falling, without being ever actually down.

Every science has its hitherto undiscovered mysteries, after which men should travel, undiscouraged by the failure of former adventurers. Every new attempt serves, perhaps, to facilitate its future invention. We may not find the Philosopher's stone, but we shall probably hit upon new inventions in pursuing it. We shall perhaps never be able to discover the longitude, yet perhaps we may arrive at new truths in the investigation.

Were any of those sagacious minds among us (and surely no nation, or no period, could ever compare with us in this particular) were any of those minds, I say, who now sit down contented with exploring the intricacies of another's system, bravely to shake off admiration, and, un-dazzled with the splendour of another's reputation, to chalk out a path to fame for themselves, and boldly cultivate untried experiment, what might not be the result of their enquiries, should the same study that has made them wise make them enterprising also? What could not such qualities united produce? But such is not the character of the English; while our neighbours of the Continent launch out into the ocean of science, without proper stores for the voyage, we fear shipwreck in every breeze, and con-sume in port those powers which might probably have weathered every storm.

Projectors in a state are generally rewarded above their deserts; projectors in the republic of letters, never. If wrong, every inferior dunce thinks himself entitled to laugh at their disappointment; if right, men of superior talents think their honour engaged to oppose, since every new discovery is a tacit diminution of their own preeminence.

To aim at excellence, our reputation, our friends, and our all must be ventured; by aiming only at mediocrity, we run no risk, and we do little service. Prudence and greatness are ever persuading us to contrary pursuits. The one instructs us to be content with our station, and to find happiness in bounding every wish; the other impels us to superiority, and calls nothing happiness but rapture. The one directs [us] to follow mankind, and to act and think with the rest of the world: the other drives us from the crowd, and exposes us as a mark to all the shafts of envy or ignorance: " Nec minus periculum ex magna fama quam ex mala."—TACIT.

The rewards of mediocrity are immediately paid, those attending excellence generally paid in reversion. In a word, the little mind who loves itself, will write and think with the vulgar, but the great mind will be bravely eccentric, and scorn the beaten road, from universal benevolence.

A CITY NIGHT PIECE.[1]

" Ille dolet vere qui sine teste dolet."—MART.

THE clock has struck two, the expiring taper rises and sinks in the socket, the watchman forgets the hour in slumber, the laborious and the happy are at rest, and nothing now wakes but guilt, revelry, and despair. The

---

[1] This paper, re-written, appeared as Letter CXVII. of the 'Citizen of the World' (which see). There, however, the striking last paragraph—" But let me turn," &c., which is thought to have a personal application, is omitted.—ED.

drunkard once more fills the destroying bowl, the robber walks his midnight round, and the suicide lifts his guilty arm against his own sacred person.

Let me no longer waste the night over the page of antiquity, or the sallies of contemporary genius, but pursue the solitary walk, where vanity, ever changing, but a few hours past, walked before me—where she kept up the pageant, and now, like a froward child, seems hushed with her own importunities.

What a gloom hangs all around! The dying lamp feebly emits a yellow gleam; no sound is heard but of the chiming clock, or the distant watch-dog. All the bustle of human pride is forgotten, and this hour may well display the emptiness of human vanity.

There may come a time when this temporary solitude may be made continual, and the city itself, like its inhabitants, fade away, and leave a desert in its room.

What cities, as great as this, have once triumph'd in existence; had their victories as great as ours; joy as just, and as unbounded as we; and, with short-sighted presumption, promised themselves immortality. Posterity can hardly trace the situation of some: the sorrowful traveller wanders over the awful ruins of others; and, as he beholds, he learns wisdom, and feels the transience of every sublunary possession.

Here, stood their citadel, but now grown over with weeds; there their senate-house, but now the haunt of every noxious reptile; temples and theatres stood here, now only an undistinguished heap of ruin. They are fallen, for luxury and avarice first made them feeble. The rewards of the state were conferred on amusing, and not on useful members of society. Thus true virtue languished, their riches and opulence invited the plunderer, who, though once repulsed, returned again, and at last swept the defendants into undistinguished destruction.

How few appear in those streets which but some few hours ago were crowded; and those who appear, no longer now wear their daily mask, nor attempt to hide their lewdness or their misery.

But who are those who make the streets their couch, and find a short repose from wretchedness at the doors of the opulent? These are strangers, wanderers, and orphans, whose circumstances are too humble to expect redress, and their distresses too great even for pity. Some are without the covering even of rags, and others emaciated with disease; the world seems to have disclaimed them; society turns its back upon their distress, and has given them up to nakedness and hunger. These poor shivering females have once seen happier days, and been flattered into beauty. They have been prostituted to the gay luxurious villain, and are now turned out to meet the severity of winter in the streets. Perhaps, now lying at the doors of their betrayers, they sue to wretches whose hearts are insensible to calamity, or debauchees who may curse, but will not relieve them.

Why, why was I born a man, and yet see the sufferings of wretches I cannot relieve! Poor, houseless creatures! the world will give you reproaches, but will not give you relief. The slightest misfortunes, the most imaginary uneasiness of the rich, are aggravated with all the power of eloquence, and engage our attention; while you weep unheeded, persecuted by every subordinate species of tyranny, and finding enmity in every law.

Why was this heart of mine formed with so much sensibility! or why was not my fortune adapted to its impulse! Tenderness, without a capacity of relieving, only makes the heart that feels it more wretched than the object which sues for assistance.

But let me turn from a scene of such distress to the sanctified hypocrite, *who has been talking of virtue till the time of bed,*[1] and now steals out, to give a loose to his vices under the protection of midnight; vices more atrocious, because he attempts to conceal them. See how he pants down the dark alley, and, with hastening steps, fears an acquaintance in every face. He has passed the whole day in company he hates, and now goes to prolong the night among company that as heartily hate him. May his vices be detected; may the morning rise upon his shame! Yet I wish to no purpose: villany, when detected, never gives up, but boldly adds impudence to imposture.

---

[1] " Then talk'd of virtue till the time of bed."—PARNELL.—B.

THE BEE.

UPON POLITICAL FRUGALITY.

FRUGALITY has ever been esteemed a virtue as well among Pagans as Christians : there have been even heroes who have practised it. However, we must acknowledge, that it is too modest a virtue, or, if you will, too obscure a one, to be essential to heroism ; few heroes have been able to attain to such a height. Frugality agrees much better with politics ; it seems to be the base, the support, and, in a word, seems to be the inseparable companion of a just administration.

However this be, there is not, perhaps, in the world a people less fond of this virtue than the English ; and of consequence, there is not a nation more restless, more exposed to the uneasinesses of life, or less capable of providing for particular happiness. We are taught to despise this virtue from our childhood ; our education is improperly directed, and a man who has gone through the politest institutions, is generally the person who is least acquainted with the wholesome precepts of frugality. We every day hear the elegance of taste, the magnificence of some, and the generosity of others, made the subject of our admiration and applause. All this we see represented, not as the end and recompense of labour and desert, but as the actual result of genius, as the mark of a noble and exalted mind.

In the midst of these praises bestowed on luxury, for

which elegance and taste are but another name, perhaps it
may be thought improper to plead the cause of frugality.
It may be thought low, or vainly declamatory, to exhort
our youth from the follies of dress, and of every other
superfluity; to accustom themselves, even with mechanic
meanness, to the simple necessaries of life. Such sort of
instructions may appear antiquated; yet, however, they
seem the foundations of all our virtues, and the most effi-
cacious method of making mankind useful members of
society. Unhappily, however, such discourses are not
fashionable among us, and the fashion seems every day
growing still more obsolete, since the press, and every other
method of exhortation, seems disposed to talk of the
luxuries of life as harmless enjoyments. I remember, when
a boy, to have remarked, that those who in school wore the
finest clothes, were pointed at as being conceited and
proud. At present, our little masters are taught to consider dress betimes, and they are regarded, even at school,
with contempt, who do not appear as genteel as the rest.
Education should teach us to become useful, sober, disinterested, and laborious members of society; but does it
not at present point out a different path? It teaches us
to multiply our wants, by which means we become more
eager to possess, in order to dissipate, a greater charge to
ourselves, and more useless or obnoxious to society.

If a youth happens to be possessed of more genius than
fortune, he is early informed, that he ought to think of
his advancement in the world; that he should labour to
make himself pleasing to his superiors; that he should
shun low company, (by which is meant the company of his
equals); that he should rather live a little above than below his fortune; that he should think of becoming great;
but he finds none to admonish him to become frugal, to
persevere in one single design, to avoid every pleasure and
all flattery, which, however seeming to conciliate the favour
of his superiors, never conciliate their esteem. There are
none to teach him that the best way of becoming happy in
himself, and useful to others, is to continue in the state in
which fortune at first placed him, without making too hasty
strides to advancement; that greatness may be attained,
but should not be expected; and that they who most im-

patiently expect advancement, are seldom possessed of their wishes. He has few, I say, to teach him this lesson, or to moderate his youthful passions ; yet, this experience may say, that a young man, who, but for six years of the early part of his life, could seem divested of all his passions, would certainly make, or considerably increase, his fortune, and might indulge several of his favourite inclinations in manhood with the utmost security.

The efficaciousness of these means is sufficiently known and acknowledged ; but as we are apt to connect a low idea with all our notions of frugality, the person who would persuade us to it might be accused of preaching up avarice.

Of all vices, however, against which morality dissuades, there is not one more undetermined than this of avarice. Misers are described by some as men divested of .honour, sentiment, or humanity : but this is only an ideal picture, or the resemblance at least is found but in a few. In truth, they who are generally called misers, are some of the very best members of society. The sober, 'the laborious, the attentive, the frugal, are thus styled by the gay, giddy, thoughtless, and extravagant. The first set of men do society all the good, and the latter all the evil that is felt. Even the excesses of the first no way injure the commonwealth ; those of the latter are the most injurious that can be conceived.[1]

The ancient Romans, more rational than we in this particular, were very far from thus misplacing their admiration or praise : instead of regarding the practice of parsimony as low or vicious, they made it synonymous even with probity. They esteemed those virtues so inseparable, that the known expression of *Vir frugi* signified, at one and the same time, a sober and managing man, an honest man, and a man of substance.

The Scriptures, in a thousand places, praise economy ; and it is every where distinguished from avarice. But, in spite of all its sacred dictates, a taste for vain pleasures and foolish expense is the ruling passion of the present

---

[1] Compare with the author's defence of misers in " On Generosity and Justice," *ante*, p. 355.—ED.

times.   Passion, did I call it? rather the madness which
at once possesses the great and the little, the rich and the
poor: even, some are so intent upon acquiring the superfluities of life, that they sacrifice its necessaries in this
foolish pursuit.

To attempt the entire abolition of luxury, as it would
be impossible, so it is not my intent.   The generality of
mankind are too weak, too much slaves to custom and
opinion, to resist the torrent of bad example.   But if it
be impossible to convert the multitude, those who have
received a more extended education, who are enlightened
and judicious, may find some hints on this subject useful.
They may see some abuses, the suppression of which would
by no means endanger public liberty; they may be directed
to the abolition of some unnecessary expenses, which have
no tendency to promote happiness or virtue, and which
might be directed to better purposes.   Our fire-works, our
public feasts and entertainments, our entries of ambassadors, &c.—what mummery all this! what childish
pageants! what millions are sacrificed in paying tribute
to custom! what an unnecessary charge at times when we
are pressed with real want, which cannot be satisfied without burthening the poor!

Were such suppressed entirely, not a single creature in
the state would have the least cause to mourn their suppression, and many might be eased of a load they now feel
lying heavily upon them.   If this were put in practice, it
would agree with the advice of a sensible writer of Sweden,
who, in the *Gazette de France*, 1753, thus expressed himself on that subject: " It were sincerely to be wished,"
says he, " that the custom were established amongst us,
that in all events which cause a public joy, we made our
exultations conspicuous only by acts useful to society. We
should then quickly see many useful monuments of our
reason, which would much better perpetuate the memory
of things worthy of being transmitted to posterity, and
would be much more glorious to humanity, than all these
tumultuous preparations of feasts, entertainments, and
other rejoicings used upon such occasions."

The same proposal was long before confirmed by a
Chinese emperor, who lived in the last century, who, upon

an occasion of extraordinary joy, forbad his subjects to make the usual illuminations, either with a design of sparing their substance, or of turning them to some more durable indications of joy, more glorious for him, and more advantageous to his people.

After such instances of political frugality, can we then continue to blame the Dutch ambassador at a certain court, who receiving at his departure the portrait of the king, enriched with diamonds, asked what this fine thing might be worth? Being told that it might amount to about two thousand pounds,—"And why," cries he, "cannot his majesty keep the picture, and give me the money?" This simplicity may be ridiculed at first; but when we come to examine it more closely, men of sense will at once confess that he had reason in what he said, and that a purse of two thousand guineas is much more serviceable than a picture.

Should we follow the same method of state frugality in other respects, what numberless savings might not be the result! How many possibilities of saving in the administration of justice, which now burdens the subject, and enriches some members of society, who are useful only from its corruption!

It were to be wished, that they who govern kingdoms would imitate artizans. When at London a new stuff has been invented, it is immediately counterfeited in France. How happy were it for society, if a first minister would be equally solicitous to transplant the useful laws of other countries into his own. We are arrived at a perfect imitation of porcelain; let us endeavour to imitate the good to society that our neighbours are found to practise, and let our neighbours also imitate those parts of duty in which we excel.

There are some men, who, in their garden, attempt to raise those fruits which nature has adapted only to the sultry climates beneath the line. We have at our very doors a thousand laws and customs infinitely useful; these are the fruits we should endeavour to transplant; these the exotics that would speedily become naturalized to the soil. They might grow in every climate, and benefit every possessor.

The best and the most useful laws I have ever seen, are generally practised in Holland. When two men are determined to go to law with each other, they are first obliged to go before the reconciling judges, called the *peace-makers*. If the parties come attended with an advocate, or a solicitor, they are obliged to retire, as we take fuel from the fire we are desirous of extinguishing.

The peace-makers then begin advising the parties, by assuring them that it is the height of folly to waste their substance, and make themselves mutually miserable, by having recourse to the tribunals of justice: "Follow but our direction, and we will accommodate matters without any expense to either." If the rage of debate is too strong upon either party, they are remitted back for another day, in order that time may soften their tempers, and produce a reconciliation. They are thus sent for twice or thrice; if their folly happens to be incurable, they are permitted to go to law, and, as we give up to amputation such members as cannot be cured by art, justice is permitted to take its course.

It is unnecessary to make here long declamations, or calculate what society would save, were this law adopted. I am sensible, that the man who advises any reformation, only serves to make himself ridiculous. What! mankind will be apt to say, adopt the customs of countries that have not so much real liberty as our own!—our present customs, what are they to any man; we are very happy under them! This must be a very pleasant fellow, who attempts to make us happier than we already are! Does he not know that abuses are the patrimony of a great part of the nation? Why deprive us of a malady by which such numbers find their account? This, I must own, is an argument to which I have nothing to reply.

What numberless savings might there not be made in both arts and commerce, particularly in the liberty of exercising trade, without the necessary prerequisites of freedom! Such useless obstructions have crept into every state, from a spirit of monopoly, a narrow selfish spirit of gain, without the least attention to general society. Such a clog upon industry frequently drives the poor from labour, and reduces them by degrees to a state of hopeless

indigence. We have already a more than sufficient repug-
nance to labour; we should by no means increase the obstacles, or make excuses in a state for idleness. Such
faults have ever crept into a state, under wrong or needy
administrations.

Exclusive of the masters, there are numberless faulty
expenses among the workmen; clubs, garnishes,[1] free-
doms, and such-like impositions, which are not too minute
even for law to take notice of, and which should be
abolished without mercy, since they are ever the inlets to
excess and idleness, and are the parent of all those outrages
which naturally fall upon the more useful part of society.
In the towns and countries I have seen, I never saw a city
or village yet, whose miseries were not in proportion to the
number of its public-houses. In Rotterdam, you may go
through eight or ten streets without finding a public-
house. In Antwerp, almost every second house seems an
alehouse. In the one city, all wears the appearance of
happiness and warm affluence; in the other, the young
fellows walk about the streets in shabby finery, their fathers
sit at the door darning or knitting stockings, while their
ports are filled with dunghills.

Alehouses are ever an occasion of debauchery and excess,
and, either in a religious or political light, it would be our
highest interest to have the greatest part of them suppressed. They should be put under laws of not continuing open beyond a certain hour, and harbouring only
proper persons. These rules, it may be said, will diminish
the necessary taxes; but this is false reasoning, since what
was consumed in debauchery abroad, would, if such a regu-
lation took place, be more justly, and perhaps more equit-
ably for the workman's family, spent at home; and this
cheaper to them, and without loss of time. On the other
hand, our alehouses being ever open, interrupt business;
the workman is never certain who frequents them, nor can
the master be sure of having what was begun finished at
the convenient time.

A habit of frugality among the lower orders of mankind

---

[1] A garnish was an entertainment given on entering a workshop. The
word used now is "footing." In Goldsmith's days a "garnish" or
"footing" was expected even from a prisoner entering a prison.—Ed.

is much more beneficial to society than the unreflecting
might imagine.   The pawnbroker, the attorney, and other
pests of society, might, by proper management, be turned
into serviceable members; and, were their trades abolished,
it is possible the same avarice that conducts the one, or
the same chicanery that characterizes the other, might, by
proper regulations, be converted into frugality and com-
mendable prudence.

But some [who] have made the eulogium of luxury, have
represented it as the natural consequence of every country
that is become rich.   Did we not employ our extraordinary
wealth in superfluities, say they, what other means would
there be to employ it in?   To which it may be answered, if
frugality were established in the state, if our expenses were
laid out rather in the necessaries than the superfluities of
life, there might be fewer wants, and even fewer pleasures,
but infinitely more happiness.   The rich and the great would
be better able to satisfy their creditors; they would be
better able to marry their children, and, instead of one
marriage at present, there might be two, if such regulations
took place.

The imaginary calls of vanity, which, in reality, contribute nothing to our real felicity, would not then be attended to, while the real calls of nature might be always
and universally supplied.   The difference of employment
in the subject is what, in reality, produces the good of
society.   If the subject be engaged in providing only the
luxuries, the necessaries must be deficient in proportion.
If, neglecting the produce of our own country, our minds
are set upon the productions of another, we increase our
wants, but not our means; and every new imported delicacy for our tables, or ornament in our equipage, is a tax
upon the poor.

The true interest of every government is to cultivate the
necessaries, by which is always meant, every happiness our
own country can produce; and suppress all the luxuries,
by which is meant, on the other hand, every happiness imported from abroad.   Commerce has, therefore, its bounds;
and every new import, instead of receiving encouragement,
should be first examined whether it be conducive to the
interest of society.

Among the many publications with which the press is every day burthened, I have often wondered why we never had, as in other countries, an Economical Journal, which might at once direct to all the useful discoveries in other countries, and spread those of our own. As other journals serve to amuse the learned, or, what is more often the case, to make them quarrel, while they only serve to give us the history of the mischievous world, for so I call our warriors, or the idle world, for so may the learned be called, they never trouble their heads about the most useful part of mankind, our peasants and our artizans. Were such a work carried into execution, with proper management and just direction, it might serve as a repository for every useful improvement, and increase that knowledge which learning often serves to confound.

Sweden seems the only country where the science of economy seems to have fixed its empire. In other countries, it is cultivated only by a few admirers, or by societies which have not received sufficient sanction to become completely useful; but here there is founded a Royal Academy, destined to this purpose only, composed of the most learned and powerful members of the state; an academy which declines every thing which only terminates in amusement, erudition, or curiosity, and admits only of observations tending to illustrate husbandry, agriculture, and every real physical improvement. In this country, nothing is left to private rapacity, but every improvement is immediately diffused, and its inventor immediately recompensed by the state. Happy were it so in other countries! By this means, every impostor would be prevented from ruining or deceiving the public with pretended discoveries or nostrums, and every real inventor would not, by this means, suffer the inconveniences of suspicion.

In short, the economy equally unknown to the prodigal and avaricious, seems to be a just mean between both extremes; and to a transgression of this at present decried virtue it is that we are to attribute a great part of the evils which infest society. A taste for superfluity, amusement, and pleasure bring[s] effeminacy, idleness, and expense in their train. But a thirst of riches is always proportioned to our debauchery, and the greatest prodigal is too frequently found to be the greatest miser; so that the vices which seem the most opposite, are frequently found to produce each other; and, to avoid both, it is only necessary to be frugal.

" Virtus est medium vitiorum et utrinque reductum."—Hor.

[*The Fame Machine.*]

Scarce a day passes in which we do not hear compliments paid to Dryden, Pope, and other writers of the last age, while not a month comes forward that is not loaded with invective against the writers of this. Strange, that our critics should be fond of giving their favours to those who are insensible of the obligation, and their dislike to those who, of all mankind, are most apt to retaliate the injury.

Even though our present writers had not equal merit with their predecessors, it would be politic to use them with ceremony. Every compliment paid them would be more agreeable, in proportion as they least deserved it. Tell a lady with a handsome face that she is pretty, she only thinks it her due; it is what she has heard a thousand times before from others, and disregards the compliment: but assure a lady, the cut of whose visage is something more plain, that she looks killing to-day, she instantly bridles up, and feels the force of the well-timed flattery the whole day after. Compliments which we think are deserved, we only accept as debts, with indifference; but those which conscience informs us we do not merit, we receive with the same gratitude that we do favours given away.

Our gentlemen, however, who preside at the distribution of literary fame, seem resolved to part with praise neither from motives of justice or generosity; one would think, when they take pen in hand, that it was only to blot reputations, and to put their seals to the packet which consigns every new-born effort to oblivion.

Yet, notwithstanding the republic of letters hangs at present so feebly together; though those friendships which once promoted literary fame seem now to be discontinued; though every writer who now draws the quill seems to aim at profit, as well as applause, many among them are probably laying in stores for immortality, and are provided with a sufficient stock of reputation to last the whole journey.

As I was indulging these reflections, in order to eke out the present page, I could not avoid pursuing the metaphor of going a journey in my imagination, and formed the following Reverie, too wild for allegory, and too regular for a dream:—

I fancied myself placed in the yard of a large inn, in which there were an infinite number of waggons and stage-coaches, attended by fellows who either invited the company to take their places, or were busied in packing their baggage. Each vehicle had its inscription, showing the place of its destination. On one I could read, "The Pleasure Stage Coach"; on another "The Waggon of Industry"; on a third, "The Vanity Whim"; and on a fourth, "The Landau of Riches." I had some inclination to step into each of these, one after another; but, I know not by what means, I passed them by, and at last fixed my eye upon a small carriage, Berlin fashion, which seemed the most convenient vehicle at a distance in the world; and, upon my nearer approach, found it to be "The Fame Machine."

I instantly made up to the coachman, whom I found to be an affable and seemingly good-natured fellow. He informed me, that he had but a few days ago returned from the Temple of Fame, to which he had been carrying Addison, Swift, Pope, Steele, Congreve, and Colley Cibber: that they made but indifferent company by the way; and that he once or twice was going to empty his berlin of the whole cargo: "however," says he, "I got them all safe home, with no other damage than a black eye, which Colley gave Mr. Pope, and am now returned for another coachful."—"If that be all, friend," said I, "and if you are in want of company, I'll make one with all my heart. Open the door; I hope the machine rides easy."—"Oh, for that, Sir, extremely easy." But, still keeping the door shut, and measuring me with his eye, "Pray, Sir, have you no luggage? You seem to be a good-natured sort of a gentleman; but I don't find you have got any luggage, and I never permit any to travel with me but such as have something valuable to pay for coach-hire." Examining my pockets, I own I was not a little disconcerted at this unexpected rebuff; but considering that I carried a number of the BEE under my arm, I was resolved to open it in his eyes, and dazzle him with the splendour of the page. He read the title and contents, however, without any emotion, and assured me he had never heard of it before. "In short, friend," said he, now losing all his former respect, "you must not come in: I expect better passengers; but as you seem a harmless creature, perhaps, if there be room left, I may let you ride a while for charity."

I now took my stand by the coachman at the door; and since I could not command a seat, was resolved to be as useful as possible, and earn by my assiduity what I could not by my merit.

The next that presented for a place was a most whimsical figure indeed.[1] He was hung round with papers of his own composing, not unlike those who sing ballads in the streets, and came dancing up to the door with all the confidence of instant admittance. The volubility of his

---

[1] Sir John Hill, whom Churchill in the 'Rosciad' describes as—

> "The Proteus Hill—
> Actor, inspector, doctor, botanist."

Davies, in his 'Life of Garrick,' says, that Dr. Hill was a "quack in medicine, and not to be depended on in science."—B. One of Garrick's smartest epigrams thus describes him—

> "For physic and farces his equal there scarce is,
> His farces are physic, his physic a farce is."

When Goldsmith wrote of him he was Dr. Hill; the King of Sweden knighted him about two years before his death, which took place in 1775. Among his numerous writings and compilations was a series of papers called 'The Inspector,' which he contributed to the *Daily Advertiser*, and, it is said, the cookery book of "Mrs. Glasse."—ED.

motion and address prevented my being able to read more of his cargo than the word 'Inspector,' which was written in great letters at the top of some of the papers. He opened the coach-door himself without any ceremony, and was just slipping in, when the coachman, with as little ceremony, pulled him back. Our figure seemed perfectly angry at this repulse, and demanded gentleman's satisfaction. " Lord, Sir! " replied the coachman, " instead of proper luggage, by your bulk you seem loaded for a West-India voyage. You are big enough, with all your papers, to crack twenty stage coaches. Excuse me, indeed, Sir, for you must not enter." Our figure now began to expostulate: he assured the coachman, that though his baggage seemed so bulky, it was perfectly light, and that he would be contented with the smallest corner of room. But Jehu was inflexible, and the carrier of the Inspectors was sent to dance back again, with all his papers fluttering in the wind. We expected to have no more trouble from this quarter, when, in a few minutes, the same figure changed his appearance, like harlequin upon the stage, and with the same confidence again made his approaches, dressed in lace, and carrying nothing but a nosegay. Upon coming near, he thrust the nosegay to the coachman's nose, grasped the brass, and seemed now resolved to enter by violence. I found the struggle soon begin to grow hot, and the coachman, who was a little old, unable to continue the contest; so, in order to ingratiate myself, I stept in to his assistance, and our united efforts sent our literary Proteus, though worsted, unconquered still, clear off, dancing a rigadoon, and smelling to his own nosegay.

The person[1] who after him appeared as candidate for a place in the stage, came up with an air not quite so confident, but somewhat, however, theatrical; and, instead of entering, made the coachman a very low bow, which the other returned, and desired to see his baggage; upon

---

[1] Probably Mr. Murphy.—B. Arthur Murphy, who afterwards wrote a ' Life of Johnson.' ' The Orphan of China ' is the tragedy alluded to. It was produced at Drury Lane in this year (1759). The review of it in the *Critical Review* (and in our vol. iv.) is supposed to be by Goldsmith.—ED.

which he instantly produced some farces, a tragedy, and other miscellany productions. The coachman, casting his eye upon the cargo, assured him, at present he could not possibly have a place, but hoped in time he might aspire to one, as he seemed to have read in the book of nature, without a careful perusal of which none ever found entrance at the Temple of Fame. "What!" replied the disappointed poet, "shall my tragedy, in which I have vindicated the cause of liberty and virtue!—" "Follow nature," returned the other, "and never expect to find lasting fame by topics which only please from their popularity. Had you been first in the cause of freedom, or praised in virtue more than an empty name, it is possible you might have gained admittance; but at present I beg, Sir, you will stand aside for another gentleman whom I see approaching."

This was a very grave personage,[1] whom at some distance I took for one of the most reserved, and even disagreeable figures I had seen; but as he approached, his appearance improved, and when I could distinguish him thoroughly, I perceived that, in spite of the severity of his brow, he had one of the most good-natured countenances that could be imagined. Upon coming to open the stage door, he lifted a parcel of folios into the seat before him, but our inquisitorial coachman at once shoved them out again. "What! not take in my Dictionary?" exclaimed the other in a rage. "Be patient, Sir," replied the coachman, "I have drove a coach, man and boy, these two thousand years; but I do not remember to have carried above one dictionary during the whole time. That little book which I perceive peeping from one of your pockets, may I presume to ask what it contains?"—"A mere trifle," replied the author; "it is called the *Rambler*." "*The Rambler!*" says the coachman, "I beg, Sir, you'll take your place; I have heard our ladies in the court of Apollo frequently mention it with rapture; and Clio, who happens to be a little grave, has been heard to prefer it to the *Spectator*; though others have observed,

---

[1] Mr., afterwards Dr., Samuel Johnson, whose 'Dictionary' was four years old at this time. His 'Rasselas' was published in this year. Goldsmith did not know Johnson personally at this time.—ED.

that the reflections, by being refined, sometimes become minute."

This grave gentleman was scarce seated, when another,[1] whose appearance was something more modern, seemed willing to enter, yet afraid to ask. He carried in his hand a bundle of essays, of which the coachman was curious enough to enquire the contents. " These," replied the gentleman, " are rhapsodies against the religion of my country."—"And how can you expect to come into my coach, after thus choosing the wrong side of the question?"—" Ay, but I am right," replied the other; " and if you give me leave, I shall, in a few minutes, state the argument."—" Right or wrong," said the coachman, " he who disturbs religion is a blockhead, and he shall never travel in a coach of mine."—" If, then," said the gentleman, mustering up all his courage, " if I am not to have admittance as an essayist, I hope I shall not be repulsed as an historian; the last volume of my history met with applause."—" Yes," replied the coachman, " but I have heard only the first approved at the Temple of Fame; and as I see you have it about you, enter, without further ceremony."[2] My attention was now diverted to a crowd who were pushing forward a person[3] that seemed more inclined to the Stage-coach of Riches; but by their means he was driven forward to the " Fame Machine," which he, however, seemed heartily to despise. Impelled, however, by their solicitations, he steps up, flourishing a voluminous history, and demanding admittance. " Sir, I have formerly heard your name mentioned," says the coachman, " but never as an historian. Is there no other

---

[1] David Hume.—B. Goldsmith similarly viewed Hume twelve years later, when he wrote, and, as he acknowledges, founded, his ' History of England ' upon Hume's work. See the Preface to Goldsmith's ' History of England ' in our vol. iv.—ED.

[2] The first part of Hume's ' History of England ' which was published, was his History of the Stuarts, of which the first volume appeared in 1754, and the second in 1756; his History of the House of Tudor did not appear till 1759.—B.

[3] Probably Dr. Smollett. This essay is supposed to have led to Goldsmith's friendship with both Johnson and Smollett, from which, as regards the latter, almost immediately proceeded Goldsmith's engagement to write for the *British Magazine*—started in January, 1760, under the control of Smollett. See ' Life,' p. 19.—ED.

work upon which you may claim a place?"—"None,"
replied the other, "except a romance; but this is a work
of too trifling a nature to claim future attention."—"You
mistake," says the inquisitor, "a well-written romance is
no such easy task as is generally imagined. I remember
formerly to have carried Cervantes and Segrais;[1] and if
you think fit, you may enter."

Upon our three literary travellers coming into the same
coach, I listened attentively to hear what might be the
conversation that passed upon this extraordinary occasion;
when, instead of agreeable or entertaining dialogue, I found
them grumbling at each other, and each seemed discontented with his companions. Strange! thought I to myself, that they who are thus born to enlighten the world,
should still preserve the narrow prejudices of childhood,
and, by disagreeing, make even the highest merit ridiculous. Were the learned and the wise to unite against
the dunces of society, instead of sometimes siding into
opposite parties with them, they might throw a lustre
upon each other's reputation, and teach every rank of
subordinate merit, if not to admire, at least not to avow
dislike.

In the midst of these reflections, I perceived the coachman, unmindful of me, had now mounted the box. Several
were approaching to be taken in, whose pretensions, I was
sensible, were very just; I therefore desired him to stop,
and take in more passengers: but he replied, as he had
now mounted the box, it would be improper to come down;
but that he should take them all, one after the other,
when he should return. So he drove away; and for myself, as I could not get in, I mounted behind, in order to
hear the conversation on the way.

(*To be continued*[2].)

---

[1] A curious coupling. But in those days the French tales of Segrais
were viewed as models of style in such composition. Segrais was born
at Caen in 1624; and there he also died in 1701.—ED.
[2] But it, probably, never was continued.—ED.

A WORD OR TWO ON THE LATE FARCE CALLED ' HIGH LIFE BELOW STAIRS.' [1]

Just as I had expected, before I saw this farce, I found it formed on too narrow a plan to afford a pleasing variety. The sameness of the humour in every scene could not at last fail of being disagreeable. The poor affecting the manners of the rich might be carried on through one character, or two at the most, with great propriety; but to have almost every personage on the scene almost of the same character, and reflecting the follies of each other, was unartful in the poet to the last degree.

The scene was also almost a continuation of the same absurdity; and my Lord Duke and Sir Harry, (two foot-men who assume these characters,) have nothing else to do but to talk like their masters, and are only introduced to speak, and to show themselves. Thus, as there is a sameness of character, there is a barrenness of incident, which, by a very small share of address, the poet might have easily avoided.

From a conformity to critic rules, which, perhaps, on the whole, have done more harm than good, our author has sacrificed all the vivacity of the dialogue to nature; and though he makes his characters talk like servants, they are seldom absurd enough, or lively enough, to make us merry. Though he is always natural, he happens seldom to be humorous.

The satire was well intended, if we regard it as being masters ourselves; but probably a philosopher would re-joice in that liberty which Englishmen give their domes-tics; and for my own part, I cannot avoid being pleased at the happiness of those poor creatures, who, in some mea-sure, contribute to mine. The Athenians, the politest and best-natured people upon earth, were the kindest to their slaves; and if a person may judge, who has seen the world,

---

[1] At first ascribed to Garrick, but now known to have been written by the Rev. James Townley, master of Merchant Taylors' School, and afterwards Vicar of Hendon. The play was produced at Drury Lane, Oct. 31, 1759 ; so, no doubt, Goldsmith's article was upon the first per-formance.—ED.

our English servants are the best treated, because the generality of our English gentlemen are the politest under the sun.

But, not to lift my feeble voice among the pack of critics, who, probably, have no other occupation but that of cutting up every thing new, I must own, there are one or two scenes that are fine satire, and sufficiently humorous; particularly the first interview between the two footmen, which at once ridicules the manners of the great, and the absurdity of their imitators.

Whatever defects there might be in the composition, there were none in the action; in this the performers showed more humour than I had fancied them capable of. Mr. Palmer and Mr. King were entirely what they desired to represent; and Mrs. Clive—(but what need I talk of her, since, without the least exaggeration, she has more true humour than any actor or actress upon the English or any other stage I have seen)—she, I say, did the part all the justice it was capable of.[1] And, upon the whole, a farce, which has only this to recommend it, that the author took his plan from the volume of nature, by the sprightly manner in which it was performed, was, for one night, a tolerable entertainment. This much may be said in its vindication, that people of fashion seemed more pleased in the representation than the subordinate ranks of people.[2]

UPON UNFORTUNATE MERIT.

EVERY age seems to have its favourite pursuits, which serve to amuse the idle, and to relieve the attention of the industrious. Happy the man who is born excellent in the

---

[1] Palmer played Sir Harry, King my Lord Duke, and Mrs. (Kitty) Clive was Kitty.—ED.

[2] This still favourite farce was a success in London; but its performance in Edinburgh caused a riot in the footmen's gallery; the result being the withdrawal of the free-admission to servants attending their employers to the theatre, which was until then general: vide Genest's ' History of the Stage,' &c.—ED.

pursuit in vogue, and whose genius seems adapted to the times he lives in. How many do we see, who might have excelled in arts or sciences, and who seem furnished with talents equal to the greatest discoveries, had the road not been already beaten by their predecessors, and nothing left for them except trifles to discover, while others of very moderate abilities become famous, because happening to be first in the reigning pursuit.

Thus, at the renewal of letters in Europe, the taste was not to compose new books, but to comment on the old ones. It was not to be expected that new books should be written, when there were so many of the ancients either not known or not understood. It was not reasonable to attempt new conquests, while they had such an extensive region lying waste for want of cultivation. At that period, criticism and erudition were the reigning studies of the times ; and he who had only an inventive genius, might have languished in hopeless obscurity. When the writers of antiquity were sufficiently explained and known, the learned set about imitating them : from hence proceeded the number of Latin orators, poets, and historians, in the reigns of Clement the Seventh and Alexander the Sixth. This passion for antiquity lasted for many years, to the utter exclusion of every other pursuit, till some began to find, that those works which were imitated from nature, were more like the writings of antiquity, than even those written in express imitation. It was then modern language began to be cultivated with assiduity, and our poets and orators poured forth their wonders upon the world.

As writers become more numerous, it is natural for readers to become more indolent ; from whence must necessarily arise a desire of attaining knowledge with the greatest possible ease. No science or art offers its instruction and amusement in so obvious a manner as statuary and painting. From hence we see, that a desire of cultivating those arts generally attends the decline of science. Thus the finest statues and the most beautiful paintings of antiquity, preceded but a little the absolute decay of every other science. The statues of Antoninus, Commodus, and their contemporaries, are the finest productions of the chisel, and appeared but just before learning was destroyed by comment, criticism, and barbarous invasions.

What happened in Rome may probably be the case with us at home. Our nobility are now more solicitous in patronizing painters and sculptors than those of any other polite profession; and from the lord, who has his gallery, down to the 'prentice, who has his twopenny copperplate, all are admirers of this art. The great, by their caresses, seem insensible to all other merit but that of the pencil; and the vulgar buy every book rather from the excellence of the sculptor than the writer.

How happy were it now, if men of real excellence in that profession were to arise![1] Were the painters of Italy now to appear, who once wandered like beggars from one city to another, and produced their almost breathing figures, what rewards might they not expect! But many of them lived without rewards, and therefore rewards alone will never produce their equals. We have often found the great exert themselves, not only without promotion, but in spite of opposition. We have often found them flourishing, like medicinal plants, in a region of savageness and barbarity, their excellence unknown, and their virtues unheeded.

They who have seen the paintings of Caravagio, are sensible of the surprising impression they make; bold, swelling, terrible to the last degree,—all seems animated, and speaks him among the foremost of his profession; yet this man's fortune and his fame seemed ever in opposition to each other.

Unknowing how to flatter the great, he was driven from city to city in the utmost indigence, and might truly be said to paint for his bread.

Having one day insulted a person of distinction, who refused to pay him all the respect which he thought his due, he was obliged to leave Rome, and travel on foot, his usual method of going his journeys down into the country, without either money or friends to subsist him.

After he had travelled in this manner as long as his strength would permit, faint with famine and fatigue, he

[1] Had Goldsmith written a few years later, he would probably have allowed this excellence to his friend Sir Joshua Reynolds, the great ornament of the English school.—B.

at last called at an obscure inn by the way-side. The host knew, by the appearance of his guest, his indifferent circumstances, and refused to furnish him a dinner without previous payment.

As Caravagio was entirely destitute of money, he took down the innkeeper's sign, and painted it anew for his dinner.[1]

Thus refreshed, he proceeded on his journey, and left the innkeeper not quite satisfied with this method of payment. Some company of distinction, however, coming soon after, and struck with the beauty of the new sign, bought it at an advanced price, and astonished the innkeeper with their generosity ; he was resolved, therefore, to get as many signs as possible drawn by the same artist, as he found he could sell them to good advantage ; and accordingly set out after Caravagio, in order to bring him back. It was night-fall before he came up to the place where the unfortunate Caravagio lay dead by the road-side, overcome by fatigue, resentment, and despair.

---

[1] In an obscure village in Fifeshire is an alehouse sign painted by the Scottish Teniers, Wilkie. We are not aware that the artist had the same motive to exertion with the unfortunate Caravagio.—B.

THE BEE.

No. VI.—SATURDAY, NOVEMBER 10, 1759.

ON EDUCATION.[1]

To the author of " The Bee."

SIR,—As few subjects are more interesting to society, so few have been more frequently written upon, than the education of youth. Yet it is a little surprising, that it has been treated almost by all in a declamatory manner. They have insisted largely on the advantages that result from it, both to individuals and to society; and have expatiated in the praise of what none have ever been so hardy as to call in question.

Instead of giving us fine but empty harangues upon this subject, instead of indulging each his particular and whimsical systems, it had been much better if the writers on this subject had treated it in a more scientific manner, repressed all the sallies of imagination, and given us the result of their observations with didactic simplicity. Upon this subject the smallest errors are of the most dangerous consequence; and the author should venture the imputation of stupidity upon a topic where his slightest devia-

---

[1] This constituted No. VII. of the 'Essays,' where the author placed at its head the following:—

" N.B.—This treatise was published before Rousseau's Emilius: [1762] if there be a similitude in any one instance, it is hoped the author of the present essay will not be deemed a plagiarist."

There are a few other slight differences in the two editions. Here we give the 'Essays' text (as being the improved one); but retain the heading, letter form, &c., of the original 'Bee' issue.—ED.

tions may tend to injure posterity.[1] [2] However, such are the whimsical and erroneous productions written upon this subject. Their authors have studied to be uncommon, not to be just; and, at present, we want a treatise upon education, not to tell us anything new, but, to explode the errors which have been introduced by the admirers of novelty. It is in this manner books become numerous; a desire of novelty produces a book, and other books are required to destroy this production.[2]

The manner in which our youth of London are at present educated is, some in free-schools in the city, but the far greater number in boarding-schools about town. The parent justly consults the health of his child, and finds an education in the country tends to promote this much more than a continuance in town. Thus far he is right: if there were a possibility of having even our free-schools kept a little out of town, it would certainly conduce to the health and vigour of perhaps the mind as well as the body. It may be thought whimsical, but it is truth,—I have found by experience, that they who have spent all their lives in cities, contract not only an effeminacy of habit, but even of thinking.

But when I have said, that the boarding-schools are preferable to free-schools, as being in the country, this is certainly the only advantage I can allow them; otherwise it is impossible to conceive the ignorance of those who take upon them the important trust of education. Is any man unfit for any of the professions, he finds his last resource in setting up a school. Do any become bankrupts in trade, they still set up a boarding-school, and drive a trade this way, when all others fail: nay, I have been told of butchers and barbers, who have turned schoolmasters; and, more surprising still, made fortunes in their new profession.

Could we think ourselves in a country of civilized people —could it be conceived that we have a regard for posterity,

---

[1] The first, or ' Bee,' edition has the rather stronger, and since much used, term—" the rising generation."—ED.

[2]—[2] In lieu of this the ' Bee ' issue had—" I shall, therefore, throw out a few thoughts upon this subject, which have not been attended to by others, and shall dismiss all attempts to please, while I study only instruction."—ED.

when such persons are permitted to take the charge of the morals, genius, and health of those dear little pledges, who may one day be the guardians of the liberties of Europe, and who may serve as the honour and bulwark of their aged parents? The care of our children, is it below the state? is it fit to indulge the caprice of the ignorant with the disposal of their children in this particular? For the state to take the charge of all its children, as in Persia, or Sparta, might at present be inconvenient; but surely, with great ease, it might cast an eye to their instructors. Of all professions in society, I do not know a more useful, or a more honourable one, than a schoolmaster; at the same time that I do not see any more generally despised, or men whose talents are so ill rewarded.

Were the salaries of schoolmasters to be augmented from a diminution of useless sinecures, how might it turn to the advantage of this people—a people whom, without flattery, I may in other respects term the wisest and greatest upon earth. But, while I would reward the deserving, I would dismiss those utterly unqualified for their employment: in short, I would make the business of a schoolmaster every way more respectable, by increasing their salaries, and admitting only men of proper abilities.

It is true we have already schoolmasters appointed, and they have small salaries; but where at present there is only one schoolmaster appointed, there should at least be two; and wherever the salary is at present twenty pounds, it should be augmented to a hundred. Do we give immoderate benefices to our own instructors, and shall we deny even subsistence to those who instruct our children? Every member of society should be paid in proportion as he is necessary: and I will be bold enough to say, that school-masters in a state are more necessary than clergymen, as children stand in more need of instruction than their parents.

But, instead of this, as I have already observed, we send them to board in the country to the most ignorant set of men that can be imagined; and, lest the ignorance of the master be not sufficient, the child is generally consigned to the usher. This is commonly some poor needy animal, little superior to a footman either in learning or spirit, invited to his place by an advertisement, and kept there merely from his being of a complying disposition, and making the children fond of him. " You give your child to be educated to a slave," says a philosopher to a rich man; " instead of one slave, you will then have two."

It were well, however, if parents, upon fixing their children in one of these houses, would examine the abilities of the usher as well as the master; for, whatever they are told to the contrary, the usher is generally the person most employed in their education. If, then, a gentleman, upon putting out his son to one of these houses, sees the usher disregarded by the master, he may depend upon it, that he is equally disregarded by the boys: the truth is, in spite of all their endeavours to please, they are generally the laughing-stock of the school. Every trick is played upon the usher; the oddity of his manners, his dress, or his language, is a fund of eternal ridicule; the master himself, now and then, cannot avoid joining in the laugh; and the poor wretch, eternally resenting this ill-usage, seems to live in a state of war with all the family. This is a very proper person, is it not, to give children a relish for learning? They must esteem learning very much, when they see its professors used with such ceremony. If the usher be despised, the father may be assured his child will never be properly instructed.[1]

But let me suppose, that there are some schools without these inconveniences,—where the masters and ushers are men of learning, reputation, and assiduity. If there are to be found such, they cannot be prized in a state sufficiently. A boy will learn more true wisdom in a public school in a year, than by a private education in five. It is not from masters, but from their equals, youth learn a knowledge of the world: the little tricks they play each other, the punishment that frequently attends the commission, is a just picture of the great world; and all the ways of men are practised in a public school in miniature. It is true, a child is early made acquainted with some vices in a

[1] Some think the author is here reflecting upon his own experience as an usher. If so, the strictures hardly apply to Dr. Milner's school, where, as Mr. Black has pointed out ('Goldsmith,' p. 26), Goldsmith seems to have been well treated in every respect.—ED.

school; but it is better to know these when a boy, than be first taught them when a man, for their novelty then may have irresistible charms.

In a public education boys early learn temperance; and if the parents and friends would give them less money upon their usual visits, it would be much to their advantage, since it may justly be said, that a great part of their disorders arise from surfeit,—*plus occidit gula quam gladius.* And now I am come to the article of health, it may not be amiss to observe, that Mr. Locke, and some others, have advised, that children should be inured to cold, to fatigue, and hardship, from their youth; but Mr. Locke was but an indifferent physician. Habit, I grant, has great influence over our constitutions, but we have not precise ideas upon this subject.

We know, that among savages, and even among our peasants, there are found children born with such constitutions, that they cross rivers by swimming, endure cold, thirst, hunger, and want of sleep, to a surprising degree; that when they happen to fall sick, they are cured, without the help of medicine, by nature alone. Such examples are adduced, to persuade us to imitate their manner of education, and accustom ourselves betimes to support the same fatigues. But had these gentlemen considered, first, how many lives are lost in this ascetic discipline; had they considered that these savages and peasants are generally not so long lived as those who have led a more indolent life; that the more laborious the life is, the less populous is the country: had they considered, that what physicians call the *stamina vitæ*, by fatigue and labour become rigid, and thus anticipate old age; that the numbers who survive those rude trials, bears no proportion to those who die in the experiment. Had these things been properly considered, they would not have thus extolled an education begun in fatigue and hardships. Peter the Great, willing to inure the children of his seamen to a life of hardship, ordered that they should only drink sea water, but they unfortunately all died under the trial.

But while I would exclude all unnecessary labours, yet still I would recommend temperance in the highest degree. No luxurious dishes with high seasoning, nothing given children to force an appetite, as little sugared or salted provisions as possible, though never so pleasing; but milk, morning and night, should be their constant food. This diet would make them more healthy than any of those slops that are usually cooked by the mistress of a boarding-school; besides, it corrects any consumptive habits, not unfrequently found amongst the children of city parents.

As boys should be educated with temperance, so the first, greatest lesson that should be taught them is, to admire frugality. It is by the exercise of this virtue alone, they can ever expect to be useful members of society. It is true, lectures continually repeated upon this subject, may make some boys, when they grow up, run into an extreme, and become misers; but it were well had we more misers than we have among us. I know few characters more useful in society; for a man's having a larger or smaller share of money lying useless by him, no way injures the common-wealth; since, should every miser now exhaust his stores, this might make gold more plenty, but it would not in-crease the commodities or pleasures of life; they would still remain as they are at present: it matters not, there-fore, whether men are misers or not, if they be only frugal, laborious, and fill the station they have chosen. If they deny themselves the necessaries of life, society is no way injured by their folly.

Instead, therefore, of romances, which praise young men of spirit, who go through a variety of adventures, and, at last, conclude a life of dissipation, folly, and extravagance, in riches and matrimony, there should be some men of wit employed to compose books that might equally interest the passions of our youth; where such a one might be praised for having resisted allurements when young, and how he, at last, became Lord Mayor—how he was married to a lady of great sense, fortune, and beauty: to be as explicit as possible, the old story of Whittington, were his cat left out, might be more serviceable to the tender mind than either Tom Jones, Joseph Andrews, or a hundred others, where frugality is the only good quality the hero is not possessed of. Were our schoolmasters, if any of them have sense enough to draw up such a work, thus employed, it would be much more serviceable to their pupils, than all the grammars and dictionaries they may publish these ten years.

Children should early be instructed in the arts from which they may afterwards draw the greatest advantages. When the wonders of nature are never exposed to our view, we have no great desire to become acquainted with those parts of learning which pretend to account for the phenomena. One of the ancients complains, that as soon as young men have left school, and are obliged to converse in the world, they fancy themselves transported into a new region : *Ut cum in forum venerint existiment se in aliam terrarum orbem delatos.* We should early, therefore, instruct them in the experiments, if I may so express it, of knowledge, and leave to maturer age the accounting for the causes. But, instead of that, when boys begin natural philosophy in colleges, they have not the least curiosity for those parts of the science which are proposed for their instruction ; they have never before seen the phenomena, and consequently have no curiosity to learn the reasons. Might natural philosophy, therefore, be made their pastime in school, by this means it would in college become their amusement.

In several of the machines now in use, there would be ample field both for instruction and amusement : the different sorts of the phosphorus, the artificial pyrites, magnetism, electricity, the experiments upon the rarefaction and weight of the air, and those upon elastic bodies, might employ their idle hours, and none should be called from play to see such experiments but such as thought proper. At first, then, it would be sufficient if the instruments, and the effects of their combination were only shown ; the causes should be deferred to a maturer age, or to those times when natural curiosity prompts us to discover the wonders of nature. Man is placed in this world as a spectator ; when he is tired of wondering at all the novelties about him, and not till then, does he desire to be made acquainted with the causes that create those wonders.

What I have observed with regard to natural philosophy, I would extend to every other science whatsoever. We should teach them as many of the facts as possible, and defer the causes until they seemed of themselves desirous of knowing them. A mind thus leaving school, stored with all the simple experiences of science, would be the fittest in the world for the college course; and though such a youth might not appear so bright, or so talkative, as those who had learned the real principles and causes of some of the sciences, yet he would make a wiser man, and would retain a more lasting passion for letters, than he who was early burdened with the disagreeable institution of cause and effect.

In history, such stories alone should be laid before them as might catch the imagination: instead of this, at present, they are too frequently obliged to toil through the four empires, as they are called, where their memories are burdened by a number of disgusting names, that destroy all their future relish for our best historians, who may be termed the truest teachers of wisdom.

Every species of flattery should be carefully avoided; a boy who happens to say a sprightly thing, is generally applauded so much, that he sometimes continues a coxcomb all his life after. He is reputed a wit at fourteen, and becomes a blockhead at twenty. Nurses, footmen, and such, should therefore be driven away as much as possible. I was even going to add, that the mother herself should stifle her pleasure or her vanity, when little master happens to say a good or a smart thing. Those modest, lubberly boys who seem to want spirit, become at length more shining men; and at school generally go through their business with more ease to themselves, and more satisfaction to their instructors.

There has of late a gentleman appeared, who thinks the study of rhetoric essential to a perfect education.[1] That bold male eloquence, which often, without pleasing, convinces, is generally destroyed by such an institution. Convincing eloquence is infinitely more serviceable to its possessor than the most florid harangue, or the most pathetic tones that can be imagined; and the man who is thoroughly convinced himself, who understands his sub-

---

[1] No doubt Mr. Thomas Sheridan, actor, author, &c.—the father of R. B. Sheridan. He was delivering lectures on rhetoric and elocution at this time.—ED.

ject, and the language he speaks in, will be more apt to silence opposition, than he who studies the force of his periods, and fills our ears with sounds, while our minds are destitute of conviction.

It was reckoned the fault of the orators at the decline of the Roman empire, when they had been long instructed by rhetoricians, that their periods were so harmonious, that they could be sung as well as spoken. What a ridiculous figure must one of these gentlemen cut, thus measuring syllables, and weighing words, when he should plead the cause of his client! Two architects were once candidates for the building a certain temple at Athens: the first harangued the crowd very learnedly upon the different orders of architecture, and showed them in what manner the temple should be built; the other, who got up after him, only observed, that what his brother had spoken he could do; and thus he at once gained his cause.

To teach men to be orators, is little less than to teach them to be poets; and for my part, I should have too great a regard for my child, to wish him a manor only in a bookseller's shop.

Another passion which the present age is apt to run into, is to make children learn all things,—the languages, the sciences, music, the exercises, and painting. Thus the child soon becomes a *talker* in all, but a *master* in none. He thus acquires a superficial fondness for every thing, and only shows his ignorance when he attempts to exhibit his skill.

As I deliver my thoughts without method or connection, so the reader must not be surprised to find me once more addressing schoolmasters on the present method of teaching the learned languages, which is commonly by literal translations. I would ask such, if they were to travel a journey, whether those parts of the road in which they found the greatest difficulties would not be most strongly remembered? Boys who, if I may continue the allusion, gallop through one of the ancients with the assistance of a translation, can have but a very slight acquaintance either with the author or his language. It is by the exercise of the mind alone that a language is learned; but a literal translation, on the opposite page, leaves no exercise for the memory at all. The boy will not be at the fatigue of remembering, when his doubts are at once satisfied by a glance of the eye; whereas, were every word to be sought from a dictionary, the learner would attempt to remember them, to save himself the trouble of looking out for the future.

To continue in the same pedantic strain,[1] of all the various grammars now taught in schools about town, I would recommend only the old common one; I have forgot whether Lily's or an emendation of him. The others may be improvements; but such improvements seem to me only mere grammatical niceties, no way in-fluencing the learner, but perhaps loading him with trifling subtleties, which, at a proper age, he must be at some pains to forget.

Whatever pains a master may take to make the learn-ing of the languages agreeable to his pupil, he may depend upon it, it will be at first extremely unpleasant. The rudiments of every language, therefore, must be given as a task, not as an amusement. Attempting to deceive children into instruction of this kind, is only deceiving ourselves; and I know no passion capable of conquering a child's natural laziness but fear. Solomon has said it before me; nor is there any more certain, though perhaps more disagreeable truth, than the proverb in verse, too well known to repeat on the present occasion. It is very probable that parents are told of some masters who never use the rod, and consequently are thought the properest instructors for their children; but though tenderness is a requisite quality in an instructor, yet there is too often the truest tenderness in well-timed correction.

Some have justly observed, that all passion should be banished on this terrible occasion; but, I know not how, there is a frailty attending human nature, that few masters are able to keep their temper whilst they correct. I knew a good-natured man, who was sensible of his own weakness in this respect, and consequently had recourse to the following expedient to prevent his passions from being engaged, yet at the same time administer justice

---

[1] The 'Bee' version adds " though no schoolmaster."—ED.

with impartiality. Whenever any of his pupils committed a fault, he summoned a jury of his peers,—I mean of the boys of his own or the next classes to him : his accusers stood forth ; he had liberty of pleading in his own defence ; and one or two more had the liberty of pleading against him : when found guilty by the panel, he was consigned to the footman who attended in the house, who had previous orders to punish, but with lenity. By this means the master took off the odium of punishment from himself ; and the footman, between whom and the boys there could not be even the slightest intimacy, was placed in such a light as to be shunned by every boy in the school.

¹ And now I have gone thus far, perhaps you will think me some pedagogue, willing, by a well-timed puff, to increase the reputation of his own school ; but such is not the case. The regard I have for society, for those tender minds who are the objects of the present essay, such is the only motive I have for offering those thoughts, calculated not to surprise by their novelty, or the elegance of composition, but merely to remedy some defects which have crept into the present system of school education. If this letter should be inserted, perhaps I may trouble you, in my next, with some thoughts upon a university education, not with an intent to exhaust the subject, but to amend some few abuses. I am, &c.¹

ON THE CONTRADICTIONS OF THE WORLD.

FROM VOLTAIRE.²

THE more we know of the world, the more we see of its absurdities and contradictions. To begin with the grand seignior ; he generally cuts off every head that displeases him, and can seldom preserve his own.

---

¹—¹ This last paragraph only appeared in the 'Bee' edition.—ED.
² Abridged from the opening section of the article " Contradictions," in Voltaire's 'Philosophical Dictionary.'—ED.

If from the turk we make a natural transition to the pope, he confirms the election of emperors, he has even kings for vassals, yet is not so powerful as any one of their ministers. He issues out orders for America and Africa; yet is not able to deprive even the little republic of Lucca of its privileges. The emperor is sometimes king of the Romans; but his only privileges consist in holding the pope's stirrup, and presenting him with the bason while he washes.

The English serve their kings upon the knee; but they are often found to depose them, to imprison them, and bring some of them to the scaffold.

Bishops and monks, who make vows of poverty, in consequence of such vows receive immoderate incomes; and, by virtue of their professed humility, become despotic princes.

Men who are convicted of not conforming to the religion· of their country, are burned in the market place; while the second eclogue of Virgil, which contains the most shocking obscenities, is gravely commented upon and taught by those very strenuous asserters of the divinity.

If a poor philosopher, who imagines no mischief, should teach that the earth takes an annual revolution, or that all light proceeds from the sun, should he assert that matter may have several properties, which we are entirely unacquainted with, he is at once branded with impiety, and as a disturber of public tranquillity; our modern philosophers are discouraged from delivering their sentiments, while the Tusculan questions of Cicero, and the works of Lucretius, which contain a complete course of irreligion, are put into the hands of our youth, and cried up as models for imitation.

Bayle, the sceptic philosopher, was persecuted even in Holland. Le Vayer, a greater sceptic, and a much inferior philosopher, was constituted the king's preceptor.[1] Nay, France has seen her ambassadors burnt in effigy in the streets of Paris, and the very next day honoured with the royal instructions.

The famous atheist Spinosa lived and died in peace.

[1] Francis de la Mothe-le-Vayer, 1588-1672. He was made preceptor to Louis XIV., on the advice of Richelieu.—ED.

Vanini, who wrote only against Aristotle, was burnt as an atheist. With this appellation he is branded in all the histories of the works of the learned, and biographical dictionaries, those immense archives of folly and falsehood. Consult any of these, and you will find that Vanini not only publicly taught atheism by his writings, but also that twelve of his disciples left Naples with him, in order to assist in making proselytes. After consulting those anecdotes, next consult his own works, and you will be surprised to find them replete with proofs of the existence of a God. He thus speaks in his 'Amphitheatrum,' a work equally condemned and unknown.

"God is the beginning and end, and the parent of all that was, or will be; he always exists, but not in time. To him the past has not fled, and the future will not arrive. He reigns everywhere, without being in any place; motionless, without being fixed, rapid without passing. He is all and above all; he is in all, without being confined; without all, but not excluded. Good, without quality; great, but without quantity; entire, without parts; unchangeable, yet diversified in every part of the universe. His will is his power, simple; there is no possibility with him, but all really is. In a word, being all, he is above all beings, being actually present, and existing in all." [1]

After such a confession of faith, could we think it, Vanini was declared an atheist! What were the motives to condemn him? Nothing more than the bare deposition of one Francon. In vain did his books bear witness to the falsehood of the deposer; one single enemy has cost him his life, and tarnished his character through all Europe.

Should I continue to examine the contradictions which are to be found in the republic of letters, I might perhaps be obliged to write the history of all the scholars and wits of the age. Should I extend my survey to society, I might be obliged to write the history of Europe. Should

---

[1] Vanini's accusers, however, said, with regard to the 'Amphitheatrum,' that it was a crafty attempt to cloak the writer's real opinions, as, they added, his writings, both before and after, show. But Vanini had apologists before Voltaire, and who took his view.—ED.

an Asiatic[1] come among us, what judgment could he form
of our religion ! Or would he not think that of Paganism
still continued ! The days of the week still retain the
names of heathen deities, our churches are filled with
statues of the gods of the ancients;[2] and should he sometimes be a spectator at our theatres, he might mistake the
scene for a temple to their honour, and our assiduity for
devotion.

In Spain, our Asiatic would be surprised to find severe
laws, which forbid strangers carrying on any commerce to
America; and yet he might see strangers alone in possession of that prohibited trade; and the Spaniards, in effect,
no more than factors to others, whom they enrich, while
they continue in poverty. How would he be surprised to
find our actors styled vagabonds[3] by law, yet encouraged
by the great, and kept company with as equals ! He
would find the press loaded with works which every one
condemns, and yet all are eager to purchase. He would
every where find our customs in opposition to our statutes.
He might probably laugh at our absurdities ; yet, should
we take a voyage into Asia, we might see the same absurdities practised with very little variation.

Men are every where equally fools; they have made
laws in the same manner that breaches are repaired in
the walls of a city. In one country the elder sons have
all the fortune from the rest; in another the fortune is
equally divided amongst them all. At one time the church
commands duelling; at another, it excommunicates all
who venture in single combat. They have, at times, ex-
communicated the partizans and the opposers of Aristotle;
those who wore long hair, and those who wore short.

---

[1] This speculation, possibly, with the before-going ' Turkish Spy,'
' Persian Letters,' &c., suggested to Goldsmith his ' Letters ' of the
" Chinese Philosopher" Lien Chi Altangi, afterwards collected as the
' Citizen of the World.' The latter series was commenced in January,
1760, almost immediately after the stoppage of the ' Bee.'—Ed.

[2] This is a rather free rendering of Voltaire's—" Les noces de Cupidon
et de Psyché sont peintes dans la maison des papes."—Ed.

[3] Voltaire's essay has not this remark concerning actors. It is an
interpolation of the translator, and applies to the English law, upon
which Goldsmith again comments in Letter LXXXV. of the ' Citizen of
the World.'—Ed.

We have, in this world, but one inviolable body of law, which is never infringed; I mean the laws of gaming. These never admit of exception, change, or subordination. If a man who was once a footman plays with a king, he is immediately paid, when he wins, without hesitation. Such is always the rule in this; in all other affairs, the sword is the only law, where the strong cut the weak into a thousand pieces.

Notwithstanding this, the world subsists as if all things were well ordered, and irregularity seems suited to our natures. Our political world resembles our globe, a great regular irregularity. It would be folly to expect to see our mountains, seas, and rivers assume beautiful mathematical figures; it would still be a greater folly to expect perfect wisdom in society.

ON THE INSTABILITY OF WORLDLY GRANDEUR.[1]

An alehouse keeper near Islington, who had long lived at the sign of the French King, upon the commencement of the last war with France pulled down his old sign, and put up that of the Queen of Hungary. Under the influence of her red face and golden sceptre, he continued to sell ale till she was no longer the favourite of his customers; he changed her, therefore, some time ago, for the King of Prussia, who may probably be changed, in turn, for the next great man that shall be set up for vulgar admiration.

In this manner the great are dealt out one after the other, to the gazing crowd.[2] When we have sufficiently wondered at one of them, he is taken in, and another exhibited in his room, who seldom holds his station long; for the mob are ever pleased with variety.

I must own I have such an indifferent opinion of the vulgar, that I am ever led to suspect that merit which

---

[1] This became No. VIII. in the 'Essays.'—ED.
[2] The 'Bee' has—"Our publican, in this, imitates the great exactly, who deal out their figures," &c.—ED.

raises their shout; at least I am certain to find those great, and sometimes good men, who find satisfaction in such acclamations, made worse by it; and history has too frequently taught me, that the head which has grown this day giddy with the roar of the million, has the very next been fixed upon a pole.

As Alexander VI. was entering a little town in the neighbourhood of Rome, which had been just evacuated by the enemy, he perceived the townsmen busy in the market-place in pulling down from a gibbet a figure, which had been designed to represent himself. There were some also knocking down a neighbouring statue of one of the Orsini family, with whom he was at war, in order to put Alexander's effigy in its place. It is possible a man who knew less of the world would have condemned the adulation of those bare-faced flatterers; but Alexander seemed pleased at their zeal, and, turning to Borgia his son, said with a smile, *Vides, mi fili, quam leve discrimen patibulum inter et statuum.* "You see, my son, the small difference between a gibbet and a statue." If the great could be taught any lesson, this might serve to teach them upon how weak a foundation their glory stands; for, as popular applause is excited by what seems like merit, it as quickly condemns what has only the appearance of guilt.

Popular glory is a perfect coquette: her lovers must toil, feel every inquietude, indulge every caprice; and perhaps at last be jilted for their pains. True glory, on the other hand, resembles a woman of sense: her admirers must play no tricks; they feel no great anxiety, for they are sure, in the end, of being rewarded in proportion to their merit. When Swift used to appear in public, he generally had the mob shouting in his train. "Pox take these fools!" he would say, "How much joy might all this bawling give my Lord Mayor!"

We have seen those virtues which have, while living, retired from the public eye, generally transmitted to posterity as the truest objects of admiration and praise. Perhaps the character of the late Duke of Marlborough[1] may one day be set up, even above that of his more talked-of

---

[1] The third duke, who died in 1758.—ED.

predecessor; since an assemblage of all the mild and amiable virtues is far superior, to those vulgarly called the great ones. I must be pardoned for this short tribute to the memory of a man, who, while living, would as much detest to receive any thing that wore the appearance of flattery, as I should to offer it.

I know not how to turn so trite a subject out of the beaten road of commonplace, except by illustrating it, rather by the assistance of my memory than my judgment, and instead of making reflections, by telling a story.

A Chinese, who had long studied the works of Confucius, who knew the characters of fourteen thousand words, and could read a great part of every book that came in his way, once took it into his head to travel into Europe, and observe the customs of a people which he thought not very much inferior even to his own countrymen.[1] Upon his arrival at Amsterdam, his passion for letters naturally led him to a bookseller's shop: and, as he could speak a little Dutch, he civilly asked the bookseller for the works of the immortal Xixofou.[2] The bookseller assured him he had never heard the book mentioned before. "Alas!" cries our traveller,[3] "to what purpose, then, has he fasted to death, to gain a renown which has never travelled beyond the precincts of China!"

There is scarce a village in Europe, and not one university, that is not thus furnished with its little great men. The head of a petty corporation, who opposes the designs of a prince who would tyrannically force his subjects to save their best clothes for Sundays; the puny pedant who finds one undiscovered property in the polype, or describes an unheeded process in the skeleton of a mole; and whose mind, like his microscope, perceives nature only in detail; the rhymer who makes smooth verses, and paints to our

---

[1] The 'Bee' edition adds—"in the arts of refining upon every pleasure."—ED.

[2] Ilixofou is the name in the 'Bee.'—ED.

[3] The 'Bee' version is amplified thus—"'What! have you never heard of that immortal poet?' returned the other, much surprised; 'that light of the eyes, that favourite of kings, that rose of perfection! I suppose you know nothing of the immortal Fipsihihi, second cousin to the moon?'—'Nothing at all, indeed, Sir,' returned the other.—'Alas!' cries our traveller," &c.—ED.

imagination when he should only speak to our hearts; all equally fancy themselves walking forward to immortality, and desire the crowd behind them to look on. The crowd takes them at their word. Patriot, philosopher, and poet, are shouted in their train. "Where was there ever so much merit seen? no times so important as our own! ages yet unborn shall gaze with wonder and applause!" To such music the important pigmy moves forward, bustling and swelling, and aptly compared to a puddle in a storm.

I have lived to see generals, who once had crowds hallooing after them wherever they went, who were bepraised by newspapers and magazines, those echoes of the voice of the vulgar, and yet they have long sunk into merited obscurity, with scarce even an epitaph left to flatter. A few years ago, the herring fishery employed all Grub Street; it was the topic in every coffeehouse, and the burden of every ballad. We were to drag up oceans of gold from the bottom of the sea; we were to supply all Europe with herrings upon our own terms. At present we hear no more of all this. We have fished up very little gold that I can learn; nor do we furnish the world with herrings as was expected. Let us wait but a few years longer, and we shall find all our expectations a herring fishery.[1]

SOME ACCOUNT OF THE ACADEMIES OF ITALY.

THERE is not, perhaps, a country in Europe, in which learning is so fast upon the decline as in Italy; yet not one in which there are such a number of academies instituted for its support. There is scarce a considerable town in the whole country, which has not one or two institutions of this nature, where the learned, as they are pleased to call themselves, meet to harangue, to compliment each other, and praise the utility of their institution.

Jarchius has taken the trouble to give us a list of those

---

[1] For the herring fishery mania, see 'Citizen of the World,' Letter CVII., and note to Letter CX.—ED.

clubs or academies, which amount to five hundred and fifty, each distinguished by somewhat whimsical in the name. The academies of Bologna, for instance, are divided into the Abbandonati, the Ausiosi, Ociosio, Arcadi, Confusi, Dubbiosi, &c. There are few of these who have not published their transactions, and scarce a member who is not looked upon as the most famous man in the world, at home.

Of all those societies, I know of none whose works are worth being known out of the precincts of the city in which they were written, except the Cicalata Academica —or, as we might express it, the Tickling Society—of Florence. I have just now before me a manuscript oration, spoken by the late Tomaso Crudeli at that society, which will at once serve to give a better picture of the manner in which men of wit amuse themselves in that country, than any thing I could say upon the occasion. The oration is this:

" The younger the nymph, my dear companions, the more happy the lover. From fourteen to seventeen you are sure of finding love for love; from seventeen to twenty-one, there is always a mixture of interest and affection. But when that period is past, no longer expect to receive, but to buy—no longer expect a nymph who gives, but who sells, her favours. At this age, every glance is taught its duty; not a look, not a sigh without design; the lady, like a skilful warrior, aims at the heart of another, while she shields her own from danger.

" On the contrary, at fifteen you may expect nothing but simplicity, innocence, and nature. The passions are then sincere; the soul seems seated in the lips; the dear object feels present happiness, without being anxious for the future; her eyes brighten if her lover approaches; her smiles are borrowed from the Graces, and her very mistakes seem to complete her desires.

" Lucretia was just sixteen. The rose and lily took possession of her face, and her bosom, by its hue and its coldness, seemed covered with snow. So much beauty and so much virtue seldom want admirers. Orlandino, a youth of sense and merit, was among the number. He had long languished for an opportunity of declaring his passion, when Cupid, as if willing to indulge his happiness, brought the charming young couple by mere accident to an arbour, where every prying eye, but that of love, was absent. Orlandino talked of the sincerity of his passion, and mixed flattery with his addresses; but it was all in vain. The nymph was pre-engaged, and had. long devoted to heaven those charms for which he sued. ' My dear Orlandino,' said she, ' you know I have been long dedicated to St. Catherine, and to her belongs all that lies below my girdle; all that is above, you may freely possess, but farther I cannot, must not, comply. The vow is passed; I wish it were undone, but now it is impossible.' You may conceive, my companions, the embarrassment our young lovers felt upon this occasion. They kneeled to St. Catherine, and though both despaired, both implored her assistance. Their tutelar saint was entreated to show some expedient, by which both might continue to love, and yet both be happy. Their petition was sincere. St. Catherine was touched with compassion; for lo, a miracle! Lucretia's girdle unloosed, as if without hands; and though before bound round her middle, fell spontaneously down to her feet, and gave Orlandino the possession of all those beauties which lay above it."

THE BEE.

OF ELOQUENCE [AND POPULAR PREACHING].

OF all kinds of success, that of an orator is the most pleasing. Upon other occasions, the applause we deserve is conferred in our absence, and we are insensible of the pleasure we have given; but in eloquence, the victory and the triumph are inseparable. We read our own glory in the face of every spectator; the audience is moved; the antagonist is defeated; and the whole circle bursts into unsolicited applause.

The rewards which attend excellence in this way are so pleasing, that numbers have written professed treatises to teach us the art; schools have been established with no other intent; rhetoric has taken place among the institutions; and pedants have ranged under proper heads, and distinguished with long learned names, *some* of the strokes of nature, or of passion, which orators have used. I say only *some*, for a folio volume could not contain all the figures which have been used by the truly eloquent; and scarce a good speaker or writer but makes use of some that are peculiar or new.

Eloquence has preceded the rules of rhetoric, as languages have been formed before grammar. Nature renders men eloquent in great interests, or great passions. He that is sensibly touched, sees things with a very different eye from the rest of mankind. All nature to him becomes an object of comparison and metaphor, without attending to it; he throws life into all, and inspires his audience with a part of his own enthusiasm.

It has been remarked, that the lower parts of mankind generally express themselves most figuratively, and that tropes are found in the most ordinary forms of conversation. Thus, in every language, the heart burns; the courage is roused; the eyes sparkle; the spirits are cast down; passion inflames, pride swells, and pity sinks the soul. Nature every where speaks in those strong images, which, from their frequency, pass unnoticed.

Nature it is which inspires those rapturous enthusiasms, those irresistible turns; a strong passion, a pressing danger, calls up all the imagination, and gives the orator irresistible force. Thus, a captain of the first caliphs, seeing his soldiers fly, cried out, " Whither do you run? the enemy are not there! You have been told that the caliph is dead; but God is still living. He regards the brave, and will reward the courageous. Advance!"

A man, therefore, may be called eloquent, who transfers the passion or sentiment with which he is moved himself, into the breast of another; and this definition appears the more just, as it comprehends the graces of silence and of action. An intimate persuasion of the truth to be proved, is the sentiment and passion to be transferred; and he who effects this, is truly possessed of the talent of eloquence.

I have called eloquence a talent, and not an art, as so many rhetoricians have done, as art is acquired by exercise and study, and eloquence is the gift of nature. Rules will never make either a work or a discourse eloquent; they only serve to prevent faults, but not to introduce beauties; to prevent those passages which are truly eloquent and dictated by nature from being blended with others which might disgust, or at least abate our passion.

What we clearly conceive, says Boileau, we can clearly express. I may add, that what is felt with emotion is expressed also with the same movements; the words arise as readily to paint our emotions as to express our thoughts with perspicuity. The cool care an orator takes to express passions which he does not feel, only prevents his rising into that passion he would seem to feel. In a word, to feel your subject thoroughly, and to speak without fear, are the only rules of eloquence, properly so called, which I can offer. Examine a writer of genius on the most beautiful parts of his work, and he will always assure you, that such passages are generally those which have given him the least trouble, for they came as if by inspiration. To pretend that cold and didactic precepts will make a man eloquent, is only to prove that he is incapable of eloquence.

But, as in being perspicuous, it is necessary to have a full idea of the subject, so in being eloquent it is not sufficient, if I may so express it, to feel by halves. The orator should be strongly impressed, which is generally the effect of a fine and exquisite sensibility, and not that transient and superficial emotion which he excites in the greatest part of his audience. It is even impossible to affect the hearers in any great degree without being affected ourselves. In vain it will be objected, that many writers have had the art to inspire their readers with a passion for virtue, without being virtuous themselves, since it may be answered, that sentiments of virtue filled their minds at the time they were writing. They felt the inspiration strongly, while they praised justice, generosity, or good-nature; but, unhappily for them, these passions might have been discontinued, when they laid down the pen. In vain will it be objected again, that we can move without being moved, as we can convince without being convinced. It is much easier to deceive our reason than ourselves: a trifling defect in reasoning may be overseen, and lead a man astray, for it requires reason and time to detect the falsehood; but our passions are not easily imposed upon,—our eyes, our ears, and every sense, are watchful to detect the imposture.

No discourse can be eloquent that does not elevate the mind. Pathetic eloquence, it is true, has for its only object to affect; but I appeal to men of sensibility, whether their pathetic feelings are not accompanied with some degree of elevation. We may then call eloquence and sublimity the same thing, since it is impossible to be one without feeling the other. From hence it follows, that we may be eloquent in any language, since no language refuses to paint those sentiments with which we are thoroughly impressed. What is usually called sublimity of style, seems to be only an error. Eloquence is not in the words, but in the subject; and in great concerns, the more simply any thing is expressed, it is generally the more sublime. True eloquence does not consist, as the rhetoricians assure us, in saying great things in a sublime style, but in a simple style; for there is, properly speaking, no such thing as a sublime style; the sublimity lies only in the things; and when they are not so, the language may be turgid, affected, metaphorical,—but not affecting.

What can be more simply expressed than the following extract from a celebrated preacher,[1] and yet what was ever more sublime? Speaking of the small number of the elect, he breaks out thus among his audience:—" Let me suppose that this was the last hour of us all—that the heavens were opening over our heads—that time was passed, and eternity begun—that Jesus Christ in all his glory, that man of sorrows, in all his glory, appeared on the tribunal, and that we were assembled here to receive our final decree of life, or death eternal! Let me ask, impressed with terror like you, and not separating my lot from yours, but putting myself in the same situation in which we must all one day appear before God, our judge,—let me ask, if Jesus Christ should now appear to make the terrible separation of the just from the unjust, do you think the greatest number would be saved? Do you think the number of the elect would even be equal to that of the sinners? Do you think, if all our works were examined with justice, would he find ten just persons in this great assembly? Monsters of ingratitude! would he find one?" Such passages as these are sublime in every language. The expression may be less speaking, or more indistinct, but the greatness of the idea still remains. In a word, we may be eloquent in every language and in every style, since elocution is only an assistant, but not a constitutor of eloquence.

Of what use, then, will it be said, are all the precepts given us upon this head, both by the ancients and moderns? I answer, that they cannot make us eloquent, but they will certainly prevent us from becoming ridiculous. They can seldom procure a single beauty, but they may banish

[1] Massillon, Bishop of Clermont : born, 1663; died, 1742.—B.

a thousand faults. The true method of an orator is not to attempt always to move, always to affect, to be continually sublime, but at proper intervals to give rest both to his own and the passions of his audience. In these periods of relaxation, or of preparation rather, rules may teach him to avoid any thing low, trivial, or disgusting. Thus criticism, properly speaking, is intended not to assist those parts which are sublime, but those which are naturally mean and humble, which are composed with coolness and caution, and where the orator rather endeavours not to offend, than attempts to please.

I have hitherto insisted more strenuously on that eloquence which speaks to the passions, as it is a species of oratory almost unknown in England. At the bar it is quite discontinued, and I think with justice. In the senate it is used but sparingly, as the orator speaks to enlightened judges. But in the pulpit, in which the orator should chiefly address the vulgar, it seems strange that it should be entirely laid aside.

The vulgar of England are, without exception, the most barbarous and the most unknowing of any in Europe. A great part of their ignorance may be chiefly ascribed to their teachers, who, with the most pretty gentleman-like serenity, deliver their cool discourses, and address the reason of men who have never reasoned in all their lives. They are told of cause and effect, of beings self-existent, and the universal scale of beings. They are informed of the excellence of the Bangorian Controversy,[1] and the absurdity of an intermediate state. The spruce preacher reads his lucubration without lifting his nose from the text, and never ventures to earn the shame of an enthusiast.

By this means, though his audience feel not one word of all he says, he earns, however, among his acquaintance, the character of a man of sense; among his acquaintance only, did I say? nay, even with his bishop.

The polite of every country have several motives to induce them to a rectitude of action,—the love of virtue for its own sake, the shame of offending, and the desire of

---

[1] The controversy started in 1717 by the publication (by command of George I.) of the sermon by Hoadley, Bishop of Bangor, on the text— " My kingdom is not of this world."—ED.

pleasing. The vulgar have but one,—the enforcements of religion; and yet those who should push this motive home to their hearts, are basely found to desert their post. They speak to the squire, the philosopher, and the pedant; but the poor, those who really want instruction, are left uninstructed.

I have attended most of our pulpit orators, who,'it must be owned, write extremely well upon the text they assume. To give them their due also, they read their sermons with elegance and propriety; but this goes but a very short way in true eloquence. The speaker must be moved. In this, in this alone, our English divines are deficient. Were they to speak to a few calm, dispassionate hearers, they certainly use the properest methods of address; but their audience is chiefly composed of the poor, who must be influenced by motives of reward and punishment, and whose only virtues lie in self-interest or fear.

How, then, are such to be addressed? Not by studied periods, or cold disquisitions; not by the labours of the head, but the honest spontaneous dictates of the heart. Neither writing a sermon with regular periods, and all the harmony of elegant expression—neither reading it with emphasis, propriety, and deliberation—neither pleasing with metaphor, simile, or rhetorical fustian—neither arguing coolly, and untying consequences united in *à priori*, nor bundling up inductions *à posteriori*—neither pedantic jargon, nor academical trifling, can persuade the poor. Writing a discourse coolly in the closet, then getting it by memory, and delivering it on Sundays, even that will not do. What, then, is to be done? I know of no expedient to speak—to speak at once intelligibly and feelingly—except to understand the language: to be convinced of the truth of the object—to be perfectly acquainted with the subject in view—to prepossess yourself with a low opinion of your audience—and to do the rest extempore. By this means, strong expressions, new thoughts, rising passions, and the true declamatory style, will naturally ensue.

Fine declamation does not consist in flowery periods, delicate allusions, or musical cadences, but in a plain, open, loose style, where the periods are long and obvious; where the same thought is often exhibited in several points of view: all this, strong sense, a good memory, and a small share of experience, will furnish to every orator; and without these, a clergyman may be called a fine preacher, a judicious preacher, and a man of sound sense; he may make his hearers admire his understanding, but will seldom enlighten theirs.

When I think of the Methodist preachers among us, how seldom they are endued with common sense, and yet how often and how justly they affect their hearers, I cannot avoid saying within myself, had these been bred gentlemen, and been endued with even the meanest share of understanding, what might they not effect! Did our bishops, who can add dignity to their expostulations, testify the same fervour, and *entreat* their hearers, as well as *argue*, what might not be the consequence![1] The vulgar, by which I mean the bulk of mankind, would then have a double motive to love religion; first, from seeing its professors honoured here, and next, from the consequences hereafter. At present the enthusiasms of the poor are opposed to law; did law conspire with their enthusiasms, we should not only be the happiest nation upon earth, but the wisest also.

Enthusiasm in religion, which prevails only among the vulgar, should be the chief object of politics. A society of enthusiasts, governed by reason, among the great, is the most indissoluble, the most virtuous, and the most efficient of its own decrees that can be imagined. Every country, possessed of any degree of strength, have had their enthusiasms, which ever serve as laws among the people. The Greeks had their *Kalokagathia*, the Romans their *Amor Patriæ*, and we the truer and firmer bond of the *Protestant Religion*. The principle is the same in all: how much, then, is it the duty of those whom the law has appointed teachers of this religion, to enforce its obligations, and to raise those enthusiasms among people, by which alone political society can subsist?

From eloquence, therefore, the morals of our people are to expect emendation; but how little can they be improved

---

[1] See vol. i., Essay 'On the English Clergy and Popular Preachers,' in which the author advocates this style of pulpit eloquence at greater length.—B.

by men who get into the pulpit rather to show their parts, than convince us of the truth of what they deliver; who are painfully correct in their style, musical in their tones; where every sentiment, every expression, seems the result of meditation and deep study!

Tillotson has been commended as the model of pulpit eloquence: thus far he should be imitated, where he generally strives to convince rather than to please; but to adopt his long, dry, and sometimes tedious discussions, which serve to amuse only divines, and are utterly neglected by the generality of mankind—to praise the intricacy of his periods, which are too long to be spoken—to continue his cool phlegmatic manner of enforcing every truth,—is certainly erroneous. As I said before, the good preacher should adopt no model, write no sermons, study no periods; let him but understand his subject, the language he speaks, and be convinced of the truths he delivers. It is amazing to what heights eloquence of this kind may reach! This is that eloquence the ancients represented as lightning, bearing down every opposer; this the power which has turned whole assemblies into astonishment, admiration, and awe—that is described by the torrent, the flame, and every other instance of irresistible impetuosity.

But to attempt such noble heights, belongs only to the truly great, or the truly good. To discard the lazy manner of reading sermons, or speaking sermons by rote; to set up singly against the opposition of men who are attached to their own errors, and to endeavour to be great, instead of being prudent, are qualities we seldom see united. A minister of the Church of England, who may be possessed of good sense, and some hopes of preferment, will seldom give up such substantial advantages for the empty pleasure of improving society. By his present method he is liked by his friends, admired by his dependants, not displeasing to his bishop; he lives as well, eats and sleeps as well, as if a real orator, and an eager asserter of his mission: he will hardly, therefore, venture all this, to be called, perhaps, an enthusiast; nor will he depart from customs established by the brotherhood, when, by such a conduct, he only singles himself out for their contempt.

CUSTOM AND LAWS COMPARED.

WHAT, say some, can give us a more contemptible idea of a large state, than to find it mostly governed by custom; to have few written laws, and no boundaries to mark the jurisdiction between the senate and people? Among the number who speak in this manner is the great Montesquieu, who asserts that every nation is free in proportion to the number of its written laws, and seems to hint at a despotic and arbitrary conduct in the present King of Prussia, who has abridged the laws of his country into a very short compass.[1]

As Tacitus and Montesquieu happen to differ in sentiment upon a subject of so much importance, (for the Roman expressly asserts, that the state is generally vicious in proportion to the number of its laws,) it will not be amiss to examine it a little more minutely, and see whether a state, which, like England, is burdened with a multiplicity of written laws, or which, like Switzerland, Geneva, and some other republics, is governed by custom and the determination of the judge, is best.

And to prove the superiority of custom to written law, we shall at least find history conspiring. Custom, or the traditional observance of the practice of their forefathers, was what directed the Romans, as well in their public as private determinations. Custom was appealed to in pronouncing sentence against a criminal, where part of the formulary was *more majorum*. So Sallust, speaking of the expulsion of Tarquin, says, *mutato more*, and not *lege mutata*; and Virgil, *pacisque imponere morem*. So that, in those times of the empire in which the people retained their liberty, they were governed by custom; when they sunk into oppression and tyranny, they were restrained by new laws, and the laws of tradition abolished.

As getting the ancients on our side is half a victory, it will not be amiss to fortify the argument with an observation of Chrysostom's—that "The enslaved are the fittest

---

[1] In the *Code Frederique*. Napoleon Bonaparte has made a similar digest of the French laws in his *Code Napoleon.*—B.

to be governed by laws, and free men by custom." Custom partakes of the nature of parental injunction; it is kept by the people themselves, and observed with a willing obedience. The observance of it must, therefore, be a mark of freedom; and coming originally to a state from the reverenced founders of its liberty, will be an encouragement and assistance to it in the defence of that blessing: but a conquered people, a nation of slaves, must pretend to none of this freedom, or these happy distinctions; having, by degeneracy, lost all right to their brave forefathers' free institutions, their masters will in policy take the forfeiture; and the fixing a conquest must be done by giving laws, which may every moment serve to remind the people enslaved of their conquerors; nothing being more dangerous than to trust a late subdued people with old customs, that presently upbraid their degeneracy, and provoke them to revolt.

The wisdom of the Roman republic in their veneration for custom, and backwardness to introduce a new law, was perhaps the cause of their long continuance, and of the virtues of which they have set the world so many examples. But to show in what that wisdom consists, it may be proper to observe, that the benefit[s] of new-written laws are merely confined to the consequences of their observance; but customary laws, keeping up a veneration for the founders, engage men in the imitation of their virtues as well as policy. To this may be ascribed the religious regard the Romans paid to their forefathers' memory, and their adhering for so many ages to the practice of the same virtues; which nothing contributed more to efface than the introduction of a voluminous body of new laws over the neck of venerable custom.

The simplicity, conciseness, and antiquity of custom, give an air of majesty and immutability that inspires awe and veneration; but new laws are too apt to be voluminous, perplexed, and indeterminate; whence must necessarily arise neglect, contempt, and ignorance.

As every human institution is subject to gross imperfections, so laws must necessarily be liable to the same inconveniences, and their defects soon discovered. Thus, through the weakness of one part, all the rest are liable to be brought into contempt. But such weaknesses in a custom, for very obvious reasons, evade an examination; besides, a friendly prejudice always stands up in their favour.

But, let us suppose a new law to be perfectly equitable and necessary; yet, if the procurers of it have betrayed a conduct that confesses by-ends and private motives, the disgust to the circumstances disposes us, unreasonably indeed, to an irreverence of the law itself; but we are indulgently blind to the most visible imperfections of an old custom. Though we perceive the defects ourselves, yet we remain persuaded that our wise forefathers had good reason for what they did; and though such motives no longer continue, the benefit will still go along with the observance, though we don't know how. It is thus the Roman lawyers speak: "Non omnium quæ a majoribus constituta sunt, ratio reddi potest, et ideo rationes eorum quæ constituuntur inquiri non oportet, aliaquin multa ex his quæ certa sunt subvertuntur."

Those laws which preserve to themselves the greatest love and observance, must needs be best; but custom, as it executes itself, must be necessarily superior to written laws, in this respect, which are to be executed by another. Thus, nothing can be more certain, than that numerous written laws are a sign of a degenerate community, and are frequently not the consequences of vicious morals in a state, but the causes.

From hence we see how much greater benefit it would be to the state, rather to abridge than increase its laws. We every day find them increasing; acts and reports, which may be termed the acts of judges, are every day becoming more voluminous, and loading the subject with new penalties.

Laws ever increase in number and severity, until they at length are strained so tight as to break themselves. Such was the case of the latter empire, whose laws were at length become so strict, that the barbarous invaders did not bring servitude but liberty.

OF THE PRIDE AND LUXURY OF THE MIDDLING CLASS OF PEOPLE.[1]

OF all the follies and absurdities which this great metropolis labours under, there is not one, I believe, at present appears in a more glaring and ridiculous light, than the pride and luxury of the middling class of people. Their eager desire of being seen in a sphere far above their capacities and circumstances, is daily—nay hourly—instanced, by the prodigious numbers of mechanics who flock to the races, gaming-tables, brothels, and all public diversions this fashionable town affords.

You shall see a grocer or a tallow-chandler, sneak from behind the compter, clap on a laced coat and a bag, fly to the E. O. table, throw away fifty pieces with some sharping man of quality, while his industrious wife is selling a pennyworth of sugar, or a pound of candles, to support her fashionable spouse in his extravagances.

I was led into this reflection by an odd adventure which happened to me the other day at Epsom races, where I went, not through any desire, I do assure you, of laying bets, or winning thousands, but at the earnest request of a friend, who had long indulged the curiosity of seeing the sport, very natural for an Englishman. When we had arrived at the course, and had taken several turns to observe the different objects that made up this whimsical group, a figure suddenly darted by us, mounted and dressed in all the elegance of those polite gentry who come to show you they have a little money, and rather than pay their just debts at home, generously come abroad to bestow it on gamblers and pickpockets. As I had not an opportunity of viewing his face till his return, I gently walked after him, and met him as he came back; when, to my no small surprise, I beheld in this gay Narcissus the visage of Jack Varnish, a humble vender of prints.[2] Disgusted

---

[1] First published in the 'Literary Magazine,' May, 1758. This was after Johnson had ceased to edit the magazine.—ED.

[2] Here follows in the original edition—"who had often taken a crown of me for a Teniers or a Berghem." In the next paragraph the 'Literary Magazine' had "Keep your shop, Robin," &c.—ED.

at the sight, I pulled my friend by the sleeve, pressed him to return home, telling him all the way, that I was so enraged at the fellow's impudence, I was resolved never to lay out another penny with him.

And now, pray, Sir, let me beg of you to give this a place in your paper, that Mr. Varnish may understand he mistakes the thing quite, if he imagines horse-racing recommendable in a tradesman; and that he who is revelling every night in the arms of a common strumpet (though blessed with an indulgent wife) when he ought to be minding his business, will never thrive in this world. He will find himself soon mistaken, his finances decrease, his friends shun him, customers fall off, and himself thrown into a gaol. I would earnestly recommend this adage to every mechanic in London, " Keep your shop, and your shop will keep you." A strict observance of these words will, I am sure, in time gain them estates. Industry is the road to wealth, and honesty to happiness; and he who strenuously endeavours to pursue them both, may never fear the critic's lash, or the sharp cries of penury and want.

SABINUS AND OLINDA.

In a fair, rich, and flourishing country, whose clifts are washed by the German ocean, lived Sabinus, a youth formed by nature to make a conquest wherever he thought proper; but the constancy of his disposition fixed him only with Olinda. He was, indeed, superior to her in fortune, but that defect on her side was so amply supplied by her merit, that none was thought more worthy of his regards than she. He loved her, he was beloved by her; and in a short time, by joining hands publicly, they avowed the union of their hearts. But, alas! none, however fortunate, however happy, are exempt from the shafts of envy, and the malignant effects of ungoverned appetite. How unsafe, how detestable are they who have this fury for their guide! How certainly will it lead them from themselves, and plunge them in errors they would have shuddered at, even in apprehension. Ariana, a lady of many amiable qualities, very nearly allied to Sabinus, and highly esteemed by him, imagined herself slighted, and injuriously treated, since his marriage with Olinda. By incautiously suffering this jealousy to corrode in her breast, she began to give a loose to passion; she forgot those many virtues for which she had been so long and so justly applauded. Causeless suspicion and mistaken resentment betrayed her into all the gloom of discontent; she sighed without ceasing; the happiness of others gave her intolerable pain; she thought of nothing but revenge. How unlike what she was,—the cheerful, the prudent, the compassionate Ariana!

She continually laboured to disturb a union so firmly, so affectionately founded, and planned every scheme which she thought most likely to disturb it.

Fortune seemed willing to promote her unjust intentions: the circumstances of Sabinus had been long embarrassed by a tedious law-suit, and the court determining the cause unexpectedly in favour of his opponent, it sunk his fortune to the lowest pitch of penury from the highest affluence. From the nearness of relationship, Sabinus expected from Ariana those assistances his present situation required; but she was insensible to all his entreaties, and the justice of every remonstrance, unless he first separated from Olinda, whom she regarded with detestation. Upon a compliance with her desires in this respect, she promised her fortune, her interest, and her all, should be at his command. Sabinus was shocked at the proposal; he loved his wife with inexpressible tenderness, and refused those offers, with indignation, which were to be purchased at so high a price. Ariana was no less displeased to find her offers rejected, and gave a loose to all that warmth which she had long endeavoured to suppress. Reproach generally produces recrimination; the quarrel rose to such a height, that Sabinus was marked for destruction, and the very next day, upon the strength of an old family debt, he was sent to gaol, with none but Olinda to comfort him in his miseries. In this mansion of distress, they lived together with resignation, and even with comfort. She provided the frugal meal, and he read for her while employed

in the little offices of domestic concern. Their fellow
prisoners admired their contentment, and whenever they
had a desire of relaxing into mirth, and enjoying those
little comforts that a prison affords, Sabinus and Olinda
were sure to be of the party. Instead of reproaching each
other for their mutual wretchedness, they both lightened
it, by bearing each a share of the load imposed by Providence. Whenever Sabinus showed the least concern on
his dear partner's account, she conjured him by the love
he bore her, by those tender ties which now united them
for ever, not to discompose himself; that so long as his
affection lasted, she defied all the ills of fortune, and every
loss of fame or friendship; that nothing could make her
miserable but his seeming to want happiness; nothing
pleased but his sympathising with her pleasure. A continuance in prison soon robbed them of the little they had
left, and famine began to make its horrid appearance; yet
still was neither found to murmur: they both looked upon
their little boy, who, insensible of their or his own distress, was playing about the room, with inexpressible yet
silent anguish, when a messenger came to inform them
that Ariana was dead, and that her will, in favour of a
very distant relation, who was now in another country,
might easily be procured and burnt, in which case all her
large fortune would revert to him, as being the next heir
at law.

A proposal of so base a nature filled our unhappy
couple with horror; they ordered the messenger immediately out of the room, and, falling upon each other's
neck, indulged an agony of sorrow, for now even all hopes
of relief were banished. The messenger who made the
proposal, however, was only a spy sent by Ariana to sound
the dispositions of a man she loved at once and persecuted.
This lady, though warped by wrong passions, was naturally kind, judicious, and friendly. She found that all
her attempts to shake the constancy or the integrity of
Sabinus were ineffectual; she had therefore begun to
reflect, and to wonder how she could so long and so un-
provoked injure such uncommon fortitude and affection.

She had, from the next room, herself heard the reception given to the messenger, and could not avoid feeling

all the force of superior virtue: she therefore reassumed her former goodness of heart; she came into the room with tears in her eyes, and acknowledged the severity of her former treatment. She bestowed her first care in providing them all the necessary supplies, and acknowledged them as the most deserving heirs of her fortune. From this moment, Sabinus enjoyed an uninterrupted happiness with Olinda, and both were happy in the friendship and assistance of Ariana; who, dying soon after, left them in possession of a large estate, and, in her last moments, confessed, that virtue was the only path to true glory; and that, however innocence may for a time be depressed, a steady perseverance will, in time, lead it to a certain victory.

THE SENTIMENTS OF A FRENCHMAN ON THE TEMPER OF THE ENGLISH.

NOTHING is so uncommon among the English as that easy affability, that instant method of acquaintance, or that cheerfulness of disposition, which make in France the charm of every society. Yet, in this gloomy reserve they seem to pride themselves, and think themselves less happy if obliged to be more social. One may assert, without wronging them, that they do not study the method of going through life with pleasure and tranquillity, like the French. Might not this be a proof that they are not so much philosophers as they imagine? Philosophy is no more than the art of making ourselves happy; that is, of seeking pleasure in regularity, and reconciling what we owe to society with what is due to ourselves.

This cheerfulness, which is the characteristic of our nation, in the eye of an Englishman passes almost for folly. But is their gloominess a greater mark of their wisdom? and, folly against folly, is not the most cheerful sort the best? If our gaiety makes them sad, they ought not to find it strange if their seriousness makes us laugh.

As this disposition to levity is not familiar to them,

and as they look on every thing as a fault which they do not find at home, the English who live among us are hurt by it. Several of their authors reproach us with it as a vice, or at least as a ridicule.

Mr. Addison styles us a comic nation. In my opinion, it is not acting the philosopher on this point, to regard as a fault that quality which contributes most to the pleasure of society and happiness of life. Plato, convinced that whatever makes men happier makes them better, advises to neglect nothing that may excite and convert to an early habit this sense of joy in children. Seneca places it in the first rank of good things. Certain it is, at least, that gaiety may be a concomitant of all sorts of virtue, but that there are some vices with which it is incompatible.

As to him who laughs at every thing, and him who laughs at nothing, neither of them has sound judgment. All the difference I find between them is, that the last is constantly the most unhappy. Those who speak against cheerfulness, prove nothing else but that they were born melancholic, and that, in their hearts, they rather envy than condemn that levity they affect to despise.

The Spectator, whose constant object was the good of mankind in general, and of his own nation in particular, should, according to his own principles, place cheerfulness among the most desirable qualities; and, probably, whenever he contradicts himself in this particular, it is only to conform to the tempers of the people whom he addresses. He asserts, that gaiety is one great obstacle to the prudent conduct of women. But are those of a melancholic temper, as the English women generally are, less subject to the foibles of love? I am acquainted with some doctors in this science, to whose judgment I would more willingly refer than to his. And perhaps, in reality, persons naturally of a gay temper, are too easily taken off by different objects to give themselves up to all the excesses of this passion.

Mr. Hobbes, a celebrated philosopher of his nation, maintains that laughing proceeds from our pride alone. This is only a paradox, if asserted of laughing in general, and only argues that misanthropical disposition for which he was remarkable.

To bring the causes he assigns for laughing under suspicion, it is sufficient to remark, that proud people are commonly those who laugh least. Gravity is the inseparable companion of pride. To say that a man is vain, because the humour of a writer, or the buffooneries of a harlequin, excite his laughter, would be advancing a great absurdity. We should distinguish between laughter inspired by joy, and that which arises from mockery. The malicious sneer is improperly called laughter. It must be owned, that pride is the parent of such laughter as this: but this is, in itself vicious; whereas, the other sort has nothing in its principles or effects that deserves condemnation. We find this amiable in others, and is it unhappiness to feel a disposition towards it in ourselves?

When I see an Englishman laugh, I fancy I rather see him hunting after joy than having caught it; and this is more particularly remarkable in their women, whose tempers are inclined to melancholy. A laugh leaves no more traces on their countenance, than a flash of lightning on the face of the heavens. The most laughing air is instantly succeeded by the most gloomy. One would be apt to think that their souls open with difficulty to joy, or, at least, that joy is not pleased with its habitation there.

In regard to fine raillery, it must be allowed that it is not natural to the English, and, therefore, those who endeavour at it make but an ill figure. Some of their authors have candidly confessed, that pleasantry is quite foreign to their character; but, according to the reason they give, they lose nothing by this confession. Bishop Sprat[1] gives the following one: " The English," says he, " have too much bravery to submit to be derided, and too much virtue and honour to mock others."

[1] Bishop of Rochester; the friend and biographer of Cowley.—B.

THE BEE.

ON DECEIT AND FALSEHOOD. [AND PERSECUTION FOR WITCHCRAFT, ETC.]

THE following account is so judiciously conceived, that I am convinced the reader will be more pleased with it than with any thing of mine, so I shall make no apology for this new publication:—

TO THE AUTHOR, ETC.[1]

SIR,—Deceit and falsehood have ever been an overmatch for truth, and followed and admired by the majority of mankind. If we enquire after the reason of this, we shall find it in our own imaginations, which are amused and entertained with the perpetual novelty and variety that fiction affords, but find no manner of delight in the uniform simplicity of homely truth, which still sues them under the same appearance.

He, therefore, that would gain our hearts, must make

---

[1] Almost the whole of this paper is copied verbatim from two essays on " Witchcraft," in a work called ' The Humourist,' published anonymously, and dating its third edition in 1724. What is not borrowed is evidently Goldsmith's own ; but probably a slight feeling of compunction, at the idea of appropriating what did not fairly belong to him, induced him to give the whole in the form of a communication from a correspondent.—B. Comparing this paper with the ' Humourist' articles we find that very little of it is Goldsmith's. In fact it is a mere adaptation. Some matter is left out, and some is slightly paraphrased, but it cannot be said that anything is added. Goldsmith, however, half confesses the act of appropriation in his introductory words concerning " this new publication."—ED.

his court to our fancy; which, being sovereign comptroller of the passions, lets them loose, and inflames them more or less, in proportion to the force and efficacy of the first cause, which is ever the more powerful the more new it is. Thus, in mathematical demonstrations themselves, though they seem to aim at pure truth and instruction, and to be addressed to our reason alone, yet I think it is pretty plain, that our understanding is only made a drudge to gratify our invention and curiosity, and we are pleased, not so much because our discoveries are certain, as because they are new.

I do not deny but the world is still pleased with things that pleased it many ages ago; but it should at the same time be considered, that man is naturally so much a logician, as to distinguish between matters that are plain and easy, and others that are hard and inconceivable. What we understand we overlook and despise, and what we know nothing of, we hug and delight in. Thus, there are such things as perpetual novelties; for we are pleased no longer than we are amazed, and nothing so much contents us as that which confounds us.

This weakness in human nature gave occasion to a party of men to make such gainful markets as they have done of our credulity. All objects and facts whatever now ceased to be what they had been for ever before, and received what make and meaning it was found convenient to put upon them: what people ate, and drank, and saw, was not what they ate, and drank, and saw, but something farther, which they were fond of, because they were ignorant of it. In short, nothing was itself, but something beyond itself; and by these artifices and amusements the heads of the world were so turned and intoxicated, that, at last, there was scarce a sound set of brains left in it.

In this state of giddiness and infatuation it was no very hard task to persuade the already deluded, that there was an actual society and communion between human creatures and spiritual demons. And when they had thus put people into the power and clutches of the devil, none but they alone could have either skill or strength to bring the prisoners back again.

But, so far did they carry this dreadful drollery, and so
fond were they of it, that to maintain it and themselves
in profitable repute, they literally sacrificed for it, and
made impious victims of numberless old women, and
other miserable persons, who, either through ignorance
could not say what they were bid to say, or through madness said what they should not have said. Fear and
stupidity made them incapable of defending themselves,
and frenzy and infatuation made them confess *guilty in-
possibilities*, which produced cruel sentences, and then
inhuman executions.

Some of these wretched mortals, finding themselves
either hateful or terrible to all, and befriended by none,
and perhaps wanting the common necessaries of life,
came at last to abhor themselves as much as they were
abhorred by others, and grew willing to be burnt or
hanged out of a world which was no other to them than
a scene of persecution and anguish.

Others, of strong imaginations and little understandings,
were, by positive and repeated charges against them of
committing mischievous and supernatural facts and
villainies, deluded to judge of themselves by the judgment
of their enemies, whose weakness or malice prompted
them to be accusers. And many have been condemned
as witches and dealers with the devil, for no other reason
but their knowing more than those who accused, tried,
and passed sentence upon them.

In these cases, credulity is a much greater error than
infidelity, and it is safer to believe nothing than too much.
A man that believes little or nothing of witchcraft, will
destroy nobody for being under the imputation of it; and
so far he certainly acts with humanity to others, and
safety to himself; but he that credits all, or too much,
upon that article, is obliged, if he acts consistently with
his persuasion, to kill all those whom he takes to be the
killers of mankind; and such are witches. It would be a
jest and a contradiction to say, that he is for sparing
them who are harmless of that tribe, since the received
notion of their supposed contract with the devil implies,
that they are engaged, by covenant and inclination, to do
all the mischief they possibly can.

I have heard many stories of witches, and read many accusations against them; but I do not remember any that would have induced me to have consigned over to the halter or the flame any of those deplorable wretches, who, as they share our likeness and nature, ought to share our compassion, as persons cruelly accused of impossibilities.

But we love to delude ourselves, and often fancy or forge an effect, and then set ourselves, as gravely as ridiculously, to find out the cause. Thus, for example, when a dream or the hyp has given us false terrors, or imaginary pains, we immediately conclude that the infernal tyrant owes us a spite, and inflicts his wrath and stripes upon us by the hands of some of his sworn servants amongst us. For this end an old woman is promoted to a seat in Satan's privy-council, and appointed his executioner in chief within her district. So ready and civil are we to allow the devil the dominion over us, and even to provide him with butchers and hangmen of our own make and nature.

I have often wondered why we did not, in choosing our proper officers for Belzebub, lay the lot rather upon men than women, the former being more bold and robust, and more equal to that bloody service; but, upon enquiry, I find it has been so ordered for two reasons: first, the men having the whole direction of this affair, are wise enough to slip their own necks out of the collar; and, secondly, an old woman is grown by custom the most avoided and most unpitied creature under the sun, the very name carrying contempt and satire in it. And so far, indeed, we pay but an uncourtly sort of respect to Satan, in sacrificing to him nothing but the dry sticks of human nature.

We have a *wondering quality* within us, which finds huge gratification when we see strange feats done, and cannot at the same time see the doer, or the cause. Such actions are sure to be attributed to some witch or demon; for if we come to find they are slily performed by artists of our own species, and by causes purely natural, our delight dies with our amazement.

It is, therefore, one of the most unthankful offices in the world, to go about to expose the mistaken notions of witchcraft and spirits; it is robbing mankind of a valuable imagination, and of the privilege of being deceived. Those who at any time undertook the task, have always met with rough treatment and ill language for their pains, and seldom escaped the imputation of atheism, because they would not allow the devil to be too powerful for the Almighty. For my part, I am so much a heretic as to believe, that God Almighty, and not the devil, governs the world.

If we enquire what are the common marks and symptoms by which witches are discovered to be such, we shall see how reasonably and mercifully those poor creatures were burnt and hanged who unhappily fell under that name.

In the first place, the old woman must be prodigiously ugly; her eyes hollow and red, her face shrivelled; she goes double, and her voice trembles. It frequently happens, that this rueful figure frightens a child into the palpitation of the heart: home he runs, and tells his mamma, that Goody such a one looked at him, and he is very ill. The good woman cries out her dear baby is bewitched, and sends for the parson and the constable.

It is moreover necessary that she be very poor. It is true, her master, Satan, has mines and hidden treasures in his gift; but no matter, she is, for all that, very poor, and lives on alms. She goes to Sisly the cook-maid for a dish of broth, or the heel of a loaf, and Sisly denies them to her. The old woman goes away muttering, and perhaps in less than a month's time, Sisly hears the voice of a cat, and strains her ancles, which are certain signs that she is bewitched.

A farmer sees his cattle die of the murrain, and the sheep of the rot, and poor Goody is forced to be the cause of their death, because she was seen talking to herself the evening before such an ewe departed, and had been gathering sticks at the side of the wood where such a cow ran mad.

The old woman has always for her companion an old grey cat, which is a disguised devil too, and confederate with Goody in works of darkness. They frequently go journeys into Egypt upon a broom-staff in half an hour's

time, and now and then Goody and her cat change shapes.
The neighbours often overhear them in deep and solemn discourse together, plotting some dreadful mischief, you may
be sure.

There is a famous way of trying witches, recommended
by King James I. The old woman is tied hand and foot,
and thrown into the river, and if she swims she is guilty,
and taken out and burnt; but if she is innocent, she sinks,
and is *only* drowned.[1]

The witches are said to meet their master frequently
in churches and church-yards. I wonder at the boldness
of Satan and his congregation, in revelling and playing
mountebank farces on consecrated ground; and I have as
often wondered at the oversight and ill policy of some
people in allowing it possible.

It would have been both dangerous and impious to have
treated this subject at one certain time in this ludicrous
manner. It used to be managed with all possible gravity,
and even terror; and, indeed, it was made a tragedy in all
its parts, and thousands were sacrificed, or rather murdered, by such evidence and colours, as, God be thanked!
we are at this day ashamed of. An old woman may be
miserable now, and not be *hanged* for it.

AN ACCOUNT OF THE AUGUSTAN AGE OF ENGLAND.[2]

THE history of the rise of language and learning is calculated to gratify curiosity rather than to satisfy the

---

[1] King James, in treating of this mode of trial, lays down, that as
witches have renounced their baptism, so it is just that the element
through which the holy rite is enforced, should reject them.—SIR W.
SCOTT, *Demonology.*—PRIOR.

[2] The greater part of this paper first appeared in the ' Literary Magazine,' where, however, it figured, substantially, as the last of four articles
titled " The History of Our Own Language " (' Lit. Mag.' Feb. to May,
1758). It is generally agreed that the present paper is by Goldsmith,
yet the fact of its being an excerpt, as just stated, throws, perhaps,
some doubt upon the authorship. If, however, this paper is by Goldsmith, the remaining portion of " The History of Our Language " must
surely also be by him. See Appendix to the ' Bee,' p. 456.—ED.

understanding. An account of that period only when language and learning arrived at its highest perfection, is the most conducive to real improvement, since it at once raises emulation, and directs to the proper objects. The age of Leo X. in Italy, is confessed to be the Augustan age with them. The French writers seem agreed to give the same appellation to that of Louis XIV.; but the English are yet undetermined with respect to themselves.

Some have looked upon the writers in the times of Queen Elizabeth as the true standard for future imitation; others have descended to the reign of James I., and others still lower, to that of Charles II. Were I to be permitted to offer an opinion upon this subject, I should readily give my vote for the reign of Queen Anne, or some years before that period. It was then that taste was united to genius; and as before our writers charmed with their strength of thinking, so then they pleased with strength and grace united. In that period of British glory, though no writer attracts our attention singly, yet, like stars lost in each other's brightness, they have cast such a lustre upon the age in which they lived, that their minutest transactions will be attended to by posterity with a greater eagerness, than the most important occurrences of even empires which have been transacted in greater obscurity.

At that period there seemed to be a just balance between patronage and the press. Before it, men were little esteemed whose only merit was genius; and since, men who can prudently be content to catch the public, are certain of living without dependence. But the writers of the period of which I am speaking, were sufficiently esteemed by the great, and not rewarded enough by book-sellers to set them above independence.[1] Fame, consequently, then was the truest road to happiness; a sedulous attention to the mechanical business of the day, makes the present never-failing resource.

The age of Charles II.,[2] which our countrymen term the

---

[1] So in the original edition of the 'Bee,' and in most editions since; but perhaps the word should be dependence.—ED.

[2] From this point the text is almost word for word that of the 'Literary Magazine' article; the above paragraphs having been specially written, apparently, for this paper in the 'Bee.'—ED.

age of wit and immorality, produced some writers that at once served to improve our language and corrupt our hearts. The king himself had a large share of knowledge, and some wit; and his courtiers were generally men who had been brought up in the school of affliction and experience. For this reason, when the sunshine of their fortune returned, they gave too great a loose to pleasure, and language was by them cultivated only as a mode of elegance. Hence it became more enervated, and was dashed with quaintnesses which gave the public writings of those times a very illiberal air.

L'Estrange, who was by no means so bad a writer as some have represented him, was sunk in party faction; and having generally the worst side of the argument, often had recourse to scolding, pertness, and, consequently, a vulgarity that discovers itself even in his more liberal compositions. He was the first writer who regularly enlisted himself under the banners of a party for pay, and fought for it, through right and wrong, for upwards of forty literary campaigns. This intrepidity gained him the esteem of Cromwell himself, and the papers he wrote even just before the Revolution, almost with the rope about his neck, have his usual characters of impudence and perseverance. That he was a standard writer cannot be disowned, because a great many very eminent authors formed their style by his. But his standard was far from being a just one; though, when party considerations are set aside, he certainly was possessed of elegance, ease, and perspicuity.[1]

Dryden, though a great and undisputed genius, had the same cast as L'Estrange. Even his plays discover him to be a party man, and the same principle infects his style in subjects of the lightest nature; but the English tongue, as it stands at present, is greatly his debtor. He first gave it regular harmony, and discovered its latent powers. It was his pen that formed the Congreves, the Priors, and the Addisons, who succeeded him; and had it not been for Dryden, we never should have known a Pope, at least, in

---

[1] Sir Roger L'Estrange (1616-1704) may be viewed as the founder of English journalism. He successively conducted the *Public Intelligencer*, the *London Gazette*, and the *Observator*, all ministerial papers.—ED.

the meridian lustre he now displays.[1] But Dryden's excellencies, as a writer, were not confined to poetry alone.
There is in his prose writings an ease and elegance that
have never yet been so well united in works of taste or
criticism.

The English language owes very little to Otway, though,
next to Shakespeare, the greatest genius England ever
produced in tragedy. His excellencies lay in painting
directly from nature, in catching every emotion just as it
rises from the soul, and in all the powers of the moving
and pathetic. He appears to have had no learning, no
critical knowledge, and to have lived in great distress.
When he died, (which he did in an obscure house near the
Minories), he had about him the copy of a tragedy, which,
it seems, he had sold for a trifle to Bentley the bookseller.
I have seen an advertisement at the end of one of
L'Estrange's political papers, offering a reward to any
one who should bring it to his shop. What an invaluable
treasure was there irretrievably lost, by the ignorance and
neglect of the age he lived in![2]

Lee had a great command of language, and vast force
of expression, both which the best of our succeeding dramatic poets thought proper to take for their models.
Rowe, in particular, seems to have caught that manner,
though in all other respects inferior. The other poets of
that reign contributed but little towards improving the
English tongue, and it is not certain whether they did not
injure, rather than improve it. Immorality has its cant as
well as party, and many shocking expressions now crept
into the language, and became the transient fashion of the
day. The upper galleries, by the prevalence of party
spirit, were courted with great assiduity, and a horse-

---

[1] Pope said (according to Spence)—" I learned versification wholly
from Dryden's works; who had improved it much beyond any of our
former poets." See Spence's 'Anecdotes,' 1820, p. 281.—ED.

[2] The following advertisement (from L'Estrange's *Observator*, Nov.
27, 1686) for the same still missing play seems to have been another
endeavour at finding it:—" Whereas, Mr. Thomas Otway sometime
before his death made four acts of a play, whoever can give notice in
whose hands the copy lies, either to Mr. Thomas Betterton or Mr.
William Smith at the Theatre Royal, shall be well rewarded for his
pains."—ED.

laugh following ribaldry was the highest instance of applause, the chastity as well as energy of diction being overlooked or neglected.

Virtuous sentiment was recovered, but energy of style never was. This, though disregarded in plays and party writings, still prevailed amongst men of character and business. The despatches of Sir Richard Fanshaw, Sir William Godolphin, Lord Arlington, and many other ministers of state, are all of them, with respect to diction, manly, bold, and nervous. Sir William Temple, though a man of no learning, had great knowledge and experience. He wrote always like a man of sense and a gentleman; and his style is the model by which the best prose writers in the reign of Queen Anne formed theirs. The beauties of Mr. Locke's style, though not so much celebrated, are as striking as that of his understanding. He never says more nor less than he ought, and never makes use of a word that he could have changed for a better. The same observation holds good of Dr. Samuel Clarke.

Mr. Locke was a philosopher; his antagonist, Stillingfleet, Bishop of Worcester, was a man of learning; and therefore the contest between them was unequal. The clearness of Mr. Locke's head renders his language perspicuous; the learning of Stillingfleet's clouds his. This is an instance of the superiority of good sense over learning, towards the improvement of every language.

There is nothing peculiar to the language of Archbishop Tillotson, but his manner of writing is inimitable; for one who reads him, wonders why he himself did not think and speak it in that very manner. The turn of his periods is agreeable, though artless, and every thing he says seems to flow spontaneously from inward conviction. Barrow, though greatly his superior in learning, falls short of him in other respects.[1]

The time seems to be at hand when justice will be done to Mr. Cowley's prose, as well as poetical writings; and though his friend Dr. Sprat, Bishop of Rochester, in his diction falls far short of the abilities for which he has

[1] The author must mean in respect of manner, for in acuteness and power of thinking, Barrow certainly does not "fall short" of Tillotson, or of any other writer of his age.—B.

been celebrated, yet there is sometimes a happy flow in his periods, something that looks like eloquence. The style of his successor, Atterbury, has been much commended by his friends, which always happens when a man distinguishes himself in party ; but there is in it nothing extraordinary. Even the speech which he made for himself at the bar of the House of Lords, before he was sent into exile, is void of eloquence, though it has been cried up by his friends to such a degree, that his enemies have suffered it to pass uncensured.

The philosophic manner of Lord Shaftesbury's writing is nearer to that of Cicero than any English author has yet arrived at ; but perhaps had Cicero written in English, his composition would have greatly exceeded that of our countryman. The diction of the latter is beautiful, but such beauty as, upon nearer inspection, carries with it evident symptoms of affectation. This has been attended with very disagreeable consequences. Nothing is so easy to copy as affectation, and his lordship's rank and fame have procured him more imitators in Britain than any other writer I know ; all faithfully preserving his blemishes, but, unhappily, not one of his beauties.

Mr. Trenchard and Dr. Davenant were political writers of great abilities in diction, and their pamphlets are now standards in that way of writing.[1] They were followed by Dean Swift, who, though in other respects far their superior, never could arise to that manliness and clearness of diction in political writing, for which they were so justly famous.

They were all of them exceeded by the late Lord Bolingbroke, whose strength lay in that province ; for as a philosopher and a critic he was ill qualified, being destitute of virtue for the one, and of learning for the other. His writings against Sir Robert Walpole are incomparably the best part of his works. The personal and perpetual antipathy he had for that family, to whose places he thought his own abilities had a right, gave a glow to his style, and an edge to his manner, that never has been yet equalled

---

[1] John Trenchard, son of Sir John, the minister to William III., b. 1669, d. 1723 : Dr. Charles D'Avenant, son of Sir William, the dramatist, b. 1656, d. 1714.—ED.

in political writing. His misfortunes and disappointments gave his mind a turn which his friends mistook for philosophy; and at one time of his life he had the art to impose the same belief upon some of his enemies. His 'Idea of a Patriot King,' which I reckon (as indeed it was) amongst his writings against Sir Robert Walpole, is a masterpiece of diction. Even in his other works, his style is excellent; but where a man either does not, or will not understand the subject he writes on, there must always be a deficiency. In politics, he was generally master of what he undertook; in morals, never.[1]

Mr. Addison, for a happy and natural style, will be always an honour to British literature. His diction, indeed, wants strength, but it is equal to all the subjects he undertakes to handle, as he never (at least in his finished works) attempts any thing either in the argumentative or demonstrative way.

Though Sir Richard Steele's reputation as a public writer was owing to his connections with Mr. Addison, yet after their intimacy was formed, Steele sunk in his merit as an author. This was not owing so much to the evident superiority on the part of Addison, as to the unnatural efforts which Steele made to equal or eclipse him. This emulation destroyed that genuine flow of diction which is discoverable in all his former compositions.

Whilst their writings engaged attention and the favour of the public, reiterated but unsuccessful endeavours were made towards forming a grammar of the English language. The authors of those efforts went upon wrong principles. Instead of endeavouring to retrench the absurdities of our language, and bringing it to a certain criterion, their grammars were no other than a collection of rules attempting to naturalize those absurdities, and bring them under a regular system.

Somewhat effectual, however, might have been done towards fixing the standard of the English language, had it not been for the spirit of party. For both Whigs and

---

[1] About ten years later Goldsmith wrote his 'Life of Bolingbroke,' which compare. The 'Literary Mag.' has this passage exactly as here, except that the significant words at the end—" in morals, never," are wanting.—ED.

Tories being ambitious to stand at the head of so great a design, the Queen's death happened before any plan of an academy could be resolved on.[1]

Meanwhile, the necessity of such an institution became every day more apparent. The periodical and political writers, who then swarmed, adopted the very worst manner of L'Estrange, till not only all decency, but all propriety of language, was lost in the nation. Lesly, a pert writer, with some wit and learning, insulted the government every week with the grossest abuse. His style and manner, both of which were illiberal, were imitated by Ridpath, De Foe, Dunton,[2] and others of the opposite party, and Toland pleaded the cause of atheism and immorality in much the same strain; his subject seemed to debase his diction, and he ever failed most in one, when he grew most licentious in the other.

Towards the end of Queen Anne's reign, some of the greatest men in England devoted their time to party, and then a much better manner obtained in political writing. Mr. Walpole, Mr. Addison, Mr. Mainwaring, Mr. Steele, and many members of both houses of Parliament, drew their pens for the Whigs; but they seem to have been over-matched, though not in argument, yet in writing, by Bolingbroke, Prior, Swift, Arbuthnot, and the other friends of the opposite party. They who oppose a ministry have always a better field for ridicule and reproof than they who defend it.[3]

Since that period, our writers have either been encouraged above their merits or below them. Some who were possessed of the meanest abilities acquired the highest preferments, while others, who seemed born to

[1] This is thought to have reference to the movement consequent upon the publication of Swift's 'Proposal for Correcting, Improving, and Ascertaining the English Tongue' (1712), the failure of which Sir W. Scott describes in his 'Life of Swift' (Miscellaneous Prose Works, 1841, v. i., p. 26). Johnson said of the 'Proposal' that it "was written without much knowledge of the general nature of language, and without any accurate inquiry into the history of other tongues."—Ed.

[2] These writers, excepting Defoe, would be now forgotten but for their figuring in Pope's 'Dunciad.'—Ed.

[3] "They who oppose," &c., is an addition to the text as it appears in the 'Lit. Mag.'—Ed.

reflect a lustre upon their age, perished by want or neglect. More, Savage, and Amherst,[1] were possessed of great abilities, yet they were suffered to feel all the miseries that usually attend the ingenious and the imprudent—that attend men of strong passions, and no phlegmatic reserve in their command.

At present, were a man to attempt to improve his fortune or increase his friendship by poetry, he would soon feel the anxiety of disappointment. The press lies open, and is a benefactor to every sort of literature but that alone.[2]

I am at a loss whether to ascribe this falling off of the public to a vicious taste in the poet, or in them. Perhaps both are to be reprehended. The poet, either dryly didactive, gives us rules which might appear abstruse even in a system of ethics, or, triflingly volatile, writes upon the most unworthy subjects; content, if he can give music instead of sense; content if he can paint to the imagination without any desires or endeavours to affect : the public, therefore, with justice, discard such empty sound, which has nothing but jingle, or, what is worse, the unmusical flow of blank verse, to recommend it. The late method, also, that our newspapers have fallen into, of giving an epitome of every new publication, must greatly damp the writer's genius. He finds himself, in this case, at the mercy of men who have neither abilities nor learning to distinguish his merit. He finds his own compositions mixed with the sordid trash of every daily scribbler. There is a sufficient specimen given of his work to abate curiosity, and yet so mutilated as to render him contemptible. His first, and perhaps his second work, by these means sink, among the crudities of the age, into oblivion. Fame, he finds, begins to turn her back; he therefore flies to profit, which invites him, and he enrolls himself in the lists of dullness and of avarice for life.

---

[1] See also 'Enquiry into the State of Polite Learning,' Chap. X.; the letter to Mrs. Lauder (Letters in v. i.); and the 'Citizen of the World,' Letter XCIII.

[2] This was our author's own experience even later, viz., after he had become distinguished as a poet, as is shown by his reply to Lord Lisburn. See 'Life,' p. 28.—ED.

Yet there are still among us men of the greatest abilities, and who, in some parts of learning, have surpassed their predecessors. Justice and friendship might here impel me to speak of names which will shine out to all posterity, but prudence restrains me from what I should otherwise eagerly embrace. Envy might rise against every honoured name I should mention, since scarce one of them has not those who are his enemies, or those who despise him, &c.[1]

OF THE OPERA IN ENGLAND.

THE rise and fall of our amusements pretty much resemble that of empire. They this day flourish without any visible cause for such vigour; the next they decay away without any reason that can be assigned for their downfall. Some years ago, the Italian opera was the only fashionable amusement among our nobility. The managers of the play-houses dreaded it as a mortal enemy, and our very poets listed themselves in the opposition : at present the house seems deserted, the *castrati* sing to empty benches; even Prince Vologeso[2] himself, a youth of great expectations, sings himself out of breath, and rattles his chain to no purpose.

To say the truth, the opera, as it is conducted among us, is but a very humdrum amusement; in other countries, the decorations are entirely magnificent, the singers all excellent, and the burlettas, or interludes, quite entertaining; the best poets compose the words, and the best masters the music; but with us it is otherwise : the decorations are but trifling and cheap; the singers, Matei[3] only excepted, but indifferent. Instead of interlude, we have those sorts of skipping dances, which are calculated for the galleries of the theatre. Every performer sings his

---

[1] The last four paragraphs are not in the ' Literary Magazine.'—ED.
[2] The character in which Cornacini first appeared in England.—ED.
[3] Also mentioned in No. II. of the ' Bee' : see *ante*, p. 334.—ED.

favourite song, and the music is only a medley of old Italian airs, or some meagre modern capricio.

When such is the case, it is not much to be wondered if the opera is pretty much neglected. The lower orders of people have neither taste nor fortune to relish such an entertainment; they would find more satisfaction in the "Roast Beef of Old England" than in the finest closes of an eunuch; they sleep amidst all the agony of recitative. On the other hand, people of fortune or taste can hardly be pleased, where there is a visible poverty in the decorations, and an entire want of taste in the composition.

Would it not surprise one, that when Metastasio is so well known in England, and so universally admired, the manager or the composer should have recourse to any other operas than those written by him? I might venture to say, that "written by Metastasio," put up in the bills of the day, would alone be sufficient to fill a house, since thus the admirers of sense as well as sound might find entertainment.

The performers also should be entreated to sing only their parts, without clapping in any of their own favourite airs. I must own, that such songs are generally to me the most disagreeable in the world. Every singer generally chooses a favourite air, not from the excellency of the music, but from the difficulty; such songs are generally chosen as surprise rather than please, where the performer may show his compass, his breath, and his volubility.

From hence proceed those unnatural startings, those unmusical closings, and shakes lengthened out to a painful continuance; such, indeed, may show a voice, but it must give a truly delicate ear the utmost uneasiness. Such tricks are not music; neither Corelli nor Pergolesi ever permitted them, and they begin even to be discontinued in Italy, where they first had their rise.

And, now I am upon the subject, our composers also should affect greater simplicity—let their bass cliff have all the variety they can give it,—let the body of the music (if I may so express it) be as various as they please; but let them avoid ornamenting a barren groundwork, let

them not attempt, by flourishing, to cheat us of solid
harmony.

The works of Mr. Rameau [1] are never heard without a
surprising effect. I can attribute it only to this simplicity
he every where observes, insomuch that some of his finest
harmonies are often only octave and unison. This simple
manner has greater powers than is generally imagined;
and were not such a demonstration misplaced, I think,
from the principles of music, it might be proved to be most
agreeable.

But to leave general reflection: With the present set of
performers, the operas, if the conductor thinks proper, may
be carried on with some success, since they have all some
merit, if not as actors, at least as singers. Signora Matei
is at once both a perfect actress and a very fine singer.
She is possessed of a fine sensibility in her manner, and
seldom indulges those extravagant and unmusical flights of
voice complained of before. Cornacini, on the other hand,
is a very indifferent actor—has a most unmeaning face—
seems not to feel his part—is infected with a passion of
showing his compass; but to recompense all these defects,
his voice is melodious—he has vast compass, and great
volubility—his swell and shake are perfectly fine, unless
that he continues the latter too long. In short, whatever
the defects of his action may be, they are amply recompensed by his excellency as a singer; nor can I avoid
fancying that he might make a much greater figure in an
oratorio than upon the stage. [2]

However, upon the whole, I know not whether ever
operas can be kept up in England; they seem to be entirely
exotic, and require the nicest management and care. Instead of this, the care of them is assigned to men unacquainted with the genius and disposition of the people
they would amuse, and whose only motives are immediate
gain. Whether a discontinuance of such entertainments
would be more to the loss or the advantage of the nation,

[1] J. P. Rameau, composer of 'Castor and Pollux,' &c. See also the
essay on 'Schools of Music' in vol. i.—ED.

[2] In these paragraphs, and in the 'Schools of Music' in vol. i., we
have Goldsmith as a critic of music. Compare with Hawkins, &c., on
his capabilities in this regard, 'Life,' p. 13, &c.—ED.

I will not take upon me to determine, since it is as much our interest to induce foreigners of taste among us on the one hand, as it is to discourage those trifling members of society who generally compose the operatical *dramatis personæ*, on the other.[1]

---

[1] So ended 'The Bee,' a publication not at all successful when first issued, but one having important after-results for its author. It led to Goldsmith's acquaintance with Johnson and Smollett—which led to the connexion with Newbery, to the publication of the 'Citizen of the World' letters, and to the sale and publication of the 'Traveller' and the 'Vicar of Wakefield'—all within less than seven years of the days of the 'Bee'—and these successes of course fully established Goldsmith both as a poet and a prose writer.—ED.

APPENDIX TO THIS EDITION OF THE 'BEE.'

"THE AUGUSTAN AGE OF ENGLAND."

The following few words are less an Appendix in themselves than a means of apprising the reader of what may more fairly be termed an "Appendix to the 'Bee,'" which we have to come in our fourth volume. The eighth, and last, number of the 'Bee,' it may have been noticed, though the fact is not very generally known, is much less original than are the previous numbers. Likely enough this is traceable to the doubts which naturally existed as to whether there should be a number eight at all. We can imagine the question being in debate, and the "copy" being consequently delayed; and when it was decided that there should be a number eight, which should be the little paper's last, we can further imagine Goldsmith getting his matter together hurriedly—and, in fact, borrowing its greater part. Borrowed the greater part certainly was. The first of the three articles constituting the number is, as we have shown at p. 438, borrowed from a similar miscellany of nearly forty years before, the 'Humourist.' The paper entitled 'An Account of the Augustan Age of England' is also borrowed, but with an important difference. This paper is, as we conclude, and as Prior also concluded, borrowed by Goldsmith from Goldsmith. That is to say, it is part of a longer paper or series of papers which Goldsmith published about a year before in another periodical, and with another title. The 'Account of the Augustan Age of England' is in fact the concluding portion of four papers entitled 'The History of Our Own Language' which Goldsmith contributed to the 'Literary Magazine' of 1758. When the 'Literary Magazine' started in 1756 it was edited and contributed to by Dr. Johnson; but Goldsmith's contributions came some months after Johnson had left the magazine. It is somewhat strange, seeing that the 'Bee' article on the 'Augustan Age of England' has always been included with Goldsmith's works—from Bishop Percy's collection, which was the first, down to the edition immediately preceding our own—that its other and larger part should never have been re-published. As we have remarked at p. 443, if it is a settled thing, as it seems to be, that the 'Augustan Age' article is by Goldsmith, it can hardly be doubted that the 'History of Our Own Language,' whence the 'Augustan Age' article was taken, is also by him. This being our view, we shall publish in the present edition of the 'Works of Goldsmith,' and for the first time so collected, the remainder of this 'History of Our Own Language.' It will be found with the 'Later Collected Essays, &c." in vol. iv. It may be added, that the hitherto rejected portion of the 'History of Our Own Language' is perhaps chiefly notable, as a work of Goldsmith, on account of its containing what may be viewed as a more adequate judgment upon Shakspere and Milton than occurs elsewhere in the author's writings.—ED.

THE

MYSTERY REVEALED;

CONTAINING A SERIES OF

TRANSACTIONS

AND

AUTHENTIC TESTIMONIALS,

RESPECTING THE SUPPOSED

COCK-LANE GHOST;

WHICH HAVE HITHERTO BEEN CONCEALED FROM THE PUBLIC.

—— Since none the Living dare implead,
Arraign him in the Person of the Dead.
DRYDEN.

[Mr. P. Cunningham first included this pamphlet in the works of Goldsmith, at the suggestion of the late Mr. James Crossley, of Manchester. The present is its second appearance in Goldsmith's works. Mr. Prior published Goldsmith's receipt for the amount paid for the work, but he failed to find a copy of the work itself. He found an advertisement in the *Public Advertiser* of Feb. 22, 1762, setting forth that—" To-morrow will be published, price 1s., The Mystery Revealed," &c.—the title running on just as in the preceding page—but Mr. Prior thought this advertisement referred to another pamphlet, and that the " precise title" of Goldsmith's pamphlet was, like the work itself, lost. Mr. Cunningham printed from a copy supplied to him by Mr. Crossley. Our text is from the British Museum copy, which differs as to its imprint, though not materially in the text (see note at p. 464). The imprint of the Crossley copy, as given by Mr. Cunningham, is—" London : Printed for W. Bristow, in St. Paul's Churchyard ; And C. Ethrington, York. 1762." The imprint of the copy whence comes our text is—" London : Printed for W. Bristow, in St. Paul's Church-yard, MDCCXLII." The date 1742 in the latter is manifestly a misprint for 1762, but the omission of the name of the York publisher from this copy seems to show that Mr. Crossley's was one of an issue in York. W. Bristow, the publisher, was in business a door or two from Newbery in St. Paul's Churchyard, and is known to have published things for Newbery—the early numbers of the *Public Ledger*, wherein first appeared Goldsmith's ' Citizen of the World' letters, for instance. Mr. Forster took Prior's view, viz., that the present pamphlet is not Goldsmith's, and that the one for which Newbery paid Goldsmith three guineas is lost. He says it is " very unlikely " that Newbery should have withheld his name from the pamphlet for which he paid. But we think it is still more unlikely that the two publishers, Newbery and Bristow, who often worked hand-in-hand, should upon this occasion have jostled each other with rival publications upon the same topic. The two pamphlets which Messrs. Prior and Forster deem to have existed—one being lost—are, no doubt, one, and the one is that here reprinted.

Whether this was written by Goldsmith is another question, though the following receipt in Goldsmith's own hand (from Mr. Murray's Newbery MSS.) is proof presumptive that it was :—" Received of Mr. Newbery three guineas for a pamphlet respecting the Cock Lane Ghost. Oliver Goldsmith. March 5, 1762." (See also this receipt, with Goldsmith's Letters, in our vol. i.) Goldsmith has a reference to the Cock-Lane Ghost topic in the Preface to his ' Essays,' 1765. But this says little either for or against the theory that he wrote the present pamphlet. It is likely enough, however, that, supposing our author had a hand, little or much, in the production of this work, he would never have cared to own it. Mr. Crossley thought he traced Goldsmith's style in the work. Perhaps the truth is, that the narration of facts—substantially a defence of Mr. K——, who was so cruelly aspersed in the matter—was supplied by K——, or his friends, and Goldsmith merely touched the narrative up, and added the opening and closing matter. This would account for the smallness of the sum paid for the work ; and the humble character of the whole would of course account for Goldsmith's name not being associated with it, even by repute. See also the notes at pp. 473, 474, and 476.—Ed.]

THE MYSTERY REVEALED, &c.

It is somewhat remarkable, that the Reformation, which in other countries banished superstition, in England seemed to increase the credulity of the vulgar. At a time when Bacon was employed in restoring true philosophy, King James[1] was endeavouring to strengthen our prejudices, both by his authority and writings. Scot, Glanville, and Coleman, wrote and preached with the same design; and our judges, particularly Sir Matthew Hales,[2] gave some horrid proofs of their credulity.

Since that time, arguments of this kind have been pretty much rejected by all but the lowest class. The vulgar have, indeed, upon several occasions, called for justice upon supposed criminals, and when denied, have often exercised it themselves; their accusations, however, in general, fell upon the poor, the ignorant, the old, or the friendless, upon persons who were unable to resist, or who, because they knew no guilt, were incapable of making an immediate defence.

But of all accusations of this nature, few seem so extraordinary as that which has lately engrossed the attention of the public, and which is still carrying on at a house in Cock-lane, near Smithfield. The continuance of the noises, the numbers who have heard them, the perseverance of the girl, and the atrociousness of the murder which she pretends to detect, are circumstances that were never perhaps so favourably united for the carrying on of imposture before. The credulous are prejudiced by the child's apparent benevolence: her age and ignorance wipe

[1] See the 'Bee,' No. VIII., p. 443. Where, however, it should be remembered, it is not Goldsmith who writes, but the author he quotes. See our notes concerning that particular 'Bee' paper, at p. 438.—Ed.

[2] Sir Matthew Hale, the great lawyer, Lord Chief Justice, &c.—Ed.

off the imputation of her being able to deceive, and one or two more, who pretend actually to have seen the apparition, are ready to strengthen her evidence.

Upon these grounds, a man, otherwise of a fair character, as will shortly appear, is rendered odious to society, shunned by such as immediately take imputation for guilt, and made unhappy in his family, without having even in law a power of redress. Few characters more deserve compassion than one that is thus branded with crimes without an accuser, attacked in a manner at once calculated to excite curiosity and spread defamation, and all without a power of legal vindication. If a person in such circumstances disregards calumny, and appears unconcerned, he is then accused of obstinacy and impudence; if he shrinks at the reproach, his timidity is construed as a symptom of his guilt. A writer of the life of Urban Grandier, who was maliciously accused, and burnt for being a magician, thus describes his situation : "If he spoke like an orator," says the historian, " his accusers observe that the devil inspired his eloquence; if he was silent, they looked upon it as a tacit avowal of his guilt; when he groaned aloud under the torture, they called it obstinacy; when he fainted away, they asserted that his familiar had rendered him insensible." In short, if the credulous are resolved to suspect, even opposite and improbable circumstances will serve to awaken suspicion; and then calumny shall grow, though incapable of being traced to the author, or though apparently propagated by malice, resentment, or imbecility.

It is, however, a great instance of the good sense of the public upon the present occasion, that even the vulgar have scarce given the smallest degree of assent to this deception. Though no scheme was ever laid with more low cunning, and carried on with more indefatigable application, yet it has found but very few partizans, even among the very lowest of the people, who are ready enough to believe any tale of this nature. They readily perceived that it was but a trick; they were only amazed at what could be the motives for so black an imputation ; and probably desired information ; they heard the person's character who had been accused, very freely treated in the news papers, and perhaps were not unwilling to believe a crime against a man whom they had been taught to dislike. I shall, therefore, upon the present occasion, give the public a more satisfactory account of this whole transaction than has hitherto transpired, and that without partiality or prejudice. I shall repeat nothing as a truth that will not upon the closest examination, be found *strictly so ;* living witnesses shall be appealed to in proof of each assertion. More studious of defence than recrimination, nothing is asserted that even the opponents will not confess. It is the duty of every honest man to exculpate the guiltless, and enlighten the public, and these are the only motives for my present publication.

The circumstances that gave rise to this affair, are, in short, as follows. In the year 1756, Mr. K—— was married to Miss E—— L—— of L—— in the county of Norfolk, and during the short time she lived with him, they enjoyed all the happiness a married state could bestow. But, in about eleven months after their cohabitation, Mr. K—— having taken the Post-office at S—— in Norfolk, he and his wife were scarce settled there a month, when she died in childbed. This fatal accident, therefore, determined him to lay aside all thoughts of public business, but, as he had engaged for a year certain at the Post-office, he was obliged to keep house till the expiration of that term. During this interval Miss F—— L——, the person whose ghost is supposed to appear, and who was sister to his late wife, and lived with her as a companion, at her decease continued to reside with Mr. K——, in the character of house-keeper. The frequent intercourse arising from such a situation, soon produced a very tender affection between them. Mr. K——, however, finding, that by the strictness of the canon law, he was not allowed to indulge his passion (as his deceased wife's issue by him was born alive, though it died a short time after birth), took a resolution of coming up to London, with the intentions of purchasing a place in some public office, and in hopes of finding a cure from absence and dissipation. Their affections, however, seemed to increase by absence ; he constantly received letters from the young lady, filled with repeated entreaties to

spend the rest of their lives together, and with positive
protestations of coming to London after him even on foot,
if he did not procure her a more creditable conveyance.
These instances of her regard and resolution awakened all
his passion, and at last induced Mr. K—— to comply with
her solicitations, thus at once to gratify his own inclination as well as hers. As the canon law would have allowed
him to marry her had there been no issue born alive from
his former wife, he thought himself at least, *in foro con-
scientiæ*, permitted to gratify his passion, nor could he see
why so small an obstacle as the birth of a child, that so
short a time survived its mother, should prevent his
happiness.

During their residence at S—— they had contracted an
acquaintance with one Mr. I——, a gentleman who lived
some years in the same neighbourhood. To this gentleman, who was now settled in London, Mr. K—— had
recourse as a friend; and understanding that he soon pur-
posed spending a fortnight in Norfolk, about Whitsuntide,
1759, Mr. K—— communicated the whole affair to him,
showed him her letters, and entreated him, if she persisted
in her resolution of coming to London, to conduct her up
to town upon his return. The gentleman complied, and
upon his going into the country waited upon Miss F——,
informed her of his instructions, and as his principal
business lay at a village about twenty miles distant from
her, where he intended to stay eight or ten days, he desired
to be acquainted with her final resolution by letter: accordingly, three or four days before his intended return to
town, he received a letter from her, requesting him to
meet her at S——m, a market-town exactly midway between them. Here they agreed to go for London that
night, and as the Yarmouth stage coach was going then
for London, they took that opportunity, and arrived in
town at about five in the evening.

Mr. K——, not being exactly apprised of the day of her
arrival, was at that time at his country lodgings at Green-
wich, upon which Miss F—— took a pair of oars and went
to him there. As it was Mr. K——'s intention for the
future to live with her as his wife, he had declared himself
a married man to all his acquaintance long before her

arrival, nor were any of them surprised at his bringing home a woman, whom he acknowledged as his lawful wife. She was always called by his name, and ever treated and considered as a wife by him; and from their mutual happiness and affection the contrary would have never been known, had not her relations, who by all the ties of honour and generosity, were concerned to keep it a secret, taken every opportunity of divulging it to the world, and from a pretended regard for her reputation, endeavoured to publish her shame.

As Mr. K—— could not find a house to his mind, he took her to his lodgings near the Mansion-house, where, however, they did not continue long; for, to use the expression of a gentleman who published an account in one of the public news papers, signed " J. A. L.", the people of the house where they lodged did not altogether approve their conduct; and indeed, it would be surprising if they had, for Mr. K—— was obliged to arrest his landlord for above twenty pounds that he had lent him, a step which it is probable this same landlord did not entirely approve.

From this lodging they removed to Mr. P——'s in Cock-lane, near West Smithfield. But it soon unfortunately happened that his present landlord had the very same cause of dislike to Mr. K—— that his former landlord had. Money was borrowed by this as well as the former, and the same slow disposition to repay it appeared in the new as well as the old. Mr. K—— was therefore obliged to have recourse once more to law, and to sue his new landlord for twelve pounds, after many vain solicitations for payment. This, as may naturally be expected, created uneasiness and disturbances between them, and the quarrel rose to such a height, that at last he left Mr. P——'s house at an hour's warning, and took another lodging, at a jeweller's in the same neighbourhood, an inconvenient apartment indeed, but which he expected would serve for a short time, till a house which he had taken in Bartlet-court was fitted up.[1]

---

[1] Red Lion Street, wherein was Bartlet Court, the actual scene of the death of the poor woman whose spirit was said to have been the " Cock Lane Ghost," runs at the back of St. John's Square into Clerkenwell Green.—ED.

Thus far, then, we see nothing so very culpable in the conduct of Mr. K——; there was neither inveigling nor incest in the case, as the world has been taught to believe; the lady's coming to London was almost against his consent, and his living with her after as his wife, was what the canon law would have allowed, had it not been for the child by his former wife, which was born alive. This light circumstance prevented a public marriage; but to remedy this, the young lady and he took every precaution to live faithfully together, and to unite their friendship by the ties also of interest. They made their wills mutually in each other's favour; Mr. K——'s fortune was considerable; hers only amounted to a bare hundred pound; so that if there was any advantage on either side, it was on the part of the young lady. Yet how has this been misrepresented to the public by the same gentleman in the news papers, who signs himself "J. A. L." He seems to intimate that the lady was inveigled from her friends, and then decoyed into making a will prejudicial to her own interests. But who is this Person, who so disinterestedly espouses the cause of public justice, and takes this open method of aspersing Mr. K——? There is a gentleman of K——'s acquaintance, the initials of whose name are these letters, and whether he really was or not concerned in the publication will be shortly made appear in a due course of justice.[1]

If there be anything very culpable in Mr. K——'s behaviour, the public has now seen it; perhaps a rigid moralist would censure him in some instances of it, but certain I am, there are few who, conscious of their own transgressions, could not pardon him; what the reader has seen, however, is the only indefensible part of his character; in all other respects he was entirely blameless, and what follows of his conduct is as open, and as well attested, as any evidence that was ever given, and which, instead of reproach, will perhaps merit approbation.

[1] Mr. Cunningham printed "new course of justice." This and another variation noted at p. 471 constitute the chief differences between Mr. C.'s text and our own, and these may be misprints. The "due" or "new" course of justice alluded to is of course the suit for libel which Mr. K—— afterwards instituted. See note at p. 476.—ED.

At his new lodging he had not remained above a week, when Mrs. L—— was taken ill. A physician was immediately sent for, who had occasionally visited her before; an apothecary was employed, and every precaution taken that tenderness could suggest. But the reader will best determine on the manner of her treatment by the following certificate, drawn up by the physician himself, and signed by him and the apothecary:—

"Some time in November, 1759, I visited Mr. K—— at his lodgings at Mr. P——'s in Cock-lane,[1] and was then retained to attend the deceased F—— ——, in her expected labour, she being then in the sixth month of her pregnancy. In the course of the following months, I visited her occasionally, twice or thrice in the same house; on the 25th of January following, I received a message from Mr. K——, about nine in the morning, that the lady was ill, and wanted my assistance; I found them removed from P——'s, to an inconvenient apartment in the neighbourhood. I found the lady deceived by an acute pain in the back into an opinion that she was actually in labour; but on my declaring the contrary, found not only she, but the women about her, were extremely uneasy, still suspecting I had formed a wrong judgment; after a few hours, Mr. K—— informed me he had taken a house in Bartlet's-court, near Red-lyon-street, Clerkenwell, and, if I thought there was no danger, would be glad to remove her thither; I told him, there were no signs of labour, but that, from the symptoms, she would probably be ill some time, as I apprehended an eruptive fever, though I had not, at that time, any suspicion of the small-pox, as I did not know she had never had them. In the afternoon I attended the deceased in a coach (having properly secured her from receiving any injury by cold) to the house; Mr. K—— having been before sent, to prepare the apartment. I had her immediately put to bed, ordered her to be blooded, and prescribed such cordial medicines as I thought were proper to throw out an eruption; a nurse was immediately provided, and all necessaries for the care of the sick patient. The next morning I met Mr. Jones, her apothecary, by appointment, the eruption began to appear, and from the violent lumbago of the day before, and other symptoms, we prognosticated a confluent small-pox, of a very virulent nature; Mr. K—— was informed that, in her situation, the most favourable species of that distemper would be extremely hazardous; and that hers being a bad sort, the danger was very great; we endeavoured to assist nature by early blisterings, and administered medicines of a cordial nature; the symptoms were, for the first four or five days, rather favourable; but when maturation should have been performed, the pulse flagged, the fever sunk, and the whole eruption put on a wharty pallid appearance;

---

[1] The man's name was Parsons. He was clerk at St. Sepulchre's church, now on the Holborn Viaduct. What remains of Cock-lane runs at the back of this church, from Giltspur-street to Snow-hill.—Ed.

and, as she could not swallow, but with difficulty, she could but seldom be prevailed on to take any thing; she was herself sensible of her danger, and Mr. K—— was told she could not survive three or four days; he was advised therefore to procure a minister to visit her, which was accordingly done; for the last two days no persuasion could bring her to taste any thing; so that for near fifty hours before she died she hardly swallowed a pint of any fluid whatever, and that only, when myself, or the apothecary, were present to administer it to her. The last morning of her life we found her extremely low, her eyes sunk, her speech failing, and her intellects very imperfect; we told Mr. K—— she could not then live twelve hours.—Accordingly, a short time after we left her, her speech was wholly taken from her, she became senseless, a little convulsed, and expired in the evening, viz. on the 2d of Feb. 1762.[1]

"T. C.

"The foregoing is a true relation of the case of F—— ——, which we, who attended her in her illness, are ready to attest: as witness our hands,

"THO. COOPER, M.D.,
"Northumberland-street, Charing-Cross.

"JA. JONES, Apothecary,
"Grafton-street, Soho.

"Feb. 8, 1762."[2]

By this we find the lady taken ill of a disorder in itself extremely dangerous, still more so at her mature time of life, but most of all so as the patient was now far advanced in her pregnancy. We see her treated in the most judicious manner by persons of learning and credit, her danger prognosticated with judgment and accuracy, and her disorder going through all the regular but fatal stages peculiar to the small-pox alone, together with her death foretold, and prepared for four days before it happened.

After such an attestation we may judge what credit is to be given to the supposed ghost, when, among the rest of her answers, she asserts, that she was poisoned but three hours before she died. It here appears, she swallowed nothing but in the presence of the physician, at least fifty hours before her death; and, in fact, there was no great necessity to poison her, if there had been such an intention, and if she could swallow, when the doctor

[1] and [2] The dates here are manifest misprints for 1760, as is shown by the other dates in the pamphlet, those of the trial which followed, &c. As stated at p. 469, it was nearly two years after F—— L——'s death that the "rappings" became a town talk.—ED.

and apothecary both joined in asserting she could not live twelve hours, and when the symptoms of approaching death but too visibly promised to anticipate the operations of even the strongest poison, so as to make the perpetration needless.

After such a full vindication, therefore, the reader may judge what credit is to be given to the calumny of the person who subscribes himself " R—— B——," a man, at best—but I will have more tenderness to his character than he had to that of Mr. K——; it is enough to observe, that he was connected with her relations, and saw nothing that he relates, there can be no credit therefore given to this man, when he assures the public, that she was *purely*, or in a fair way of doing well, the day before she died.

In fact, so far from being so, that she perceived herself the approaches of death, and prevailed on Mr. K—— to send for one Mr. M——s, an eminent attorney of her acquaintance, to examine her will in Mr. K——'s favour, and if not found a good one, to draw it over anew. Upon Mr. M——'s declaring the will to be good, she asked this gentleman if it could not be made still more strongly in Mr. K——'s favour: to which he replied in the negative: upon which, declaring her satisfaction, Mr. K—— asked her if she would choose to give any thing to any of her relations? to which she replied, no: he then desired to know if she chose to divide her clothes among her sisters? to which she answered with some emotion, I have nothing to give to any one but you. She was at that time sensible; and surely, had she herself suspected any foul treatment, she would never have carried her affection so far as to reward the cause of her destruction.

But she was also attended by a divine of the Church of England, Mr. A——,[1] a gentleman equally remarkable for his benevolence, learning, and morals: he was a witness to Mr. K——'s treatment and her behaviour; he declares, and has often declared, that never, during the time of his visits, did he see a grief more expressive than in Mr. K——, nor a tenderness more affecting than in the deceased.

As soon as she died, Mr. K—— sent her sister, who

---

[1] The Rev. S. Aldrich : see p. 473.—Ed.

lived in Pall-Mall, the earliest notice; ordered an undertaker to make as good a coffin as he could, both lined and covered; but being apprehensive of a prosecution, if he gave her his own name upon it, and being unwilling to give her any other, he desired that no name should be fixed; but afterwards, when called upon for to have her name registered, finding himself obliged to give some name, he gave her his own, being determined she should not suffer reproach, whatever might be the result.[1]

Her funeral was as decent as his circumstances could permit; and her sister, who was present, wept over the corpse for some time before the coffin was screwed down; by which it farther appears what credit should be given to the aforesaid B——, when he says, that " her sister was deprived of the pleasure of seeing her dear sister's body, as the coffin had been screwed down some time before she came to the house." Her sister wept for some time over the body while yet exposed, and the coffin being then screwed down, she attended it with the company to the vault in St. J—— Clerkenwell, and seemed at that time well satisfied with her sister's treatment. Mr. K——, upon their return, offered her any part of the clothes of the deceased, or the whole if she chose them; to which she replied, that she looked upon Mr. K——'s behaviour to her sister in the same light as if they had been actually married; and that he was welcome to all that he was possessed of belonging to her sister.

Such is the plain narrative of the behaviour of Mr. K—— to Miss L——, not supported by mere assertion, but by facts that will bear the strictest scrutiny; not by witnesses remote or obscure, but by persons of undoubted credit, candour, and veracity; not produced as supporters of a controversy, for the accusation is too ridiculous to admit one, but mentioned in order to carry conviction. And, indeed, it was happy for him that his conduct was observed by a greater number of persons than are gene-

---

[1] A few years ago the coffin, without a name, of poor F—— L——, used to be pointed out in the crypt of St. John's Church, St. John's Square, Clerkenwell. See Pinks and Wood's ' Hist. Clerkenwell,' where, however, the date of the Committee of Inquiry and trial is misprinted 1763 for 1762.—ED.

rally present upon such occasions; his behaviour could admit of no suspicion, and there were no suspicious characters concerned in the transaction.

A person who had behaved in so fair and open a manner, might surely have no reason to expect reproach upon this affair; he might rest in security that no accusation or calumny, arising from his former conduct, could affect him now; but he was attacked from a quarter that no person in his senses could in the least have imagined, in a manner, that but to mention, would have excited the laughter of thousands: after an interval of two years, all of a sudden, he was surprised with the horrid imputation of being a murderer, of having murdered the person he held most dear upon earth, of having murdered her by poison: and who is his accuser? Why, a ghost! The reader laughs; yet, ridiculous as the witness is, groundless as the accusation, it has served to make one man completely unhappy. The slightest evils, by frequent repetition, at last become real misfortunes, and the imputation of great crimes, however unsupported, often blacken a character more than the commission of smaller ones.

I would not choose to pall the reader with a repetition of transactions which he has already heard too often repeated, but the story of the ghost is, in brief, as follows: —For some time a knocking and scratching has been heard in the night at Mr. P——s's, where Mr. K—— and Mrs. L—— formerly lodged, to the great terror of the family; and several methods were tried to discover the imposture, but without success. This knocking and scratching was generally heard in a little room in which Mr. P——s's two children lay; the eldest of which was a girl about twelve or thirteen years old. The purport of this knocking was not thoroughly conceived, till the eldest child pretended to see the actual ghost of the deceased lady mentioned above. When she had seen the ghost, a weak, ignorant publican also, who lived in the neighbourhood, asserted that he had seen it too; and Mr. P——s himself (the gentleman whom Mr. K—— had disobliged by suing for money), he also saw the ghost about the same time: the girl saw it without hands, in a shroud; the

other two saw it with hands, all luminous and shining.
There was one unlucky circumstance however in the apparition : though it appeared to three several persons, and
could knock, scratch, and flutter, yet its coming would
have been to no manner of purpose, had it not been kindly
assisted by the persons thus haunted. It was impossible
for a ghost that could not speak to make any discovery ;
the people, therefore, to whom it appeared kindly undertook to make the discovery themselves ; and the ghost, by
knocking, gave its assent to their method of wording the
accusation ; thus there was nothing illegal on any side,
Mr. K——'s character was blackened without an accuser ;
the persons haunted only asked questions, no doubt merely
from curiosity, without any assertion that could be reprehended ; and answers by knocking could by no means be
looked upon as a legal cause of impeachment. Thousands
who believed nothing of the matter came, in order if possible
to detect its falsehood, or satisfy curiosity ; and the words
poison and murder being frequently joined with the name
of the supposed offender, that name became every where
public, joined to an accusation, which, whether believed
or not, in itself is to a sensible mind sufficient misery :
to become every where remarkable for imputed guilt is
certainly a state of uneasiness that only falls short of a
consciousness of real villany.

When therefore the spirit taught the assistants, or
rather the assistants had taught the spirit (for that could
not speak), that Mr. K—— was the murderer, the road
lay then open, and every night the farce was carried on,
to the amusement of several, who attended with all the
good-humour which the spending one night with novelty
inspires ; they jested with the ghost, soothed it, flattered
it, while none was truly unhappy but him whose character
was thus repeatedly rendered odious, and trifled with,
merely to amuse idle curiosity.

To have a proper idea of this scene, as it is now carried
on, the reader is to conceive a very small room with a bed
in the middle ; the girl, at the usual hour of going to bed,
is undressed, and put in with proper solemnity ; the spectators are next introduced, who sit looking at each other,

suppressing laughter, and wait in silent expectation for the opening scene. As the ghost is a good deal offended at incredulity, the persons present are to conceal theirs, if they have any, as by this concealment they can only hope to gratify their curiosity. For if they show either before or when the knocking is begun, a too prying, inquisitive, or ludicrous turn of thinking,[1] the ghost continues usually silent, or to use the expression of the house, Miss Fanny is angry. The spectators therefore have nothing for it but to sit quiet and credulous, otherwise they must hear no ghost, which is no small disappointment to persons who have come for no other purpose.[2]

The girl, who knows, by some secret, when the ghost is to appear, sometimes apprizes the assistants of its in-

[1] Mr. Cunningham's text reads " a too prying inquisition, or ludicrous style of thinking."—ED.

[2] Horace Walpole, writing to George Montagu, Feb. 2, 1762, says:— " You told me not a word of Mr. Macnaughton, and I have a great mind to be as coolly indolent about our famous Ghost in Cock Lane. . . . I could send you volumes on the ghost, and I believe, if I were to stay a little, I might send its *life*, dedicated to my Lord Dartmouth, by the Ordinary of Newgate, its two great patrons. . . . I went to hear it, for it is not an *apparition*, but an *audition*. We set out from the Opera, changing our clothes at Northumberland House, the Duke of York, Lady Northumberland, Lady Mary Coke, Lord Hertford, and I, all in one hackney coach, and drove to the spot: it rained torrents; yet the lane was full of mob, and the house so full we could not get in ; at last they discovered it was the Duke of York, and the company squeezed themselves into one another's pockets to make room for us. The house, which is borrowed, and to which the ghost has adjourned, is wretchedly small and miserable; when we opened the chamber, in which were fifty people, with no light but one tallow candle at the end, we tumbled over the bed of the child to whom the ghost comes, and whom they are murdering by inches in such insufferable heat and stench. At the top of the room are ropes to dry clothes. I asked if we were to have rope-dancing between the acts? We had nothing. They told us, as they would at a puppet-show, that it would not come that night till seven in the morning, that is when there are only 'prentices and old women. We stayed, however, till half an hour after one. The Methodists have promised them contributions ; provisions are sent in like forage, and all the taverns and ale-houses in the neighbourhood make fortunes. The most diverting part is to hear people wondering *when it will be found out*—as if there was anything to find out—as if the actors would make their noises when they can be discovered." See Walpole's ' Letters,' v. iii.—ED.

tended visitation. It first begins to scratch, and then to
answer questions, giving two knocks for a negative, and
one for an affirmative. By this means it tells whether a
watch, when held up, be white, blue, yellow, or black;
how many clergymen are in the room, though in this
sometimes mistaken; it evidently distinguishes white men
from negroes, with several other marks of sagacity; however, it is sometimes mistaken in questions of a private
nature, when it deigns to answer them: for instance; the
ghost was ignorant where she dined upon Mr. K——'s
marriage; how many of her relations were at church upon
the same occasion; but particularly she called her father
John instead of Thomas, a mistake indeed a little extraordinary in a ghost; but perhaps she was willing to verify
the old proverb, that "It is a wise child that knows
its own father." However, though sometimes right and
sometimes wrong, she pretty invariably persists in one
story, namely that she was poisoned, in a cup of purl,
by red arsenic, a poison unheard of before, by Mr. K——,
in her last illness, and that she heartily wishes him
hanged.

It is no easy matter to remark upon an evidence of this
nature; but it may not be unnecessary to observe, that
the ghost, though fond of company, is particularly modest
upon these occasions, an enemy to the light of a candle,
and always most silent before those from whose rank and
understanding she could most reasonably expect redress.
When a committee of gentlemen of eminence for their
rank, learning, and good sense, were assembled to give
the ghost a fair hearing, then, one might have thought,
would have been the time to knock loudest, and to exert
every effort; then was the time to bring the guilty to
justice, and to give every possible method of information;
but in what manner she behaved upon this test of her
reality will better appear from the committee's own words
than mine. Their advertisement runs thus:

"I think it proper to acquaint the Public, that the following account
of the proceedings of the committee of gentlemen, who met at my house
on Monday evening, in order to enquire into the reality of the supposed
visitation of a departed spirit at a house in Cock-lane, is alone authen-
tick, and was drawn up, with the concurrence and approbation of the

assembly, while they were present; and that the account in the *Ledger* [1] of this day contains many circumstances not founded in truth.

"   STE. ALDRICH." [2]

"Feb. 1, 1762."

"On this night, many gentlemen, eminent for their rank and character, were, by the invitation of the Rev. Mr. Aldrich, of Clerkenwell, assembled at his house for the examination of the noises supposed to be made by a departed spirit, for the detection of some enormous crime.

"About ten at night the gentlemen met in the chamber in which the girl supposed to be disturbed by a spirit had, with proper caution, been put to bed by several ladies : they sat rather more than an hour, and hearing nothing, went down stairs, where they interrogated the father of the girl, who denied, in the strongest terms, any knowledge or belief of fraud.

"The supposed spirit had before publicly promised, by an affirmative knock, that it would attend one of the gentlemen into the vault under the church of St. John, Clerkenwell, where the body is deposited, and give a token of her presence there by a knock upon her coffin ; it was therefore determined to make this trial of the existence or veracity of the supposed spirit.

"While they were enquiring and deliberating, they were summoned into the girl's chamber by some ladies, who were near her bed, and who had heard knocks and scratches : when the gentlemen entered, the girl declared, that she felt the spirit like a mouse upon her back ; and was required to hold her hands out of bed. From that time, though the spirit was very solemnly required to manifest its existence, by appearance, by impression on the hand or body of any present, by scratches, knocks, or any agency, no evidence of any preternatural power was exhibited.

"The spirit was then very seriously advertised, that the person to whom the promise was made of striking the coffin was then about to visit the vault, and that the performance of the promise was then claimed. The company, at one, went into the church, and the gentleman to whom the promise was made, went, with one more, into the vault. The spirit was solemnly required to perform its promise ; but nothing more than silence ensued. The person supposed to be accused by the spirit then went down, with several others, but no effect was perceived. Upon their return they examined the girl, but could draw no confession from her : between two and three she desired, and was permitted, to go home with her father.

---

[1] Here may be a clue to the solution of the question why Newbery, who paid for this pamphlet, gave it to Bristow to publish. (See introductory note, p. 458.) Newbery was proprietor of the *Ledger*, which, it seems, rather took the side of the Ghost party. Newbery may have wished to give both sides a hearing without committing himself to either.—ED.

[2] The Rev. S. Aldrich, of St. John's Church, St. John's-square, Clerkenwell. The crypt of this church, where F—— L—— was buried, is a part of the ancient priory of St. John of Jerusalem.—ED.

" It is therefore the opinion of the whole assembly, that the child has some art of making or counterfeiting particular noises, and that there is no agency of any higher cause." [1]

Such an account will convince those who are under the influence of reason ; but nothing can gain over some, who from their infancy have been taught to believe, but not to think. To convince such it were to be wished, that the committee had continued their scrutiny a night or two longer, by which means the impostor would in all probability be caught in the fact, or at least more thoroughly detected. For if the ghost persisted in such company to continue silent, it would then be obvious, that it was afraid of the discovery it pretended to aim at ; or if it continued to knock or scratch, the noises, by explaining themselves, could not long frustrate a judicious enquiry.

But as it is, the ghost still continues to practise as before, and in some measure remains undetected ; and it is probable, that she will thus continue for a much longer time to exhibit among friends who desire no detection, or among the curious, whose pleasure is in proportion to the deception. The ghost knows perfectly well before whom to exhibit. She could, as we see, venture well enough to fright the ladies, or perhaps some men, about as courageous as ladies, and as discerning ; but when the committee had come up, and gathered round the bed, it was no time then to attempt at deception, the ghost was angry, and very judiciously kept her hunters at bay.

[1] This account also appeared in the *Gentleman's Magazine*, Feb., 1762, and it is said to have been written by Dr. Johnson (then Mr. Johnson), who was one of the committee. This account, however, cannot have been taken from the *Gentleman's Magazine*, as the pamphlet appeared just before the February magazine was published. This is shown by the fact that, appended to the magazine paper, is a reference to this pamphlet, " The Mystery Revealed," &c., which the magazine commends to its readers' notice as " just published," and from which it gives an extract on the antecedents of Mr. K——, F—— L——, &c. The *Annual Register* also gives the above report of the committee, which, it says, was published the day after the committee's assembly, on Jan. 31st, at Mr. Aldrich's house. Dr. Johnson's part in this committee laid him open to the imputation of being a believer in the ghost—an imputation that Boswell combats (' Life of Johnson,' Bohn's edition, v. ii., p. 181)—and to Churchill's ridicule, in the character of " Pomposo," in ' The Ghost.'—ED.

But let not the reader imagine that I would seriously produce formal arguments to refute an accusation which, upon the first blush, answers itself; what was once said to a writer, who drew up a book to prove the iniquity of the Inquisition, might, in such a case, be applied to me. " Men," said he, " who read books of controversy are already convinced of the absurdity you undertake to refute; while those who believe such falsehoods never examine their own opinions, and will consequently never read yours."

The question in this case, therefore, is not, whether the ghost be true or false, but who are the contrivers, or what can be the motives for this vile deception? To attempt to assign the motives of any action is not so easy a task as many imagine. A thousand events have arisen from caprice, pride, or mere idleness, which an undiscerning spectator might have attributed to reason, resentment, and close laid design. It would not therefore become me, who have been now endeavouring to vindicate innocence, to lay the blame of this imposture on any individual upon earth, though never so rationally to be suspected. All I shall say is, that, as the reader may remember, Mr. K——has many who owe him an ill-will. His landlord at one house, whom he arrested for money lent him, had cause of resentment; his landlord in Cock-lane, the father of the child, whom he was obliged to sue from similar motives, was, it is to be supposed, willing enough to retaliate the supposed injury. But above all, Mrs. L——'s relations, who had filed a bill in chancery against him, just two months before this infernal agent appeared to strengthen their plea. This law-suit between him and the family of the deceased is of a domestic nature, and therefore unfit at present to be laid before the public; all that is necessary to be mentioned is, that their animosity has been carried to the highest pitch, and that since its commencement, they have pursued him with implacable resentment; what may be the justice of his cause, or of their anger, the proper judges and not the public are to determine; but whether it goes for or against him, the world may be assured, that the whole true state of this chancery suit (as far as is consistent with law) will be very minutely laid

before them, upon a proper occasion; for the present it
is sufficient to observe that it was commenced in November last, while Mr. K—— was upon a journey for his
brother, and that when he returned, to put in his appearance, he soon found a prosecution of a much more terrible
nature commenced against him, more terrible, as unexpected, and more dangerous, as the cause was unknown.

I have now as briefly, and indeed as tenderly as I could,
stated the whole of this most surprising transaction, and
the reader by this time sees how far Mr. K—— is culpable.
He sees him living affectionately with a woman as his wife,
whom the laws of nature allowed him to love, but the
strictness of the canon law forbade him to marry. He
sees every possible method taken to preserve this woman's
reputation and life, and the most reputable persons produced as witnesses of her end. He sees men of the highest
rank, both for birth, character, and learning, joined to
acknowledge the whole of the pretended ghost as an imposition upon the public; and lastly, he sees those who
pretend to bear witness to the accusation, persons of a
mixed reputation, of gross ignorance, great cruelty, and
what is more, armed with resentment against him. I
would not wish, however, to turn the popular resentment
upon any particular person, but I think it my duty to
divert it somewhere from the guiltless.[1]

[1] The story of this imposture is thus very fairly told up to the date of
the writing of the pamphlet, when, as is shown at p. 459, the " rappings "
were still being practised. The sequel was, the speedy discovery on the
child's person of a piece of board, whereon she was trying to produce
raps, &c. (*Annual Register* (Chronicle), p. 146), and, a little later, the
trial of Parsons and others, on the prosecution of Mr. K——, for conspiracy. The trial took place on July 10, 1762, before Lord Mansfield,
and it lasted twelve hours. Parsons, his wife, and one Mary Fraser,
with " a clergyman and a reputable tradesman," all the persons charged,
were found guilty, but sentence was deferred for seven or eight months
to give an opportunity for reparation being made to Mr. K——. At
the end of that time the clergyman and tradesman got off by paying
Mr. K—— some £600, while Parsons was sentenced to two years imprisonment, and to be put three times in the pillory, his wife was
adjudged one year's imprisonment, and Mary Fraser six months in
Bridewell. It is further recorded that, when Parsons was put in the
pillory, he appeared, or feigned, to have lost his wits, and the populace,
instead of pelting him—the usual fate of the pilloried—collected money
for him.—ED.

But still it seems something extraordinary, how this imposition could be so long carried on without a discovery. However, when we compare it to some others, which have successfully deceived the public a yet longer time, our wonder will be in some measure diminished. It was the observation of Erasmus, that whenever people flock to see a miracle, they are generally sure of seeing a miracle; they bring a heated imagination, and an eager curiosity to the scene of action, give themselves up blindly to deception, and each is better pleased with having to say that he had seen something very strange, than that he was made the dupe of his own credulity. There are many alive now who must, I suppose, remember the famous impostor Richard Hathaway, whose case is recorded in the State Trials. This ignorant creature deceived the public both successfully and long. He vomited in public crooked pins, which he had previously swallowed in private; he accused an innocent person of magic; he pretended to fast for a month together, and even in this deceived his guardians, with twenty other feats; by which means, the person he accused was actually imprisoned, and stood her trial at Guildford assizes. The circumstances are strong; but then was not the time for burning for witchcraft, as about an age before: the poor woman was acquitted, and her accuser ordered to prison in her stead; Hathaway was consigned to the care of an apothecary who lived in Guildford, if I remember, and here guarded by a maid, who pretended to be sorry for his situation, and took part in his distress: to her, therefore, he confessed all his impostures, and the apothecary actually detected him at last, through a hole in his chamber wall, either hiding more pins in his mouth, or making an hearty meal upon provisions the maid had stole for him. Richard, however, though put in the pillory as an impostor, had many partizans of credit and reputation; and some were so credulous as to suppose him sincere, even after his confession to the contrary.

The people believed in Richard; but there never was an instance in which they were in general so averse to imposture as in the present attempt to deceive them: it is not known, however, what effect a continuance of those endeavours, if not silenced by proper methods, may have: it is easy to conceive how much credulity is wrought upon by perseverance, *even pious and orthodox divines themselves have been known to give credit to the strangest falsehoods of this kind:* and Glanville declares his solemn belief in a ghost whose only business consisted in playing tricks and clattering plates and trenchers.

In fact, the people can at last be taught to believe any thing, and may probably, by perseverance, be taught to believe this; nor can I avoid deploring the easiness with which some, whose duty it is to guide them from error, suffer themselves to be led into it. A story that I am going to relate, will serve as an instance, how far the public may deceive themselves, and how far even a Protestant divine may, unknowingly, help the imposture. The account is given us by Adrian Regenvolscius, a Protestant divine, in a work entitled "A Chronological System of History, respecting the Reformation in Sclavonia," printed in Utrecht, 1652, p. 95. He mentions it as a transaction for the truth of which he can vouch; and his prudence, and the historian's veracity are confirmed still farther by Voetius, one of the most eminent theologians of his time, and who was himself the editor. The passage is this:

"In the number of these obstacles to the reformation in Poland, which we have already mentioned, we may add another, namely, about the year 1597, God permitted the appearance of a certain spirit (at first it could not be said whether it was black or white) to delude several from the true faith, after the old superstitions. There was a certain girl whose name was Bietka, who was courted by a young man called Zachary; they were both natives of Weilam, and had received their education there. This youth, though in deacon's orders, and also soon expected to be priested, was nevertheless resolved to marry Bietka, and accordingly they mutually plighted a promise to each other; but his father, in consideration of the rank which he held in the church, prevented his marriage, upon which he became melancholy, and soon after hanged himself. A short time after his death, a spirit appeared to the disconsolate Bietka, which pretended to be the soul of Zachary her lover, assuring her that he was sent by God, to apprize her of his displeasure at the rashness of his death; and that, as she had been the principal cause of his temerity, he was come to accomplish his promise to her, and to marry her. This false spirit knew perfectly how to cajole this poor girl, by promising to enrich her, so that he at length persuaded her that he was in reality the spirit of her lover; and she accordingly plighted him her marriage vow. The noise of this extraordinary match, between a woman and a spirit, was quickly spread over the whole country, and the curious, from every quarter, flocked to be witness of so extraordinary an affair.

" Many of the Polish nobility, who believed in the honesty of the spirit, became intimately acquainted with him ; and even many of them brought him home to their houses. By these means Bietka amassed a large sum of money, and so much the more, as the spirit would not return an answer, nor speak to a single person, nor foretell the smallest occurrence without his wife's consent. The spirit lived a whole year in the house of the Sieur Trepka, intendant of Cracovia ; from thence going from house to house, he went at last to reside with a certain widow lady, whose name was Wlodkow, where he remained for the space of two years, and there played all the tricks of which he was capable. The principal are as follow : He told all things, past and present. He talked in favour of the Roman Catholic religion, and assured his auditors that the Reformers were all damned. He would not even permit one of them to approach him, for he considered them as unworthy his conversation ; he rather persisted in assuring his audience that their only study was novelty, and not reformation ; and thus he brought back many again to popery.

" Hitherto not a single creature had perceived that this spirit was the devil, nor would it have ever been known, had it not been for some Polanders, who, going to Rome in the year of jubilee 1600, spread the news of the spirit through the whole country. A certain Italian, who understood magic, hearing this report, among others, and being informed that the spirit had now exhibited five years, recollected that he had lost a spirit about that time, which he had long kept confined near his person. This magician therefore went to Poland, and waiting upon dame Wlodkow, demanded his property, to the astonishment of all the spectators. He insisted that this devil, which had fled from him, should be restored back ; with which reasonable request the lady instantly complied : he once more therefore shut up his malicious spirit in a ring, and brought him back to Italy, assuring the people, that, had the devil been permitted to stay in Poland much longer, he would have drawn down numberless miseries upon the nation."

One would think that a story of this nature could hardly gain credit, and yet it deceived a whole nation for five years successively : what is still more surprising, it deceived a Protestant divine, otherwise of sense, and of learning. I cannot avoid thinking, that there are several similar circumstances between this Polish ghost and the ghost of Cock-lane. The ghost at Cock-lane answers questions, so did Zachary ; the Cock-lane ghost is visited by the nobility, so was Zachary ; the Cock-lane ghost plays tricks, so did Zachary ; the Cock-lane ghost follows a girl, so did Zachary. There is one circumstance, however, in

which the parallel will not hold good ; Zachary was believed
to be a real ghost by a Protestant divine ; but I fancy no
Protestant divine can be found among us so much the old
woman as to lend even a moment's assent to the ghost in
Cock-lane.

END OF VOLUME II.

www.ingramcontent.com/pod-product-compliance
Lightning Source LLC
Chambersburg PA
CBHW030040130726
47901CB00005BA/1178